Writing Feature Articles

D0273697

Related titles published by Focal Press

Basic Radio Journalism	Paul Chantler and Peter Stewart
Broadcast Journalism	Andrew Boyd
Broadcast News Writing, Reporting and Producing	Ted White
Flash Journalism: How to Create Multimedia News Packages	Mindy McAdams
Journalism Online	Mike Ward
Law and the Media	Tom Crone
Modern Newspaper Practice	F. W. Hodgson
Practical Newspaper Reporting	Geoffrey Harris and David Spark

Writing Feature Articles

Fourth edition

Brendan Hennessy

AMSTERDAM • BOSTON • HEIDELBERG • LONDON • NEW YORK • OXFORD
PARIS • SAN DIEGO • SAN FRANCISCO • SINGAPORE • SYDNEY • TOKYO
Focal Press is an imprint of Elsevier

ELSEVIER

For Ann, Caitlin, Huw, Daniel and Madeleine

Focal Press is an imprint of Elsevier
Linacre House, Jordan Hill, Oxford OX2 8DP, UK
30 Corporate Drive, Suite 400, Burlington, MA 01803, USA

First edition 1989
Reprinted with revisions 1990
Second edition 1993
Reprinted 1994 (twice), 1995
Third edition 1997
Reprinted 1997 (twice), 1998, 1999, 2001, 2002, 2003, 2004
Fourth edition 2006
Reprinted 2006

Notice
No responsibility is assumed by the publisher for any injury and/or damage to persons
or property as a matter of products liability, negligence or otherwise, or from any use
or operation of any methods, products, instructions or ideas contained in the material
herein. Because of rapid advances in the medical sciences, in particular, independent
verification of diagnoses and drug dosages should be made

British Library Cataloguing in Publication Data
A catalogue record for this book is available from the British Library

Library of Congress Cataloging-in-Publication Data
A catalog record for this book is available from the Library of Congress

ISBN–13: 978-0-240-51691-2
ISBN–10: 0-240-51691-5

For information on all Focal Press publications
visit our website at www.focalpress.com

Printed and bound in *Great Britain*

06 07 08 09 10 10 9 8 7 6 5 4 3 2

Working together to grow
libraries in developing countries
www.elsevier.com | www.bookaid.org | www.sabre.org

ELSEVIER   BOOK AID
International   Sabre Foundation

Contents

Illustrations   ix

Foreword: From a lecturer   x

Foreword: From a writer   xi

Preface   xii

Acknowledgements   xiii

I   PRACTISING THE SKILLS

1   **Introduction**   3
    The basic skills and resources – Gathering experience and
    networking – Assignments

2   **Getting organized**   10
    Books and equipment – Running a business – Assignments

3   **From idea to publication**   16
    The feature defined – The stages in production –
    Assignments

4   **The world of ideas**   41
    Staff writers' ideas – Freelance writers' ideas – Development
    techniques – The place of specialism – Checklist –
    Assignments

5   **Studying the print market**   59
    The world of features – Aiming at versatility – Assignments

6   Subjects and treatments   79
Likely targets – Celebrities – Children – Crime – Education – Health
and medicine – Old age or retirement – Travel – Assignments

7   The commissioning and the editing   97
The editor's point of view – Preparing to pitch – How to pitch –
Using your network – Organizing the assignment – When to
send specs – Dealing with editors – Assignments

8   Ways of finding out   115
Reliable sources – An interviewing strategy – Verification
skills – Assignments

9   Researching and writing online   142
Internet basics – Researching online – A writer's
experience – Creating your own website – Writing online – Assignments

10   Creating the best order   159
Checking for the right ingredients – Putting your file in order –
Discovering what to say – Matching order to content – Assignments

11   Making a coherent whole   174
Examples of teamwork – Titles – The intro – The ending –
Links – Appendages – Assignment

12   Developing writing techniques   197
Choose the precise word – Be simple and concise – Prefer
the familiar word to the unfamiliar – Use the concrete rather
than the abstract – Avoid clichés – Be positive and honest –
Write as you speak – Vary your pace and rhythm –
Assignments

13   The style for the purpose   215
Describing memorably – Narrating compellingly – Explaining fully –
Arguing convincingly – Finding your own style – Assignments

14   Illustrating with impact   225
Entering the market – Relevance or art? – Subjects for your
pictures – Choosing your equipment – Working with a

photographer – Pictures from other sources – Graphics –
Captions – The business aspects – A nomadic career –
Assignments

II   EXPANDING YOUR HORIZONS

15   Writing publicity   243
Advertising and PR defined – Advertising copywriting –
From PR into journalism – Obtaining publicity work –
Techniques for publicity writing – Assignments

16   Interview features and profiles   255
Choice of interviewee – Getting commissioned –
Setting up the interview – Choosing the method –
Preparing the questions – Interviewing techniques –
Editing the transcript – Formats for writing up –
Following up – Assignments

17   The regular columnist   288
Learning from the best – Getting a slot – All kinds of
discoveries – Many working methods – Assignments

18   The reviewer   307
How to become a reviewer – The reviewer's tasks – The
writing-up process – Books – Music – Art – Theatre –
Films – Television – Assignments

19   The specialists   336
Opportunities galore – A marketing strategy – Producing
specialist features – Samples published – Specialist
columns – Research and fact checking – Assignments

20   Selling overseas   357
Guides to the market – Choosing your countries – Some
likely opportunities – Syndication – Assignment

21   Law and ethics   363
Copyright – Libel – The question of attribution –
Ethical concerns

Appendix 1	Suggested responses to assignments	367
Appendix 2	National Union of Journalists – Professional Code of Conduct	371
Appendix 3	Press Complaints Commission: Code of Practice for the Press	373
Appendix 4	The Society of Authors' Quick Guide 1: Copyright and Moral Rights	379
Appendix 5	Useful contacts	385
Appendix 6	Training	391
Bibliography		**393**
Index		**403**

Illustrations

Figure 3.1   Page from *Writers' and Artists' Yearbook 2005*
(A. & C. Black)   23

Figure 3.2   Page from *The Writer's Handbook 2005* (Macmillan)   24

Figure 3.3   Page from *The Economist Style Guide*, Eighth
Edition (Hamish Hamilton/The Economist
Books Ltd)   26

Figure 3.4   Looking abroad: a page from *Freelance Market
News*, Vol. 11, No. 9, April 2005 (The Association
of Freelance Writers)   37

Figure 4.1   A mind map with the subject 'surgery'   55

Figure 5.1   W. H. Smith – opportunities galore   69

Figure 8.1   Ways of finding out: Press Cuttings Agencies from
The Writer's Handbook 2005 (Macmillan)   117

Figure 11.1   Connections that make for coherence   191

Figure 14.1   How display techniques project a feature: *Sunday
Times* travel page   230

Figure 14.2   Graphics from *Press Gazette* (30 July 2004)   233

Figures 14.3   Photographer collaborating with a writer on a TV film
and 14.4   set for *The Advocate*   238

Figure 19.1   Briefings from *Campaign's* features editor   340

Figure 19.2   Line drawing with technical detail: from *Building
Today* 24 March 1988   343

Foreword: From a lecturer

It was 1989 and I was three years into my career as a journalism educator when I read *Writing Feature Articles*. It was one of the first books about the mechanics of British journalism and came as a blessed relief. I knew how to pitch an idea and write a feature, but I had gained my skills over the years by osmosis; Hennessy gave me the theory behind those skills which finessed my craft, broke it down into manageable chunks and made it easy to deliver those skills to people hungry to clamber on to the first rung of the journalism ladder. It has stood the test of time. Other books may focus on different aspects of feature writing, but this one covers *everything* – networking, angling stories, gathering data, interviewing sources, structuring and writing.

It remains an invaluable resource for journalism and media studies lecturers, their students and for journalists who want to brush up on their craft and develop new freelance markets.

Barbara Rowlands
Deputy Head/Programme Director,
Postgraduate Diploma in Magazine Journalism
Department of Journalism and Publishing
City University, London

Foreword: From a writer

The Mary Tyler Moore Show was an American sitcom based in the newsroom of WJM-TV, a small television station in Minneapolis. Tyler Moore, although the nominal star, as often as not let herself be the foil to the kinds of inflated or disappointed egos you find in any newsroom. Among them was Murray Slaughter, the news bulletin's chief writer who had aspirations but probably not the talent to graduate to greater things (Gavin MacLeod, who played him, went on to star in *The Love Boat* – thus do the gods mock us all). In one episode, Mary brought a 15-year old who wanted to be a journalist in to see him. 'Do you like writing?' the boy asked. 'Let me see,' sighed Murray. 'I like getting paid for what I write. I like reading what I wrote. I like having written. No, I don't like writing.'

Many of us lucky enough to earn a living by our words would, if we were honest, give much the same reply, and, I suspect, feature writers would agree most strongly of all. Features are not as hard to write as a doctoral thesis, a 'Dear John' letter or a holiday postcard, but they are tricky. Unlike news stories, they rarely have an obvious beginning or an end. You want to be clear but you don't want to be patronising. Humour is good but not silliness. The author's personality should be visible but no one wants to be told they have written about themselves rather than their subject. Accuracy is important but so is the need to entertain, especially over longer lengths. So, yes, each is a puzzle that needs to be solved, and in its own way. Yet a good feature is more satisfying than almost any other form of journalism. Since it admits complexity, it is more likely to be truthful.

This is not a short book but reading it is the quickest way I know of reducing the risks in writing a profile or a review, a news feature or an opinion column. For a beginner, it would, I imagine, be invaluable. To someone who has been writing features for decades, it has, I can confirm, some tricks to impart. For all of us, Brendan Hennessy narrows the gap between the agony of the 'new document' screen and the joy of 'having written'.

Andrew Billen

Andrew Billen began his career in journalism on the *Sheffield Star* in 1980. Since 1993 he has written 'The Billen Interview' for, successively, *The Observer*, the London *Evening Standard*, and *The Times*. He has been the *New Statesman's* television critic since 1997.

Preface

This book aims to help not only students on journalism and media studies courses, but also anybody at any stage of life who wants to get into journalism, whether staff or freelance, and practising journalists who want to extend their range. The emphasis is on aspects still neglected in books on writing skills. Those aspects are: first, the need to have something to say, and second, the need to adapt content to different audiences. To put it another way, I have concentrated on how to find good ideas and how to develop them in different ways. I have therefore commented on extracts from a wide spectrum of published articles.

How to use this book

I suggest reading it straight through and then referring to specific chapters as necessary. Each chapter attempts to be fairly comprehensive about its topic so there is a little unavoidable repetition.

In this edition I have improved, and added to the number of, assignments and suggested responses. Feedback from tutors, students and practising journalists have helped me to do so. Nevertheless, these sections are intended as guides only. They have been formulated so that tutors and readers can easily adapt them to their specific requirements. I have again kept in mind the requirements of the National Vocational Qualifications (NVQs) in news and periodical journalism and the requirements of the NCTJ and other training courses. As always, feedback from readers, based on their own experience of using the book, will be welcome and should be addressed to me, c/o the publisher.

Brendan Hennessy
South Norwood
London

Acknowledgements

Extracts were taken, with permission and with copyright requirements honoured, from the following newspapers:

Daily Express, *Daily Mirror*, *Daily Telegraph*, *Dover Express*, *Edinburgh Evening News*, the London *Evening Standard*, *Financial Times*, *The Independent Review*, *The Guardian*, *Kentish Times*, *The Mail on Sunday*, *The Mirror*, *The Observer*, *South London Press*, *The Star*, *The Sunday Express*, *The Times* and *Western Morning News*.

Extracts were taken, with permission and with copyright requirements honoured, from the following magazines:

Arena, *British Journalism Review*, *Choice*, *Empire*, *FHM*, *Financial Times Magazine*, *Geographical* magazine, *Gramophone*, *GQ*, *The Independent Magazine*, *Loaded*, *Marie Claire*, *Mojo*, *Money Observer*, *New Internationalist*, *New Statesman*, *The Observer Magazine*, *Philosophy Now*, *Private Eye*, *Reader's Digest*, *Saga*, *The Spectator*, *Sunday Express Magazine*, *Sunday Times Magazine*, *The Telegraph Magazine*, *Time Out*, *The Week*, *What's On*, *Woman*, *Woman's Own*, *Writers' Forum*, *Heat*, *You* (*The Mail on Sunday Magazine*).

The following authors and publishers allowed me to take extracts, with copyright requirements honoured, from the following books:

Francis Wheen and Guardian Books/Atlantic Books (2002), from *Hoo-Hahs and Passing Frenzies. Collected Journalism 1991–2001*; Christopher Silvester and Penguin Books (1993), *The Penguin Book of Interviews* (published in the USA as *The Norton Book of Interviews*, 1996).

I am indebted to the following sources for reproducing pages from publications, photographs and other illustrations, as listed on page ix:

Natasha Babaian and *The Advocate Building Today*, *Campaign*, *The Economist Style Guide*, *Freelance Market News*, John Rooney and *Press Gazette*, *The Sunday Times*, *Writers' and Artists' Yearbook*, *The Writer's Handbook*.

Permission was kindly granted for the reproduction of The NUJ Professional Code of Conduct for the Press, and the Society of Authors' Quick Guide: Copyright and Moral Rights.

Special thanks are due to Freddie Hodgson, my editor for three editions, whose guidance is still evident in this one; John Morrish for keeping me on track and up to date; Georgia Kennedy of Focal Press, for helpfulness and patience throughout; and Frank Wynne for making the best sense possible out of Chapter 9.

1 Practising the skills

1　Introduction

Journalists ... fellows with, in the main, squalid and unfulfilling lives, insecure in their careers, and suffering a considerable degree of dependence on alcohol and narcotics ... (The late Alan Clark, MP, 'Why I hold journalists in low regard', *The Penguin Book of Journalism. Secrets of the Press*, Penguin Books, 1999)

A man may write at any time, if he will set himself doggedly to it. (James Boswell, quoting Dr Samuel Johnson)

You have to be prepared to be unpopular if you're a journalist or a politician. The important thing is that you've become unpopular for the right reasons. You've tried to tell the truth as you see it. It will help if you can keep off the booze.

Dr Johnson meant women too, of course. It's a wonderful way to earn a living. You can write at any time of day and at any time of life. Within limits, you can write even when ill. Some writing talent must be assumed, but there is much scope for development. But you also need that doggedness, plenty of curiosity and a strong desire to communicate.

Doggedness means the determination to improve your skills by constant practice, and in particular the perseverance to write and rewrite (time allowing) until the article comes right. In journalism 'coming right' means satisfying not only yourself but your editor and the readers aimed at.

Curiosity means being interested in the human condition. You feed it by reading, meeting a wide variety of people; you keep it alive by thinking and writing. You maintain a lively interest in many subjects, however specialized the field you write about.

The desire to communicate is the fuel for the engine. You may be driven by a 'mission to explain' (not to preach though), or by a fire in the belly that makes you want to correct wrongs and demand retribution. You may be most interested in getting readers' attention by entertaining them, perhaps making them see the funny side of things. Journalism, however, demands that imparting accurate information is the essential task that underpins those laudable aims.

THE BASIC SKILLS AND RESOURCES

The essential journalistic skill is reporting. You also need to have a shorthand system of some kind, even if it's one that you've made up yourself. You need to be computer-literate with keyboarding skills and you need to know how to use the Internet. These subjects are the concerns of various chapters.

Getting trained

Most newcomers to journalism are armed with degrees these days, some with media studies degrees that include journalism practice. Newcomers may have in addition or alternatively National Council for the Training of Journalists' (NCTJ) qualifications, or a diploma from a College of Further Education or private college. Appendix 6 gives guidance on training courses, some of which organize work placements as part of the curriculum. You don't get paid but with luck you might get valuable experience in reporting, subediting and feature writing, as well as in making the tea and buying a birthday present for the boss's wife. If you're even luckier the work placement might lead to a staff job.

If your objective is freelance feature writing, a staff job for a while will enable you to build a network of contacts. The job is more likely to be subbing than writing at the outset.

Getting sorted

If you haven't already done so, you need to turn your study at home into a well-equipped office, whether you're a staff writer doing freelance work for non-competitive publications or a freelance (or prospective freelance). See Chapter 2.

GATHERING EXPERIENCE AND NETWORKING

Whatever degrees or diplomas you've got, whatever training and work experience you've had, it may still be difficult to find the post you want or get established as a freelance. When the economics are difficult and publications are downsizing, both staff and freelance work is harder to find. The staff made redundant join a growing freelance pool. The main lesson to be learnt, especially as a freelance, is that you have to promote yourself rigorously and suffer rejections without losing your self-confidence.

If you've had some work experience you may be able to develop the relationship forged with a publication, perhaps by some casual subbing. To repeat: it's usually best to work in a salaried post for a while before making the plunge into freelancing.

Take any opportunity to network. Go to parties and other social events where there will be journalists who may be useful contacts, who may give you work or introduce you to someone who may give you work. Try getting personal recommendations from friends, relations, former fellow-students, colleagues who have connections with the business. But don't pitch too strongly and desperately to an editor at a social event. Your later pitch will benefit from even the briefest of introductions. Discover the best means of pursuing your claim to attention.

Make the most of any opportunity offered to meet an editor to discuss ideas. A young journalist, having got printed in a woman's magazine, was invited to meet the editor with ideas. She gave forth with passion.

But they weren't what he was looking for. 'What I have in mind,' he said, 'for example, is a feature on "20 things every woman wants in a man".'

She said, 'That sounds a bit banal to me.' The meeting was not a success and he published no more of her work. The lesson is that at an early stage give editors what they ask for when they won't take what's better (and riskier) from you. Later, when you've proved your worth, you'll get more of your own ideas accepted.

Editors are looking for feature writers who have some kind of profile and who can provide evidence that they can write. Getting into print so that you have something to show and being persistent will help you to get into editors' sights. At first you may have a thin portfolio containing photocopies of one or two pieces in a student or parish magazine. Select the best pieces and send them to targeted editors to back up your approaches. As time goes by you'll be able to broaden your range and you will have gathered a more impressive portfolio to back up your pitches.

Getting printed

Editors are looking for writers who have some specialist knowledge within their publications' areas of interest and who know how to communicate it to their readers. As a new writer you will find it easier to break in with those qualifications. It's a good idea to select one or two publications that you enjoy reading, select one or two areas of interest to specialize in, market-study the publications (see Chapter 5), and prepare to pitch. Make sure your selected subjects are not dealt with regularly by staff writers or established columnists. Your close study of several issues of your target publication will reveal those subjects.

Unless advised otherwise, send a proposal rather than a piece 'on spec' (speculatively). Find out in what form and how long a publication wants a proposal to be, and whether they want it by post, by fax, email or on the phone. If by post, do they want a proposal to be backed up by cuttings of features published (likely) and a brief c.v. (perhaps, if you've not much else to show)? You may be asked to fax copies of pieces published. If a pitch by email is wanted, does it have a link to your website containing some published articles?

One way to get knowledgeable about both the selected subject areas and the latest controversies about them, and about the readership, as well as to become noticed by the editor, is to become a letter writer.

Writing for the letters page

Writing letters also trains you to study the ways in which a publication's features, and especially controversial columnists, are followed up or argued about in the letters page.

You might want to experiment by widening your range of topics and readerships, to see what works best for you: social problems, human rights, class conflicts, the failures in the education system and the National Health Service, your views on TV programmes, especially the 'soaps'?

Of course there are eccentric letter writers, some of whom notoriously write in green ink and who are printed to create controversy or amusement. So choose your publications carefully and type.

After getting several letters published, you may be getting into correspond-ence with the editor, paving the way for you to propose a feature.

Staff and freelance

You may prefer to remain a staff writer where your features may be spin-offs from, or an essential part of, your job; you may prefer to go freelance with little or no staff experience; or you may select any of the degrees in between. Let's get a flavour of the differences.

Melody Ryall is Group Editor of the *Kentish Times* series. She graduated in drama and theatre studies. How did she get started in journalism?

'I wrote letters to every editor in the land until I was offered "indentures": a trainee reporter's job with the *Kentish Times* under the proviso of the National Council for the Training of Journalists (NCTJ).'

She obtained the NCTJ Proficiency Certificate after covering Magistrates' and Crown courts, council meetings and human interest stories. She began her career on the *Kentish Times* in 1989. She did general news reporting, arts editor, theatre reviewer, celebrity interviews and campaigns. As a freelance she has won awards as a campaign journalist, and worked as an assistant producer on a series of network documentaries for ITV.

Her features are mainly interview-based. 'Easiest is the writing part of it. Most difficult can be sussing out the mood of the interviewee and extract-ing exactly what you want to angle the piece. Once my personality radar has given me an inkling of how my interviewee is feeling I know how the feature should go. As a feature writer I plan my day around the interviews I've fixed up, get the research done, arrange for pictures and then organize the time to write the piece.' Initially she researches online but 'I avoid recycling the Internet information that everybody has access to. I'm always looking for a fresh perspective.'

She has a free rein in finding and developing her own ideas. The Group Editor's job is a matter of quality control. It's hard work but she clearly couldn't be doing anything else. The future? To paraphrase, she wants to get better at what she does.

Press Gazette's regular feature 'Seven Days' gives you working weeks described by a selection of staff writers and editors, and freelance journalists in print and broadcasting. There are also full-page features from time to time on the world of the freelance. What comes through most strongly in those pieces is insecurity, and the remedy – willpower.

Writer's block tends to be more of a freelance's problem. Remedies: write anything, just keep going until you get it right. Or: plan the piece first.

Tim Lott, long-standing and highly successful columnist for London's *Evening Standard*, interviewed by Dan Roberts in *Press Gazette* of 23 July 2004, says, 'I don't have to pitch any more, but I was a journalist for twenty years before people started ringing me to offer work.'

Encouragement from Dan Roberts? 'As any creative person knows ... crises of confidence and bouts of self-criticism are indicative of a serious, committed approach to writing. If you're a perfectionist, a little misery is part of the deal.' Read on for some more encouragement.

ASSIGNMENTS

1 *Assess yourself.* Journalists, as well as other kinds of writers, and physicians, need to know themselves. Knowing yourself helps you to avoid inflicting your prejudices on others and to focus on what your readers need to know. This assignment will help you to know yourself and to select the areas of interest you'll find it rewarding to write about. Total about 800 words.
   (a) Try to see yourself as others see you. Write an account of yourself in the third person. Include your appearance, family background and education, character (strengths and weaknesses), main interests, likes and dislikes, beliefs and political views.
   (b) What attracts you to journalism as a career? What are your ambitions?
   (c) List the publications you regularly read in one column, together with their main areas of interest, and your own interests and activities in an opposite column. Match up the publications you most enjoy reading with your main interests. Select one match where you detect a possibility, study the publication closely as advised, and when you're ready start pitching.
   (d) List the skills (keyboarding, etc.) that you possess that are useful for journalists and those that you need to develop further.

(e) List some of the books, both fiction and non-fiction, that you have read recently. Consider their usefulness for your career as a journalist, and whether your reading should be widened/deepened.

2 Study the current issues of *The Daily Telegraph* and your local paper. Reply to one letter to the editor in each (300 and 200 words respectively). Agree or disagree with the opinions expressed. Add to the content if you agree.

3 Indicate (200 words for each) how you would develop your letters into 800-word feature articles for those markets. Give a summary of the proposed content and suggest someone you might interview in each case when preparing such features.

2 Getting organized

If you're a staff writer much of the organizing that makes your work possible will be done for you and the necessary equipment will be at hand. But increasingly staff writers do some of their work at home and operate from two offices. Freelance writers have often worked as staff writers (and/or as editors/subeditors) before making the plunge.

Whether your interests are mainly as a staff writer or as a freelance, whether the freelance work is full time or part time, you need to be well organized at home (perhaps in a rented office away from home). You need to decide on the shape you have in mind for your career in journalism, your immediate and longer-term objectives. Then you will want those objectives to be reflected in the way you organize your time, equipment and all the business aspects.

BOOKS AND EQUIPMENT

A suggested list of reference books to start with is on pages 397–8. You will add to this according to the way your interests and commissions develop.

Publications vary in the way they want features to be submitted. By email (increasingly), on disk, by fax, by post? It's best to be prepared, so make sure your desk or work station is large enough to accommodate your computer and other equipment. A telephone, answering machine, fax machine and photocopier can be all in one package if you prefer. It's advisable to have broadband – a separate line for the Internet, making access much faster and allowing you to send and receive large files. Furthermore, although you can have an answering service on the line used for the Internet, editors don't like leaving messages.

You need a mobile phone, through which you can access your answerphone for messages when you're on the move. When emailing files your system doesn't have to be compatible with anyone else's. But some publications may insist on your using particular software, usually Microsoft Word but perhaps Quark if you are doing any subbing.

If you do much work while on the move, you will consider buying a laptop computer or even a palm/hand-held computer. On the latter you can currently write your features, visit websites, access emails, keep records of contact, and so on. Accessories include a full-size folding keyboard that fits into your pocket, modems and hand-held scanners. Take a look: the technology is advancing fast.

Your desk should be large enough to spread papers out and have sufficient drawers for stationery, including headed notepaper, business cards if you find them useful, and other essentials. It's a good idea to have a filing cabinet or two close at hand as well as shelves containing reference books.

Backing up

Losing important work on your computer (through a power cut for example) can be a disaster. Save on to your hard disk as you go. Then be prepared for any failure of your hard disk by archiving important work on floppy disks. You can be even more secure by using an online file storage service.

Have a tape recorder that you can connect to a telephone. You plug one end of a short cable into your tape recorder and at the other end is a rubber suction plug that you stick under the handset. For travelling use the telephone pickup (made by Olympus) consisting of a microphone that goes into your ear and records your interviewee and your own voice recycled through the handset. Ask permission before you tape people's telephone conversations.

Much of your secretarial work, keeping lists of clients and contacts and of negotiations with editors, and so on, can be done on catalogue cards or in a filofax system. Two organizers, whether desk diaries or filofax systems, are used by some writers, one for their personal lives and one for their work. Other writers use their computers for lists or a pocket-sized digital diary. Keep a telephone log to record the results of telephone calls relating to work, being careful to make full notes of briefings and (for tax purposes) the duration of the calls. Confirm briefings and agreements in writing.

RUNNING A BUSINESS

In the freelance writing business, like any other, you have a product to sell. Your features won't sell themselves. Unless you have been a staff writer and are starting off as a freelance with a regular contract or two you need to keep up a supply of ideas and features that are better than those of your competitors. True, the most important way to cultivate clients is to store up goodwill with editors by keeping to deadlines, working to the briefs, writing well and being accurate. But neglect the business aspects and you can watch lesser talents who don't neglect them become far more successful. Invest in some basic business training, get well organized, and in the long run you will save precious time.

In this chapter I'm assuming that you have to be:

- organizing your time
- constantly finding work
- keeping records
- taking care of financial matters
- making sure that you're operating legally and professionally.

What follows are the basic techniques that will help you achieve these goals.

Keeping records

As a freelance you need to keep a record of time spent on producing features (not forgetting that spent on research), so that you can chart your earning power as the years go by. Record expenses that have been agreed with editors, which may include travel and hotel and restaurant bills. Such records I keep in a hardbacked exercise book spread over two pages, with columns for titles, the publications, the time spent, dates of starting and finishing, where published, fees paid. On 4 April each year I draw a line across and total up fees, etc., for the tax year.

A record of pitches can be kept on 6 in. × 4 in. cards, one for each article (or in a ring binder, with one page for each title). Cross-reference these with another set of cards or pages each devoted to a target publication, contains its contact names, phone numbers and email addresses (kept up to date). Look at the history of your dealings when about to make the next pitch. There are various programs of course for computerizing such information.

Finding work

Develop ideas and pitch them to publications you've studied, as described in Chapters 3 to 6. Before you've established an effective network of clients and contacts (see Chapter 1) you may find it useful to promote yourself in more general ways. Try advertising and look for feature writing jobs advertised. The *Press Gazette* is a good place. But advertising in the press can be expensive, so experiment with other methods. Try sending out a mailshot – a flier or a brochure – if you can refer to some features published.

Note that on the whole punters, in whichever way they're pitching, emphasize what they specialize in, and most refer to websites where samples can be accessed. As described in Chapter 9, create your own website with a c.v. emphasizing journalistic experience and link it to articles published. It can also help to register with freelance directories online.

You may need to allocate a day or two weekly to finding work. Aim to get regular commissions from at least one or two clients. When one source of work dries up find another to replace it, diversify to keep up with current trends, and follow up a successful sale with new ideas.

Organizing your time

Schedule writing into the day first at a time when you're freshest. Slot in the other activities round it: the market study, reading on your subjects, researching your features, interviewing, corresponding, telephoning, managing the business. When arranging deadlines, calculate the time likely to be required for the various tasks. For a complex feature the actual writing may take up about a fifth or less of the total time whereas some features may be written off the top of your head in an hour or two. Does the fee proposed reflect the work involved? Make sure you have a comfortable chair that keeps your back straight. Don't spend too long at your desk in one session. Take breaks from your desk and find time for fresh air and exercise. Do some arm-stretching while still in your chair. Close your eyes for a minute or two occasionally. Circle your head slowly, drop your head on to your chest and raise it again several times. Do some deep breathing exercises.

A keyboard speed of 40 minutes is often recommended but somewhat less than this is adequate if you do your thinking as you work straight on to the keyboard. Touch typing will increase your speed but be careful to avoid back and neck strain, or even Repetitive Strain Injury (RSI). There's good advice online from Patient UK (www.patient.co.uk) and RSI/UK (www. demon.co.uk/rsi).

Financial matters

For your freelance activities you need to keep a check on time spent on writing and money earned. Records of all expenses incurred in your freelance work are required for income tax purposes. Find a computer program to keep your accounts in order and consider using a tax accountant.

Negotiate payment for an article when commissioned, before writing it. Although you may be unfussy about fees early in your career, eager for the opportunities, demand the proper price for work accepted once you have something of a portfolio to show. The proper price means at least the minimum rate that the publication should be paying for features, which is based on the advertising rates per page. If you accept lower fees, you will be doing other freelances out of work. Give a fair estimate of any expenses that will be incurred and make sure that they will be covered.

The *NUJ Freelance Guide* lists varying minimum rates for feature articles, news reporting, casual subbing, book royalties, and radio and TV scripts. These are the rates agreed with various book publishers, newspapers, magazines, the BBC, the Association of Independent Radio Contractors (commercial radio) and Independent TV Contractors Association (commercial TV). Most freelance work is negotiated directly with editors, and once you are established, you should be obtaining rates higher than the minimum ones.

Normally you indicate First British Serial Rights (FBSR) are being sold. If you sell world rights (English language) to a magazine, the fee should be doubled, and general world rights add 150 per cent. The booklet indicates that 50 per cent of an agreed fee is payable for work cancelled before it is begun. Delivered work which was definitely commissioned should be paid for in full, whether it is used or not. Get commissioned in writing: 'We'll have a look at it' on the phone is not a commission. And don't complain if you haven't fulfilled what was promised. Chapter 7 pursues this matter.

If there is no definite publication date for ordered work, try to negotiate a date of payment – perhaps within a month of submission of the work. Send an invoice with your copy, or at least a few days afterwards. If you negotiate a regular contract to produce work, you should try to get an agreement for a severance payment – usually one month's expected earnings for every year of contributing – and for some paid holiday time. The magazine business is volatile. If payment is not forthcoming for an article, ring the accounts department and you should be able to deduce from its reaction whether delay is common. As a last resort, you can consider taking out a summons through the small claims court.

Literary agents (see the *Writers' and Artists' Yearbook*) are rarely interested in short scripts, unless from the clients whose full-length works they are handling. Dealing with articles is not likely to be profitable for them, though a series of articles for a high-paying market, or the serialization of a book, might be.

Being professional

Membership of a professional organization will be a source of valuable support. The National Union of Journalists (NUJ) promotes and defends the incomes and conditions of employment of journalists, and provides various benefits and legal assistance. It is the largest member of the International Federation of Journalists, which links journalists throughout the world. Apart from the Fees Guide the NUJ publishes *The Journalist*, with its articles about trends and strikes, management problems and future prospects for the industry; *Freelance*, a news sheet giving details about branch meetings and updated information on agreements about fees and conditions made with various publishing houses; and the *Online Freelance Directory*. Other useful contacts, including online resources, are listed in Appendix 5.

ASSIGNMENTS

1 Read a news story of about 100 words three times, then put it away and reproduce it as faithfully as you can. Compare your version with the original. How does your order compare? Did you leave anything out? Was it important? Is your version clear and did you get the main point of the story across compellingly? If not, why not?
2 Read the intro to a feature, about 100 words. Follow the instructions to assignment 1.

---

3 From idea to publication

'Why are you here? Why aren't you sitting at home writing?' John Steinbeck said. The author of *Of Mice and Men* and *The Grapes of Wrath* and Nobel Prize winner was addressing his writing class at their first meeting.

He had started with the most important bit of advice he had to give. You have to develop your writing skills by doing it. All the rest – the lectures, the books like this one – is advice that you must adapt and apply to your particular purposes, to what you write, and the important thing is to write regularly. You don't become a good cook by reading cookbooks.

This chapter covers the whole process of producing a feature from idea to the piece on the published page. The following chapters expand on the different tasks.

THE FEATURE DEFINED

First, we'd better ask: what exactly is a feature? The best approach, I think, is to compare and contrast it with a news report.

Skills that are common to the production of news reports and features are the need to appeal to a wide audience and to be readable, in the sense of purveying accurate information in an interesting way as well as following correct usage, including grammar. Other forms of writing, for example the essay, of the pupil at school or the undergraduate, the business report and many other kinds of writing, must testify to knowledge of the subject tackled and must communicate clearly. But they don't have to appeal to a wide audience and the journalistic kind of readability is not a high priority. University graduates often find it difficult at first to leave an academic style and frame of mind behind.

Those common skills for reporting and feature writing are employed to satisfy a particular readership. That may be vast and varied, as for the popular national newspapers, or it may be narrowly specialized, as for professional journals. The writers on the staff of a publication soon get to know their readers and how to address them. They get to know their age group, educational level, lifestyles, and so on. Freelance writers have to make a special effort to market-study a publication they aim to write for, in the ways described in Chapter 5.

But we have to start with reporting and then see how feature writing builds from that basic skill: examine what features add to news content and the different structures they employ.

Content

Still the neatest way to illustrate what's news and what isn't is: 'man bites dog' is, 'dog bites man' isn't. News is about recent events, previously unknown, says the dictionary. Expanding somewhat, news has the qualities of conflict, human interest, importance, prominence, proximity, timeliness and unusualness, in varying degrees. News may be merely of public interest but it may also be, more importantly, in the public interest – of public concern.

Ideally, a news story is objective. The facts are ascertained by the reporter's five W questions (Who, What, When, Where and Why) plus How. That formula is a valuable guide to determining what any piece of writing is about. You ask whichever of the questions will fit, and sometimes they all fit.

News is often classified as either 'hard' or 'soft'. Hard news is about something important and sticks to the facts, as far as possible. Ideally, it is objective. Soft news is written round entertainment, personalities and human interest stories, and takes up most of the space in some of the national tabloids. You still need those questions.

A feature, says the dictionary, means something distinctive, or regular. Where does that 'regular' come in? Well, features on particular subjects tend to have regular places in a publication, with familiar and sometimes renowned bylines.

'Distinctive'? In journalism a feature, like a news story, aims to inform, but it may also narrate, describe, explain, persuade or entertain, and sometimes all five. It may aim to inspire or stimulate the reader to think or provoke to action. It has distinctive characteristics that add something to the facts.

Many features in newspapers and weekly news magazines fill in the background to the news and help us to put the news into perspective. They explain why events happened and may speculate on the consequences. Even features in the lifestyle sections of newspapers and in general interest magazines that aren't directly related to the news normally have a topical peg of some kind. For example, pieces on gardening, cooking, DIY and travel will get some topicality out of the seasons; other pieces will latch on to an anniversary, after looking up a Dictionary of Dates. But of course everybody's doing that, so do it sparingly and cleverly. Please don't even mention Christmas.

There is usually more space for a feature and therefore more scope for subjectivity, imaginative ways of gaining information, or for originality of expression. But features must be based on accurate reporting of the facts.

Subjectivity cannot be completely restrained, however, even in what sets out to be straightforward relaying of the facts. It's hard to be objective about the horrors of war. Robert Fisk, reporting 'this filthy war' in Afghanistan for *The Independent*, made it clear where his sympathies lay, and after being badly beaten up at an Afghan refugee camp in Pakistan declared that he would have behaved like his attackers if he had been an Afghan refugee.

Such 'point-of-view reporting' has increased since the broadcast media became the main purveyors of the news as it breaks. When the main news is televised at night the morning paper has to try to add something to the news and comment creeps in. Middlebrow papers have features reflecting on the social issues underlying TV's sitcoms. Popular papers give much space to the private lives of the stars of TV soaps. Thus the distinctions between hard and soft news and between news stories and features have become blurred.

The feature writer should make it as clear as possible where facts end and point of view begins. But it's not a simple matter. Subjectivity is in every breath you take and is behind every selection you make of the facts.

Structure

News structure in newspapers is often an inverted pyramid shape, the most important point coming first, explained by answering those six questions (or as many of them as are relevant). Readers short of time can content themselves with the first paragraph. As the news comes in items have to be cut to make room, and the structure described makes it easy for subeditors to cut from the bottom. This doesn't always work because breaking news may require changes and the subeditor may have some rewriting to do.

The danger in relying too much on the inverted pyramid shape is that the reporter may produce a first paragraph or two that is overloaded with detail. Something like:

> Joe Quinn, who comes from Cork, is preparing to complete a sponsored walk on July 25, setting off at 10.30 am from Tooting Bec in London with the aim of raising funds for The Greater Chernobyl Cause (GCC), which will go to the Ayagus orphanage in the town of Seipalatinsk, Kazakhstan, children having regularly been abandoned there since the atom bomb testing in the region in 1949.
>
> The side-effects remain today and children are still being born with multiple deformities.

That first par certainly gives you who, what, when, where, why and how, but it should start with the what, the story in a nutshell, and bring in the details later. Something like:

> A London-based Irishman is walking to raise funds for the severely deformed children in an orphanage in Kazakhstan.

The rest should be covered in shorter sentences, avoiding subordinate clauses ('who comes from … which will go to …') and participial phrases ('having regularly been abandoned').

The term *news story* reminds us that there must be an angle to a report: the facts must be selected and ordered to make the point concisely and readably.

While the reporter is told to 'kiss' (keep it short and simple), the feature writer is allowed more scope for individuality in structure as well as content, as long as the prescribed length is adhered to, and words are not wasted. In other words a feature should need only light subbing, and sometimes the writer is contacted to do any necessary subbing or to agree to a cut. Features, in their greater complexity, take many different shapes. A common shape is the pyramid the right way up, with a conclusion of some sort at the end.

A word here about the basic differences between the newspaper feature and the magazine article. The former is generally urgent in tone with information being used to work out viewpoints or conclusions. The latter is more inclined to spread itself, giving more attention to colour and readability; it

19

may be more inclined to raise questions or doubts and to leave you to come to your own conclusions.

THE STAGES IN PRODUCTION

Which is the best route from idea to the feature on the published page? There will be several shortcuts once you've got editors ringing you to ask for a thousand words next Monday. If you have, you can skip this chapter. If you haven't, let's assume you want to get published a feature of, say, 600 to 800 words. How would you go about it?

There are features of this length you can do out of the top of your head: personal experience, humorous columns, a day at the races. Jot down a few points, indicate the best order for them and get on with it is the norm. Or do a draft and polish it up for a final version. Even then you might find it better to work from a brief outline: provisional title, intro, body, conclusion, indicating a few linking devices.

But few good features come straight out of your head, even modest-length ones. So let's assume that you'll have to do some information gathering and make a few notes before planning and writing up. On the way you'll have to deal with editors, and there may be ways of following up. Here are the stages you might want or need to go through:

- From idea to market
- Getting commissioned
- Gathering information
- Simple outlining
- Writing up methods
- Vetting and rewriting
- Submission
- Spin-offs.

From idea to market

A subject for a feature is not enough: you need an idea. An effective title can make it clear how good an idea it is. 'Giving doctor a taste of his own medicine', a *Guardian* article, is a study of how barriers to communication between doctors are being broken down. 'The education of doctors' would have indicated the general subject only.

An idea is a specific angle or approach to a subject. Ideas for features tend to deal with a specific problem, tension, drama, struggle, conflict, question, doubt or anxiety. The subject 'Police in Britain Today' may become the idea 'The Police: Are They Racist?' Editors consider not only whether their readers would like the idea, or want it, but whether they *need* it.

Ideas may come at any time – on a bus, in a pub or restaurant, while watching TV. This means that you should carry a notebook and pen wherever you go (or a dictaphone). Have your notebooks paced at strategic points in your home – in the bathroom, kitchen, sitting room, on your desk, on your bedside table. Surf the net for ideas, via newsletters and discussion groups. As a staff feature writer ideas will come out of the news and features currently of interest to the readers of the publication you work for. Many of them may be suggested by your editor. As a freelance you have to be constantly producing ideas and pitching them.

Sometimes the idea comes to you first. You work out what the likely market is, and then narrow it down to a target publication or two. Sometimes your ideas may be suggested in the course of your market-study of likely targets. Whichever order they come in, you have to attune your ideas carefully to target publications. You will be reshaping some of the rejected ideas for other targets.

At an early stage in a writing career, depending on how much choice you have in the matter, it's best to concentrate on subjects that you know something about so that you don't get bogged down in research that slows down your rate of production. But keep in mind that what journalists can find out is more important than what they know. It is specialists that are in greater demand, so develop a few specialisms as you go.

Carry out basic market study by consulting the marketing guide books mentioned in Chapter 2, but that is no substitute for studying several issues of any target publication. As well as recording your dealings with publications (see page 12), file pages out of newspapers and magazines that indicate their policies and formulas – for example, letters pages, editorials and the contents pages of magazines. Newspapers and magazines can take up a lot of space and hoarding them indiscriminately in the hope that this constitutes market study can be counter-productive. It's also a good idea to file pages (photocopy newspaper pages) that you find good models of different kinds of articles, good models of writing techniques, especially those that deal with your interests. Make a few notes in the margins. Sample likely publications online, including ezines – but note how much, if anything, they pay.

From market to idea

The above implies a move from idea to market and of course it's often the other way round. Ideas suggest themselves while you're looking through publications.

You find a woman's monthly magazine interesting so you take a closer look, by studying the past six months' issues or more. Much can be learned from the Contents page. You note which features are contributed by staff – you look for the regular columns and the pieces that are set up by the magazine for the staff writers.

The pieces by freelances, you note, include a fair number of interviews, thickly quoted ones. Many of the interviewees are women with unusual jobs. The interviews run between 800 and 1400 words. It so happens that you've just read a news story in your local paper about a woman who built up a mail-order business from home after being struck down by multiple sclerosis. You work out a way of developing this story for *She*, by doing some research into the disease and by finding out what help is available for the disabled to work in this way.

So, in whichever order you found them, you have an idea and a target publication. Where do you go from here?

Getting commissioned

You will have done just enough preliminary research into that disease before you pitch your idea to *She*. A main selling point will be that you can indicate that you have an interesting angle on it for those readers. You can't afford to spend much time on research without a commission behind you. As you progress in a particular field, your commissions will require you to update information-filled files rather than start from scratch.

Figures 3.1 and 3.2 show sample pages from the *Writers' and Artists' Yearbook* and Macmillan's *Writers' Handbook*. These are basic guidelines on how to get commissioned. The American *Writer's Market* gives much more detail and is accessible online. You have to be careful to update the information by studying current and recent issues of the publications. Many magazines provide up-to-date guidelines online. Some magazines (again, more notably American ones) will supply, automatically on

Editor Francesca Rhydderch
Quarterly £5.40 (£20 p.a., £38 2 yrs)

Literary – critical articles, short stories, poems, book reviews, interviews and profiles. Especially, but not exclusively, concerned with Welsh writing in English. Theatre in Wales section. Length: up to 3000 words (articles). Illustrations: colour. Payment: £50 per 1000 words (articles); £25 per poem, £75 per short story, £40 per review, £60 per illustration. Founded 1988.

New Woman

EMAP Élan, Endeavour House, 189 Shaftesbury Avenue, London WC2H 8JG
tel 020-7437 9011 *fax* 020-7208 3585
email lizzi.hosking@hotmail.com
website www.newwoman.co.uk
Editor Sara Cremer
Monthly £2.60

Features up to 2000 words. Occasionally accepts unsolicited articles; enclose sae for return. No fiction. Payment: at or above NUJ rates. Illustrated. Founded 1988.

The New Writer

PO Box 60, Cranbrook, Kent TN17 2ZR
tel (01580) 212626 *fax* (01580) 212041
email editor@thenewwriter.com
website www.thenewwriter.com
Editor Suzanne Ruthven *Publisher* Merric Davidson
6 p.a. £3.95

Features, short stories from guest writers and from subscribers, poems, news and reviews. Seeks forward-looking articles on all aspects of the written word that demonstrate the writer's grasp of contemporary writing and current editorial/publishing policies. Length: approx. 1000 words (articles), longer pieces considered; 1000–2000 words (features). Payment: £20 per 1000 words (articles), £10 (stories), £3 (poems). Founded 1996.

The Newspaper

Young Media Ltd, PO Box 121, Tonbridge, Kent TN12 5ZR
tel (01622) 871297 *fax* (01622) 871927
email editor@thenewspaper.org.uk
website www.thenewspaper.org.uk
Editor Jenny MacDonald
6 p.a. Free

Newspaper aimed at 8–14 year-old schoolchildren for use as part of the National Curriculum. Contains similar columns as in any national daily newspaper. Length: 800–1000 words for features and short stories (non-fiction). Payment: £250 per item. Illustrations: colour. Founded 1999.

Now

IPC Media Ltd, King's Reach Tower, Stamford Street, London SE1 9LS
tel 020-7261 7366 *fax* 020-7261 6789
Editor Jane Ennis
Weekly £1.10

Showbiz magazine of celebrity gossip, news, fashion, health and cookery. Most articles are commissioned or are written by in-house writers. Founded 1996.

Nursery Education

Scholastic Ltd, Villiers House, Clarendon Avenue, Leamington Spa, Warks. CV32 5PR
tel (01926) 887799 *fax* (01926) 883331
email earlyyears@scholastic.co.uk
website www.scholastic.co.uk
Editor Susan Sodhi
Monthly £3.75

Practical theme-based activities for educators working with 3–5 year-olds. All ideas based on the Early Learning Goals. Material mostly commissioned.Length: 500–1000 words. Illustrations: colour and b&w; colour posters. Payment: by arrangement. Founded 1997.

Nursery World

Admiral House, 66–68 East Smithfield, London E1W 1BX
tel 020-7782 3120
Editor Liz Roberts
Weekly £1.30

For all grades of primary school, nursery and child care staff, nannies, foster parents and all concerned with the care of expectant mothers, babies and young children. Authoritative and informative articles, 800 or 1300 words, and photos, on all aspects of child welfare and early education, from 0–8 years, in the UK. Practical ideas, policy news and career advice. No short stories. Payment: by arrangement. Illustrations: line, half-tone, colour.

Nursing Times

EMAP Healthcare, Greater London House, Hampstead Road, London NW1 7EJ
tel 020-7874 0500 *fax* 020-7874 0505
Editor Rachel Downey
Weekly £1.10

Articles of clinical interest, nursing education and nursing policy. Illustrated articles not longer than 2000 words. Contributions from other than health professionals sometimes accepted. Press day: Monday. Illustrations: photos, line, cartoons. Payment: NUJ rates; by arrangement for illustrations. Founded 1905.

Figure 3.1
Page from *Writers' and Artists' Yearbook 2005*. © A. & C. Black, London, 2004

Circulation 16,500

Founded 1962. MONTHLY. Aimed at Brownie members aged 7–10.

ARTICLES Crafts and simple make-it-yourself items using inexpensive or scrap materials.

FICTION Brownie content an advantage. No adventures involving unaccompanied children in dangerous situations – day or night. Max. 650 words. PAYMENT £50 per 1000 words pro rata.

Build It

1 Canada Square, Canary Wharf, London E14 5AP

☎020 7772 8440 Fax 020 7772 8584

✉ buildit@mrn.co.uk

www.buildit-online.co.uk

Owner *Inside Communications*
Editor *Catherine Monk*

Founded 1990. MONTHLY magazine covering self-build, conversion and renovation. Unsolicited material welcome on self-build case studies as well as articles on technical construction, architecture and design and dealing with builders. Max. length 2500 words. Approach by phone, post or e-mail.

The Burlington Magazine

14–16 Duke's Road, London WC1H 9SZ

☎020 7388 1228 Fax 020 7388 1230

✉ editorial@burlington.org.uk

www.burlington.org.uk

Owner *The Burlington Magazine Publications Ltd*
Managing Director *Kate Trevelyan*
Editor *Richard Shone*
Associate Editors *Bart Cornelis, Jane Martineau*

Founded 1903. MONTHLY. Unsolicited contributions welcome on the subject of art history provided they are previously unpublished. All preliminary approaches should be made in writing.

EXHIBITION REVIEWS Usually commissioned, but occasionally unsolicited reviews are published if appropriate. Max. 1000 words.

ARTICLES Max. 4500 words.

SHORTER NOTICES Max. 2000 words.

PAYMENT articles, £140 (max.); shorter notices, £80 (max.).

Business Brief

PO Box 582, Five Oaks, St Saviour JE4 8XQ

☎01534 611600 Fax 01534 611610

✉ mspeditorial@msppublishing.com

Owner *MSP Publishing*
Editor *Peter Body*

Circulation 6,500 (Jersey & Guernsey)

Founded 1989. MONTHLY magazine covering business developments in the Channel Islands and how they affect the local market. Styles itself as the magazine for business people rather than just a magazine about business. Interested in business-orientated articles only – 800 words max. Approach the editor by e-mail in the first instance with telephone follow-up. PAYMENT negotiable.

Business Traveller

Nestor House, Playhouse Yard, London EC4V 5EX

☎020 7778 0000 Fax 020 7778 0022

✉ editorial@businesstraveller.com

www.businesstraveller.com

Owner *Euromoney Institutional Investor Plc*
Editor-in-Chief *Tom Otley*
Circulation 500,000 (worldwide)

MONTHLY. Consumer publication. Opportunities exist for freelance writers but unsolicited contributions tend to be about leisure travel rather than business travel. Would-be contributors are strongly advised to study the magazine or the website first. Approach in writing with ideas.

PAYMENT varies.

Camcorder User

Highbury Entertainment London, 53–79 Highgate Road, London NW5 1TW

☎020 7331 1000 Fax 020 7331 1242

✉ rob.hull@highburywv.com

www.camuser.co.uk

Owner *Highbury WV*
Editor *Robert Hull*
Circulation 15,000

Founded 1988. MONTHLY magazine dedicated to camcorders, with features on creative technique, shooting advice, new equipment, accessory round-ups and interesting applications on location. Unsolicited mss, illustrations and pictures welcome. PAYMENT negotiable.

Campaign

22 Bute Gardens, London W6 7HN

☎020 8267 4683 Fax 020 8267 4914

✉ campaign@haynet.com

www.brandrepublic.com

Owner *Haymarket Publishing Ltd*
Editor *Caroline Marshall*
Circulation 17,700

Founded 1968. WEEKLY. Lively magazine serving the advertising and related industries.

Figure 3.2
Page from *The Writer's Handbook 2005*. © Macmillan Publishers Ltd., 2004, ed. Barry Turner

commission or in response to a request, more detailed guidelines, which may include:

- How to pitch: by telephone, fax, email, letter.
- How detailed the pitch should be: whether they want a summary, a brief outline, a detailed outline.
- What personal details are required: a c.v., a brief summary of career outlining qualifications for tackling the idea proposed?
- What evidence of writing skill is required: by fax, by email (where they may be linked to your website), cuttings by post, or bring your portfolio to an interview?
- The publication's house style, the forms of words and phrases that a particular publication insists on. It may refer to *The Times Style Book* or *The Economist Style Guide* (Figure 3.3) but may add some special preferences (see below).
- Details of the publication's readership, policy/philosophy, the formulas they want their features to adhere to, lengths and treatments required for particular subjects, the cooperation with subeditors required, and so on. A good example of this is the booklet *Writing for Reader's Digest* which you can buy (see page 403).
- How to submit: for example, if by email attachment, should it be in .rtf (rich text format)?

Gathering information

At this stage let's survey some sources of information and the techniques for using them on a fairly basic level.

There are four main sources for getting (and updating) information: from your own knowledge and experience; by legwork; by printed sources; and by interviews and conversations.

Participators in an event are first-hand sources. These include your own observation and experience, and interviews or surveys carried out at an event at the time. Second-hand sources include interviews with eyewitnesses and opinion surveys taken after the event when the recall may be less accurate; official sources such as PROs of companies, spokesmen for institutions and their publications and publicity materials; experts' views; and all the other printed sources.

Punctuation

APOSTROPHES. Use the normal possessive ending **'s** after singular words or names that end in **s: boss's, caucus's, Delors's, St James's, Jones's, Shanks's.** Use it after plurals that do not end in **s: children's, Frenchmen's, media's.**

Use the ending **s'** on plurals that end in **s – Danes', bosses', Joneses'** – including plural names that take a singular verb, eg, **Reuters', Barclays', Stewarts & Lloyds', Salomon Brothers'.**

Although singular in other respects, the United States, the United Nations, the Philippines, etc, have a plural possessive apostrophe: eg, **What will the United States' next move be?**

Peoples' = of peoples. **People's** = of (the) people.

Try to avoid using **Lloyd's** (the insurance market) as a possessive; it poses an insoluble problem.

The vulnerable part of the hero of the Trojan war is best described as an **Achilles** heel.

Do not put apostrophes into decades: the **1990s** not the **1990's.**

BRACKETS. If a whole sentence is within brackets, put the full stop inside.

Square brackets should be used for interpolations in direct quotations: **"Let them [the poor] eat cake."** To use ordinary curved brackets implies that the words inside them were part of the original text from which you are quoting.

COLONS. Use a colon "to deliver the goods that have been invoiced in the preceding words" (Fowler). **They brought presents: gold, frankincense and oil at $35 a barrel.**

Use a colon before a whole quoted sentence, but not before a quotation that begins mid-sentence. **She said: "It will never work." He retorted that it had "always worked before".**

Use a colon for antithesis or "gnomic contrasts" (Fowler). **Man proposes: God disposes.**

COMMAS. Use commas as an aid to understanding. Too many in one sentence can be confusing.

It is not necessary to put a comma after a short phrase at the start of a sentence if no natural pause exists there: **On August 2nd he invaded. Next time the world will be prepared.** But a breath, and so a comma, is needed after longer passages: **When it was plain that he had his eyes on Saudi Arabia as well as Kuwait, America responded.**

Figure 3.3
Page from *The Economist Style Guide,* Eighth Edition. Hamish Hamilton/The Economist Books Ltd., 1993 (first published as *The Economist Pocket Style Book* by The Economist Publications Ltd., 1986)

Personal experience

When you can bring some personal experience into your knowledge of a subject it's unique and can be valuable. It will often be unconsciously employed. You may be able to write an occasional article almost entirely based on personal experience. How you faced extreme danger, or conquered anorexia, or established a club to keep disaffected youths off the streets, or started a new career as a freelance journalist in middle age should provide good bases for features.

To repeat, though, recognize that it's what you find out that's interesting rather than what you know. Work out how your subject is illuminated by having other experience, from other sources, used as a commentary on your own.

Legwork

You go somewhere and find out for yourself: that is the basic legwork activity of the journalist. You visit a fire, a factory, a mental hospital, a prison, a café, a pub or a government department, and you make notes on what you see and hear there. You'll take a notebook and perhaps a tape recorder as well.

Printed sources

Appendix 5 lists some organizations with materials and facilities available for researching journalists. It's worthwhile putting yourself on the mailing list of organizations, including companies in business, that are concerned with your specialisms or interests.

Time allowing, get informed on a subject from:

- Your cuttings. Replace your cuttings with information that updates them. Have a regular clear-out of old cuttings, keep your files manageable and don't cast your net too wide.
- The library: books, newspapers, magazines.
- The library: electronic databases.
- Handouts, brochures and other materials from business organizations and voluntary associations.
- Scripts or back-up information from broadcasting organizations.
- The Internet.

Find the time to read enough to be able to select information that is significant and striking, to argue well, and to avoid leaving the reader with the feeling there's a gap or that your treatment is superficial.

Readers new to researching techniques will find Kenneth Whittaker's *Using a Library* (Andre Deutsche) and Ann Hoffmann's *Research for Writers* (A. & C. Black) useful. A good encyclopedia in book or CD form can get you started into a subject and the entries provide brief bibliographies.

Find out from the indexes to publications which articles relevant to your subject have been published recently. The *British Humanities Index* (BHI) covers the broadsheet national papers and a selection of magazines. The broadsheets and several magazines produce their own indexes. Once you have noted published features you can access some of them on CD-ROM or microfilm and print them out. Some publications, however, have replaced these facilities by giving access to material online and some of this you have to pay for. Access Amazon online for titles of books on your subject.

Organization indexes such as the *Directory of British Associations* (DBA) list pressure groups of all kinds that will provide you with literature. Put yourself on the mailing list of organizations in whose activities you are interested and which are potential sources of material. PR companies, PROs and press contacts are listed in *Hollis Press and Public Relations Annual*.

Interviews and conversations

Even for the briefest interview during legwork or the five-minute phone call, prepare your questions carefully (ones that elicit useful answers: see Chapter 8). When researching a feature you might find good case study material in Internet chatlines. Talk to anybody who might have an interesting contribution to make, online or anywhere.

The oldest idea can be given fresh impetus by a well selected interviewee. That may be an acknowledged expert who has been difficult to corner, or an unusual choice who has a revelation to share.

Reference books for names you might need to interview include *DBA*; *Who's Who*; the various extensions of *Who's Who* (*Who's Who in the Theatre*, etc.); The Central Office of Information's directory of press and PROs in government departments and public corporations; film and TV annuals, *Spotlight* for agents of showbiz/film/theatre celebrities; *Willing's Press Guide*, whose back pages list hundreds of specialized magazines; *Keesing's Record of World Events*; and *The Statesman's Yearbook*.

Give authoritative sources for facts and figures especially where they might be queried. If in doubt, say 'according to' or 'allegedly'. Editors appreciate a separate list of key sources attached to an article in case there is checking/updating to be done in the office. But keep your confidential sources to yourself.

For picture research see Chapter 14.

Note-taking basics

Some notes may be taken on the move, in your reporter's hard-backed notebook, and that may suffice for many features.

The NCTJ and other training organizations require journalism students to gain a shorthand qualification, for lack of accurate notes of an interview can lose libel cases. Transcripts of a taped interview and the tape itself should be kept for at least a year after publication of the piece in case an interviewee claims misrepresentation. For an interview of any length take notes as well as tape recording. Record what the number indicator says at key points, for example, or note where you feel you've got an incomplete answer that you might like to follow up later.

If you have not learned shorthand, work out some system. Journalists use Teeline, easy to learn from a book and/or evening classes, and more convenient than the more elaborate traditional systems. If you need to increase your note-taking speed, practise at lectures, meetings, or from radio talks.

You may have thoughts as you go about the points you're noting. If so, put them under the notes in square brackets. Note the source at the end of each note thus glossed so that you can return to it later for checking. Compile a list of sources with full details so that you can easily locate them. Details might include authors, titles of books or articles, publishers or titles of publications with dates published, page numbers, names of interviewees with dates of interviews, events attended with dates. Editors might want your list of sources in case checking in-house is needed at the time of publication.

For complex tasks resulting in long features (say 3000 words or more) you may find it difficult to put those notebook notes in order, and you may also have a pile of original or photocopied source materials. Try transferring notes regularly to A4 sheets or to 6 in. × 4 in. cards, written on one side only so that you can shuffle them into the order required. Then do a logical outline like the one on pages 165–6, indicating where your various materials will slot in. There are computer programs that can help with this kind of organizing.

In your own words

Paraphrase when making notes so that you do not repeat other writers' words and risk being accused of plagiarism. Do a complete job of this immediately. Put quotation marks round significant statements that you may want to reword later or use as quotes because the point is being expertly expressed, or because you want to show that the manner of expressing it is revealing of the writer.

Noting selectively

Don't make too many notes. Read and digest background material, then select only those points that are central to your purpose. Over-researching, as already suggested, encourages procrastination – the feeling that you don't know enough and must examine further.

Checking the facts

Facts and figures should be double-checked before submission of the final version. If you've extracted some figures from a newspaper report, for example, you should check what you've said against that report, and then check against the original source, if known – the government department or local authority or statistical publication or whatever. Check also doubtful spellings of names.

When figures don't look quite right, a check against the original source may reveal that the figures themselves are correct, but that other facts or figures that were needed to put them into context are lacking. For example, we often learn that the figures for certain crimes are increasing. But does this mean that the crime is being committed more often or that more people are reporting it, or that police activity and success in bringing offenders to account are increasing?

Simple outlining

As a child (and sometimes much later) what you had to say all spilled out, along with several other things. 'Yes dear, but what do you want to say exactly?' you were asked. Eventually, with luck, you learned that to make clear what your main point is and what backs it up you must put what you have to say in order.

We do it unconsciously in our heads all the time. One way of describing this order is: 'Hey! You! See! So!' We can rely on this ability for short features and it's not a bad basic formula. Let's take a closer look:

- Hey! You! – grab your readers' attention and show why they should be interested (intro, teaser, hook, beginning). 'You' turns into 'we' when a general argument is being pursued.
- See! – this is what I have to say (body, middle).
- So! (conclusion, summary, clincher, ending).

A feature in the *Western Morning News* supporting organic farming begins by telling readers that 'we humans are a part of the natural life cycle of the planet'. The body gives evidence of health benefits from organic foods and relates conversations with people in shops and market stalls selling organic, and customers buying it. The conclusion is that we need a return to traditional farming methods containing 'a high percentage of organic farming'. It would be 'a huge step forward for the human race and our wellbeing'.

You'll have your own ways of bringing about a good structure. You may prefer to work towards it in drafts, improving the shape each time, although most journalists tend to do all their tinkering or tweaking on the computer as they go. You may prefer to work it all out before you start with an elaborate outline that has the feature almost written before you start. Or you may like to saturate yourself in your material, make a substantial outline, put it aside, plunge into the writing and check with the outline when you come to the end. Does the outline suggest that there's a better structure or does what you've written improve on it? Does the outline reveal that you've left important points out?

Whichever, there has to be a sense of freedom somewhere in the act of writing up, so that your imagination, where it is needed, can flourish, fresh ideas can be generated, and serendipity can happen. Too rigid or too elaborate outlines can be repressive. So be prepared to reject or redo an outline that doesn't work well and start again.

Among the simplest formulas is the list. A 500- to 600-word piece on a Science Museum or the attractions of a city for a travel/holiday page works perfectly as a list of selected attractions to appeal to the readership. A brief hello at the start and goodbye at the finish will serve as intro and conclusion. Travel pieces at greater length, of the service kind, can have the same approach: for example, places to visit, places to avoid; or things to see, things to do; or day life, night life; or combinations.

You can use a simple formula for ordering a short or simple feature. Note the different points or aspects you have to cover. Then number them, say 1 to 4, according to how interesting or important they are. You may find 1, 4, 3, 2 the best formula, or if you have a great ending 2, 4, 3, 1. A longer article might work with 1, 6, 3, 4, 5, 2. Making a circle can produce a satisfying pattern. The conclusion echoes the intro, like a snake swallowing its tail.

Writing up methods

As mentioned computers have made rewriting as you go easier, however badly change is required: tweaking, tinkering, editing, rewriting are terms that suggest from little to much effort. The process of rewriting and reordering is made so easy. On the other hand that facility brings the danger that you may tinker too much and, especially if it's a longish piece, that you might lose sight of the whole. It's wise anyway, when you get to the end of a piece, to make a printout or two of the whole to edit. Keep earlier versions so that if you decide against certain changes you can easily reverse them. If at the editing stage you find a faulty structure, cutting the pars out and reordering them may work well. Paste or staple them on to sheets in the order wanted before rewriting.

Others have to get the intro right before they can get going. They write and rewrite it over and over again until they're completely satisfied. They then find that the rest of the article comes easily. Others find that if they get hung up on the intro it slows them down badly. They find that for them it's best to put something down to start so that they get going into the middle, and that the intro will come when they get to the end.

You may find that some of your best writing is done in overdrive. You're full of your subject, passion is driving you on, the unconscious is let off the rein and you allow the sentences to flow. Collect from the shores of your consciousness like a river picking up debris as it runs. When the flow has subsided, remove any rubbish and put things in order. Some of the ideas yielded by the unconscious may be so valuable that you will revise your outline to include them.

Vetting and rewriting

Your way of revising on paper or on screen will depend on the way you put your draft together in the first place. If you tend to work from a detailed plan you may find the piece well structured but too predictable: you may need to inject surprises – in the content or in the language. If you tend to write now, worry later, you may find too many surprises and a lack of clarity and structure. Assume you share the faults of both writers when considering drafts.

Editors say about a feature they like that 'it reads short', and about a feature they don't that 'it reads long'. Articles with the faults described above read long. Even if they're only 600 words they can be boring or wordily confusing. An article of 2000 words can read short, as if it were 600. A readable piece holds the attention throughout. Readability is achieved essentially by:

Content:

- making it interesting (entertaining, thought-provoking, etc.) for the target readership
- making it accurate and convincing (check facts and figures again in case errors were made in the writing up).

Structure:

- linking clearly (see Figure 11.1 for an example).

Language:

- making it as simple and direct as possible
- creating pace
- supplying excitement, passion, inspiration, etc.

Before your final version, put the latest draft of your article aside for an hour or two, or a day or two if you have the time. It will then be easier to read it with the eyes of an editor, freshly and objectively. Read it more than once, concentrating on particular aspects: first for content, second for structure and then again to look closely at the language.

Checklist

1 Is the overall *purpose* and *audience* clear? (Why did you write the piece? What did you hope to achieve by it? Was it effectively communicated to the readers you had in mind?)
2 Is the *content* adequate for the purpose? Is it significant enough? Was some information inaccessible? Did you manage to replace it?
3 Is the *idea* clear and compelling? Have you said exactly what you wanted to say?
4 Does the *form* (structure and language) match the *idea* and the *content*? Does it pass the readability test for interest, directness, pace and linkage?

For those who like code words you have PACIFIC.

Submission

When commissioned you will be told how to submit or given alternatives: by post, as email (attachment on disk?). Send two scripts ('hard copies') with a disk. Give a daily paper two weeks to consider your work, a weekly about six weeks, and a monthly about three months before sending a reminder to the editor, and have a list of other targets prepared so that rejected work is immediately sent out again (adapting or rewriting as necessary).

As a freelance, when work has been sent off it is advisable to start something new immediately: the best consolation for rejection is new work progressing well.

Following house style

As part of your market study of a publication you note its house style, the particular forms and usages preferred. If you receive writer's guidelines from a publication you may be given the advice that in general *The Times Stylebook* or *The Economist Style Guide* is followed, plus a list of such preferences as '-ise' rather than '-ize', the forms of dates used and the way military ranks are printed.

Spin-offs

Clearly it helps if you can decide on possibilities at as early a stage as possible. When you open a file for a feature idea immediately note any spin-off potential. Ideas for spin-offs may come at any stage of the feature production. You might consider:

- multiple submissions, using a syndication agency perhaps
- multi-purposing from the start
- reshaping for different targets
- a script for radio or TV
- a book.

Multiple submissions

If your feature has a fairly timeless theme, you may want to send it out to one publication at a time rather than to several. You want to avoid two publications publishing, or wanting to publish, your feature at the same time (if this happens they may not be keen to use your services in the future). If you can be patient and decisions don't take too long, and if you're reasonably successful in getting features printed, sending out to one at a time is the best policy.

Point out that an early decision is needed, because if it's not wanted you will want to try another target. Another advantage of one-at-a-time is that if rejected there's an opportunity to rewrite the piece before sending it on.

On the other hand, if you have a piece that needs an early publication date because of a topical peg, you may want to send it out to several publications at the same time. Some feature editors may take months to decide on submissions. Play it by ear, find out how different editors react, establish relationships with editors that allow you to discuss this question of timing candidly.

Multi-purposing from the start

Most obviously a feature must be multi-purposing in the sense that it must both inform and entertain. It may serve other purposes, such as move the reader emotionally, persuade, amuse. As has also been pointed out, a feature has to engage with a large audience. That probably means both sexes and certainly a wide range of age groups, educational levels, interests, and so on.

Syndication

But multi-purposing can be taken much further. Written in a certain way the same feature can be syndicated all over a country, and worldwide.

You can do it on your own: offer the same feature to local newspapers, including freesheets, all over the country. Specify release time and date and indicate that you have not offered to other newspaper groups in the same circulation area. Each publication pays a small fee because of the restricted rights.

A syndication agency is worth considering. A regular feature used by many targets can bring substantial rewards, but you're likely to need a syndication agency (see the *Writers' and Artists' Yearbook*). But domestic syndication is more easily achieved in large countries, such as the United States, Canada and Australia, where there are many regional papers. Notable examples are the humorous columns of the Americans Art Buchwald (the Washington Post) and Russell Baker (the New York Times), who syndicate extensively in the USA and abroad.

In a small country such as the UK, writers tend to look for overseas syndication possibilities. *Freelance Market News* is aimed at the beginner (Figure 3.4 shows a sample page). More in Chapter 20.

Reshaping for different targets

When the publications you want to reach with your subjects are quite different reshaping may be needed. Suppose one of your subjects is mentally handicapped. You have done a fair amount of research and have plenty of notes and cuttings on file (you may already have published an article or two). The subject for various reasons gets into the news so you decide

Overseas Markets

Fantasy & Science Fiction is an American magazine which issues the following guidelines: "We are looking for stories that will appeal to science fiction and fantasy readers. The SF element may be slight, but it should be present. We prefer character-oriented stories. We receive a lot of fantasy fiction but never enough science fiction or humour. Do not query for fiction; send the entire manuscript. We publish fiction up to 25,000 words in length. We do not accept electronic submissions. Please type your manuscript on white paper, double spaced, with one inch margins. Writers from abroad are encouraged to send recyclable manuscripts with IRCs or 80 cents in US postage. We prefer not to see more than one submission from a writer at a time. Payment is 6-9 cents per word on acceptance."
Address: Gordon Van Gelder, Editor, Fantasy & Science Fiction, P.O. Box 3447, Hoboken, NJ 07030, U.S.A.

Body & Soul is an American magazine which is published eight times a year. They say, "Our editorial objective is to serve as an inspirational guide for all those who want to live healthier, more balanced lives. We cover a wide range of subjects: integrative medicine, nutrition, self-help psychology, spirituality, the mind/body connection, work and money issues, and organic living. We provide the information readers need to take an active role in improving their lives and preserving the planet. We are looking for quality writing and thorough reporting to inform and entertain our audience. We publish four features per issue (1,500 to 3,000 words); and around 16 relatively short (250 to 1,200 words) consumer-centric items. Our payment rates range from $50 for a short news piece to $1,500 or more for a feature story. Fees are determined on an individual basis. It is best to send a query letter with clips of recent work and a resumé. We cannot consider submissions sent via e-mail."
Address: Body & Soul, Editorial Department, 42 Pleasant St, Watertown, MA 02472, U.S.A.
Website: www.bodyandsoulmag.com

Van Gogh's Ear is an anthology series devoted to publishing excellent poetry in English by major voices (which have included John Updike and Yoko Ono) and innovative new talent from around the world. They welcome all forms of poetry, from traditional to experimental. Submit up to five poems at a time with a cover letter and SAE/IRCs. Published poets receive a copy of the issue in which their work appears.
Address: French Connection Press, 12 rue Lamartine, 75009 Paris, France.
Website: www.frenchcx.com/frenchcxn.press.html

Traveltalk Australia is a quarterly publication which has recently made the transition from a Perth-based Western Australian magazine to a national publication. It includes international travel articles about places that Australian travellers like to visit, so this may be a good opportunity for UK-based freelancers to do some travel writing without having to move too far from home. The editor, Jane Hammond Foster, suggests you contact her by e-mail with a list of article suggestions and if she likes your ideas she will then contact you to discuss payment, article lengths etc.
Address: Jane Hammond Foster, Editor, Traveltalk Australia, 1st Floor, National Australia Bank Building, 104 Erindale Road, Balcatta, WA 6021, Australia. Tel: (08) 9240 3883
E-mail: editorial@traveltalk.biz
Website: www.traveltalk.biz

MAD is an American comedy magazine which says it is actively looking to expand its freelance writing staff. They are looking for writers who are clever, off-beat and, most importantly, funny. They want to infuse new life, energy and a fresh look into the magazine. Articles can be on anything which you think is funny, especially if it is about a current trend. Send a synopsis of the article. Rough sketches are also welcome. Do not send just text as MAD is a visual magazine. Do not fax or send submissions by e-mail.
Address: MAD Submissions Editor, 1700 Broadway, New York, NY 10011, U.S.A.
Visit the website for further details:
www.warnerbros.com/madmagazine

Figure 3.4
Looking abroad: a page from *Freelance Market News*, Vol. 11, No. 9, April 2005 (The Association of Freelance Writers). With kind permission of *Freelance Market News*

to devote a few features to it. First you can divide your subject by listing various ideas suggested by your materials. Then you can consider the marketing.

You might interest your local paper in a story about problems of abuse in a local home. You might then use some of this in a piece for a national paper that shows how the wider care-in-the-community policy is working, pegging the feature to yesterday's speech by the Health Minister in the House of Commons.

A general interest magazine might accept a piece summarizing the newspaper article and following it up with accounts of how one or two regional health authorities interpret the policy. This could be done effectively by case studies contrasting treatments inside and outside institutions in each area.

Research sources will include MENCAP and the British Institute of Medical Handicap, which produces the journal *Mental Handicap Research*.

If you have time to take plenty of notes on a subject, you may want to make a list of the publications you read, and write for, and ask yourself what aspect or angle they might be interested in.

While developing ideas and studying the market as described in the following chapters you will see more precisely how a feature can be reshaped in different ways and, after a pause, updated.

A script for radio or TV

This is outside the scope of this book, but see the Bibliography for guides to writing for broadcast.

Books

The outline for a feature of length and complexity can easily be expanded to provide the framework for a book. An example is given on page 165.

Ideas for non-fiction books will come when you have devoted a fair amount of time to a specialism. After publishing a dozen or so articles on a how-to subject, for example, you may well decide you can develop the material for a book.

ASSIGNMENTS

1 Take three articles (approximately 500, 800 and 1500 words) from different publications. Produce a clear outline of the content of each by listing the main points in note form (not sentences), one point for each paragraph. Point out where you think the structure could have been improved.
2 Change each of the above to a sentence outline, indicating links.
3 Rewrite the following paragraphs, the intro to a student's article, 'Euthanasia: Mercy Killing or Murder?'. Reduce to 80–90 words. Improve the structure and make it less academic. (For a popular woman's magazine.)

Whatever area of nursing nurses find themselves in, from geriatrics to hospice or intensive care, as nurses, they are confronted by patients whose condition is so severe, or whose quality of life so questionable, that thoughts of euthanasia inevitably cross their minds. These thoughts can throw into turmoil all that their training has taught them about the preservation of life and cause them to confront their most deeply cemented ethical beliefs. This article attempts to explore the differing opinions on euthanasia, from a nursing perspective. The primary question is whether it is in our society's interest to change the current law against euthanasia in Britain. This has far-reaching implications, outlined later in the article.

I have spoken to Philippa, a senior nurse with several years experience of working with the terminally ill, who remains unconvinced that causing the premature death of a patient is a viable option in the ongoing quest to relieve suffering. I have also spoken to Anne, a retired nurse who endorses 'active euthanasia'. From these opposing viewpoints, I hope this article will provide the basis for further discussion and research into this very difficult and emotive subject. It is my personal belief that 'active' euthanasia goes against the very grain of nursing standards of practice, which endeavour to provide dignity, comfort and support to those suffering long-term and terminal illness.

4 *Workshop.* All students of a small group (up to eight) write an article of 600 words at home with the same title and target publication.The completed scripts are collected and distributed so that

each writer gets someone else's. Each writer now becomes an editor, subs the article and writes a letter suggesting how it might be improved and possibly commissioned. The editors may be anonymous or not: try it both ways. Each student then reports on the editing done to their script, indicating their response. The tutor guides group discussion on each script.

A large group can split up into two or three small groups, each operating as above, each with a different title/target, after which the tutor can work through the scripts immediately, guiding the group discussion.

4   The world of ideas

Editors want ideas, not subjects. Racism, and Racism in London are subjects: if you propose either to an editor you will be asked what your idea is. Or your viewpoint, or angle, or slant. The synonyms and near-synonyms for 'idea' in journalism are many.

The idea is extracted from a subject. The Ignorance that is Racism is an idea. The angle or viewpoint is clear. But it sounds more like the title of a book than of an article. It might make an essay type of column for an intellectual weekly but it is too large an idea for most publications.

Narrow it down geographically (The Ignorance that is Racism in Bradford's Schools) and you may have a likely idea for a local paper in the Bradford area if it hasn't been aired there recently. Narrow it down thematically (Pre-School Infants Are Not Racist) and you may have an acceptable idea for the education section of a national paper or for a women's magazine. You twist a subject into focus, you make an angle. The Danger of Noise can become Discos Can Make You Deaf, The Police in Britain – When Should the Police be Armed?

This chapter describes:

- staff writers' ideas
- freelance writers' ideas
- development techniques
- the place of specialism.

STAFF WRITERS' IDEAS

The staff writer has the advantage of living in a familiar world of ideas that has built up round the publication. There may be editorial meetings where feature writers can bounce ideas off each other, or this may happen informally. Press releases and other literature, arriving daily, suggest possible topics for features. Staff writers can judge immediately which ideas fit the publication they work for. Furthermore, staff writers are backed up by extensive resources. Ideas come to staff and freelance writers in different ways, but they can learn from each other.

If you're a freelance, put yourself in the editor's shoes. If an idea is going to need plenty of time, expense and resources, it will probably be given to a staff writer. This will tend to happen if there's a risk inherent in the idea – that it might not come off, for instance – or if it will need careful day-by-day developing in the office.

Ideas out of news

Reporters on local papers begin to turn into feature writers when they develop straightforward news reports into news features. For example, a reporter is covering a landslide into the sea. Cracks have appeared in houses near a cliff edge. The district council says the houses will now have settled and that it is planned to shore up the bank with some boulders to prevent further erosion. End of news story. But the editor tells the reporter that ten years ago the same reassurances were given to people living in an isolated house near a cliff edge some miles farther down the coast. Their house collapsed in the middle of the night, and they were lucky to escape with their lives. A sea wall was eventually built.

'Investigate it,' the editor says. 'It may be that the sea wall will have to be extended. Get as much as possible from the cuttings, then go back to the surveyors on the council.'

The reporter might discover from cuttings sources that might be contacted, not only to update on the topic but to extend it and develop a more ambitious backgrounder: the Department of the Environment, the Professor of Geology at the nearest university, the local secretary of the Farmers' Union perhaps. The editor is persuaded to allow more time. A feature has been born.

A sudden spate of foxes killing chickens, burglaries on an inner-city housing estate, road accidents on a dangerous corner and the selling of gifted players by the local football team though its performance is deteriorating are other stories that might similarly suggest background features on a local paper. Some might be worth a freelance rewriting, after widening the research, as spin-offs for national publications.

Ideas out of press releases

Press releases may yield a feature rather than a news story. A local paper receives a brief one about a novelty act called The Three Charlies, based locally, which involves clowns combining playing instruments, juggling and contortions. The release mentions that the trio has achieved some national success and has TV and film engagements lined up. Without much change, the release makes a news item.

But a feature writer is asked to get more. The paper's cuttings library and microfilm are studied, the publicity agents are contacted, the performers interviewed. The show, it is discovered, is based on a famous music hall act at the turn of the century. There are articles on the original troupe performing at the now defunct theatre in the area. A local antiques shop has posters that can be reproduced. The feature makes a page.

From the inside

On a regional paper of some standing and on nationals ideas are both originated and developed in editorial meetings: preliminary meetings of section editors with their writers will often precede the main editorial conferences of newspapers. At these the editor checks on the progress of news and feature projects with section editors. Everyone will have read the morning papers.

Ideas will be expressed about how to follow up, improve on, or scoop the stories rival publications contain, as well as ideas about how to move forward the projects that originated in-house and that they hope their rivals haven't got wind of.

Decisions will be made about whether a story is better treated as straight news or, with more space and analysis, on news review or 'Focus' pages, or whether it is general feature material. A project may begin in one camp and end up in another. A features editor will watch current news stories.

Ideas out of the letters page

Ideas from staff writers or suggested to them are especially valued if they encourage feedback from readers, and a debate can, with skilful subbing, be continued for several issues. Readers are sometimes invited to respond to controversial pieces, by email to the writer if not in a letter to the editor. *The People* engineered a debate in this way:

> Last week *The People* told the heartbreaking story of tragic Dad Nigel Nelson whose brain-damaged baby daughter Naomi died after he increased her dose of pain-killing drugs. We asked you to tell us whether intolerable suffering justifies mercy killing. Your verdict was an overwhelming Yes, and our postbag contained some of the most moving letters we have ever received. Here is a selection …

FREELANCE WRITERS' IDEAS

The distinction between staff and freelance ideas is blurred to some extent. On the one hand freelances have access to increasingly sophisticated resources such as the Internet, and on the other hand staff writers increasingly write at home. A freelance closely associated with a publication will operate in much the same way as the staff writer described above. And although what follows has the freelance mainly in mind, a staff writer is often working as, or like, a freelance.

Some freelances have launched themselves out of staff jobs and have inside knowledge to carry with them. Some specialize as columnists or reviewers for one two publications. But the tyro freelance may have to be adept at finding different kinds of ideas and at matching them to different targets, and will have to provide their own back-up resources at home or in libraries.

With targets in mind

Professional golfers about to compete on a golf course spend many hours getting to know the course in practice rounds. They get to know the shape of it well, every bump in the ground, the contours, the gradients, the length of the grass in different parts. They can then play it in their minds. Professional feature writers about to compete for space on a publication do a market study of the publication.

Suppose you want to tackle Bullying in the Workplace. Suppose you make this list of target publications: the *Daily Mail, The Guardian, The Economist, Business, New Statesman, Woman's Own, Marie Claire, The Lady, Men Only, GQ* and your local paper. You realize that you haven't got one potential feature but many. Unless you have an impressive track record, of course, you would find many of the publications difficult to break into.

Here's a suggestion for how to proceed. Take a close look at your list and decide which are the most likely prospects for you. Each publication will require a different treatment: it will require you to answer the questions about the subject that its audience would ask, in such a way as to command its attention. Treatment involves angle, content, structure and style. You study each publication carefully (several recent issues) and decide on the kind of treatment that will work.

You will consider, for example, which publications will be most interested in the effects of the bullying on the efficiency of the company, which on the psychologies of bullies and victims, and you will decide what range of workplaces would be covered by each publication. Which will want drama, which cool reasoning? What lengths do features in each publication run to? Which go for humour, which lean towards academic seriousness?

As examples, the *Daily Mail* and *The Guardian*, you deduce, will bring politics into it, *The Guardian* (having many teachers among its readers) will relate it to bullying at school. *The Economist* will be interested in the damaging effects of bullying on the efficiency of businesses, *Woman's Own* in how parents can help victims. Would your local newspaper do a survey of the local schools, perhaps using a questionnaire that both teachers and pupils would be asked to complete? How would you develop the idea for each of the other publications? Having chosen a target, you check that the subject hasn't been dealt with recently and that their editorial policy for features hasn't suddenly been changed (for example, by a new appointment).

You may prefer to do it more the other way round, to concentrate on getting ideas developed before looking for targets. (You want to make sure you will produce something that fits but is somewhat different from the usual fare perhaps.) Whichever, once established as a regular writer for a publication, the whole process will be more of a collaboration with the editor, who will adapt a briefing policy to what they know you're capable of. These are matters for the following chapters. Let's get back to the ideas.

Finding the idea

Freelance writers have the advantage that they can come up with the more unusual ideas. Publications can get in a rut sticking too rigidly to a formula.

Editors can then be excited by the passion and commitment of a freelance with fresh ideas and above-average writing ability.

Freelances are sometimes paid for a good idea, especially by newspapers, when a staff writer is considered to be better placed with connections, and better qualified generally, to develop the article. But don't give too much away before getting a commission: ideas can be pinched as well as pitched.

You need to be open to ideas and ready to capture them. The poet Louis MacNeice spent 25 years learning how to write poetry, then suddenly one day realized he had poems flying past his right ear. All he had to do was move his head a bit to the right. The German poet Schiller found ideas came more rapidly if he had rotting apples in a drawer of his desk. Ernest Hemingway sharpened a lot of pencils before starting to write. You will find your own ways of getting into a receptive state of mind. Be as mystical about it as you like if it works. For the moment we're on a practical level.

As journalists, you need to be practical, in terms of size (seriousness, importance) of idea, in kinds of market aimed at, and in day-to-day procedure. To repeat: carry a notebook and pen everywhere and leave them around your home. For many ideas will come when you least expect them. Some will come in the form of a word or a phrase or a sentence, perhaps a title. Others will demand a page or more of your notebook. Transfer likely ideas to a folder where they can be developed by adding notes, cuttings and other printed materials or start computer files for them. (See Chapter 2.)

Where should you look for ideas? Here are some likely sources.

Personal experience

Features can be written about first- or second-hand experience of, for example, the domestic upheaval of moving house, a change of career, office politics, dangerous dogs, a conversion to Buddhism. And so on.

It's probably best to develop such a piece with a target in mind. In which case, make sure that it will appeal to the readership aimed at. It's too easy to assume that what has deeply affected you will interest others. There have been numerous articles published on such topics as those listed above, so what have you got to add? Can you think of a fresh treatment? Can you combine your experience with that of others gleaned from your cuttings files? Can you think of interviewees who would add a dimension or two?

Conversations noted

At a party you've been identified as a good listener by a woman of a certain age who is being lengthy about her studies as an Open University student. You are edging away when she says, 'I had to do something when I lost my husband and two children in a car crash.' You begin to contribute to the conversation. You won't whip out your notebook right away but you may ask if she would mind your taking a few notes for an article you see on the horizon.

In a pub you hear two men in the tiling business discussing how they avoid the tax man. You may get some ideas for an article on moonlighting. You may like to make some surreptitious notes on the newspaper you are carrying, since using a notebook might arouse suspicion. You may get into conversation with them if you don't look too much like an income tax inspector, or if they aren't too big, and you can choose your words carefully.

Events observed

Deepen your particular interests and areas of knowledge by attending associated events. If you want to write features for a local newspaper, find out which organizations and activities are not covered by the paper. Scouts, street entertainers, swimming galas, surviving rural skills, amateur dramatics, restaurants guide? Then develop convincing arguments for their inclusion and send those arguments to the editor with some samples of your writing.

If you are taken on as a regular contributor (which could lead to the offer of a staff job), not all your reports are going to be used, but you might be able to negotiate a retainer fee. Put yourself on the mailing lists of the organizations. Attend some meetings and make yourself known to the chairmen, who will telephone you with the dates or results of future ones. Having contributed news items to the paper on this basis for a while, you may find it easier to get space on the feature pages.

Editorial departments of newspapers and magazines have a printed or computer-screened diary of forthcoming events that staff reporters and feature writers will cover. The diary includes anniversaries that may provide a ready-made news peg: of the birth or death of a famous resident, for example. Past issues will be studied to make sure the resident hasn't been dealt with too recently and that the new story has freshness.

Freelances often keep their own diary or concertina file for forthcoming events they may decide to write up, noting especially those related to their particular interests and the kinds of events that have been overlooked by publications considered likely markets.

Broadcasts

Radio phone-in programmes, like the letters pages of newspapers and magazines, are natural homes for the cranky and the quirky and can be a fertile source of ideas. Child abusers should be castrated, you may hear someone say, or sterilized, or nothing at all should be opened on Sundays, or the public schools should be abolished and the buildings used to house the mentally ill. Such remarks may amuse or annoy: they probably start you thinking about the subject.

Be on the lookout for broadcasts that deal with topics you're thinking about or have begun to write about. Radio and TV documentaries on such subjects as drug addiction, the prison system, immigrants, increasing obesity and business frauds may throw up some aspect that grabs you: then you grab your notebook. Such programmes will suggest possible contacts. Note that tonight's TV documentary may have been made a year ago: check and update the material.

Printed sources

Read widely for ideas and develop a system for extracting them: from newspapers and magazines, from books, and from other literature – publicity material from business organizations, for example.

Newspapers and consumer magazines

Let's get back to your cuttings library and look at it more closely.

Read the popular as well as the quality prints. Collect cuttings that add something new to one of your subjects, that may suggest future features or provide facts for them. Collect also cuttings of articles you consider good models for particular kinds: for a celebrity interview, a political background piece, a film review or whatever. Paste the most useful on A4 sheets, photocopy (to preserve them) and file. Indicate origin and date, so that you will know how to update them when the time comes. Make comments in the margins so that you won't wonder several months later why you cut them.

Do all this regularly and avoid hoarding whole publications, which can soon take up a lot of space. Read in libraries and use their photocopiers. You may want to file the sheets of cuttings in subject files, or collect them in envelopes, with some means of reference. Have a clear-out occasionally, replacing cuttings with fresher material. It's a good idea also to collect cuttings of articles that you consider models of effective techniques – for structure, for an original use of language, in the employment of anecdotes and quotes, or whatever.

The contents pages of discarded magazines can suggest new ideas in themselves. A good tip when extracting an idea from one market is to reshape it for another where it will be less familiar. A medical breakthrough analysed in an upmarket weekly may lend itself to a more light-hearted human interest treatment for a popular paper or magazine. Conversely an interview with a young woman in a local paper who has survived a dysfunctional family and drug addiction and launched a career in television may suggest how some researching will discover stories that might add up to a feature for a national magazine.

Subscribe to *Press Gazette* to keep up to date with the journalism business, and a writers' trade magazine for up-to-date market information and articles on idea forming and writing techniques.

Returning to the letter pages, note that subjects come and go in cycles. The following were aired in the mid 1990s but are on the go again in 2005 (so you may want to keep informative cuttings on your favourite themes until they're quite superseded): ironical letters about farmers claiming to be defenders of liberty when footpaths are blocked to ramblers by barbed wire; letters adamant that young offenders (under 18) are best dealt with in the community than by locking them up. When you have cut an article expressing a strong view and the following week a letter responding forcefully with the opposite view, you can be well on the way to your ideas on the subject.

Don't over-file though. You can access much up-to-date material, including newspaper and magazine features from archives, quickly on the Internet. Note what's free and what isn't.

File when you see an idea lurking in a subject rather than when you see a subject that might, or might not, produce an idea.

For example, file when you see information that's unusual, not readily available elsewhere, or which appears in an article where you didn't expect it. You read the run-of-the-mill travel or tourism piece and what catches your attention is a remark about the difference in the ways hotel managers treat guests in different countries. Just a remark but, wait a minute, file it: that could be developed.

Business-to-business magazines and professional journals

Some news stories don't break in newspapers but in business-to-business magazines and professional journals. Keep an eye on them. You can corner ideas worth wider dissemination.

You spot in a catering magazine, for example, that a famous hotel company, in its bid to take over another, accuses the latter of various management faults. One fault mentioned is a failure to use efficiently technology new to hotels. You note that this aspect has not been covered by newspapers or the business magazines, which have concentrated on the financial aspects of the conflict. Names are mentioned in the catering magazine article that could help you to write a piece on the new technology, or lack of it, in hotels. A national newspaper or a consumer magazine might be interested.

Such ideas frequently revolve around new products or new technology. Information in a business-to-business or technical journal about a new kind of computer for use in schools, or about a court case concerning an accident caused by a department store escalator breaking down, may have wider implication. The news media may not immediately realize the news value of such stories or see how to interpret them to a wider audience.

Ideally placed to do so would be part-time freelances whose main jobs are in hotels, computer technology and store management. In journalistic terms, they are the 'experts'. But your most valuable trick is in knowing who the experts are and in getting them to talk to you.

Books

Reference books of various kinds are worth digging into. Consider *Chambers Dictionary of Dates*. Take the section 25th March: '1843 – The 1300 foot Thames tunnel, from Wapping to Rotherhithe, was opened. 1867 – Arturo Toscanini born. 1975 – King Faisal of Saudi Arabia assassinated by his nephew.' Some library research into these subjects will develop ideas about famous tunnels, musicians, assassinations. Staying with anniversaries, reference books of different kinds can tell or remind you when Mothers' Day is and Fathers' Day, National Condom Week, Wake up to

Birds Week, and so on. But avoid the anniversaries all those other freelances pick up.

Looking through the London South East Yellow Pages telephone directory I find the following intriguing entries: chimney sweeps, diamond sawing, fallout shelters, gold blockers, hairpiece manufacturers and importers, naturopaths, noise and vibration consultants, pawnbrokers, portable buildings, robots, ship breakers, toastmasters. Nothing stirs you? Have a go yourself in your local Yellow Pages.

Other literature

Newsletters, pamphlets and press releases from government departments and non-governmental organizations (NGOs), including charities and pressure groups, academic institutes and business organizations are other sources of ideas and information. Such literature pours into newspaper and magazine offices. As a freelance, put yourself on mailing lists. A word of warning here. The ideas those organizations are promoting won't easily fit into feature articles without your assessing their validity. You will recognize particular agendas. You will, for example, check what the Department of Health says against what MIND says, what the Department of the Environment says against what Greenpeace and Friends of the Earth say.

An advert for a special luxury object catches your eye. 'Two fine examples of Chinese lacquer. The larger can be found in the British Museum, the smaller in the High Street.' What are the other uses of lacquer today, you wonder. Who else uses techniques over 2000 years old? Is there an article in it? Who would be interested in such an article?

An advert for unit trusts in *The Financial Times* is headed 'Why the Meteorological Office should be staffed by giraffes'. That is a good title. It makes you wonder what other animal habits, as well as those of giraffes, signify changes in the weather, and what angle could be given to that. Or perhaps you're more interested in pursuing the idea in the advert. You may ask yourself how reliable are the predictions of stock market movements made by analysts who believe they come in cyclical patterns.

Computerized sources

A computer gives you access to a great deal of journalism and the indexes to publications to enable you to locate articles dealing with your subject.

At the research and development stage you can key your subject word or a related one into your search engine and you will be led into worlds of possibilities. You will be able to locate quotes, anecdotes, extracts, article and publication titles, book titles, names of experts, websites of likely contacts.

The websites of organizations that relate to your areas of interest and that give out up-to-date news of their activities may be good sources of ideas.

DEVELOPMENT TECHNIQUES

Whether you're a staff writer or a freelance, or both, you need techniques to make your ideas grow. Ideas are tender plants. Some you've just got to let grow; others you've got to feed and watch over; others are beyond any surgical intervention. You will find your own ways, but you may want to experiment with the suggestions below and discover what sort of activity works best for you.

The growing process, as described earlier, is probably best done inside a folder. Start off a folder by collecting as many cuttings/notes as you can, add to the folders when you can, and go through them regularly to remove the out-of-date ones and decide when you've got a good idea to sell.

At any stage of this development, however, you may want to experiment with different brainstorming methods to see what fits the idea or your way of thinking. Here are a few suggestions.

Putting the imagination to work

Imagination is, generally speaking, putting things together in new ways. In journalism the originality of an idea resides in treatment – in the angle, in the style, in the structure, in avoiding the obvious content. You gather your information from places not too familiar, you find your own contacts if you can that know more than has been revealed, you talk to the not-so-obvious sources.

On a simple level: you read that a country horse event is to take place next Saturday. You decide to attend and write an account of the event as seen by a man who cleans out the stables. You are angered by a shop assistant's lack of interest and courtesy, and you decide to write an article about it, perhaps comparing the British worker with the French or Spanish counterpart. But you do a bit of research and discover that this view has been aired frequently. You decide to develop the theme from the point of view of the shop assistants.

On a more complex level the power of imagination helps you to yoke together disparate notions in inventive ways. As a feature idea grows and you have notes from various sources you need to use your imagination to experiment with them, juxtapose them in different ways, to liberate yourself from the weight of information, to let illumination in. Sometimes you will find yourself on an unrewarding journey, and you may have to abandon the trail and start again with another brainstorming method.

Using formulas and word associations

An idea can begin with a word or phrase that lodges in the mind for no particular reason.

'Animal' can turn into 'Animals Anonymous', and that might suggest animals with behaviour problems being organized for some kind of treatment, or more sinisterly, for genetic experiments.

There are formula ideas, hundreds of them, that work well for popular markets: What Your … Should Tell You About Yourself (hand, handwriting, earlobes), What Is The Best …? (age, diet), The … Of The Future (toys, careers, bodies), Behind The Scenes At The … (opera, TV centre, film studio, football stadium), The World's Biggest …, The World's Smallest …, Can … Survive? (personality, conversation).

Some intriguing lists can be turned into articles: The Great Bars of the World, The Best Hotels. But of course most of them are overdone, so turn the ideas on their heads: The Worst …, The Cheapest …

Putting two subjects together can make an idea. The police by itself is a subject. Ideas are there already in the police and arms, the police and race, or rape, or TV, or interrogation techniques, or the law, or football hooliganism, or politics.

Looking at a subject's contrary can make a possible idea: for example, Fortunate Accidents, Unhappy Millionaires, Ingenious Mishaps, Tragic Trifles. Such phrases at least start you thinking.

As some of these formula examples show, a good idea can come to you in the shape of a good title. But a good title is sometimes hard to find, and the ones that immediately suggest themselves may be well worn. Work at finding a good title because that will help you develop the idea and keep you on track. Experiment by listing possible titles on a piece of paper or on your screen. Try to make them reflect your angle and suit the publication aimed at.

You might have a problem interesting an editor in a piece on The Danger of Noise; Discos Can Make You Deaf will perhaps have a better chance. Such alliteration helps to make them memorable, as do rhythm and puns and other verbal tricks. On the other hand, you have to avoid using these factors in predictable ways.

Many titles are changed by the subeditors. Your title has to harmonize with the other titles in the issue, and if you aren't a subeditor you cannot usually anticipate them, nor the design of the page where your article will appear and therefore the size wanted. The subeditors are closer to the readers and may have special expertise. Nevertheless, work at creating a good title, or at least a good provisional title, because it will help you to sell the idea or the article, and to keep you on track. When the piece is accepted, the subeditor will have something to work on.

Linear-logical thinking

Developing a feature outline from a subject in a linear-logical way can unleash a few ideas. You see the possibilities and can select an aspect that strikes you as fruitful. Suppose the subject is surgery and your angle the question: is it skilful enough? You might discover such a pattern as:

- Medical training for surgeons
- Where technology is up to date
- Where lacking
- Cutbacks in the Health Service
- Priorities in budgeting
- Criteria?
- Too many errors?
- Law
- Ethics
- Compensation
- Insurance.

If you're knowledgeable about a subject and know more or less where you're going this way of thinking is productive. If you need to be open to different possibilities, if you want to discover how you see a subject, to stimulate your thinking about it, the linear-logical approach can be restrictive and a brainstorming technique is recommended.

Lateral thinking

Try putting 'surgery' in the middle of an A4 page and fan out the promising associations as they come into your mind: make a mind map. Keep a measure of control. Then compare the result with Figure 4.1. You will find that the words and phrases will work on each other, and you will be encouraged to make unusual and interesting associations. Your thinking is encouraged to become more original. You can then select that part of the map that you want to concentrate on.

Free association with words and phrases can produce a similar effect. Still with 'surgery' as my subject, I open a dictionary and write down words at random: candle, cry, danger, fence, left-handed, meeting, nerve, pact.

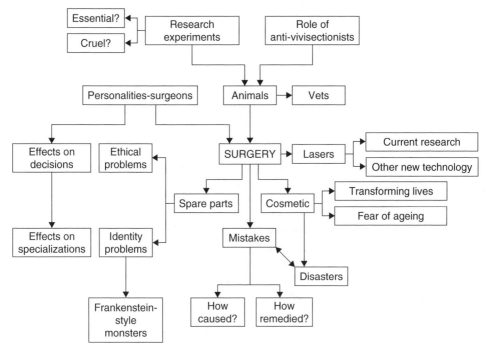

Figure 4.1
A mind map with the subject 'surgery'

'Candle' makes me wonder about any out-of-date equipment, 'cry' what proportion of victims of errors complain. What would a list of recent surgical errors suggest are the most likely dangers? What is being done to avoid them? Are many errors hushed up? Left-handed – how often do physical weaknesses contribute to errors? What screening is made of surgeons? Do they have to undergo tests periodically? After a mishap, what meetings take place? Who are present? What pacts are made? Nerve – how often does the anaesthesia go wrong? Once you have gathered questions or points by brainstorming, you can allow logic back in to outline your article.

Computerized brainstorming

There are computer programs that generate ideas by word association brainstorming. A sophisticated one is the American IdeaFisher. This is an interactive database of questions and an ideas thesaurus (you can get more than a thousand associations for one word) used by a great variety of companies for which communication, problem solving and strategy are priorities. This is expensive but you may want to explore such aids. They may not suit the way you work.

IdeaFisher combines with Tony Buzan's mind maps organization. Have a look at www.mind-map.com.

In general you can simply key a word into your search engine and you'll be able to follow up various pathways via associated ideas, contacts, book titles, quotes and quotations.

You can use your computer to brainstorm as you scroll through a feature, having your text on the left of the screen and using the right side to generate ideas or jot down notes that may be incorporated later.

Try trawling through the newsgroups and other discussions. Subscribe to likely mailing lists, but select wisely and don't get overwhelmed with emails that you don't find interesting.

THE PLACE OF SPECIALISM

Subjects are in and out of fashion, magazines come and go, so feature writers are wise in the early stages of their career to develop ideas out of a variety of interests. In any case your interests will vary as you get older, and a lively curiosity about the world in general and in people of different age groups is needed if you are to communicate with wide readerships effectively.

Write about what you know, especially perhaps when starting out, but keep in mind that it's what your readers need or want to know, and that you can find out, that's important rather than what you happen to know. An idea is a paltry thing unless it can be supported by facts and put across persuasively.

At the same time it's good to have a specialism or two because specialist magazines are numerous. Newspaper editors will begin to remember your name. They will begin looking for you when your subjects are in the news, and you will welcome the time you can subtract from selling and add to writing. Making a mark in specialist writing can lead to work in broadcasting.

Of course, once you are well established with a specialism or two, you may need to concentrate on them. But don't let specialisms take you over completely. Theatre and music critics, for example, can impress with their analytical powers yet disappoint if they show few signs of knowing much else.

CHECKLIST

You can waste a lot of time not only writing pieces that are rejected but outlining ideas that are rejected. After doing some market study but before proposing an idea to an editor, put it through a test. Here's a checklist to help you decide whether your idea has potential or not:

- Is the idea too broad, or too narrow?
- Is it fresh, or has it been overdone recently?
- Can you update the published information you've seen recently on the subject?
- Is fresh information readily available? Where from?
- Will the idea appeal to the target readers?
- Are the facts likely to be of the kind that the readers will need or want?
- Is there a clear theme/angle/point of view?
- Is the idea significant, important, relevant, timely?
- If not timely, does it have enough timelessness about it?
- Is it a good time for you to handle it. Why?
- Are there any dangers of libel, or other legal or ethical considerations?
- Do you really want to write the feature or do you think of it as a chore?
- How much will the feature cost you in money and time?
- If it doesn't work for your target editor, might it appeal to others?

ASSIGNMENTS

1 Try a mind map with one of the following subjects: noise, dyslexia, fox hunting, earthquakes.

2 Use the mind map you've created to extract an idea for a feature of 600 words and write it, indicating the target aimed at.

3 Your subject is Good Manners. Here's a list of words taken at random from the dictionary. Do any of them, or any combination of them, suggest an interesting angle/approach to the subject? (If they don't, try making your own list.) Produce three possible ideas for three possible targets:

cynical, fingering, gazump, hostile, injure, linear, passable, segregate, spy, trance, unfortunate, war dance.

5 Studying the print market

Grace is given of God, but knowledge is bought in the market. (Arthur Huw Clough, 1819–61)

It is normally best to offer ideas and wait for a commission before you write a feature. But if you're a beginner you may find editors slow to commission on the basis of a proposal (until you have a reasonable track record), or even reluctant to give you a 'we'll have a look at it but no promises'. You'll find it hard to get an editor jumping at the idea of you doing a piece about getting lost in the Brazilian jungle and being mistaken for an Indian, or about your life-after-death experience, or about your wanting to describe a child's first day at school from the child's point of view, in the child's language. But if you believe you could do something brilliant with one of these, then go ahead and do it. This chapter should help you through all degrees of orthodoxy.

And there is a market for 'specs' – magazines and small ones rather than newspapers. It's worth looking for them, and writing the occasional piece on spec is beneficial anyway. It can get you out of a rut, liberate your creativity, open your mind to more possibilities, increase your potential. Needless to say, the riskier your venture, the more careful is the market study you do to prepare.

Try everything, but most of your time has to be spent on preparing and writing commissioned features. Note what was said in earlier chapters about networking and develop that activity as you progress. Keep a close watch, as described in Chapter 2, on how much time you spend on different activities.

The most common reason for rejection is not defects in the content, structure or writing, but unsuitability for the market. Be prepared to learn from rejection, to rewrite if asked to or to submit to another market. You may want to file away some of your rejects and rewrite them at a later date.

This chapter provides a general guide to market study and suggests ways of deciding which subjects and which publications you are likely to find favour with.

THE WORLD OF FEATURES

For convenience newspaper editorial matter is labelled 'news' or 'features' although the lines of demarcation can be blurred. With the increased need for background to the news already broadcast there are hybrids such as 'news features'. We'll stick to the obvious candidates for the title of feature.

Background or 'current situation' articles deal with politics, the economy and social questions, and include the Op Ed and the similar pieces that follow them in the middle of the qualities. They may be called think pieces or opinion formers.

Research features at some length and depth may be called investigative. They have in the past covered such themes as dangerous drugs put on the market with insufficient testing and aeroplane accidents due to negligence at trial stage (notably in *The Sunday Times*). Such features are often linked with campaigns to obtain better compensation for victims. They may be running stories produced by a team of reporters, feature writers and researchers.

Human interest stories ('people journalism') are rated high in most newspapers. They deal with people being victimized, being abused, struggling against illness or misfortune rather than with the statistics of social problems because that's the way to get readers' interest. The expert on social problems draws on such material, of course, for case studies. Similarly it's usually more interesting to read about people being successful than organizations being successful. Notice how business section features hunt out the human angles. Notably 'human interest' are the great number of interview features and profiles in the press.

Colour pieces are descriptions of such events as the Oxford–Cambridge boat race or an account of a visit to a prison. Their effect depends on an imaginative use of language to create atmosphere and on qualities such as humour and pathos.

The new emphasis on features

There's a constant interbreeding process between the print and the broadcasting media. Since there is 24-hour broadcasting of news, on radio, TV and on the Internet, morning newspapers, unable to compete in topicality, have to add something to what's already known. They have moved from an emphasis on news to an emphasis on features.

The distinction between the two (especially in the UK) is often blurred. Newspapers do, mainly with features, what it's more difficult for the other media to do. Newspapers do the background to the news – involving analysis, various investigations, social problems, extra angles, thoughtfulness, human interest. They compete with the political weeklies and magazines in some of these areas. Print remains the best medium for investigations in depth and for sustained argument. The depth varies greatly over the range.

It's a two-way breeding process, of course. A complex TV documentary may take months to research and put together, and when broadcast will not be an up-to-the-minute account. That may be provided by the next morning's follow-ups in the form of reviews or commentary or background features in the papers. The arguments may then be sustained in the weekly papers and magazines. These trends mean that the feature writer is increasingly valued for writing techniques, creativity and viewpoint. The traditional Op Ed page in the quality nationals has spawned several pages of comment.

Some publications accept these challenges and some don't. When broadcast media are getting most of the hard-news scoops, some newspapers go for the soft-news ones – the love lives or disgraces of celebrities. Popular papers give much space to the private lives of the stars of the TV 'soaps', sometimes blurring the distinction between these actors and their lives as fictional characters.

The democracy of the electronic media, with interaction via telephone and email, has invaded the print media. Feature writers, especially columnists, get much feedback from, and stay close to, their audiences when they encourage correspondence via email. There is much gain. On the other hand columnists can lose sharpness and individuality if they forget where they left their high horses, and there are justified complaints about dumbing down.

Specialists in demand

Freelances in particular have a much better chance of getting work for newspapers if they're pitching as a specialist. They may need more than one specialism. Generally they have to be versatile, adapting to different audiences. Let's have a closer look.

Specialist features include Parliamentary sketches, arts reviews, expert commentaries on law, medicine, science and technology, education, fashion, and so on. Then there are the regular service columns, giving advice on shopping, holidays, DIY and so on, most conveniently done by staff.

Specialists know exactly when it's time to analyse a trend, propose an article and start researching it in their or in a newspaper's cuttings files or databases. The likeliest opportunities are in areas where it's difficult for a staff writer to keep up. The content is the thing, but success is assured if they can develop the popularizing, jargon-free writing skills required, as described in Chapter 19.

The obvious candidates for such openings are scientists, doctors and professionals in general who can make a useful second income by writing. Full-time freelance writers are advised to specialize in one or two areas so that their knowledge and experience of them can quickly be called upon when required. They can ask themselves which subjects they're particularly interested in and check on the coverage given to them in the national papers and specialist magazines. Is the subject coming into or going out of fashion? Are there too many writers jostling for space or too few?

Local papers

About 80 local, also called regional or provincial, newspapers are sold daily and about 1300 weekly, plus hundreds of free papers or freesheets, almost all of them distributed weekly. The analysis of local papers done by Ian Jackson in *The Provincial Press and the Community* (Manchester University Press) in 1971 is still useful. He identifies four functions of local paper features: reflector, booster, watchdog and pump-primer.

The reflector function is carried out, says Jackson, by articles on local history that 'deepen the sense of community identity'. Booster features are stories of local heroes, champions of local causes, sports champions. Watchdog campaigns are frequently started off or sustained by public annoyance or concern. Attempts to stop a planned motorway spoiling a particular area is an example of a watchdog campaign that has been waged all over the country for years. In rural areas the risk of genetically modified crops contaminating the fields of organic food growers sounds many an alarm. Pump-priming includes those general environmental concerns over urban developments, local transport problems, lack of recreational facilities for children. Here are some samples of local paper topics that range over the past decade, with the more recent ones quoted from.

Samples of local topics

1 'Will this hero win the war on litter?' by Aroha Webster, *Edinburgh Evening News*. Computer-generated animated adverts are part of a campaign about to be launched on TV and cinema screens. They will urge teenagers to log on to a website condemning litter vandals. The adverts feature a Terminator-style robot who will educate them – saving them from the sentence of death passed on them by the army of robotic waste management wardens who were losing the battle. (Watchdog/pump-priming function.)

Intro:

> It is the year 2002 and the city is about to be taken over by artificially intelligent litter wardens who have turned against humans:

> Tired of fighting a losing battle trying to keep the streets clean of dropped litter, the waste management wardens have now decided it is easier to keep on top of the problem by wiping out humans instead.

> Sounds like the stuff of films, but if you think the plot could have been penned by a Hollywood scriptwriter, think again.

2 'Luxuries in store for London rubber-neckers' by Anne Cowan, *The Herald* (Glasgow). This guide to shopping reflects the growing confidence of Glasgow as a cultural centre. (Booster.)

3 'The great north-south divide built with bricks and mortar' by Eric Baird, associate business editor of the Glasgow *Herald*, about the problems caused by the vast differences in property prices between Scotland and England.

4 'Hook's Eye View', a column by Lib Dem Antony Hook, *Dover Express*. Tells the story of an elderly woman who will shortly need a great deal of care that only a private nursing home could provide, and that will require the raising of thousands of pounds by her family. Local Age Concern chairman Gordon Lishman is praised for his untiring

campaign for this care to be made available on the NHS as the Lib Dems have engineered in Scotland. (Watchdog.)

Intro and ending:

> The measure of a civilized community is how we support one another in living life to its fullest. An important feature is provision we make for the sick and infirm ...

> Please support our petition. If we put enough pressure on the Government we might just get the civilized community that the elderly and infirm deserve. If you want to help us call me on ...

5 On another page of the *Dover Express*, in the Memories series, Bob Hollingsbee quotes from a century-old account of a visit to an estate containing magnificent ancient trees. (Reflector.)

Intro:

> Something I promised myself I would do in semi-retirement was to go and see the legendary 'Fredville Oak' at Nonington, a favourite subject of many photographers and postcard views in days gone by.

6 'Author recalls bygone era of the old village' by Anne Leask, *Beckenham and Penge Advertiser*. Reviews a book with illustrations about old Beckenham, on sale at the local bookshop. (Reflector.)

7 'Josie flies home from Olympics' by Maria Croce, *Croydon and Purley Advertiser*. Interview with Mrs Jill Horton about the welcome awaiting daughter Josie who had gained world ranking of fifth in her judo class in the Barcelona Olympics. (Booster.)

8 'Lost stories celebrate the true voices of Cornwall' by Frank Ruhrmund, *Western Morning News*. The article celebrates the publication of a book, *Chasing Tales: The Lost Stories of Charles Lee*, by a neglected author of the late nineteenth century. It is hoped that the book will establish him as one of the greatest of writers about Cornwall. In an illustrated double-page spread there are extracts from the stories and a column of Cornish dialogue. (Booster.)

Intro:

> There was a time, and not all that long ago, when one could walk the streets of the towns and villages of Cornwall, the paths of its country-side and coasts, from Saltash to St Just, without hearing a single English, or any other foreign, voice – a time when all the accents that one heard would be Cornish.

9 'No Room at the Inn' by Will Smith, *South London Press*. Foreign tourists avoiding South London because the hotels are full of homeless families. This costs South London boroughs millions of pounds a year in lost tourism. (Watchdog.)

This is another familiar subject for local papers wherever immigrants are conspicuous. Welcoming attitudes can of course also be found.

Freesheets (free newspapers) are local, so much that has been said about writing for local papers is relevant. They can offer a promising market for the local freelance. Their dependence on advertising, however, gives them a different outlook.

New-product pieces and other news items are often connected to advertisers' businesses, but most freesheets try to compete with paid-for newspapers, however small their staff.

Reporting experience

If you are aiming at contributing features to a local paper, experience of straight reporting will be invaluable. You will collect useful contacts for a start. Make a note of groups, societies, associations, clubs and committees in your area. Consult your friends and acquaintances, and notice-boards in libraries, town halls, church halls and other public places. Don't, however, approach the paper's regular sources – the police station, local council, town hall, fire brigade and so on – without checking with staff reporters first.

Plug the gaps. Find out which local organizations and activities are not covered by the paper, develop convincing arguments for their inclusion and send those arguments to the editor with some samples. If you have any success, put yourself on the mailing lists of the organizations. Attend some meetings and make yourself known to the chairmen, who will telephone you with the dates or results of any future ones. The contacts should soon provide a few feature possibilities.

National papers

A politician in the TV sitcom *Yes Minister*, a great success in the 1980s, said:

The Times is read by the people who run the country.
The Guardian is read by the people who think they ought to run the country.

> The *Daily Mail* is read by the wives of the people who run the country.
> The *Financial Times* is read by the people who own the country.
> The *Daily Express* is read by the people who think the country ought to be run as it used to be run.
> The *Daily Telegraph* is read by the people who still think it is.
> The *Sun* readers do not care who runs the country provided she's got big tits.

There is still some truth in these labels and they do give an idea of the vast differences in the national papers of Britain. It is enough to compare the circulation figures of the qualities and the populars (*Press Gazette* regularly gives the circulation figures and readership figures are roughly three times these) to appreciate how different the contents are going to be, in length, depth, complexity and language.

- Qualities: *The Times, The Guardian, The Independent, The Financial Times, The Sunday Times, The Sunday Telegraph, The Observer* and *The Independent on Sunday.*
- Middlebrows: the *Daily Mail*, the *Daily Express*, the *Mail on Sunday*, the *Sunday Express.*
- Populars: the *Daily Mirror, The Sun, The Star*, the *Sunday Mirror*, the *News of the World, The People.*

Among the special interest papers are: the *Jewish Chronicle*, the *Catholic Herald*, the *Socialist Worker.*

Features with topical pegs

Articles for national newspapers (particularly) must have topicality. A feature tends to be pegged to a news event. Readers want to know the background, or the ramifications, or the possible consequences.

A feature writer scrutinizing a news item about a company collapse may notice a hole in it. Something is being held back, covered up. The writer digs further, finds more figures, finds the real story, perhaps, that the reporter, being busy, missed. There may have been misappropriation of funds, or some rapid and unreported changes of staff.

The following news story was followed up by articles in many nationals. A 16-year-old youth was detained for life after attempting to rape a 10-year-old girl and leaving her bleeding and unconscious. His father blamed the sex and violence on video films the family watched.

Among the questions raised were the following: Who or what is to blame? Was the father right? How should the blame be shared? What's going wrong with family life? What's the law about selling and hiring videos? What kind of censorship is in operation? Some of the articles stayed close to the story, whereas others took off into other aspects of censorship, pornography, rape, family life, using the story merely as a starter.

National papers call on specialist writers, especially for background-to-the-news features, even though the current tight budgets require staff writers to be used whenever possible.

Local and national interaction

Look for stories in your local papers that might, or must, have national implications or be of interest outside the area covered. It might be a certain kind of pollution of river water, faulty building construction, nepotism in the awarding of local council contracts, wildlife dying a mysterious disease. You wonder how widespread such cases are, why they are not being investigated on a national level, what are the loopholes in the law that make them difficult to prevent?

A celebrity living locally can provide an opportunity for an interview for a national paper, for a rewrite for a local paper, and if you got a lot on your tape you may have aspects that can be written up for various other markets.

The proliferation of the media has meant a welcome reduction in newspapers of pomposity and dogmatism. On the debit side some papers have allowed circulation-boosting attitudes to result in a loss of authority. Feature writers have the opportunity to redress the balance.

Magazines galore

Most magazines are heavily dependent on advertising. As much as two-thirds of the space in a consumer magazine may be devoted to it, and the advertising itself is often as much part of the reader appeal as the editorial content. Editors and advertising directors monitor their readership market. Surveys collect a great deal of information about their readers, which supports the promotional literature sent to advertisers discussed below. An intelligent study of the pages remains, however, the best guide for the writer.

The study of a magazine should reveal continuity. It was launched to meet an observed demand and it has to steer a course carefully by the formula established. A subtle shift in direction might be made to increase or hold a circulation, stave off competition or recognize new trends, but only as much as will not disturb the existing body of loyal readers. A new gap in the market will be quickly filled, as happened with computer magazines; some of those came too late and failed to thrive.

Feature writers, especially freelance, become familiar with the volatility and keep abreast of the trends.

While the content of newspaper features tends to be urgent in tone, with information being used to work out solutions, magazine features may reflect more time on research, or give more room to colour and more attention to readability. It may tend to deal in questions rather than answers.

Subjects for all tastes

There are about 6000 periodicals in the UK, providing a world of opportunities (Figure 5.1). Consider as targets first the magazines you enjoy reading, read more widely for ideas, and add to your targets by market study.

The matching of ideas with markets undertaken in the next chapter is largely concerned with specific magazines. Here we are concerned with the general picture.

There is great variety. They are labelled general interest or consumer, business-to-business, customer, technical, hobby, ethnic minority, house magazines for companies, and so on.

There are magazines for almost every conceivable subject. There are weekly reviews, staying closer to the news, and there are professional and academic journals. At the popular end, there are magazines that aim largely at entertainment.

There are magazines for all social, ethnic and age groups. While newspapers are mostly for large general audiences, even the non-specialist magazines need to aim at more specific readerships: young people on the

Figure 5.1
W. H. Smith – opportunities galore. With kind permission of Periodical Publisher's Association

town, oldies slowing down, housewives and house husbands, young executives, and so on.

Varying the treatment

In Chapter 4 we looked at how to identify targets for your ideas and that analysis will be taken further in Chapter 6. Meanwhile, let's take a general subject, mental handicap, and consider more closely how the treatment given by magazines would probably vary from that given by newspapers.

A local paper would cover a story about problems in a local care home. A national paper might come up with figures showing the national prevalence of mental handicap and might analyse the way the care-in-the-community policy is working, pegging the feature to yesterday's speech by the Health

Minister in the House of Commons. A general interest magazine might follow up a fairly brief summary of the problem nationally with accounts of how several regional health authorities interpret the policy and put it into effect, with descriptions of the care provided in two or three examples of homes run by the authorities contrasted with the care given outside them.

Both a newspaper and a general interest magazine might be interested in publishing a profile of a mentally handicapped person or a professional carer, or in a story built round two or three case studies. But the treatment would vary because of the differences in audiences, and the difference between the magazine formula and the newspaper features policy. The newspaper furthermore will be much more interested if the article can be published on Mental Handicap Day or if there is a strong topical peg, such as a recent scandal involving the mentally handicapped.

A professional journal, *Mental Handicap Research*, published by the British Institute of Mental Handicap, printed an article under the heading 'Changes in the lifestyle for young adults with profound handicaps following discharge from hospital care into a "second generation" housing project'.

To write for various publications requires a versatility that can only be learned by constant practice. At first you may understand the need to vary content and treatment but find it difficult to adapt your style. If you're a freelance without regular commissions it is well worth persevering, because magazines come and go, and because of the business sense in multi-purposing.

Free publications

Free magazines are born in the same way as any other magazine. A gap in the market is noticed and someone plunges in with a free magazine to fill it. Targeting of the readership is careful so that advertisers are keen and the distribution is simplified. *Ms London* led the way in London. With many pages of situations vacant and a fair number offering pregnancy advice, it is aimed at 18- to 25-year-old office workers pouring into London's railway and tube stations daily. The copies are handed out. Articles are on entertainments, pop stars, other celebrities, fashion and London life. This was followed by *Girl about Town* and others.

There are many customer magazines among the frees. British Airways' *Highlife*, and those who advertise in it, similarly recognized the advantage of a captive audience passing through airports and travelling by plane. There are now many in-flight magazines. Each has its particular area of contents and reader-targeted style. They are mostly interested in well-illustrated articles. In general, keep in mind that your ideas must have an international angle and outlook, and if the airline producing your target in-flight magazine is in a Muslim country, your range of subjects is restricted accordingly. Take Royal Brunei Airlines' magazine *Muhibah*, for example. The PR department has advised writers that they cannot refer to alcohol, religions other than Islam, dogs, pigs, political commentary, human body parts or women in revealing clothing.

AIMING AT VERSATILITY

It may take time before you find the area of the market in which you're most comfortable and successful. Whenever that happens, it's best to keep your options open and to be understanding and appreciative of different areas. Read the popular nationals. (Even if you have no desire, for example, to work for *The Sun*, it's a good idea to keep in touch with what it's doing because it has the highest circulation of the national dailies.) You may not like their policies or styles but their writers are highly skilled and you can learn much at any stage of your career from the way they get straight to the point.

Carol Sarler, who straddles both quality and popular camps, has a most perceptive essay in *The Penguin Book of Journalism*, 'Why Tabloids are Better', first published in *British Journalism* review in 1998, before qualities started going tabloid. She can do 8000 words on homeless youth for *The Independent on Sunday*, but also 30 words for the *Sunday People* on the general reaction to some news from Peru:

> Much cross-cultural outrage this week at the discovery that Peruvians eat guinea-pigs. 'How could they?' came the cry. 'They're so SWEET.'
>
> Yes. And lambs aren't?

She points out that she could have done a thousand words easily enough for a quality but she would have made the same point. That 'cross-cultural' contains the gist of those thousand words.

This is expressing a difference dramatically. Let's take a closer look at your potential targets.

Market guidance

You can supplement the marketing guidebooks, journalists' and freelance writers' magazines, media pages of the papers and your own analyses with promotional literature and contributors' guidelines, some of which is online.

Promotional literature

This is aimed at and sent to prospective advertisers in the form of media packs. Fliers are sent to prospective subscribers. Writers can also find promotional literature useful. Media packs normally include a recent copy of the publication, the advertising rate card, an analysis of the readership by age, class and profession, and a statement of the formula. This information will help you to fill up the framework for publication analysis recommended in the next section.

Some media packs are generous with readership information. You may discover how many cars are owned by the average family subscribing, the average number of plane flights a year, the educational level of the average reader, and the estimated numbers of single, married and divorced readers.

The fliers, which may include a subscription form, emphasize the personality of the publication formed by the mix of subjects and writers.

Contributors' guidelines

These come directly from some publications on request, from authorship magazines and books, and from the Internet.

From publications directly

Many publications provide a sample issue to potential contributors with or without a specially printed list of guidelines. Figures 3.1 and 3.2 show samples of guidelines from the *Writers' and Artists' Yearbook 2005* (A. & C. Black) and *The Writer's Handbook 2005* (Macmillan). Otherwise, features editors can be forthcoming with advice, especially when you have embarked on a commission.

From authorship magazines

Authorship magazines (listed on pages 404–5) often extract contributors' guidelines from publications either in the form of a full-scale interview with a commissioning editor or as brief notes. They pay particular attention to new launches, which are looking for new writers (and fresh ideas). Diane Parkin, under the rubric Market Index for *Writing Magazine* of December 2001–January 2002, interviewed Kerry Parnell, associate editor of the recently launched *Glamour*, a monthly glossy covering fashion, beauty and lifestyle. It was described as 'aspirational, glamorous, upbeat and fun', the target audience as 'the 27-year-old woman with a boyfriend, no kids, and lots of disposable income'. Potential contributors were advised to study the magazine first and then to come up with an idea that will work in a particular section.

Its first ABC results put it number 2 after *Cosmopolitan*. What's the difference? 'A *Cosmo* feature and a *Glamour* feature may both be about sex, or relationships, but will be approached very differently. It's up to you to work out what the magazine's formula is, and then send in ideas that work for it.' The harder the idea is to research, she said, the more likely it is you'll get the commission. She might have added: work out whether you have contacts that are unusual or access to information not readily available – always a plus in your favour.

Have a look at these two magazines now. Does that advice need updating?

The article, 'Easy as ABC', also dissected *Cosmopolitan, Hello!, Take a Break, Heat, Ideal Home* and *Top of the Pops*.

Press Gazette has regular pages that help with analysis. 'Expert Eye' examines publications in the same sector, concentrating on whether it's thought the formula is working or not.

From authorship books

Keep in mind, when using the marketing books or books on writing techniques like this one, that it is essential to update any market information by studying current issues and checking names of current commissioning editors and their requirements.

Writer's Digest produces a booklet, *Writing for Reader's Digest*, which can be ordered from the company. A model of clarity and conciseness, the magazine's hallmarks, it concentrates on the kind of language and structure looked for and explains the close collaboration undertaken between writer and commissioning editor.

From the internet

Note which market guides give updated information online. *WritersMarket.com*, for instance, gives constantly updated listings. Marketing features for electronic distribution is dealt with in Chapter 8.

Here are suggested headings for the profiles analysis. You will have one or two headings of your own, no doubt, to add to them.

A framework for analysis

Type of publication

Popular paper … middle … quality … general interest magazine … professional … business-to-business …

Frequency and price

Weekly, monthly, quarterly …
Retail price … subscription …

Prospects for freelances

Note which subject areas in a publication are covered by staff members or regular freelances. For example, note the bylines in several issues of a magazine and compare them with the lists of staff members on mastheads. In other words don't send speculative book reviews to markets that have well-established lists of reviewers regularly commissioned. Be realistic. Where you do see an opening, send samples of your writing, preferably published ones, plus a c.v., to back up proposals.

Readership

Study the promotional literature sent out by publications to prospective advertisers and any other forms of market guidance you can collect (see that section above). Study the advertisements in a target publication and exploit the research the advertisers have used to make sure they are on target.

This research includes the various compilations of circulation and readership statistics and specially commissioned surveys. The Audit Bureau of Circulations (ABC) publishes quarterly the circulations of numerous publications owned by member publishers. The National Readership Survey (NRS) calculates readership figures, which is based on the number of readers per copy, are about two to three times circulation figures, though they can be much higher for some magazines. Readership is socially described by a combination of letters from the group $ABC_1 C_2 DE$, representing kinds of occupation (and by implication spending power), from the top company chairman to the lowest earners and non-earners.

The advertising agency that fails to reach the target audiences desired by the clients for whom it designs and places adverts will be out of business, so much time and expense is devoted to the task. Whether or not the adverts in a publication individually succeed or fail to sell the product or the image, they collectively indicate the readership.

Readers of course talk to you out of letters pages, service, agony aunt, health and other advice columns. You see how the writers talk to their readers. You see the assumptions made about the readers underlying the editorials, the features, the general level of discussion, the pitch of the language.

What's the average age range? Proportion of male to female readers? Educational level?

Main kinds of article

Travel … personal experience … think pieces … reviews?

Note average *lengths*: of articles, paragraphs, sentences, words. Type out a sample paragraph and your computer can give you the last three measures. You now have a good idea of the level of difficulty. Aim for a variety of sentence lengths, but an average of 15 to 20 words per sentence suits most markets. The counts for the first part of this chapter are:

Number of sentences	6
Average word length	4 letters
Average words per sentence	24
Maximum words per sentence	57

That long sentence has produced a high average of words per sentence. The average for the chapter as a whole is 15.

Treatment

What are the preferred treatments? Note the sorts of treatment – factual, instructional, humorous, use of quotes, anecdotes, illustrations, boxes, …

Language

Abstract … vivid … chatty … thoughtful … use of metaphor …? Note the house style of a publication when doing your market study as advised in Chapter 4. (It is sometimes available from a publication, and/or a request to follow one of the style guides listed on pages 397–398.)

Note in particular the language style that seems to be favoured for titles, intros and endings.

Structure

Note the way the trio of title/intro/ending provides a framework for article structure. Note any striking combinations, and the publication's general policy.

Timelessness and timing

When discussing the pre-testing of an idea, the quality of *timeliness* was mentioned. The question is: is the time ripe for the idea, or has it been aired often enough recently? Indexes of article titles such as the *British Humanities Index* and the *Clover Index* will give you general guidance. If you propose a topic to a monthly magazine and the response is that an article on that topic appeared three or four months ago, you will probably be reminded, if the editor has time, that you should study the market before proposing. That means studying about two weeks of dailies, three months of weeklies, a year of monthlies.

Timing is the more specific aspect. When you have followed up in an article a controversy that has been raging in a publication and your effort has been politely rebuffed, it may be because you have not noticed that, while you have been writing, interests have shifted to other matters. Or it may be that while you've been writing there has been a change of editor or a change of policy which has suddenly made your idea or article less appealing.

In other words, however many issues you study, make sure you study the current issue.

Lead times for articles

Note your experience of:

- time taken to consider a proposal
- time allowed for the writing once a proposal is accepted
- time taken between acceptance of commissioned article and publication
- time taken between article sent on spec and publication.

Make notes on your experiences and decide when a reminder is appropriate.

Formula

Of magazine or feature articles policy of newspaper. Try to sum it up. Think in terms of recipe. What does the editor aim at in the particular magazine or newspaper you've been examining?

Keep a record of your dealings with target publications as described in Chapter 2. You may want to adapt the above framework on A4 page profiles of your targets, updating from your experience of them.

ASSIGNMENTS

1 Develop feature ideas from six news stories in a national quality newspaper. Choose the shorter page 2 or page 3 stories rather than the ongoing political stories on page 1. Include one or two 'nibs' (news in brief items).
   Write a total of 200 words for each idea. Indicate length of proposed feature, target publication, why it would be of interest to its readers. Summarize content and angle.
   Indicate possible sources, including one interview.

2 Coming events listed by local papers can suggest plenty of ideas for features as well as for straight reporting. Here are a few from my local paper:

- Dead Poets Society
- Shiatsu (spiritual healing): free consultation (telephone number)
- Speakers Club: improve and enjoy yourself, six basic lessons for £12
- Ferret racing
- Heritage Group meeting.

Discover what events are coming up in your area, from your local paper, library, wherever. Choose three, attend them, and write up three 500-word light-hearted features aimed at your local paper.

3 The English are not good at complaining. Write a how-to service article of 1000 words with the title 'To Complain is a Duty'. Use humour rather than bile, but bring out your points forcefully.

Some points

The English are not good at complaining. Why? Examples of services that need complaining about, but are not complained about enough: overcharging in general, house repairs, badly cooked restaurant food, flat beer, faulty goods, poor hotel accommodation, unfriendly sales assistants, airport services, service from telephone companies. Give examples of companies that attach great importance to encouraging complaints and following them up.

What points would you add to the above?

Some sources

Add/update:
Advisory Committee on Telecommunications (Oftel)
Association of British Travel Agents (ABTA)
National Consumer Council
Office of Fair Trading, publishers of a 60-page booklet, *A Buyer's Guide*
Office of Gas Supply (Ofgas)

4 Write a proposal (500 words) for a new magazine. Indicate the formula, target readership, frequency, price, likely advertisers, staff and freelance required. Find out how to create a dummy for a magazine and do one for your first issue.

6 Subjects and treatments

Grasp the subject; the words will follow. (Cato the Elder, 234–149 BC)

You get a sharper insight into publications when you see how differently a particular subject is treated. There follows a list of subjects with mileage, indicating varied treatments, and making some comparisons among publications. Keep in mind that subjects and types and formulas and magazines are constantly changing to meet the demands of the time. To repeat: magazines are born to reflect new interests, and die when their remit is out of date.

Journalism is all about what you can find out rather than what you happen to know – what you can find out in what's published or on the Internet or by the legwork of reporting, but also what's in people's heads. You may want to do one or two contrasting interviews – an academic expert, perhaps, plus one of the streetwise kind. You then need to take time to think out, in the end, how your original attitude to a subject has been changed by your exploration, and to decide where you want to take your readers.

Make sure you come to an agreement on such expenses as hotel accommodation and travel when you have a proposal accepted. If your feature is going to provide valuable publicity for an organization, it may provide you with a 'freebie' – for example, free or discounted hotel accommodation, meals, travel.

A word here about illustration. If you are sending photographs with a script find out whether the publication wants black and white or colour, and if colour whether transparencies or slides. How many pix do they want to select from? Give each picture a reference number and attach a printed caption to the back. Provide a separate list of captions.

LIKELY TARGETS

My matching of subjects and treatments, therefore, though valid at the time of writing, needs to be modified by what you can discover from current marketing guides and current and recent issues of the publications mentioned. If you're planning a piece on any of the subjects listed below you may also want to consult (under the subject headings) a directory of publications (see pages 399–400) and an index or two of articles to discover how and where the subject has been covered in the past year or so (see page 404). Do some surfing as well.

Digging out the relevant articles may be part of your research: you'll be able to ensure that your idea and treatment are fresh, and you'll see what sort of material needs to be updated. If you're planning to write about crime you will probably want to get the latest statistics from the Home Office and to contact one or two of the relevant agencies (see Directory of Organizations, page 399).

Develop your own preferences too. In your capacity as a freelance would you prefer to write for *Cosmopolitan* or *Glamour*, *New Statesman* or *Spectator*, *The Guardian* or *Daily Telegraph*, *Active Life* or *The Oldie*, *Woman* or *Woman's Own*? Deal with a manageable number of subjects and publications.

Develop a keen sense of the preferences you detect in what different publications demand. They each want a certain kind of subject, treatment, language. Nevertheless, note that one of those preferences is for something original, something different from the general run of what they publish and yet which fits.

Occasionally make your own particular demands. As well as writing for the publications that have commissioned you, sometimes find publications for the features you have written. You need to impose yourself on your material in your own way, develop your own style, sometimes take the risk that a feature won't come off or will be rejected. Put it away then and try rewriting it later on. Furthermore, use your familiarity with an audience courageously on occasions, to put across truths you know it may find unpalatable.

You will find your own way of studying how different publications cover subjects you've marked as your own. The list that follows, provides, I hope, a useful formula. It contrasts the varied approaches of different publications to a particular subject. It points to the pitfalls inherent in dealing with the subjects listed. And it suggests how to vary your own approach when selling a subject/idea to different editors.

CELEBRITIES

Journalism has been awash with feature articles within and about the celebrity culture for some years. You may deplore the obsession with celebrity and the vacuousness of gossip magazines, and you may believe that the vicariousness encouraged by celebrity culture has replaced the real values once provided by religion and political convictions.

You may, on the other hand, note that the culture pervades all social levels and consider the above attitude elitist and verging on the absurd. Cosmo Landesman in *Prospect* magazine believed that 'for most people celebrity culture is escapist fun. You tune in to celebrity soap operas – Robbie and Geri or Posh and Becks – and you tune out and get on with life'.

Different approaches

Between these two viewpoints there are many complexities to explore. There is cynical pandering to low expectations. Way back in 1996 Richard Barber, editor of *OK!* magazine, interviewed for *The Guardian* by Andrew O'Hagan, summed up his market of C1 and C2 women between 25 and 44 as 'a fairly bog-standard female audience in terms of who they are and where they live. Well, their biggest form of entertainment is clearly the television sitting in the corner of the living room, isn't it?' I note that there have been two or three changes of editor since then.

The colour pictures of these magazines leap off the page while much of the writing assumes a captive audience. An article in *Heat* about the domestic arrangements of David and Victoria Beckham following an alleged kidnap plot ends:

> … More often than not, the homebodies stay in, put some R&B on the stereo while David cooks Victoria her favourite salmon dinner. Or, if neither can be bothered to cook, an Indian takeaway. 'They really are normal,' reveals a close friend of the couple. 'A perfect day for them is going to Sainsbury's, coming back, making dinner and watching a DVD.'

Reader's Digest joined the club in October 2001, adding pages of celebrity interviews and a lifestyle section in order to attract readers aged 35 plus to its then core readership aged between 40 and 60. They are upbeat accounts, in that magazine's wholesome manner. Meg Grant finds Pierce Brosnan ('Bond Unbound') 'a superstar in his role of family man … compelled to provide for his children the childhood he never had'.

Newer celeb mags do that balancing act perfected by the populars of giving the wicked as well as the wonderful. *Here!* makes a point of reflecting the complexity of our (or if you prefer, its readers') fascination. There's prurience and envy mixed up with love and admiration, and the insults and the accounts of celebs' excesses and misfortunes can be funny and occasionally thought-provoking. Further upmarket, writers can probe greater depths and these are given space in Chapter 16.

The Internet is less regulated. An example is Popbitch (satirical music gossip). It was started by Neil Stevenson (who became editor of *The Face*) because he was frustrated by the way celebrities are overprotected by publicists. A welcome change from vacuity, perhaps, or as media pundit Stephen Glover called it in the *Daily Mail* 'an open sewer running with lies'. If you haven't already, have a look and see what you think.

Pitfalls

PR companies, studios, record companies and their clients put pressures on editors and writers. They may want to make such editorial decisions as which writer, which photographer, the length, the date of the issue in which the celeb interview will appear. Editors of newspapers and general consumer magazines can learn to negotiate with some success, but editors of celeb magazines have less bargaining power.

Your approach

Writers clearly have to work closely with editors when making arrangements to interview a celeb, especially when there's a demand by the interviewee or agent for copy approval. See John Morrish's *Magazine Editing* on this and other editor–writer collaborations (especially Chapter 5, The Right Words).

Celebrity can be shortlived these days and any enduring talents are soon overexposed. To fill the gap reality TV in the *Big Brother* and suchlike shows produces a kind of processed celeb out of would-be celebs without any particular talent, and they get into the papers and the mags as well. Yet another complexity for the writer to come to terms with, to come up with the right attitude for the target chosen.

Competition of course is fierce. Apply with your idea by phone or fax initially. *Hello!* says they are 'interested in celebrity-based features with a newsy angle and exclusive interviews from generally unapproachable personalities'.

To sum up, if you're going to start writing about the celebrity culture you have a wide spectrum: where would you fit in, where do your sympathies lie?

CHILDREN

Writing about children looks easier than it is. You may be a parent, a teacher, social worker or child psychologist: that will be a great help. What is essential is that you have an imaginative insight into children's worlds and an ability to establish a rapport and to interpret what they say.

Different approaches

Current themes are illiteracy at various levels, with much of the blame accruing to computer games or too much television, lack of discipline at home and school, the increase in truancy, drug use and too early sex, and the dangers from paedophiles. On the positive side, it is said that interaction with computers has raised IQ levels, that listening to them more than was the habit in the past has helped children to grow into more confident and more enterprising adults. It is also said that more imaginative parenting is prevalent today, requiring much more effort than the parenting of the past, that this is commendable and that children's general behaviour speaks of self-expression that should be encouraged rather than bad manners.

A *Guardian* article deplored the fact that too many schools concentrated on cramming in order to keep up with the National Curriculum. British children were bombarded with tests, and compared with American children lacked confidence and powers of self-expression because too little time was devoted to their encouragement.

On the other hand, self-expression can be overdone. There are horror stories of women teachers brought over from Australia, Canada and Jamaica,

83

accustomed to well-disciplined pupils, being subjected to streams of bad language and threats of rape. Their sojourns can be brief. Why are the children so badly behaved? 'Boring,' the children sometimes say. Sometimes they are justified in this. Too many temporary (stop-gap) teachers can mean a bewildering lack of continuity.

A *Tatler* article on dyslexia and associated conditions in children by Jonathan Margolis dispelled 'the myth that a learning difficulty equals failure'. This was followed by an article about his own dyslexia by the prolific columnist A. A. Gill.

An article in *She* by Paul Keers ('Hero today, gone tomorrow') analyses the effects on children of their heroes disgracing themselves, of athletes taking drugs, for example, or footballers or boxers taking bribes. This was based on case studies, with a large section in the middle containing the comments of a child psychologist at London's Tavistock Clinic.

Pitfalls

Pension-book holders must take care to avoid thinking (too often): when I was a child we were taught how to behave. If you're just out of college, you may be tempted too often to discount the views of anyone over 40.

Your approach

Interviews with experts together with case studies and your own experience make a common combination. If you have no children of your own, get to know some and learn from them.

CRIME

Crime is compelling story, drama, conflict, passion, and in its aftermath are inspirational messages, triumphs over adversity. The media are swamped with crime; the papers, the magazines and the broadcast media (documentaries, docudramas, series). There are the thrillers, the many feature films. All this means that there's plenty of information and well-informed audiences. There are pros and cons in this situation for the writer. The facts have to be separated from prejudices, passionate convictions backed up by good evidence. The territory is a rewarding one for the experts, who include ex-senior policemen, sociologists, psychologists and fiction writers. If you're not an expert, it's a good specialization as long as you can keep up.

Different approaches

In the London *Evening Standard* Paul Barker, Senior Research Fellow at the Institute of Community Studies, under the title 'Send the police out alone on the beat', wondered why police so often work in pairs. While street crime was rising in every London borough and the London Metropolitan Police pleaded lack of resources, this was a waste of resources he said. If they were on their own we would be 'twice as likely to see one of them in action'.

He talked to Glen Smyth, chairman of the Metropolitan branch of the Police Federation. The problem was diagnosed as 'our public services' paramount (and paranoid) safety culture'. Recent changes in safety legislation have 'undercut thorough policework … The NHS is riddled with the disease known as defensive medicine, whereby consultants throw every possible test at a patient to cover themselves legally. The police, in their pathetic pairings, are going in for "defensive policing".'

This is a good model of an Op Ed piece carrying a strong point of view on a controversial subject and ending up by proposing a solution. It aroused interest and provoked different points of view, and inspired a continuing debate in the letters pages.

As well as including personal experience, an expert's pronouncement and the evidence of a safety culture, the author backed up his thesis by reference to an American police novel, the Health and Safety Executive, the TV police series *Inspector Morse*, and statements made by the Home Secretary and the head of the Metropolitan Police Authority.

Features dealing with the social problem and human interest aspects of crime regularly appear in general interest magazines. They draw on the research sources of such organizations as NAPO (the National Association of Probation Officers), the Howard League for Penal Reform, NACRO (the National Association for the Care and Resettlement of Offenders) and Women in Prison. Some of the statistics and brief case studies are put in boxes.

Pitfalls

You have to be careful with the statistics. There's vastly more awareness of crime than there used to be, which can lead to false assumptions. The number of people in prison has greatly increased, prisons are overcrowded, more are being built. But with the increase of telephones and computers more crimes are being reported and recorded. Detection is aided by much media coverage and hampered by some.

The facts have to be separated from the prejudices, passionate convictions backed up by good evidence.

Your approach

If you're not an expert, it's essential to base your writing on interviews with experts, case studies and legwork, and to check and check again.

EDUCATION

The subject is riddled with controversies and arguments are constantly raging. At the time of writing there is a drastic shortage of teachers in state schools (see the Children section) and heated discussions on how the greatly increased numbers entering higher education are to be funded. But there have been unresolved problems since the Education Act of 1944, with each new government trying various ruses, seemingly bereft of a coherent policy.

Different approaches

An article by Jenni Russell in the left-wing *New Statesman* ('The Secret Lessons', 8 April 2002) revealed the absurdity of the league tables of schools being distorted by the increase in private tutoring. The league tables of test and examination performance are supposed to reflect the quality of the teaching in the schools. But the tutoring 'disadvantages working-class children and undermines any pretensions to a comprehensive school system'. The problem is compounded by parents moving house to get their children into better schools, including selective ones. The mother of a 10-year-old, when she asked a teacher why the class rarely had maths homework, was told, 'I don't tend to give homework any more, because I know most of the children are being tutored'.

Rachel Johnson in the right-of-centre *The Spectator*, following up, scored points in 'A Private Affair' (6 July 2002) by juxtaposing some of the Labour brass condemning Conservatives for their reliance on private schools and private tutoring with the Blairs and other brass making use of such topping up.

She had to be sympathetic (she did it herself): 'Why should [the Blairs] be subject to the doctrinaire requirement that the offspring of Labour Party top brass receive their education entirely at the hands of the state?' Yet she brought up the disadvantaged working-class children again and ended up on an apologetic note: 'Wouldn't it be better and fairer if we (me included) just let the schools get on with it without the intervention of parents and tutors?'

Pitfalls

Again, as in the subject of children, it's easy to pontificate, to get involved with abstractions. Talk to different kinds of parents with children at different kinds of schools, especially if you haven't any children.

Your approach

If you are a teacher or lecturer in Further Education and have offspring being educated at various levels, you might well make education a specialism. If you want to dive in occasionally, get up to date with the Education sections of the national broadsheets. There is also the weekly *Times Educational Supplement* and *The Times Higher Educational Supplement*.

HEALTH AND MEDICINE

Specialist features written by medical professionals are discussed in Chapter 19. There are not enough of these experts, however, to cope with the great interest in the subject, so here we are concerned with the non-expert who wants to write about various aspects. There are many non-experts who write well – some particular experience or unusual angle will make acceptance easier.

Different approaches

Science, and more specifically biotechnology, constantly invades the subject so that new ideas are not hard to find. Angela Wilkes had a fascinating account in Sainsbury's *The Magazine* of the prospects for effective treatment of common disorders via pharmacogenetics. This means tailoring drug treatments to our genetic profiles. A box ('Gene Talk') explained in jargon-free language the meaning of genes, genome, genotype and the DNA spiral.

Articles about illnesses need case studies. Teenage anorexia victims have been well documented. A *Marie Claire* article by Deborah Holder tackled more unusual cases: a 12-year-old girl whose weight went down to 3 st. and a 42-year-old woman (2 st. 9 lb). The interviewees spoke for themselves: the girl and her mother, the woman and her husband. A panel of information explained the help available from the Eating Disorders Association.

The popular women's magazines draw largely on case studies and question-and-answer pages giving expert advice. Judy Kirby's Here's Health section in *Saga* keeps that mature audience up to date with health matters. A typical monthly content covered articles on NHS patients going abroad for treatment, on a radio producer's experience of various hearing aids, how keeping a dream diary can foretell illness, dangers detected in some electric toothbrushes, and how listening to baroque music has helped cancer patients.

Alternative medicine is getting increasing space, with sections in the newspapers and popular magazines, and the launches of specialized magazines. Lisa Howells, the Features Editor of the monthly *Here's Health*, says they want pieces on 'alternative/natural health and living and related therapies'.

While many alternative medicine practices such as hypnotherapy are recognized as valuable by the orthodoxy, readers should be kept aware of the dangers of going for treatment to people who are inadequately qualified. It is reassuring to list within articles one or two dependable organizations which can supply the names of properly qualified practitioners. Many articles about alternative medicine are written in-house or by qualified therapists who fill a regular slot. Check this out by market study.

Pitfalls

If you get into questions of diagnosis and treatment a minor inaccuracy of yours could have woeful results for your readers so you must get it right.

That means a good medical encyclopedia on your shelves, a good biology textbook, study guides for the aspects that particularly interest you, and the ability to locate the necessary experts. For such contacts you will need at least ready access to the *General Medical Council's Register* and *The Medical Directory*, which gives the background and experience of doctors. Some aspects, such as dieting, though covered widely, must be regarded as specialist: careful checking with the experts is essential. Obesity: has there been enough on eat less and exercise more? Please.

Your approach

Where will the ideas come from and where will you sell them? As with most specialist subjects that lend themselves to popularization, a good principle is to go downmarket for the research and upmarket with the idea (see the specialist chapter) or upmarket for the research and downmarket with the idea. That way your audience will not be too familiar with the material on which your article is to be based.

Thus you will get ideas from the medical-specialist *The Lancet* and the *British Medical Journal* that you may be able to shape for general interest magazines and more than one popular magazine – among the men's, the women's, the parents', the teenagers', the elderly's. When, for example, an article in the *British Medical Journal* said that female sexual dysfunction was 'the corporate-sponsored creation of a disease' to profit from the drugs manufactured to treat it, there was follow-up far and wide. The over-prescription of drugs in orthodox medicine continues to have mileage.

OLD AGE OR RETIREMENT

Around 12 million people have at the time of writing reached retirement age: formidable 'grey power', as the advertisers were quick to recognize, that an increasing number of magazines and feature pages have to cater for. People are 'retiring' at 55 (or taking company pensions then and starting another life, some of them a writing life) and living to 85. This is a wide age range to accommodate. Furthermore, some retirees are comfortably off, have paid off their mortgages and enjoy a substantial income, while other retirees suffer from the dwindling value of the inadequate state pension. Some 'oldies' are very active, physically and mentally, others are bedridden.

Articles for most targets have to be multi-purposing enough to interest this spectrum.

Different approaches

Contrast the following magazines: *Choice, Active Life, The Oldie.*

Pitfalls

You may want to watch for fashions in nostalgia: there are sudden revivals of the tastes of the 1940s or the 1950s. But of course the revivals are short-lived, so the timing has to be just right.

You are of course most often addressing the elderly/retired directly. You'd be unwise to have a picture of your 85-year-old grandad or grandmother in your sights, however active they might be, when many retirees are aged 55.

Your approach

A few practical points when making comparisons between then and now. Be specific and accurate. Do the necessary research. Get some names (who was Prime Minister at the time?). Get dates to pinpoint periods exactly. Make price comparisons only after you have calculated the effects of inflation.

TRAVEL

Travel belongs to a huge market full of opportunities. True, and therefore it gets the lion's share of the space here. But because so many writers want to get into it, it's a tough, highly competitive area too. To specialize in it is hard work. If you don't specialize, you'll probably need to become skilled at multi-purposing.

Readers of travel magazines and the travel sections of the papers have vastly different interests, so that your readership analysis needs to be at its sharpest. How much have they got to spend, what rank of hotels/restaurants should you be talking about, how old are they, how adventurous? Is it two weeks at a beachside resort for a family or a month in the Borneo jungle for a twenty-something between jobs? Is it a package holiday in which much practical advice about insurance, health risks, etc. will be provided by tour operator or travel agent, or will you need to provide it? When most of your readers are going to be armchair travellers, you have to bring something extra out of the bag – try to make the piece entertaining in its own right, try to recreate the experience instead of merely describe it.

Different approaches

Travel articles can be classified under:

1 *Destination pieces*, the readers practical, probably planning to go there on holiday.
2 *Evocative pieces*, readers including tourists but also armchair travellers.
3 *Exploratory pieces*, which may be written by writers who are trying to understand and describe a country or countries in some depth (and perhaps themselves and the human condition at the same time). Some of these writers also produce books. Most readers will be armchair travellers. Both evocative and exploratory articles may be more concerned with the travelling than the arriving.

The above is of course a drastic oversimplification but it does help me to get through this section. The three kinds overlap, and there are numerous sub-sections. Consider the factors of time and money available to the readers aimed at: age, sex, single or married, with or without children, mode of transport, and so on. Not every reader wants to ride on a yak.

A completely honest account of a trip of the more unusual kind with a mixture of suffering and exhilaration can be refreshingly unpredictable. Stephen Pile on an adventure holiday in Peru (*Sunday Times Magazine*) describes how the group tasted the Indians' beer, made from chewed yucca and women's spit. ' "It's a script between somebody's home-brew and gone-off yoghurt," said the couple from Leicester ...'

The Leader asked the Indians if they were worried about losing their traditional ways when a road was built into the jungle. ' "No," came the reply. "We're going to open a restaurant." ' (If you're going down this road, however, make sure the experience hasn't already been done over a few times and is no longer so unpredictable.)

More off-the-beaten-track in both content and style are the travel articles in the men's magazines. (Contrast *Esquire* and *Loaded*.)

Pitfalls

Accepting 'facilities' from organizations, which means certain expenses paid or discounts on air fares and hotel bills, otherwise known as 'freebies', can be restrictive. If you tell the truth about deficiencies in a generous company's services, your relations with that company and even with an editor may be soured. But you are right and they are wrong to expect you to turn into a publicist. That principle holds for all journalism. If you're writing travel articles for a prestigious expensive glossy magazine, they may prefer to pay all expenses so that you won't have to accept free trips and be tempted to bias in what you say.

Avoid brochurespeak, which is a strong temptation if you're doing a destination piece to be written after a short visit with a pressing deadline. Clichés are fewer than they used to be and you won't get away with them. Make a note to avoid those that still slip through the net. What does 'authentic cuisine' mean?

Avoid stretches of description unless the scene is extraordinary and remote. Bring a scene to life with new facts, action, revealing dialogue, anecdotes that add drama.

Your approach

Build a travel article round a theme: finding a good title can be a good start. If you can't find a theme, try to sum up the place or the journey in a pithy sentence. Will that do as a theme? Often a theme can be turned into action – a story with a beginning, middle and end. Whatever the theme, be careful to keep the readers' needs uppermost. What will they particularly enjoy in the places described? What will they want to avoid?

Do the necessary research in guidebooks, travel books, perhaps novels, then put your notes aside when you write. If you're going to a resort, using a travel agent, ask to see that voluminous directory they keep under the counter that tells the truth about building work round the hotel or problems with air conditioning or central heating. When you visit anywhere for any length of time, read the local papers if you know the language or get someone to translate such news as how tourism is polluting the environment or how local people have recently been ripping off or mugging the tourists. If you send up the tourists, include yourself among them.

On the other hand, follow E. M. Forster's advice (about the best way to see Alexandria): 'wander aimlessly about'. Be on the alert for serendipity. Dig out the unexpected, see what other people haven't seen or probably won't see, and you won't end up sounding like your guidebook. Be knowledgeable with a light touch. Don't be a *bon vivant* or come out with foreign phrases to impress. Please allow me that one.

Avoid stretches of description unless you can astonish. Find action, new facts, revealing dialogue. Use fictional techniques.

Use a camera or take a sketch book. Your photographs or sketches will help you to be precise in your descriptions. Don't use the camera as a crutch. Note your impressions as they come, otherwise your photographs, a day or two later, may gaze back at you blankly, or freeze your imagination instead of stimulating it and reminding you of precise detail.

If you are a good photographer you will sell many features on the quality of your pictures. If you have a camera with fully automatic equipment and a good eye you don't have to be an expert to satisfy many markets. But find out whether a publication prefers to use its own picture library or a picture agency or its own photographers.

For longer trips it's a good idea to take a tape recorder as well, for note-taking, interviewing and for recording the sounds of a seedy night club in Bangkok or the croaking of frogs outside your hotel window. You may also want to take a laptop computer, and an AC adaptor and converter.

Bring back menus, brochures and leaflets that you pick up during your stay. Note striking reactions as you go to capture the edges of fresh reactions but it may be best to leave the writing up until you get back.

See Chapter 2 on expenses in general. Travel is expensive and the fee for an article may fall far short of the cost in time and money. You may be able to make use of freebies if you can avoid the pitfalls mentioned. They are not so easy to obtain these days though. It will help if you have been commissioned.

Freebies come in various forms. You may want to get on a press trip or obtain tourist-office hospitality. On press trips you are highly organized in a group. They are tiring but you can benefit from the opportunities to network with the other writers, some of whom will be travel magazine or section editors. Tourist-office hospitality can involve free hotel accommodation and meals, and sometimes help with air travel as well. But don't accept freebies with conditions that curb your independence in any way.

If you're lacking help with expenses, you may be able to sell the same article to several markets. Make the most of any trip by making notes on various aspects of the place to be written up into various articles. Read any English language publications and the local ones if you know the language. A trip to Milan might find you visiting art galleries, old churches and rundown estates as well as La Scala, talking to drug addicts and illegal immigrants and one or two British expats as well as getting businessmen's views on what the EU does for them.

Think of the publications you read, and write for. What would their readers want to know about Milan? A woman's magazine might want to know how Italian families cope with two parents working, a men's magazine a contrast between London and Milanese nightclub bouncers, and so on. See the Multi-purposing section below.

Destination pieces: readers looking for holiday ideas trawl the travel pages in newspapers for holidays they can afford and they want the prices of everything. Use charts or boxed information where appropriate. Indicate where readers can get further information, about excursions and so on.

Evocative pieces: work out which approach works best for you. Are you the traveller with personality, perhaps some eccentricity, concerned to express your reactions to what you find, whether humorously or painfully? To study this technique have a look at Redmond O'Hanlon's *Into the Heart of Borneo* and Bill Bryson. Are you, in contrast, the traveller who succeeds in blending into your surroundings, so that the scene comes vividly and purely to life and the reader is transported. (Read the travel books of Norman Lewis.)

Exploratory pieces: the epic dimensions of the quests of the renowned twentieth century travellers are lacking today, but one can learn some valuable techniques from reading Wilfred Thesiger, Laurens Van Der Post, T. E. Lawrence and Gavin Maxwell. There may be no more lost worlds or forgotten tribes to be discovered, but there are evils to be unmasked and glories to be unearthed.

The disruptive effects of industrialism and tourism on some cultures can make a serious exploratory theme. The attention paid to this issue by *Geographical Magazine* has been mentioned, but it's covered by the more escapist travel articles as well.

Books

Sampling the great travel writers listed in the Bibliography will be worth-while whatever your market, but essential if you aim to write books. You may want to write as a contributor among several for the books that approach the subject through design, diagrams and striking illustrations rather than through words. See Dorling Kindersley's series and the Insight Guides, for example. Wonderful tasters, but you may be frustrated by the need to hone your piece down to 30 words when you feel it needs a hundred.

The book with your byline, depending on your writing skill rather than illus-tration, may be your aim. As with many other subjects, if you pull it off you then have more chance of getting commissioned for features.

ASSIGNMENTS

1 Do a market analysis following the format described on pages 74–6 of the following publications:
   (a) *Daily Mail*
   (b) *The Times Educational Supplement*
   (c) *GQ*
   (d) *Cosmopolitan*
   (e) *She*
   (f) *Arena*
   (g) *Spectator.*
2 Select three of the above publications and find a suitable idea for a proposed feature of 800 words. Under a proposed title describe each idea in a paragraph of 100 words. Mention one person you would interview and what other research you would do.
3 Write the feature proposed in assignment 2.
4 Suppose you have been commissioned to write a piece about Cape Town for the Holiday page of your local paper. Suggest three other ideas for features on aspects of Cape Town but not on holidays you could write for:
   (a) *Marie Claire*
   (b) *Choice*
   (c) *Loaded.*

Under a proposed title describe each idea in 100 words, suggesting what research you could do.

5 *Group assignment* (can be done by a class or part of a class or by two or three students working together). Each student writes a 500-word how-to piece on the same subject (choose from 'How to start a magazine', 'How to travel comfortably on a long-haul flight', 'How to prepare a three-course dinner for six', 'How to write a c.v.'). Each piece is read out to the group; the reader is questioned about anything not clear. Notes are taken by the reader to help a rewrite. After discussion it is decided which was the clearest exposition and why.

7 The commissioning and the editing

An editor: a person who knows precisely what he wants – but isn't quite sure. (Walter Davenport, quoted by Bennett Cerf in *Saturday Review Reader*, No. 2)

Good editing is about knowing when to ... 'drag the readers into a story that they would never before consider reading'. (From Henry Porter, 'Editors and Egomaniacs', an essay contributed to *The Penguin Book of Journalism. Secrets of the Press*, edited by Stephen Glover, 2000)

What editors overwhelmingly want are good ideas. There's no use being a skilled writer if you have nothing to say. Walter Davenport's editors are quite sure what they want when presented with a fresh idea well expressed that fits the features formula of their publication and yet is different in some way from anything that has already appeared in it. Henry Porter is emphasizing that the good editor should have the imagination and leadership to sell the quite unfamiliar, perhaps complex and challenging piece from time to time. That unfamiliar product is sometimes a speculative ('spec') article, one that any proposal or outline could not have described satisfactorily.

This chapter sets out the ground you need to cover between studying a publication and seeing a feature of yours printed in it:

- understanding the editor's point of view
- preparing to pitch
- pitching methods
- using your network
- organizing the assignment
- sending specs
- dealing with editors.

THE EDITOR'S POINT OF VIEW

Features editors are keenly aware of the market they're in and of their publication's needs. They must be able to respond rapidly to changes in needs and to successful moves by competitors. On newspapers such responses are most likely to mean commissioning staff writers or freelances whose work is well known. The young outsider must develop strategies for breaking in.

Commissioning involves choosing the right person for the right job, not as easy as it sounds. Choosing 'the safe pair of hands' is the tendency when the pressure is on, but can lead to a predictable set of feature pages. The trick is to know when the safe is the best, and when you need an unusual combination to lift a feature out of the ordinary; when to send, for example, a fat, middle-aged, chain-smoking humorist who knows nothing about sport rather than a sports buff to interview a quirky and egotistic star athlete.

Features editors must commission and give follow-up briefings clearly or there will need to be much rewriting, by themselves, or by subs or by the authors. A news-pegged article on a national paper has to be as near as possible right first time. There may not be time for much rewriting: promising material may have to be spiked. Commissioning policy on any publication will be influenced by the special requirements of different subjects, by the traditional ways of dealing with them, and by the relationship that has been developed between editor and writer, in the course of trying to get on the same wavelength.

One writer may need to know how the feature is to be projected on the page, may need an idea of the likely headline and some precise questions that should be asked of interviewees. Another is spurred on perhaps by being given a clear idea of how the typical reader will feel after reading the article, or in what way their attitude to the subject is expected to be changed.

The processing of a newspaper staff writer's feature may have to be done in a day or two, or in an afternoon. The space requirement may change, pictures may be found that the writer didn't anticipate, breaking news may require some rewriting at the last moment. Section editors and subs may have to work on it in the middle of the night.

Freelances (and staff writers on magazines) are more likely to be given the extra time and extra briefing to make the changes themselves, or at least to be consulted. On the other hand, staff writers are more likely, provided there are none of the above emergencies, to get it right first time. They can instinctively anticipate exactly what their publication wants.

What all commissioned writers have to understand is that editors, despite the insight described above, will often not know exactly what they want until they see what they don't want. An editor and a writer must work effectively as a team. A staff writer can strengthen that teamwork by informal chat and by participating in the formal conferences and group meetings. The freelance may have to make judicious use of phone conversations, fax and email. In the end an article is a finely judged compromise – having to satisfy editor, readers, writer, lawyer and, to varying degrees, proprietors.

PREPARING TO PITCH

The commonest way to get commissioned is to sell the idea with your proposed content and treatment and illustration (if appropriate) to the editor first. If you're not known to the editor you have to sell yourself as well: explain why you are the best person to write the article, backed up by some indication of your relevant experience, including if possible cuttings of articles you've published.

Make sure you've done the market study described in Chapter 5, and have included in this study, if available, the website, media pack, editorial calendar and writers' guidelines. Having the idea and the target in mind, you must first find out both the title and the name of the person you must deal with. If there are editors of different sections of the publication, work out which section should get your query. First ask the switchboard for the name and title of that editor. The editor may be described in several different ways: features editor, commissioning editor, assistant editor, for example. For convenience we shall refer to the editor.

You will also want to know how the editor prefers to receive proposals: on the phone, by email, by fax, by letter? If you're keeping records as described in Chapter 3, note your experiences. Emails can be disregarded or forgotten if there's a daily onslaught.

A few editors want to see c.v.s, but brief ones, relevant to your ability to perform what you promise; published cuttings; printouts of online pieces; a brief summary of the proposal; or an outline of the proposed feature (or any combination of these). Writers' guidelines may specify your giving such information to back up your initial contact, whereas some editors will initially want only the idea on the phone and will accept or reject it after a minute or two.

Be ready on the phone with 25 words to make your proposal. To sell your idea at that length is a good test of its merit. If the idea is accepted, then you might be asked for all the rest. You may be taken up on an offer to provide illustrations, or you may be told that the publication will provide them.

Some American publications have changed their submission procedures since the contamination of mail by anthrax spores that followed the terrorist assault on the Twin Towers of New York. There are also widespread fears of contamination by computer virus. Don't send anything as an email attachment unless asked to.

Check that your idea meets the criteria listed in Chapter 5. What about that timeliness? Don't query too soon for you may find you cannot perform – there may be too little information available, or it may be too expensive to obtain, for example. Don't query too late, after spending much time on research, only to find that the idea has been taken up by someone else, whether for the target or for a competitor. Query when you've done just enough preliminary research to be fired by the idea and sure you can deliver.

Choose the best time if you want to get straight through to your editor. The switchboard or a secretary may be able to advise. There are unpropitious times: first thing in the morning, just before lunch or an editorial conference, between, say, 4 p.m. and 7 p.m. on a newspaper when pages are going to press, on a Thursday press day on a weekly magazine (try Friday).

There are many reasons why a proposal might be rejected. It may have been covered recently. (That shouldn't happen if you've done the necessary market study.) The idea may be considered boring or potentially libellous; the proposed treatment may be considered inappropriate, or sound too much like a 'scissors-and-paste' job. That is where your proposed content is clearly to be collected from files of newspaper cuttings and where there is no sign that it will be transmuted by some kind of originality.

If you're new the editor is unlikely to commission straight away, but if your idea appeals you may be encouraged to send the piece in and 'we'll have a look at it'. You may be given valuable suggestions about treatment. If your idea is rejected you may be told why it doesn't appeal to the market. In any case you will be able to scrutinize the idea and the target again, and consider sending the proposal to another publication. You must avoid expending time and energy on producing and sending off unsaleable features.

HOW TO PITCH

As every businessman knows there's no point in having a good product if you lack salesmanship. A good idea can be buried under an ineffective proposal. Here are some suggested techniques for querying:

- by telephone or email
- by fax or letter
- face to face.

By telephone

Be precise. Vagueness will irritate the busy executive you are talking to and, apart from losing you the commission you are aiming at, might leave an unfavourable impression.

The travel magazine editor receives a phone call

The caller has had a few articles published in a students' magazine and a local paper and has a pleasant voice and manner. A young writer worth encouraging perhaps?

'Tell me about it.'

'I'm going on holiday to Vienna for two weeks. I wonder if you'd be interested in a feature when I get back.'

'We had a feature about Vienna six months ago. Didn't you see it?'

'I'm afraid not … But I thought I'd do something a bit unusual, like describing the places where Beethoven lived and there's a museum …'

'Our feature covered that. Sorry.'

'Actually I'll be visiting Salzburg as well and …'

'What have you got in mind for Salzburg? Mozart's haunts? We've done that as well.'

'I wonder if you could suggest something I could look into while I was there?'

'Not really.' The features editor has already been too kind. 'If you think you've got something that might interest us, send it in. But study the magazine first.'

The features editor had to be vague because the caller was vague. The caller was unwise to query with even the subject only vaguely in mind and no sign of an idea.

The woman's magazine editor receives a call

The caller is also young, and has had a couple of pieces on sports background published.

'What's your idea?'

The caller refers to a summary jotted down in 23 words. 'How parents push their children to win at various sports. To damaging effect. Title perhaps: 'Champion Children – But Is The Price Too High?'

'It sounds interesting. What facts have you got?'

'The Sports Council has just published some research on effects on children of different ages. Quite academic stuff. I thought a composite piece, interviews with four or five children and their coaches and parents.'

'Send me your cuttings and a bit more – a brief outline and an intro. I don't promise but I like it so far.'

By email

When you pitch by email (unless required otherwise) try to keep the whole message short enough to be visible on the screen. Although less formal than a letter the email should give an idea of an appealing writing style and the presentation must be polished. The danger with the casualness encouraged by emails is that grammatical and spelling errors can creep in.

If sent by email the above proposal would be set out in the core paragraph, perhaps with a little more detail. Above would be the normal 'Dear (name)' greeting, followed by a subject line such as 'Article proposal' with the provisional title. A first paragraph might refer to a telephone call being followed up, in which case the briefest reminder of qualifications will suffice. If the email is the first approach, the first paragraph can give some background, perhaps a summarized c.v., and grab the editor's attention in some way. A third paragraph can ask for any details required from the editor of submission requirements. After signing off (perhaps with 'Best wishes'), give your contact details.

By fax or letter

Letters pitching to editors look more businesslike on headed notepaper with your name and address printed elegantly. Make sure you address the commissioning editor by name. As well as the normal contact information on your letterhead (home/work phone numbers, mobile phone numbers, email address, website), include at the end of the letter any other useful contact numbers, such as those of sources that the editor might want to check with. You may want to state times when you can be contacted in different places.

If the letter follows up a telephone conversation or meeting with the editor, you may not need to say much more about yourself, but you may be expected to give more elaborate descriptions of ideas already discussed.

Here are two samples of query letters sent as initial contacts:

To a magazine dealing with ecological/environmental issues

Dear …

I believe I have an excellent idea for an article that would appeal to your readers. It will be about a new social movement that has been called the 'DIY Culture'. An increasing number of people, mainly young, are working out an alternative lifestyle outside the mainstream of conventional commercial culture.

I am not sure, before I have done some research, what my own attitude to these people is or whether they will succeed or not. I shall describe the ways in which they are opposed to the conventional culture of 'economic growth' after interviewing those practising this different lifestyle. I will also look into LETS (Local Exchange and Trading Schemes) used as an alternative to money in places where this is carried on. Have you heard of this? If so, and you have some information, I'd be grateful if you'd send it on to me.

Yours sincerely

There's potential in this idea, but not enough preliminary research has been done. The first sentence of the second paragraph should be indicating knowledge, not ignorance, an attitude, not a lack of attitude. LETS should already have been looked into and the proposer should have at least an initial reaction, preferably favourable. The proposer's asking whether the target has heard of LETS suggests that any market study has been cursory. It's hardly a good start to be asking your target for information about your subject.

To a consumer magazine

This pitch succeeded, I would guess, out of its sheer enthusiasm:

Dear ...

A new leisure pursuit is sweeping Britain – walking! Everyone is getting into it and there are all kinds of snazzy gear to do it in – so it could prove an 'ad-get' for you. I am an experienced hiker and journalist (brief c.v. and relevant cuttings enclosed). About 1500 words, with illustrations if required.

Here is a suggested intro:

Walking is fast eclipsing fishing as the number one leisure pursuit in Britain today. Britons are taking to the hills in vast numbers each weekend and the sport is getting so popular that some of the favourite routes, like the Pennine Way and the Coast to Coast, are beginning to be so well trodden you hardly need a map. They join the Ramblers Association or ad hoc groups, or they like to do it in pairs, or they strike off on their own, but however they do it, they like to be well and truly togged.

How about a standfirst?:

Manufacturers are cashing in on the walking boom with all kinds of expensive kit on offer in a growing number of High Street stores – I took to the hills to investigate.

If this sounds interesting to you, please give me a call on the above number.

Yours sincerely

The writer then went on to suggest other features, on different aspects of the walking boom, to several of the dozen or so specialist walking and outdoor pursuits magazines. One article was more to do with gadgets (computer digitization of maps and navigational aids), another contrasted walking expeditions alone with doing it in groups, another explored the potential dangers in unknown territory and how to be prepared for them. All three were published. He had discovered that these magazines had not covered these aspects much.

If you want to suggest several ideas at the same time, it will probably be best to write a short covering letter with a separate ideas sheet.

Query/outline combined

After briefly following up any previous discussion, here is the way you might propose an article on 'The London homeless: what are the answers?' Note that such a subject is constantly changing and any outline would have to be updated every time you sent it out. American publications are keener on this detailed approach – see *Writers Market*.

1 *Proposed length, angle, treatment.*
2 *Suggested intro*:
   There are ... homeless people in London. They shuffle through the streets, despondent and weary. They keep moving so that they do not have to be moved on. At night they creep under railway arches, motorway flyovers, building complexes. Homeless used to be considered synonymous with alcoholics, misfits, feeble-minded, feckless, useless, old and resigned. Many of them still are, but an increasing number of them are young, only very recently unemployed and desperate to find a way back. Some of them succeed. Many more would succeed if they did not feel their family or society had rejected them.
3 *Summary of proposed article*:
   There are short-term answers ... A housing policy that takes account of the homeless is one answer. But success with an important long-term goal, to restore to the homeless a sense of community, is elusive, despite the efforts of government and the voluntary associations. (Compare the efforts to treat the mentally ill and the mentally handicapped within the community, abortive when the services provided there are inadequate.)
4 *Background*:
   Definition of homelessness (Act of 1967). Those who deserve the title and those who don't. Causes: family breakdowns, fragmentations of social

structures, unemployment, drug addiction and alcoholism, housing policy. Economic anomalies: bed and breakfast costs.

5 *Past attempts to solve problems*:
Successes and failures of housing policies, and of the efforts of voluntary associations.

6 *The task ahead*:
The particular problems of the time of writing.

7 *Conclusion*:
Up-to-date situation and prospects.

Sources: Shelter (National Campaign for Homeless People, CHAR (Campaign for the Rootless and Homeless), local government housing department, case studies.

When you've produced a structured pitch letter like the above and have been commissioned you can often develop your outline from that and quickly produce a first draft while your head is full of the subject. If you've collected material in a subject file you might have, as well your pitch, an editor's briefing, cuttings, notes and references to sources.

Use the points listed, expanding them as you write, leaving gaps where you may want to expand with an interview, anecdote, quote or other supporting material.

Multiple proposals

Chapter 3 discussed multi-purposing and syndication. Let's look at this more closely. You may want to send the same ideas to various non-competing publications, in different cities perhaps, or different countries. Indicate clearly what rights you're offering, as explained on page 14. If you receive an embarrassing number of acceptances, be sure you have prepared plans to adapt the ideas in different ways for the various publications.

If your pitches/idea sheets are not working, scrutinize them for specific detail. Lack of detail gives a feeling of blandness. Beware, however, of sticking rigidly to any formula given here or in any similar text for any stage in the pitching process.

It's a good idea to have several targets in mind for an idea, so that when it's rejected by one you can try it on another. Suppose you get interested in dubious cults being followed in your area (which not many people know about). With a local weekly in mind you do some preliminary research including interviewing. You discover some multi-purposing is going to be feasible. The local weekly might like 'When Bingo bored they turned to witchcraft' at 1000 words, with some pegging to local history. For an occult magazine you propose 'Strange Rites in Backwoods England'. This, at similar length, will incorporate various manifestations of the cult and mention similar cults in the UK. A national monthly might consider 1500 words on 'Sects can easily damage your health', with a promise to investigate cults that are hostile to the family and that use brainwashing techniques, or that claim association with charities where no connection exists, or where no proper accounts are produced.

USING YOUR NETWORK

Your ultimate aim, if you haven't already achieved it, is to have friends in high places. Then, when you have a great idea for an article, you ring up your 'friend', the features editor on a national paper, and in a minute or two you've got your assignment. A week later you have another great idea and you fix up another assignment by ringing your friend on a weekly magazine. And so on. A daunting thought for the tyro.

You can develop such friendships by telephone calls and correspondence. But it can take a long time. And you can easily blow it if you occasionally spell a name wrongly or send a query aimed at *Marie Claire* addressed to *Vogue*, because you are sending the same query to several women's magazines without any attempt to adapt them, and this time forgot to change the address.

From time to time, take the opportunity to meet editors face to face. The advantage to you is that you can soak in the atmosphere of the publication's offices created by the publication and the people who work for it. Something special will be added to what you've learnt by market study. From the editor's point of view, putting a face to your name will help to fix you in the memory.

A friendly relationship will then develop rapidly through subsequent contacts, and no doubt further commissions. You first make your customer a friend and then you sell to your friend.

Don't try this from cold, of course. If you have had a fruitful telephone conversation with a commissioning editor and impressed with an idea or two, or if you have published one or two good articles, you might be asked up to the publication's offices. If you're little known to the editor, you could take along a portfolio of any published work.

You can use a cuttings book to make a portfolio, pasting up photocopies of your printed articles, heading them with publication and date, alongside the title page of the newspaper or magazine. Don't use original cuttings, which will soon fade. Any front cover of a magazine that features or mentions your article, even going back to school or college magazines, could be pasted opposite. Some writers prefer a display book of the kind used by travelling salesmen, with cuttings inserted above a back-up sheet in a transparent plastic envelope. The cuttings may then be moved or replaced with better ones. Another kind of portfolio is loose-leafed, so that reordering of the content is easier. Once you've produced a fair number of articles you may want to use two or three portfolios each devoted to a different subject area.

If you are already writing for a publication regularly it is useful to meet your editor anyway. Depending on how far you live from the publishing address and whether you need to visit the town (to buy books and equipment or do research), allot days for the purpose in your timetable, once a month or even once a year. Plan your visits well so that you go with several ideas to discuss for the particular market, having perhaps broached them in a letter or telephone call. You will thus not be starting cold.

You've got to work at friendships. When your friend the editor complains that your feature needs a complete rewrite, try to agree. Cooperate cheerfully and promptly if asked to find better evidence for your argument not later than 4 p.m. today. Don't assume you can be a day later than the deadline because the editor's your friend, or that you can ring up for a friendly chat in the middle of a busy day, or that you can ask for the highest fee.

ORGANIZING THE ASSIGNMENT

At the moment you are commissioned to write an article you may be in the middle of several other assignments. It is advisable to write down the main instructions clearly, so that when you start the new assignment, you will not be trying to decipher yet another illegible note.

You can use your desk diary or a special telephone logbook for notes of phone conversations at home. You may want to have two desk diaries or two personal organizers: one for your personal life and one for your professional. Keep a note of the time you're paying for on the phone; the cost will be allowable for income-tax purposes. Above all, note the deadline. Work out your own deadlines: for example, for completing the reading, for completing the interviewing, for completing the writing.

If you received your assignment verbally, you should note it down, adding anything that occurs to you while the adrenaline is flowing and the discussion is fresh in your mind. You may, of course, get a letter or email containing clear instructions on what kind of article and content is wanted, and you should certainly get a letter confirming the terms. If you do not, and if you are not quite sure of the instructions, compose a letter that sets out the agreement as you have understood it and send it off. Some writers use a specially prepared form for this. If you are in this situation you may want to telephone first. Specialist features may require detailed briefing. See Figure 19.2.

The NUJ will advise on minimum fees for articles based on advertising rates and you should not accept less than the minimum. Once you have a track record you should expect more.

Starting a feature file

On being commissioned, immediately open a document (wallet) folder for the article. Use different colours of folders for articles in progress and articles published. Put any material you have into the current folder, including cuttings and the letter or note containing the assignment. If your head is full of it, you could exploit all that mental energy by typing a first short draft.

Use the points or brief paragraphs from your query letter or outline, expanding them, and leaving gaps where you might develop with interviews, anecdotes, quotes from experts, pithy quotations or other researched material. This ensures that the points you have put up will be covered. Work out as soon as you can what time you will have to spend on the piece, make any necessary phone calls to arrange interviews, and note these particulars in your desk diary.

Every writer produces a dud occasionally, and it should have a lesson to teach. You will avoid producing them too frequently by being as clear as you can at every stage about what you are doing. A dud teaches you to plan more carefully, to achieve greater control over the information you are gathering. It also teaches you to get right in your own mind what it is you are trying to say.

If you have any doubt about the editor's requirements or about what you are aiming at, clear this up before you start researching in earnest, so that you get your line of enquiry right. Some articles fail because despite apparent agreement between writer and editor about the assignment, there has been a failure in communication. The best of editors and the best of writers can end up with the wrong idea of what the other has in mind.

A wise editor judges which writers need a lot of guidance and which little: it is a delicate balance. Flexibility in the commissioning policy is necessary: there must be scope for imagination, second and third thoughts may turn out to be best, and some writers do not work well feeling hamstrung or over-briefed. On the other hand, new writers might prefer a fairly detailed briefing.

WHEN TO SEND SPECS

There are occasions when it's good to send specs:

1   *Unusual content.* You had an unusual experience. You got lost, perhaps, for a week in a Brazilian jungle and barely survived, meanwhile having a life-after-death experience. Or you cared for your grandmother who had Alzheimer's disease, or you were converted to Buddhism after hearing voices. Now you want to write a feature about it but you find it difficult to describe briefly, nor are you sure how it will turn out until you write it. So you write it and then decide who might want to print it: you send it on spec.

2   *Unusual treatment.* It may be the treatment rather than the content that will be incalculable. You may want to vaunt your way-out sense of humour in a personal lifestyle column (undaunted by the fact there are already too many such columns). You may decide to describe a child's first day at school from the child's point of view, in the child's language, or you may want to introduce the surreal, or borrow other fictional techniques, to transmute otherwise ordinary, familiar content. Almost certainly you will do these things on spec.

3   *Gatecrashing.* Writing an exceptionally good and original piece straight off, after studying the market thoroughly and making sure you have something to say, can be a good way of breaking through the barrier. Don't aim too high too soon. Some editors, it has to be said, are reluctant to respond positively to beginners' queries, even when they sound promising. They may have found that such articles have proved unsatisfactory in the past. Or it may simply be that they are overstocked.

Such editors can be delighted to find a new talent beaming up at them, an article unexpectedly well researched and well written, in tune with everything in the publication and yet having a distinctly fresh voice – and they will make room for it.

4 *The need to experiment.* You need to experiment sometimes and not be always guided by the rules, even if it means some of the wilder 'specs' do not come off. These can be filed away and perhaps rewritten at a later date. You will have learnt valuable lessons on the way and it will help you to find a distinctive voice.

5 *After a nod and a wink.* A long-established friend in an editor may commission after a pitch of a few sentences on the phone: you may be trusted to make all the right decisions about how to develop the idea. Such an editor may also consider sympathetically a piece coming in from you without warning. But don't count on it.

It can be useful to get some feedback on spec features before trying them on editors, if you know a good critic or two whose views you respect. They are probably not members of your family (though how convenient if they are), and they don't grow on trees.

DEALING WITH EDITORS

In the course of preparing a feature you may find that your original promise or the editor's briefing cannot be fulfilled for some reason. Perhaps you have failed to obtain a crucial interview or you realize that you are not sure what the editor wants exactly. Keep in touch with the editor. Explain any problem about completing in the manner agreed. There's nothing worse than producing an article on the deadline which is so far from the brief that it's too late to do anything about it.

The piece you've got might be accepted but it might not. If not, you might get a kill fee. The editor may feel that you've communicated your difficulties well and that you've done your best, or may accept some of the blame for any misunderstanding.

Make sure you submit your feature as agreed when commissioned. If you're not sure, check before submission. Some magazines (for example, *Geological Magazine*) require you to send an SAE to receive detailed instructions on how to lay out their work. Is a disk required (for example, Mac or PC format or .txt file in Word or WordPerfect) as well as hard copy? Does the publication want the article in the form of a document sent as an email attachment, or copied and pasted as text into the body of the email? How should photographic and other illustrations be submitted?

When submitting, explain any minor divergences from the query letter or briefing, or give any other explanation that may be necessary. Include a separate, brief cover letter for this if submitting by post.

A reminder: give details of sources with telephone numbers and email addresses in case any information from them needs to be checked or updated by the publication. But build up your own 'exclusive' database of contacts: don't give away all your contacts and ideas.

Proofreading

If you are sent page proofs you may be charged for any corrections you make that are second thoughts, additions or deletions, or restructuring. Be sure to use British Standard Institute (BSI) proof marks for copy preparation and proof correction. Printers' errors or errors attributable to the publication will be charged to the publication.

Editors may ask you to cut to fit their space or you will agree to their doing so. The better established you are, the more likely it is that little will be changed without your approval. The sense of your article must not be changed.

When editors reject

Editors can rarely find the time to give detailed reasons for rejecting an article. A rejected spec article sent by post will be returned if you've sent an SAE, accompanied usually by a standard rejection slip.

If there has been interest shown in your idea with some communication about it (including 'We'll have a look at it'), you might get something on why it was rejected. For example:

- The idea of describing the first week in England of a refugee from Zambobwe was a good one. Unfortunately the interviewee hasn't much to say and you haven't managed to get into his mind and soul.
- Five refugees from Iranaqwait, covering their first week in England, is two more than you promised. The result is too much detail, and I'm not sure what it all adds up to in the end. If you can send me a detailed outline, covering two refugees and one theme, we'll be prepared to give it another shot.

- Your brisk, light-hearted style doesn't suit the theme of domestic violence.
- You've written an elegant literary essay. If you study the magazine, you'll see that we never publish elegant literary essays.

If there has been some detailed discussion about the proposal, with an outline approved and a full briefing, some sympathy might accompany a kill fee. For example:

- I'm sorry but I'm afraid it hasn't quite come off. We don't become involved with the people suffering from the environmental disaster. You've become bogged down in the intricacies of the legal case against the multinational company responsible. We need to see these people and their deformities, their wrecked hopes. I enclose a cheque for $xx because I know you've put in a lot of work on it.
- I love your English irony and sense of humour. You've also got a vivid descriptive passage in the middle. But the average American reader is not *au fait* with your foreign words and phrases, nor with the history of Goa. Thanks for trying. I see that you've decided to subscribe, so we've decided to give you a year's subscription free of charge.

Responding to rejection

Respond positively. If a commissioned feature is rejected with such flaws identified, read it through to decide on future action. Assuming you have not been encouraged to rewrite it, you may be able to identify another publication that might welcome it. Then you decide whether the new editor would react in the same way and how to improve the piece.

If no comments arrive with a returned spec feature, try to work out yourself exactly why it was rejected. There may not be much wrong with it. Three or four pieces on the same theme as yours may have arrived at the same time. Yours was good, but one of the others was better. Or two pieces on the same theme arrived: yours was better, but the other was commissioned and yours wasn't. Or the editor changed while you were writing your feature and has different criteria. You may be able to try other targets.

Some features can be rewritten immediately for another target, others can be filed away to be considered at a later date. A news peg may appear after a month or two that may restore life to the material.

ASSIGNMENTS

1 Find three feature ideas and pitch them to three targets. Exchange with a fellow student or colleague who acts as editor.

2 Take three features (approximately 500, 800 and 1500 words) from different publications. Produce a clear outline of the content of each by listing the main points in note form (not sentences), one point for each paragraph. Produce a pitch letter for each, aimed at other publications, adapting the idea appropriately.

3 Change each of the above outlines to a sentence outline, indicating links.

4 You have written a feature 'To Complain is a Duty' for a customer magazine (Chapter 5, assignment 3). Work out how you could reshape it for three other target publications. Produce the three pitches in letter form. Include in your pitches three different proposed intros to grab the editors' attention.

5 Write an essay of 1000 words entitled 'The Roles of Writer and Editor: How They Differ'. Re-read this chapter to pick up any points, then find other printed sources. Talk to a feature writer and an editor, and collect an anecdote and a quote or two. Include any relevant experience of your own in dealing with editors.

6 *Workshop.* All students of a small group (up to eight) write a feature of 600 words at home with the same title and target publication. The completed scripts are collected and distributed so that each writer gets someone else's. Each writer now becomes an editor, subs the feature and writes a letter suggesting how it might be improved and possibly commissioned. The editors may be anonymous or not: try it both ways. Each student then reports on the editing done to their script, indicating their response. The tutor guides group discussion on each script.

A large group can be split up into two or three small groups, each operating as above, each with a different title/target, after which the tutor can work through the scripts immediately, guiding the group discussion.

8 Ways of finding out

The media have no choice but to ask questions of the government of the day or the state of the moment, not because they are special, not because they are better, not because they are arrogant, not because they are self-appointed, but because if they do not do it, nobody else will. (John Tusa, former Managing Director of the BBC World Service)

We have established that the basic skill of journalism is reporting – collecting and giving the facts – and that their news value consists in the facts being of public interest and sometimes in the public interest. Reporters have to identify the information that has news value, locate reliable sources of information, gather accurate (verified) information and communicate it accurately, effectively and quickly. The last requirement means that they fulfil the other objectives as well as they can within the deadline.

Feature writers must build on those skills. They may have more time, deadlines may at times be extended, and they may have less excuse for unverified data. They normally add to the reporting skills greater language skills in order to describe, analyse, argue and persuade, but these are the concerns of other chapters. This chapter concentrates on the techniques that will help you to employ to good effect:

- reliable sources
- an interviewing strategy
- verification skills.

RELIABLE SOURCES

Which are the best sources for your purpose? I presume you have a provisional title before you start gathering and know what you're looking for. The first thing to do is find out as much as you can about the topic of your feature so that you will be able to ask fruitful questions (those that get fruitful answers), and so that you will understand what interviewees are talking about and make illuminating comparisons. That study may benefit from your own personal experience and legwork.

It's worth reminding yourself, in the course of research, of the truism that you may be able to leave out things you know without spoiling your story, but if you leave something out *because* you don't know it, there will be a hole in the story.

For anything complex you may be able to get fairly detailed briefing and recommended sources from a commissioning editor.

Background study

First see what you've got in your cuttings files. If they are lacking, you may want to make use of a press cuttings agency (see Figure 8.1.) but they can be expensive. Try informal exchanges – your friends and colleagues, and chatrooms. Move around with a reporter's notebook. You may get something out of broadcast programmes and sometimes background information can be acquired from producers or press offices. Note that TV programmes may have been a year in the pipeline.

You can then decide what reference materials and the Web can't tell you that an interviewee can, who you would like to interview, and what questions you need or want to ask.

Information is now so easily available via the Internet that it's less necessary to travel and incur other expenses to gather it. For example, whereas 10 years ago you might have paid a colleague in Glasgow to do some on-the-spot research to give you notes on the Scottish aspects of your subject, or organized a network of colleagues exchanging such services, or inserted classified adverts asking for information, you'd be more likely today to go to the Web, to a newsgroup or chatline or to publications or services online. It will be worth subscribing to some publications and services online that deal with your specific interests. But avoid becoming deskbound.

Personal experience and legwork

If your magazine piece for a woman's magazine is to describe how the headmaster of your local primary school rescued it from the bottom of the

Press Cuttings Agencies

Durrants

Discovery House, 28–42 Banner Street,
London EC1Y 8QE
☎020 7674 0200 Fax 020 7674 0222
✉ contact@durrants.co.uk
www.durrants.co.uk

Wide coverage of all print media sectors plus
Internet, newswire and broadcast monitoring;
foreign press in association with agencies
abroad. High speed, early morning press cuttings from the national press e-mailed to your
desktop. Overnight delivery via courier to
most areas or first-class mail. Well presented,
laser printed, A4 cuttings. Rates on application.

International Press-Cutting Bureau

224–236 Walworth Road, London SE17 1JE
☎020 7708 2113 Fax 020 7701 4489
✉ ipcb2000@aol.com

Contact *Robert Podro*

Covers national, provincial, trade, technical
and magazine press. Cuttings are normally sent
twice weekly by first-class post. Basic charges
are £60 per month + 60p per cutting.

Romeike Media Intelligence

Romeike House, 290—296 Green Lanes,
London N13 5TP
☎0800 289543 Fax 020 8882 6716
✉ info@romeike.com
www.romeike.com

Contact *Alistair Hails*

Monitors national and international dailies and
Sundays, provincial papers, consumer magazines, trade and technical journals, teletext services as well as national radio and TV networks.
Back research, advertising checking and Internet
monitoring, plus analysis and editorial summary
service available.

We Find It (Press Clippings)

40 Galwally Avenue, Belfast BT8 7AJ
☎028 9064 6008 Fax 028 9064 6008

Contact *Avril Forsythe*

Specialises in Northern Ireland press and magazines, both national and provincial. Rates on
application.

Xtreme Information

89½ Worship Street, London EC2A 2BF
☎020 7377 1742 Fax 020 7377 6103
✉ info@news.xtremeinformation.com
www.news.xtremeinformation.com

Newcastle office: Earl Grey House, 75–85 Grey
Street, Newcastle upon Tyne NE1 6EF
☎0191 203 1020 Fax 0191 203 1010

National and European press monitoring
agency. Cuttings from national and all major
European press available seven days a week,
with early morning delivery. Also monitoring
of internet and newswire channels. Delivery
available online; account management available
24 hours a day.

Figure 8.1
Ways of finding out: Press Cuttings Agencies from *The Writer's Handbook 2005*. © Macmillan Publishers Ltd.,
2004, ed. Barry Turner

league table you might start by thinking about your own schooldays, and
about the current experiences of your children or of children you know.
Then you might read newspaper and magazine features on the national
picture (consult the BHI and other indexes of articles published). You
might follow that up with legwork – a visit to the school and the area to see
what you can observe for yourself – and interviews with the headmaster
and some of the children. You might fill up with some information about

the area's schools in general from the Local Education Authority (press releases?, booklet?, reports?).

From legwork report to legwork feature

Supposedly filed from the war zone in Iraq, reports in the *New York Times* from an American journalist were concocted in the US on his computer.

Assume you'll also be found out if you fake legwork or misrepresent any of your sources. The temptation to use the resources of the computer instead of legwork increases. Naturally so, since for some purposes the Internet is vastly superior. You can speedily collect case studies to illuminate your theme that might have required time-consuming legwork and telephone calls: the informal kind from chatroom discussion, and formal ones out of the reports from professional journals that are reproduced online.

Harold Evans, editor of *The Sunday Times* when it produced acclaimed investigative journalism about such scandals as the deformities caused by the drug Thalidomide, has said: if only we could have used chatrooms at that time. Don't be too ready, however, to advertise yourself as a journalist in a chatroom – you could be frozen out.

Avoid being too dependent on Internet sources (and make sure you know exactly what you're looking for when you go online). Getting out of the house or the office to talk to flesh and blood people should be done more often by feature writers as well as reporters. And sometimes, if you can pardon the pun, you can make a feature out of it. You might have the time and inclination to combine personal experience (literally) with legwork to argue a case and it may be the best way to do it. Let's call it a legwork feature.

It's a year or two ago now, a newspaper reported that you could earn up to £7.00 an hour on the streets of Aberdeen as a 'bogus beggar'. It was said that in London you could earn £100 a day and that many did. Police departments, town councils and charities come up with such figures from time to time. Steven Bowron in *The Sunday Post* of Dundee recounted an attempt to find out what it's like to beg. In tattered clothes and a cardboard notice ('hungry and homeless') he collected, as well as taunts, £3.13 in eight hours outside Euston Station in London (and somewhere else when moved on by the police). It was a drizzly day.

He talked to Shelter Scotland whose advice to people who wanted to help beggars genuinely in need was to give to the various charities concerned with the homeless. Well, in terms of getting to the truth, Mr Bowron's experience was useful in the casting of doubt on the assertions of the no-nonsense brigade and in getting across the miserable experience begging is, and in a sense that was getting a little nearer to the truth. He didn't make any greater claims than that.

The above account shows how careful you have to be when figures are involved. How were those original figures arrived at? How large were the samples? As for Mr Bowron's winnings, if he had done a week on the street, might he have collected more than one day's takings suggested? Could he have got better at it? Was the weather responsible for people hurrying past? Do you have to build up a presence before people start giving? Be a particular shade of grey? And so on.

You will compound any problems of interpretation if you fail to take notes and quotes accurately. Ask your interviewee to repeat anything you're not sure of. Was that 'fifteen' or 'fifty'? Would you spell that name please?

Another variation of the case-study feature was 'You can't judge a woman by her cover' in *You*, the lifestyle magazine of *The Mail on Sunday*. It was experimental theatre of a kind. The writer, Joan Burnie, accompanied model Trudie Joyce to London establishments: on two shopping expeditions to Harrods, two trips to the American Bar at the Savoy and two trips to the nightclub Stringfellows. For each visit Trudie dressed in different clothes, once as a slag and once elegantly.

The contrasting reactions of employees – doormen, sales assistants, waiters, barmen, barmaids and of the public – make an amusing account 'in the interests of sexual science and journalism'. Colour pictures of the model in different clothes and situations reinforce the thesis expressed in the title, together with suggestive captions. The thesis, you might argue, is imposed on the material rather than supported by it. Readers may guess that other encounters that didn't fit were omitted. But the first-hand experiences have impact and readers will accept the general psychological truth about human nature behind it all.

Selection of contacts

Collect good contacts as you go, for the features you write, in your own contacts book. You may find a filofax type of book ideal. One contact leads to another. Before you leave a contact, ask 'Who else shall I talk to?'

Indicate the particular expertise of your contacts ('good on progress of Parliamentary bills'). Include such entries as libraries, their specialisms, hours of business and the names of friendly librarians. *Press Gazette* produces an electronic database and regularly lists press officers.

Get on the mailing list of organizations you're interested in so that you will receive advance information about developments. Manufacturers will send you handouts and free photographs if you write about new products.

Official sources may be generous with time and information, especially if they know your work and if you have established good relationships. But talk to enemies as well as friends, consumers as well as producers.

When you've collected a fair number of contacts in your contacts book (many of whom will be experts in the particular subjects you cover), you might well start your research planning for a feature with one of them. If they don't know what's the current situation, the latest development (or problem), they may be able to put you on the right track quickly, point you to the latest book or features or most knowledgeable source.

Assessment of sources

There are three essential criteria by which your sources must be judged. Are they *accessible*; are they, where necessary, *multiple*; are they the *best informed*?

Are they accessible? If your feature would benefit greatly from your visiting an institute in New York or Paris, there may not be time and expenses might not be agreed. Think of alternative sources.

Multiple? How authoritative are your sources? Some eyewitnesses remember certain things, others remember other things. Figures given in press accounts can be wrong and the errors repeated. Cross-check one kind of expert against another.

But which are the best informed, the most credible, the most reliable? This requires some thought. The traps are endless. There are unreliable sources whose judgement is clouded or whose memory is impaired. There are hoaxers who delight in ringing up newspapers to give them false stories. There are convincing gossipers, liars, slanderers, people bearing grudges, seeking revenge at any cost. There's a limit to how much cross-checking you can do, so you must select with care. When you're not sure of the truth of statements you can attribute them in a qualified way: 'Certain people believe that …' or 'The impression has been gaining ground that …'.

For a feature about bullying in the workplace you wouldn't depend on an interview with one victim, but would supplement it with other interviews, with observers for example, and with some reading about the subject. Look for the names of experts in encyclopedia articles and recent books on your subject. Circle names of experts quoted in published features or check them out in your local library. Trade magazines (business to business) contain the names of experts in many fields. If you want a wide choice of experts find them by going online and typing in your search terms. Experts depend on being recognized as such and will grant interviews readily (if you pitch your request for one effectively).

Sometimes you can find a disaffected expert ready to tell you more than a happy one. Why are there such long delays in, say, hip replacement operations? The happy hip replacement surgeon in your local hospital may give you an interview. But you may find some questions unanswered or avoided and you may find a whistleblower to complete the picture. One such whistleblower, also a surgeon doing hip replacements, complained that a fellow surgeon was admitting private patients before NHS patients who had waited longer and was getting paid twice. The NHS Trust decided that she needed further training.

It was two years later that she was interviewed by a journalist. She had done six months further training, after which no more training had been available and she had been on full pay for two years. She had seen no patient in this period and wanted her job back. Of course, the truth isn't a simple matter. Does the other side have more of a case than you suspected? Find another source to check.

You can assess a contact's reliability from the replies to questions to which you know the answer. You know for certain, let's say, that your contact's firm has had to withdraw three products this year after being arraigned under the Trade Descriptions Act. But you ask, 'Sometimes in your business firms have trouble keeping in line with the Trade Descriptions Act. Has that ever happened to your firm?' Your readers must make their own judgements about how reliable your contacts are, and your questions and treatment should establish their confidence in your judgement.

You can be over-cautious in choosing the obvious experts. They may have been overused elsewhere. Remember that the best stories can come from an unusual angle and that can come from matching your topic with one or two out-of-the-way sources, as described in Chapter 3.

In your feature don't neglect to give sources of official figures and of unusual information, facts that might be queried, so as to lend them authority.

AN INTERVIEWING STRATEGY

For a productive interview for information you need to:

- make effective approaches
- organize your notes
- question creatively
- use techniques of persuasion
- elicit good quotes
- choose the best method
- acknowledge your sources
- establish bonds with your contacts.

Effective approaches

Don't depend on switchboard operators to guide you to a likely source of information. Work out from your initial study the name and job title of a likely contact.

If you're not known or haven't got a commission from a well-known publication it can be difficult to get past the secretaries, assistants, deputies, the various kinds of gatekeepers. It helps if you can engineer an introduction, something like: 'Brian so-and-so suggested you might be able to tell me about …'.

Decide which method of interview would be most appropriate for your subject but be ready to go along with the preference of your contact. Explain the project you're working on and why your contact's contribution would be important. If there is reluctance, remember you're giving free publicity.

You may be able to indicate (tactfully) in what way the published interview will benefit the contact and their work, and that a 'no comment' might be harmful. Tell people you want to 'talk' to them, not 'interview' them. Don't get annoyed if in spite of tactful persistence you fail to gain an interview. It happens to the best of us. Be ready with alternatives.

Dos and don'ts

Suppose you, fairly new to the game, are asked on Monday to find out why a renowned editor and several other staff had just mysteriously resigned from a highly successful magazine, and to write a feature about the magazine, explaining its success and what has gone wrong. Your deadline is Thursday, 1000 words. You've been given by your editor the name of the most promising contact, let's call him Arnold Baxter, a journalist who worked with the proprietor for 15 years and left six months ago to become the director of a School of Journalism. You have an interview on Tuesday with the Advertisement Director of the group, who will tell you something of the group's history and in particular the history of the magazine in question.

What you shouldn't do

You fix up a telephone interview with Mr Baxter for the Monday. You haven't had time to get acquainted with the magazine – it's not one you're familiar with – but you decide you'll do that after the Tuesday interview. Mr Baxter is surprised to discover that you know nothing at all about the magazine, nor its history, nor anything about the resignations. You say he's your first interview and that you'll fill in the details from your Tuesday interview. He suggests you find out about these things, do the Tuesday interview and return to him on Wednesday. But now that he's on the end of the phone you want to make the most of it so you plough on: what was it like working with that proprietor and why do you think things have suddenly gone wrong with so many of the staff?

Mr Baxter is very articulate and talks quite quickly. You're writing it all down but you have to ask him to pause frequently. You wish you'd learnt shorthand. Mr Baxter is sympathetic at first but becomes frustrated by the constant need to pause and is anxious to get the interview over. You can't expect an interviewee to talk at the speed at which you write longhand.

'Can I see the script?' asks Mr Baxter, worried that you're going to misquote him. You say it's not the policy of your magazine to show interview scripts before publication. At least, read over to me from your final script what you're quoting me as saying, he says. I'll check with my editor, you

say. The interview ends with little rapport and you have lost a good opportunity to obtain illuminating commentary. When you've gone Mr Baxter
realizes that you have failed to ask the specific kinds of questions that
would have produced that illumination. Such as: what problems did you
have with the proprietor while you were an employee? You can't expect an
interviewee to tell you what questions should be asked. You recognize that
you've done a duff interview, but Mr Baxter regrets that he's too busy to
give you another chance.

What you should do

1 Find out as much as you can about Mr Baxter, probably by interviewing briefly one or two others first. Ask the editor why he's the main prospect if you weren't told. Talk to any current or ex-colleague who knows
   Mr Baxter well. Decide on two or three main interviewees and the best
   order to interview them.
2 Buy at least the current issue of the magazine and read some of it so that
   you know what it's all about, what sort of audience it has, etc., and look
   through the others in the group. (Access them online or in a good library.)
3 Find any recent articles about the company and about the magazine in
   particular.
4 Find out as much as you can about Mr Baxter's career with the company
   and his relationship with the proprietor.
5 Since you have no shorthand, ask for permission to tape the interview,
   via a telephone hook-up. I have found that most interviewees welcome
   it, feeling there's less chance of being misquoted. (Of course, it doesn't
   always work that way because you'll do a little editing when transcribing and that may result in the interviewee feeling misrepresented. Some
   interviewees will tape the interview at their end.) If you are asked not to
   tape, you should do a crash course in shorthand.

Organize your notes

Poorly organized notes can cause much trouble when it's time to write the
piece. Here are a few essentials.

You may want to use separate sheets or cards for separate themes. You can
then experiment by shuffling them into different orders when you want to
produce an outline. Whatever the source of your notes, keep in mind that
the published article must get the acknowledgements right. Indicate name

of interviewee and date of interview or event; and authors and titles of books and articles, dates of publication, and page numbers for the references so that you can verify later that you've quoted or reproduced statements correctly. Back up points that need an authority by acknowledging the source. Well-known facts don't need acknowledgement.

Note sources for figures, especially official figures, to give them authority. Date everything: not only those mentioned above, but also any event mentioned in the course of conversation. If your interviewee says something happened 'recently', ascertain the date so that you'll know how you (or a subeditor) will refer to it on the date your piece is published. Inaccurate notes can bring trouble.

Quoting and paraphrasing

Put quote marks in your notes round significant statements. You may want to use the quotes in your feature. You may want to establish the credibility of a statement made by an expert. If you quote and attribute factual statements that might be considered disputable, you might want to use a caveat such as 'according to …'. Such care in distinguishing opinion from fact will help to establish trust in your readers. But if there are libel dangers, get legal advice on such statements.

At a local council meeting the reporter hears the water company representative, asked about the recent water shortages, say that there is no problem. In the reporter's contact book, however, is a water engineer who has been helpful with leads in the past. He says that there are leakages and that more money needs to be spent on maintenance. The reporter is asked by the editor to check cuttings and do an investigative piece. It is agreed that the engineer will be described as 'a reliable source'. The story develops into a campaign. After several investigative pieces over the course of a year culminating in a feature by a water engineer who contributes to business-to-business magazines, the funds are provided and the water supplies restored.

Make sure your notes make it clear where you're quoting and where paraphrasing. Quotes in notes (with 'paraph' in brackets) can simply remind you to paraphrase when writing up and so avoid the risk of being accused of plagiarism. (It's easy to copy material directly into your notes and forget they are the original words when writing up.) 'Style' in brackets after quotes can remind you to use the words in your piece to indicate the writer's or speaker's style.

You may have thoughts about the points you are noting. If so, put them under the notes in square brackets. Note the source at the end of each note, so that you can return to it later, if necessary, to check: author, title of book or article, publisher or title of publication, date, page number; or name of interviewee with date of interview; or event attended, with date.

Quote that significant statement when writing up even if it's in the form of a phrase included in otherwise paraphrased material and your own commentary. For example, 'Twenty years ago Paul Harrison wrote that crime rates were highest in the inner city, which was "Britain's most dramatic and intractable social problem" and perhaps the same could be said today.'

Paraphrase facts that are repeated in various sources and introduce them by saying something like 'Most experts/historians/footballers agree that …'. Chapter 10 shows how well-organized notes are developed into a well-organized feature.

Logging and ordering

If you're going to interview several people for a news feature, you may be able to work out a good order to do them in, so that your understanding and your questions are good. After perhaps some reading for background you'll probably, as we've seen, start with people most knowledgeable about the current situation, with overview; move on to people able to comment on specific detail; ending if necessary with summing up and if appropriate speculation about the future. When your interviews are done, you will think about different ways of ordering the material for interest and effect. Make sure your reporter's notebook carries your name and phone number in case it gets lost.

Let's take a fictitious example. In the county of Jaytonshire, the town of Rowdyborough is about to establish an alcohol control zone in the city centre in a month's time. It will be a trial for six months. If it works, the scheme will be repeated in other towns in the county. Already the city of Peacewick in the neighbouring county of Beldonland, also visited by many tourists, has transformed its centre by creating a dry zone by means of a by-law.

You're a feature writer for the Jaytonshire Gazette and you've been asked to write a feature of 900 words, provisional title 'Will a dry zone work in Rowdyborough?' The town suffers more from drunks and hooliganism than Peacewick did. You decide on an order of interviews and you will organize the results of your research so that the story can be clearly seen in summary. It's a good idea to keep a separate logbook as well for all your phone calls. I'm assuming the telephone interviews listed are not too time-consuming and that you know exactly what questions you should ask. Here's how it might look (F = face-to-face):

Item	Source (dates would be given)	Data
1	Coverage in the Rowdyborough Gazette, press releases from the council	Background: The Criminal Justice and Police Act 2001 and the Local Authorities (Alcohol Consumption in Designated Places) Regulations 2001 give local authorities the power to restrict anti-social drinking in designated places and to provide the police with the power to enforce this legislation.
2	(R) Council Report on Consultation with local residents and businesses	140 responses, 137 in favour, two don't knows and one in disagreement. Reference also made to noise pollution, street lighting, skateboards, mountain bikes and beggars
3	Email from R Councillor Joy Luckock, Community Safety Department	'We want to protect R's rich heritage for everyone to enjoy. The alcohol control zone is just one measure we're introducing to make R safer. We're not killjoys. Publicity? Posters, handbills, street signs, warnings from clubs, pubs and shops.'
4	Phone: Deputy Leader of R Council Norman Finch	'We've picked R for this pilot scheme because it's a great attraction for tourists and we can learn from what happened in P. In the evenings people can be intimidated by the drunks.'
5	Phone: Jaytonshire Police: Inspector Roy Bartlett	'We have talked to our colleagues in Beldonland and Sgt Michael Higgins of Peacewick will be helping us at R for a period.'

(Continued)

Item	Source (dates would be given)	Data
6	Phone: (P) Sgt Higgins	'In the two years our scheme has been operating there have been only three arrests. People drinking in public are asked to move, and they know about the by-law and they move.'
7	F: (R) Margaret Baker, National Association for the Care and Resettlement of Offenders (NACRO)	'The situation in P is not entirely satisfactory. There has been insufficient back-up from agencies like ours for people moved on. Sometimes the police could cooperate more with us. Some of the drinkers in town centres have recently been released from prison, some are alcoholics who badly need help and we lose sight of them. They take their problem somewhere else. You could talk to Shelter.'
8	F: (R) Shelter: David McManus	'There are day and night shelters for the homeless and the scheme will work if people moved on are referred to us.'

This follows the facts-gathering order I suggested would be good. In the writing up you could lead in with some colour, set the scene: a typically noisy Rowdyborough centre in the evening (you would go and have a look). Perhaps you could note an incident that reveals the scale of the problem and the need for action. Or you might want to start with the quote from Mr McManus if it sums up your own viewpoint. And in your lead-in you'd probably introduce as a link the doubt that comes with the question of the title. The laws and the consultation report would have to come early but you'd have to get readers interested in the situation first.

Question creatively

However well you do your preliminary research, however clear you are about what you want to find out and about the shape of the final story, however well you prepare your questions, however interested you are in people, however good a listener you are, however good you are at keeping your interviewee from rambling away from the subject, and at juggling your notebook, pen, telephone receiver, tape recorder and whatever else you have to juggle, however good you are at organizing your notes, you've got to add some creativity. That involves understanding people, adapting your techniques to their personalities, knowing how to phrase a question in different ways to get the facts out of an introvert, an extrovert, a workaholic, an alcoholic, people with their own agendas very different from yours, people suspicious of your intentions, people with something to hide, and so on.

Creativity also involves, as all that implies, that you're ready for the unpredictable. You'll discover facts, whole stories sometimes, different from what you expected. You often have to adapt or change your prepared questions on the hoof to take account of those unexpected answers. At the same time, an interview for information isn't like a conversation where you're delighted by completely new vistas opening up to be explored. You've already got your vista and must not be deflected by facts, however interesting, that are irrelevant for your purpose.

This kind of creativity will improve by practice, and by studying good research interviews. The following is a list of tactics of a general kind.

- Prepare on the whole *simple questions*, open-ended, not requiring yes or no: use your who, what, when, where, why and how.
- Prepare some *good specific questions*, suggested by your knowledge of the interviewee and of the current situation. Generalities create a fog. You want specifics which make for clarity and readability. Ask for specifics in an appropriately polite and natural manner. To 'were there communication problems within the company?' you're in danger of getting the answer 'yes'. Engineer a polite sequence in a natural conversation. Something like: 'I know that in 1998 you were unhappy about the lack of communication between departments and even within departments … Did you find that friendly relations were at a low ebb when you resigned? Was there any socialization after working hours? Have you kept in close touch with your ex-colleagues that remain on the magazine?'
- *Ask for examples/anecdotes/quotes*. A Detective Inspector tells you that very personal information about people has been obtained by talking to their neighbours. 'Have you got important evidence this way? Can you give me an example – without mentioning any names of course?'
- *Exploit revelations*. ('I wasn't feeling myself at the time … but we won't go into that.') Avoid being totally occupied with keeping up with the

note-taking. Follow up any unguarded remarks that promise a seam worth digging into, but emotions and opinions must be essential to the story if you're going to follow them up. You're not doing a profile.

- *Collect some colour when relevant.* A little usually is. The rowdy evening scene in Rowdyborough (with a description of the participants, unkempt beards perhaps and beer cans), was a suggested intro to that story. If leg-work isn't possible, you can collect the colour and perhaps one or two anecdotes and quotes from the people you talk to.

- *Check some facts as you go.* Get names of people and places you're not sure of spelled out. Get anything you don't understand repeated or explained, especially jargon.

- *Get more information than you need.* You're much less likely to have holes in your story.

- *Keep the person on track.* Politely. Your interviewee may prefer to talk about something else. You've got the list of questions, you're making the notes, you're in charge, or you should be.

- *Loosen the person's reserve.* When you get 'I don't like talking about it' or 'I've no patience with that kind of activity. Full stop', just asking 'Why do you say that?' or 'Why do you feel like that?' can open the gate. You may be able to loosen the reserve by showing your genuine interest and concern. Instead of firing another question try reacting emotionally: the lack of a question can have a relaxing effect. For example, 'I can understand why you may be reluctant ...' or 'How wonderful that you can still have a positive attitude!' or 'Criminal! I'm not surprised you couldn't put up with that.' (I did say genuine: don't overdo it.)

- *Find time for a review at the end of the interview.* Are there gaps in the story you can plug with another question. Is there something that doesn't quite add up?

Questions not to ask

- How did you feel when your grandmother fell off a cliff?
- How did you feel when you were told you had won such a prestigious award?
- Were you ready for the amount of fame that suddenly enveloped you?
- Your last play was panned mercilessly by the critics. Don't you think you should try another medium? Or is it too late in your career? Have you ever thought of giving up writing altogether?

- You're obviously the most promising writer of your generation. Are you on a roll, or do all the accolades put too much pressure on you?
- You've been called the most beautiful bum in the world. Are interviewers always bringing that up, and if so is it beginning to irritate you a bit?
- You are well known for your large donations to charity. Do you try to keep them quiet or is it good for your career/business? (It may be a good question if drastically rephrased.)
- How are the share prices of your company going on the stock market at the moment? (You should already know how and have some idea of why.)
- Have you stopped beating your wife? Don't ask any version of the famous trick question, encouraging an answer, whether yes or no, that implies he used to.

Use techniques of persuasion

The more difficult interviewees, especially those with much experience of being interviewed by journalists, present another kind of challenge. Even securing the interview in the first place may require much more obstinacy than is healthy. Secretaries and assistants will tell you he or she is at a meeting, is not in the office, will ring you back, will ask if you will ring back next week, and so on, which may sometimes be true, but are often ways of fobbing you off. Keep trying until your target realizes that cooperating will be easier than resistance.

PROs, information officers and press officers, in particular, start from different premises. The quid pro quo nature of the encounter is tacitly accepted. The publicists avoid giving information that may be compromising, the journalist tactfully avoids being used as a vehicle of publicity.

The publicist may give facts that put a product or service in a good light and omit several other facts that do not. Multiple check sources, as has been suggested, may be the answer to this ploy, but the journalist may be hamstrung by the deadline. Try giving the impression that you know those other facts but that you might make them out to be worse than they are.

Spokesmen of business organizations, like politicians, are highly skilled in giving you the information they have decided to give you, cunningly evading your questions while apparently answering them. Bringing them back on track may require firmness with 'You have not answered my question' or 'Interesting, but that's not exactly what I asked'.

When firmness is not enough

'Are you keeping back information that the law says I can have?'

'Do I have to tell my readers that you personally declined to give me this information? Won't a "no comment" look bad for your organization, make the situation look worse than it is? Make it look as if you've got something to hide?'

'Do you refuse to let taxpayers (or ratepayers) know what you're doing with their money?'

Such veiled threats are, however, the last resort. They can lose their bite anyway if you can't determine exactly where accountability lies.

Go on the hunt for elusive figures

The insurance company's director says he can't give you the rise expected in the premium from next January. Try guessing too high.

'About 25 per cent I've been told?'

'That's too high.'

'15 per cent?'

(Pause.) 'Perhaps a little more.'

'If I said about 20 per cent I wouldn't be far off?'

'You can say what you like.'

That gets the director off the hook and you've got a good figure.

Produce an awkward silence

Produce an awkward silence. You ask an awkward question. You get an awkward, incomplete answer. You wait. Your interviewee will probably feel more uncomfortable than you and may start filling the silence with what you want.

Leave embarrassing questions that must be asked till later. Don't start with 'Funds gone missing! All the red-tops after you! I thought you wouldn't want to talk to me right now!'

Look for signs of something to hide

You ask for an opinion about athletes taking illegal drugs to enhance their performance. Your athlete says he has never done so, and explains why he was once suspected of doing so. Guilty conscience? Or if you have strong evidence that a parent has punched a teacher, ask him why he did it and you might get an admittance rather than ask did he do it and get a denial.

When to get legal advice

If an interviewee asks you to keep a statement 'off the record', ask if you can use it without attribution. Explain why you feel it's vital to your feature and would not be a problem. If you think publication is in the public interest, you may want to include the statement; if you think there's a legal danger, alert the publication's legal expert.

A case of bureaucratic stalling

You have embarked on a special feature on race relations for your local weekly, induced by a report published two months ago by the local branch of the National Union of Teachers. This indicated that black teenagers were victims of discrimination and failing to get jobs. The local careers service promised figures to give a clear picture and have failed to produce, despite several letters and phone calls. The NUT and the Council for Community Relations have also failed to get figures.

You try the Principal Careers Officer again. She says the Chief Education Officer 'is not available for comment, but is working on it'. Later the careers service inform you that separate statistics are not kept but that 'a special report on black teenagers is being written, although there is no deadline for it'.

The Chief Education Officer next tells you that the department has not had time to extract the figures. But the Council for Community Relations was told a different story, you discover. It was told that the officer had not approved the use of resources to collect the figures. The pressure groups' scope for action is limited until they get the figures. Your deadline is approaching and it looks as if you won't get the figures for the current feature. What you say in your article, though, may make them arrive more quickly. You will no doubt fight on, with others, against the bureaucratic ramparts, making your notes. There will be revelations in due course but for another special feature.

Elicit good quotes

Good quotes from the subject mean those that:

1 are needed to give authority
2 are interesting and illuminating for the reader
3 make interviewee's opinions stand out
4 are given a fair interpretation.

1 Quotes can indicate that the subject has the knowledge or experience to give a statement authority, to deserve readers' attention. Readers will trust that any facts quoted will be correct, for example. Well-known or easily checked facts, of course (the company's turnover last year was £12 million), don't need quotes.
2 Interesting quotes will come out of who the subjects are, what they do in life, their personalities. Charm, quaintness or oddity rapidly wear thin on the printed page unless there's also some insight into an interesting character. It's up to the writer to awaken readers' interest in the subject, to ask questions that stimulate interesting answers and to provide the context that will make the quotes not only interesting in themselves but relevant to the piece and illuminating.

You can build up interest in a subject before you start quoting. Looks after his widowed mother with Parkinson's disease? Keeps a dozen snakes as pets? Believes she has psychic powers? You can incorporate an interesting factor within a quote: 'I was summoned to the manager's office,' said Andre Baines, who had risen through the ranks meteorically in six months. 'He told me I was dismissed.'

A long stretch of quote can be boring unless the reader is hooked by the speaker. The writer can help by breaking it up with paraphrasing, summarizing, changing the pace by continuing with the main narrative, and so on. More in Chapter 16.

3 Quoting can make it clear that a speaker's words are what the speaker believes and that the view is not necessarily shared by the writer. For example: 'The manager had referred to Mr Baines's "personality defects" and "lack of commitment to the company".' Leaving out the quote marks

would imply that you agreed with the verdict, and you would get into trouble with Mr Baines, if not the law.

4 You must make sure that you represent a speaker faithfully. People say things in anger, or with humour or irony that they would express quite differently if they were writing for publication. People who are not used to being interviewed may have little idea of the impression their words will make when they appear in print. They may need to be warned, 'Do you really want me to print that?' On the other hand, when speakers inadvertently reveal the truth, which doesn't show them in a good light, and it's the truth you're after, and you're asked 'You're not going to print that, are you?' there has to be a compelling reason not to say yes.

Things are said during an interview that need to be put into the whole context of the interview if they are to be interpreted correctly. Since only you, the interviewer, knows all your subject has said, you must ask yourself whether what you have selected gives a fair impression. If Mr Baines makes one derogatory reference to the manager's character ('he was vindictive'), referring to a particular event, and three other references that are complimentary, you will be doing them both an injustice if all you select is the derogatory one without even giving its context.

The writer may need to turn interpreter when the speaker misuses the language. A malapropism may be used: 'psychotherapy' instead of 'physiotherapy', for example. Or a word used may be ambiguous in the context, such as 'trendy'. Is it being used in a complimentary or in a derogatory sense? Such matters need to be cleared up in the course of the conversation. You don't, however, correct the kind of grammatical errors or odd turns of phrase that reveal a distinctive way of speaking unless they would cause misunderstanding.

Choose the best method

Telephone, email, letter, questionnaire, face to face? You're more likely to be using the results of a questionnaire (survey, poll) than organizing one yourself, so this is dealt with in the facts checking section. To repeat: if you interview fairly lengthily by phone or face to face, use both tape recorder and notes. Ask for names, technical terms, and so on, to be spelled out.

There are techniques common to all methods. Your loyalty is to the truth as far as you can ascertain it, not to anybody else's agenda. You must be friendly but firm, professional and persuasive.

You might need more than one method of interviewing for facts. Before making your choice (or after having the choice made for you) consider the advantages and disadvantages of the chosen medium. However reluctant your interviewee, anticipate that you may want to make contact again at writing-up stage. You may want to clarify a point or two, and even ask one or two more of those vital, specific questions, so ask for the privilege. With good judgement you should have achieved enough rapport for that to be granted. You may need home phone and mobile numbers at that time: you may have a looming deadline.

When it's not face to face, remember that the people you're addressing cannot see the encouragement on your face. For email and the post put that encouragement (inspiration?, empathy?, friendliness?) into your words. On the telephone put it into your voice as well.

By telephone

This is best for brief interviews for facts and you can establish rapport with your voice. If you play it skilfully you will get unguarded moments. After a phoned interview, people worry that you're going to misquote or misrepresent them. You should be able to reassure them either that you've taped it, and/or that you will read over before publication what you're intending to quote.

By email

This is an advantage when you want your interviewee to be completely at ease, having time to prepare considered answers, and when that is exactly what you want. You will lack colour and intimacy that come with tone of voice. You can't pursue the strategy of building on early answers to inform difficult questions left to the end. You display all your armoury at once. You may be able to follow up with further emails, but that's not quite the same thing.

By post

This is often requested by academics and occasionally by writers when the interview is going to probe areas that need careful responses. If you have plenty of questions that go beyond mere facts, this method may be best. But it is normally reserved for a full-scale interview feature.

Face to face

The advantages have already been suggested: you get body language, tone of voice, surroundings. You can manipulate the proceedings, adapt your questions and their order and phraseology to the personality, create the scenario as you go, adapting to each answer. When you come to the end, and there's still an important question you've failed to get answered, you can switch off the tape recorder or put away your notebook and even be accompanied to the lift, both of you quite relaxed, and you can rephrase that question and get a relaxed answer. Make a note of it later.

Let's leave the rest of the psychology until Chapter 16.

Acknowledge your sources

As described, your notes should alert you to the sources you need to acknowledge. We're now taking acknowledgement a stage further, to where you need to obtain the source's permission to use quoted extracts, as well as to acknowledge.

Appendix 4 gives the Society of Authors' Quick Guide to Copyright. Copyright under the current law expires 70 years after the author's death. Before then, as a general rule you can quote an extract up to a short paragraph without permission as long as you acknowledge it.

But the current tendency is to charge for reproducing short extracts and publications vary in their demands.

Establish bonds with contacts

Two professionals have met with different agendas. You have to negotiate, mark out the boundaries, make compromises perhaps. You have to establish a rapport, with the future in mind, without making too many promises. You may be asked to explain, for example, how the subject covered will be treated, exactly how what was said will be used in the forthcoming feature. Even if you have some idea, it will be wise not to comment, and to say that the editor must be contacted on that question.

You may be asked to show your interviewee the script of your feature, however brief their contribution. Avoid this. Seeing their words in typescript makes some people regret the frankness and want to substitute platitudes. If the material is highly technical, however, or liable to be misunderstood, you may want to agree to sending a script for verification on condition that changes are made only for reasons of accuracy or to aid understanding. Sometimes reading a script over the phone, resulting in a few minor changes of emphasis, may satisfy both parties.

It's a matter of trust. If you come across as vague or disorganized, you may find it hard to persuade anyone that sending a script for checking is not usual. If your interviewee comes across as hostile or suspicious, you will be reluctant to continue the association in any way.

A most regrettable situation, which should arise only rarely. You have worked at establishing a rapport because you may have to make contact again. Something may not be clear, or you may have left out an important question, or your editor comes up with one you hadn't thought of. The name is in your contacts book and you may find it a useful contact for future articles.

VERIFICATION SKILLS

Find reliable sources, we have said, to avoid needing too much cross-checking. Let's consider the verifying first of facts, then of figures.

Verifying the facts

Five facts you've discovered suggest that Mr A is alone responsible for some corrupt procedure. If you had more time you might discover five more facts from other sources that show the blame should be shared between Mr A and Mr B. With even more time you might discover that Mr C should share the blame too. But your deadline is tomorrow so you talk to your editor. If Mr B and Mr C live in Paris, will the editor pay for travel/hotel/meals and for your time if you're staff? Will phone calls suffice? If it's decided that the story isn't worth the expenses and risks being libellous if based on current information you might be paid a kill fee.

How many facts make the truth?

A news story can run and run in the papers. New evidence arrives daily. The news writer cannot preface too many statements with 'as far as we know'. If you're writing a feature based on a running news story you can describe evidence as 'circumstantial' to indicate that there are a number of facts that appear to arrive at a certain conclusion although one of the facts by itself would not be proof. If the conclusion seems less certain you can use the term 'anecdotal'.

It's natural to make extensive use of media sources. Keep in mind that they in turn often depend heavily on previous reports and articles. Anyone who has spent an hour or two in a newspaper cuttings library will testify to the danger therein. Going back over the life of Elvis Presley, say, or the United Nations' use of force, you are struck by the way an error can be made in an issue of one newspaper and be repeated by that paper and other papers and magazines for months or years. The original may have been a printer's error.

Some of the misuse or misinterpretation of facts perpetrated by the media is careless reporting. For example, the terms used to refer to refugees are confused. There's a tendency at the time of writing for much of the media, and much of the population, to lump together refugees, economic migrants and asylum seekers with illegal immigrants. Refugees have a genuine fear of persecution in the countries they came from. Economic migrants have been encouraged to come here to fill skill shortages. Asylum seekers are awaiting a Home Office decision to qualify as a refugee. Illegal immigrants are not asylum seekers: they are here without official authorization.

Verifying the figures

Paul Donovan in the *Press Gazette* of 26 July 2002 ('Siege mentality') gave some figures collected by MORI Social Research Institute in a poll for Amnesty International, the United Nations High Commission for Refugees (UNHCR) and other agencies. How many of the world's refugees and asylum seekers ended up in the UK? Most people thought between 10 and 19 per cent. The second most popular guess was between 20 and 29 per cent. The actual figure was 1.98 per cent.

The backing of those agencies makes us feel that we can trust those figures. There are, however, many weaknesses in the way questionnaires are set up and used that can make the results of the polls of little use. How big was the sample, how representative, how many failed to answer, what was the effect of these considerations on the results? – these well-known checks are still often ignored. If you're so bold as to want to use a questionnaire in your research, check the Bibliography for a guide to how to use them.

Don't miss Darrell Huff's classic *How To Lie With Statistics*, which reveals the flaws to look for in figure crunching. That 'average' we hear so much about: is it a mean average, a median or a mode? Quite different matters, and sometimes the distinction is crucial. Be wary, similarly, of IQs, the charts and graphs sometimes used by companies to give misleadingly favourable pictures of their progress, and percentages. Percentages of what, exactly?

ASSIGNMENTS

1 Write a 900-word feature based on the notes for 'Will a dry zone work in Rowdyborough?' for *The Jaytonshire Gazette*.

2 Wind Farms – The Energy of the Future?
  Wind Farms – Who Wants Them?
  Wind Farms – A Foolhardy Policy?

  Research and write a 1200-word feature on wind farms targeted on a national paper or consumer magazine. One of the above titles may reflect your point of view, but you may prefer to choose your own title. The current situation at your time of writing will determine your approach and your facts and figures. At the time of writing Britain is running out of gas, which accounts for 40 per cent of the electricity produced. There are predictions of increasing power cuts ahead. The Government has proposed building giant wind farms in three places off the coast of Britain. The electricity industry considers they will not solve the problem.

  Possible sources
  Scottish Power
  Manweb
  National Windpower Ltd
  Wind Development UK
  Centre for Alternative Technology
  Friends of the Earth

  Suggested group work
  After some preliminary study of the topic, divide the group into For and Against teams. Each team could divide up research and

---

drafting work, with a spokesperson to present the team's case in debate. The debate can then be open to the floor. Finally each member of the group can write the feature, without any obligation to keep to the viewpoint of their team.

3 Write a feature of 1200 words entitled either 'We Need Identity Cards' or 'We Don't Need Identity Cards' for a selected target. Make sure you give a clear description of the bases for such discussion.

Research will include, for example, explaining the Data Protection Act. In particular, what information that is held by organizations about yourself have you the right to discover? What information does the Act forbid you to discover?

Authors recommended: David Randall (*The Universal Journalist*, Chapter 10); books by David Northmore and John Pilger on investigative reporting.

9 Researching and writing online

> We've all heard that a million monkeys banging on a million typewriters will eventually reproduce the entire works of Shakespeare. Now, thanks to the Internet, we know this is not true. (Robert Wilensky Conference Speech, 1996)

The Internet offers the writer a wealth of information, some valuable research tools, an opportunity to promote your work and a potential market for your writing. The sheer scope can seem overwhelming. No one knows how many web pages are out there since more than 7.3 million pages appear every day. In January 2004, Google had an index of more than 4 billion pages; by November 2004, this had doubled to over 9 billion. The effortless experience the Internet offers can be seductive. At the click of a mouse you can consult library catalogues, order the latest bestseller, read newspapers, books and government documents, watch movie trailers, listen to radio stations from far-flung countries. Most importantly, you can communicate with people all over the world. You can even file your copy from almost anywhere in the world.

But although it can inform and entertain, educate and amaze, the Internet is also a minefield of poorly researched writing, half-truths and invective masquerading as journalism. With such a wealth and diversity of material, what tools should you use, how do you go about searching, and how do you know that you can trust the information you find?

INTERNET BASICS

The Internet is a publicly accessible worldwide network of interconnected computers. Users communicate, search and browse using email, online chat, instant messaging, newsgroups and the World Wide Web. Sixty per cent of Britons are already connected to the Internet. If you're not among them, don't panic: if you have a computer and a phone line, all you need is an Internet Service Provider (ISP).

Connecting

Internet guidebooks, computer magazines and newspaper surveys will offer advice on the best Internet Service Providers, most of whom offer both dial-up access and broadband.

Dial-up access, though cheaper than broadband, has significant disadvantages. It ties up your phone line each time you need to log on and, more importantly, it is slow, so webpages may take a long time to load, and downloading a large file may take hours. The alternative, broadband, is faster and more reliable. There is no need to dial up – you are permanently connected to the Internet and a typical broadband connection is 10 times faster than dial-up access, drastically reducing the time it takes to send and receive files. It is essential if you want to take advantage of the audio and video content offered by many sites. Cable broadband, offered by cable TV companies, connects using a set-top box. DSL (Digital Subscriber Line), like dial-up, uses a phone line to connect, but 'splits' the line so that you can use the Internet and still make and receive telephone calls.

When deciding on an ISP, read the fine print: compare not only the monthly charge for the service but the speed of connection. Broadband services may have a monthly 'cap' on how much data you can send and receive, and charge an additional fee if you exceed this limit, but these terms are generous enough for most users.

Wireless access

If you travel frequently and use a laptop you might consider investing in a 'wireless card' (many new laptops come with this as standard), making it possible for your laptop to connect to the wireless 'Wi-Fi hotspots' increasingly available in airports, cafés and hotels worldwide without worrying about cables and wires. Wi-Fi hotspots are sometimes offered free of charge, but many charge an hourly or daily rate. Your wireless card can also be used at home, in conjunction with a wireless router, allowing you to work from any room in the house – or even the garden.

Useful software

Your service provider will supply you with the basic software necessary to access your email, browse the Web, use 'instant messaging' and read newsgroups.

Email

There are dozens of software programs which allow you to send and receive, store and organize email – the most popular of which are Microsoft Outlook, Eudora and Netscape Messenger (Windows) and Apple Mail (Mac). Remember many mobile phones and most palmtops (PDAs) can be configured to send and receive email. When you travel abroad, you can send and receive email using your ISP's webmail facility, or use a service such as www.mail2web.com.

Web browsers

The billions of pages of treasures and clutter that make up the World Wide Web are accessed using a web browser. The most popular (though its share has recently declined slightly) is Microsoft's Internet Explorer; others include Netscape's Mozilla Firefox, Opera (Windows) and Safari (Mac). All of these browsers perform much the same functions.

Instant messaging

Instant messaging allows you to communicate in real time with one (or more) people – something closer to conversation than to email. It can be a useful way of conducting online interviews, as the software can 'record' the whole conversation and save it as a text file. Popular instant messenger software includes Jabber, AOL Instant Messenger, Yahoo! Messenger and .NET Messenger.

Newsgroups

Newsgroups are collections of messages posted by users interested in a specific subject. There are specialized newsgroups on almost every topic imaginable, though it may take time and experimentation to familiarize yourself with the arcane newsgroup hierarchies. The email clients Outlook and Eudora will allow you to search and browse newsgroups, but it is worth investigating more specialized News Reading software which will allow preview of image files before downloading, decipher the obscure encryption often used by newsgroup posters and handle multi-part files (news groups cannot handle large files – sound files, movies, software, etc. – so posters 'split' large files into multi-art files which later need to be 'concatenated'). Popular News Reading software includes News Rover, NewsBin Pro, News Pro (Windows) and Unison (Mac).

RSS

One of the most exciting recent developments on the Internet, RSS (Really Simple Syndication), syndicates content from websites to a desktop 'RSS reader'. The RSS is used on news sites like the BBC, The New York Times and News.com, but is also used on personal pages and weblogs. The RSS reader allows you to add your favourite sites and choose how often you want to check for updates. This means you don't have to visit your favourite websites to check for updates, the content is streamed directly to your desktop. Popular Windows readers include NewsGator and Sharpreader; Mac users can use NewsFire.

RESEARCHING ONLINE

It will take time to master the various tools you can use on the Internet. While you do, you can dip in, have fun and brainstorm. Billions of pages cover topics from aardvarks to zymurgy, making it seem like the ideal research tool for the writer or journalist. Surfing can offer fresh non-linear and surprising associations of ideas, and you may be blessed with exciting serendipity. But although finite, the Internet is vast – how much time have you got?

When you begin to research a feature or article, it may be best to start with printed sources. In the words of Jane Dorner (*The Internet: A Writer's Guide*), the Internet 'does not replace the post, the telephone, going into libraries, browsing in bookshops, attending literary events or talking to people face to face. It is as well as.' Using tried and trusted sources will guide you to people, periodicals or other books and sources quickly. They may often refer you to websites that will be relevant and reliable.

Reliability is a crucial consideration when dealing with the Internet. The democratic nature of the technology means that anyone can publish anything they like, without worrying about trivialities like accuracy, impartiality and truth. This can make it difficult to sort the wheat from the chaff. Furthermore, on the Internet, not everyone is who they say they are. The anonymity of the medium means that, in the words of the legendary *New Yorker* cartoon, 'On the Internet, no one knows you're a dog.' As from any source, information discovered on the Web should be checked and cross-checked. This important caveat shouldn't stop you from using the Internet as a research tool: it offers a wealth of reliable information and, more importantly, offers the writer a way of contacting people who are the lifeblood of any feature.

Search engines

Unlike a library or a bookshop, the Internet is not helpfully indexed. The most basic tool for a writer, therefore, is the search engine, a program to find web pages which meet your specific criteria. The most popular search engines currently are Google, MSN Search and Yahoo!

To search for information, simply enter a word or words related to the topic and the search engine will return a page of 'results': pages which contain the words you specified. The more specific your search criteria, the more precise the results. Let's say you are doing a feature on the anniversary of the Kennedy assassination and want to see Abraham Zapruder's famous footage. Searching using the words KENNEDY ASSASSINATION produces an unmanageable 700,000 results; however, searching for KENNEDY ASSASSINATION 'ZAPRUDER FILM' DOWNLOAD gives only 1400: the first of which takes you directly to the footage you want to see. By default, most search engines give results that contain *all* your search terms, so if you get few or no results, try a more general search with fewer criteria. You can search for an 'exact phrase' by putting the words in quotation marks. Metasearch engines send queries to several different search engines, allowing users to enter their search criteria only once to get results from several search engines simultaneously. Popular metasearch engines include Clusty, Dogpile, Ez2Find and Metacrawler.

If you are researching a highly specialized topic and want to avoid the clutter of personal pages and commercial websites, you could use one of the many specialized search engines on the Web which allow you to search books in print, periodicals and movies. Many libraries (including the British Library and the American Library of Congress) have searchable online catalogues. Copac provides free access to the merged online catalogues of 24 major university research libraries in the UK and Ireland, including the British Library.

Web directories

Unlike search engines, web or subject directories organize Internet sites by subject. They do so by employing editors to categorize and index the wealth of information on offer, making it easier to find relevant subject matter. The expense of this approach has meant that in recent years web directories have all but disappeared; however, LookSmart, About.com and dmoz (the Open Directory Project) remain useful tools.

Like any form of research, with time and experimentation you will become more adept at searching, and as you find interesting or reliable sites you can 'bookmark' them in your browser so that you can return to them easily.

Evaluating online sources

Since, as we've noted, almost anyone with access to a computer can create a website, it is important to decide how authoritative and reliable an online source is. This is not an easy task and even reputable agencies like the BBC have been caught out. So, when you find that piece of earth-shattering, unbelievable, exciting information on a website, you first need to decide:

- Is it dated, current, timely?
- Is information cited authentic?
- Does the author have a bias? Is he or she affiliated with a particular organization or institution?
- Could the page be ironic – a satire or a spoof?

Even if you are satisfied that the information seems authentic, up-to-date and unbiased, how can you be sure the author is who they say they are.

Some clues can be found in the following:

- Look at the URL (the 'web address').
- Is this a 'personal web page'? If the page is being hosted on free web-space provided by an ISP, this should be obvious from the web address, which will contain the user's name and often a tilde (~) or per cent sign (%) (aol.com/members/%joebloggs, geocities.com/users/~joebloggs). This does not mean the information is necessarily unreliable, but undermines its authority.
- Does the web page claim to be an authorized source? Educational, non-profit, government or other agencies use specific domain suffixes for their sites. Is your web page genuinely the site of a governmental (.gov/.gov.uk), educational (.edu), universities (.ac.uk) or non-profit organization (.org/.org.uk)?

Ask yourself: who is the author? Does the page give contact details where you can verify the writer's bona fides? Have you heard of this person or organization before? If so, search engines might help to check what has been written by or about them. Is the author qualified to comment on the subject? What background information (education, profession, credentials) is offered? If there is none, you might want to ask why.

Lastly, read the piece carefully: is there sufficient evidence to support the facts it presents? How does the information compare with other sources you have consulted? Does the author seem to have an axe to grind? If you have doubts about any of these issues, take care to check the source: you can do this by contacting the writer, verifying information using trusted sources or searching using the name of the author or organization to see.

Trusted sources and premium content

As a feature writer you may be particularly interested in online versions of newspapers and magazines or reference works available on the Internet.

UK and foreign newspapers and magazines offer online versions of print publications, from *The Times* and *The Spectator* to *Time Magazine* and *Newsweek*. Search for the contents of those that cover your subject areas. Both newspaper and magazine features accessed online often give valuable links to related features in the archives. While most, however, allow you to browse recent content free of charge, they charge for access to archived material. Some, like the *New York Times*, allow you to buy individual articles, others insist on a monthly or annual subscription.

The news agencies which supply news reports to newspapers, magazines, and radio and television broadcasters (Associated Press, Bloomberg, Reuters, The Press Association) all have comprehensive, searchable websites. Like newspapers and periodicals, however, some charge a fee for reading or downloading archived articles.

A vast array of standard reference works are available online, from the *Encyclopaedia Britannica* and the *Oxford English Dictionary* to dictionaries of quotations, world history or classical music. Though they may offer a time-limited 'free trial', to continue using them you have to pay a subscription, so you will need to consider how useful such a resource will be to you.

A recent – free – addition to online reference works is *Wikipedia*, an encyclopedia that anyone can edit. While this has become a hugely popular resource, with scholarly information on a vast array of subjects, remember that 'anyone can edit' *Wikipedia* entries, so it would be wise to cross-check information found here against other sources.

Finding experts

If you need to find an expert on a specific subject you are researching, you might try www.ibiblio.org. If you're not sure where to turn for help, submit a query to www.profnet.com, a network of news and information officers commonly used by journalists searching for expert sources, and an expert in the field will contact you.

Virtual communities

If the Internet is a vast store of knowledge, it is also and just as importantly a community made up of people from every walk of life. For the most part, they are a talkative bunch, from idle gossipers to eloquent experts who communicate not only by email and instant messenger, but through newsgroups, web forums, mailing lists and chatrooms. Online communities give you access to a breadth of human experience, and may provide you with ideas, sources for stories, contacts and support.

Use your newsgroup software or search Google Groups for newsgroups on subjects that interest you, or join the message boards on websites you have found to trade information, ask advice (or offer it). Many sites have mailing lists to which you can subscribe and will send you email digests of new and current topics on the site. Chatrooms allow you to talk to people currently logged into a website: thousands of these are aimed mainly at gossiping and flirting, but there are thousands more on specialized topics from Agoraphobia to Yu-Gi-Oh. Chatmag.com provides a useful list. Finally, websites focused on a specific subject or theme may be part of a webring, a group of voluntarily interlinked websites registered with the webring.org.

In time, you will come to find your way through the sometimes labyrinthine world of the Internet. If you feel in need of support or advice, you can find a community of journalists at www.holdthefrontpage.co.uk.

A WRITER'S EXPERIENCE

John Morrish has a broad experience of online and offline journalism. Former editor of *Time Out* and commissioning editor for Telegraph Magazines, he has worked on *Private Eye* and is a prolific freelance writer. His *Magazine Editing* is not surprisingly as useful to writers needing to understand editors as it is to editors needing to understand writers. His website www.journolist.co.uk offers guidance and new resources for journalists using the Internet. I had two questions for him.

Which have been the most important benefits of the Internet for you?

It gives me access to background material and current information from all over the world. The trick is doing intelligent searches in the first place and then learning to sift what you find so you don't get swamped. It is important not to let your background reading overwhelm your own sense of the story: you can look over it but you don't have to use it. Mainly, though, I try to use the Internet to find the right people to speak to. I find people who have had interesting things to say in the web pages I have found, or I look around newsgroups and forums.

It is important to recognize, however, that the Internet can't do everything. In many ways it has simply transferred the burden and costs of research from the publication to the individual freelance. It still helps if the magazine or newspaper you are writing for is willing to help with your research.

The Internet can't give you the full text of all newspapers and it can't help with forthcoming events: for both of those you need to subscribe to specialist services that are beyond your reach as a freelance writer.

Three questions in one. Have you interviewed by email to produce a feature? What do you reckon to be the main advantages and disadvantages? For what sort of interview is it best and for what sort is it often inadequate?

> I have, but I try not to. On the whole, I like lively quotes that sound like they came from a conversation, and I like to be able to challenge what people are saying to me. But email quotes can be good if you are dealing with people in awkward time zones: you can put in your query overnight and the quotes are there in the morning. I find they can work well with academic subjects where you need not only the general gist of something but a precise, complex form of words.

> People who are habitual email users (and fluent typists) can write in a very conversationalist way, and then the results are almost indistinguishable from spoken quotes. Instant messaging is even better for this: you can get your instant messenger to record the whole typed "conversation" as you go, and then you have it as a text file to incorporate in your story.

> Good writers can also produce pithy, pointed email quotes, although they are artificial, rather than conversational. Not bad, though, if you want a string of polished *bons mots* in your pieces.

> Email quotes from company spokesmen, PR people, politicians and the business world are useless. They will have been pored over by many hands (?) to ensure they are absolutely "on message" and will consequently be almost without interest.

CREATING YOUR OWN WEBSITE

Whether you are just starting out, or have a portfolio of articles, you may find it useful to create your own website to showcase your work and hopefully to encourage new commissions.

Before you begin, you need to decide on the purpose of your website. Is it a showcase of your work, a bid to obtain commissions, do you want to offer editing, proofreading or tutoring services? How do you persuade people you have something to offer? Study the websites of other journalists and make notes. The Bibliography contains titles of Internet guides for writers.

You will want your first website to be as simple and inexpensive as possible. The cheapest way to create a website is to use web space provided by your ISP, e.g. AOL (http://hometown.aol.co.uk/bjphennessy), but all ISPs provide between 5 and 25 Mb of free space and most offer tools and support to help you build your website. The software offered is usually very basic and you may have to follow a fairly rigid template, but it will probably serve your purpose. You might choose to have several pages outlining your experience, including samples of your feature writing. On a simple, single-page website, the author of this book was able to give a summarized c.v., with details of the features and books published and the tutoring services offered. Email and postal addresses, telephone numbers and links to publishers were included.

The disadvantage of using free webspace is that your URL (web address) will be something unwieldy and unmemorable, like http://www.service-provider.com/members/yourname/index.htm; service providers also reserve the right to put their logo and advertising on each of the pages you build. To avoid this, you can register a unique domain (www.yourname.co.uk). There are dozens of companies which will allow you to register a domain (search for 'domain names UK', or check the list available at http://www.internic.net/origin.html), and most also offer to host your website. You will need to pay for hosting as unique domains cannot be hosted on an ISP's free webspace. Registering a domain name is relatively cheap: about £15 per year for a '.co.uk' domain. If you register with a US company, you can often get a '.com' domain for as little as $4.95 per year. Hosting the domain will incur additional charges depending on how much space you need.

If you want to buy your own domain but don't fancy learning to code HTML you'll need a website design editor. There are many commercially available software packages, though you'll probably find that freeware or a shareware package like Arachnophilia are sufficient for your purpose. Though it is a cumbersome process, you can even build and save web pages using Microsoft Word. Whichever tool you choose will take you a little time to master, but you can easily find a helpful online tutorial.

Remember to keep your site simple and coherent. No website at all is better than a poorly designed one, or one that is out of date, or boring. It is best to avoid gimmicks, animations, and things that flash and ping. A few simple, minimally designed pages detailing your c.v., your professional experience and including some samples of your writing is enough. Don't forget to include your qualifications, membership of any associations and – most importantly – your contact details.

Blogging

If you have the time and commitment to write for your site regularly, create on online diary or weblog – often called a 'blog'. Blogging is personal; like a commentator with a byline, you have the opportunity to stamp your individual voice on events and issues that you are passionate about. The most important thing is that you write and keep writing: a blog that is not updated is wasted space. Check out Blog.com for advice and useful tools. A blog can be something you create for an existing blogging community such as Blurty or Live Journal, or you can put your blog on your own website and promote it through Blogger and Blogwise.

The incredible success of blogging demonstrates an audience's hunger for human stories, but it also means that blogging is no longer simply used by individual writers; political campaigns and corporate PR use blogging to spread their message. Most bloggers give readers the opportunity to leave their comments, and there have been hugely successful blogs which have catapulted their authors to national attention, but don't be impressed by stories of bloggers being snapped up by mainstream publishers. Just because the Baghdad Blogger and the 'Washington sex blogger' were offered lucrative book deals doesn't mean it's a shortcut to fame. Treat your blog simply as an opportunity to write regularly, of giving yourself a byline and making your voice heard.

Promoting your website

However beautifully designed and perfectly pitched your website, if anyone other than your Mum is to find it, it must be optimized and indexed by search engines. Before you submit a site to be indexed, it should be optimized. Search Engine Optimization (SEO) involves using keywords and phrases, both in the body copy of your pages and in invisible headers (called metatags), and ensuring that simple things like page titles and external links to your site properly reflect the site.

The software you use to build your web pages will allow you to insert keywords and a description of your site in the metatags. Include 10 to 30 keywords directly related to your work (e.g. journalism, journalist, sports journalist, technical writer, copywriter, subeditor), each separated by a comma. Some search engines – notably Google – ignore keywords, but still include page titles and the description metatags when indexing your site. Make sure all your page titles include one of these keywords or phrases. The description is a short paragraph (200 words) that will appear on the search result. Make it simple and clear, and avoid using 'sales pitch' jargon.

When writing the body copy of your site detailing your work and your experience, remember to use these keywords and phrases. If you are not sure which words to use, there are a number of Keyword Suggestion Tools on the Web.

Even optimizing your site, however, is not quite enough. Nowadays search engines rank a page depending on the links into and out of your site. In theory, the more pages which link to you, the higher your ranking. However, simply exchanging links with lots of friends may not help your ranking, since most search engines analyse the importance of the sites providing the links to your site. Focus on linking with sites with good rankings. Have your site included in the sites of professional associations or agencies of which you are a member and ask colleagues to include a link to your site. Remember that search engine spiders read the text of the link and this may help your rankings for those keywords. So a simple link like www.myweb-site.com, even if followed by a description, is less effective than if the words 'Experienced Technical Writer' contain a link to your site. Search engines assume that if people are linking to you with those words, they must be relevant to your site.

Once your site is optimized, it should be submitted to a number of search engines for indexing. There are a number of websites and software programmes (Virtual Stampede, or Microsoft's Submit-it!) which provide help in doing this for a fee. You can submit your site personally (look for Submit URL or Submit your Site) but search engines do not make it easy. At Google, for example, you must first click About Google to find a link where you can submit your site. It is a time-consuming task, but well worth doing. Submit your site to three or four major search engines, and to any specialized search engines you feel appropriate. Remember to submit each page of your site. Then wait: all this takes time, often about four to six weeks to be indexed.

WRITING ONLINE

Feature writers in the press often have a reputation, a byline that brings them respectful attention. They have earned their column inches. They have often discovered important facts that they are pleased to dispense to a selected audience. Their analyses or arguments are often highly valued, even when disagreed with. Online writers have to recognize they're in a different world.

Print journalists can be reluctant to adapt to writing for the Internet, feeling that it lacks the kudos of serious journalism, or that online journals sap some of the writer's authority. But online editors have begun to recognize that better words bring more hits. They are often aiming to serve several purposes simultaneously: inform, educate, entertain, interest (well, we know about that), but also promote and sell. It's another challenge for the feature writer.

Understanding the market

Though the Internet is full of shovelware – useless information, usually from print sources, that has been cut and pasted onto web pages – there are many opportunities for the writer: specialized journals of every stripe need features, and copywriters are needed to fill the websites of government departments, educational institutions, tourist boards and business organizations. These opportunities are global and there are bulletin boards and websites which specialize in listing jobs for freelance writers, including Elance, Journalismjobs.com, Writers Weekly, Dice (for technical writers) and MediaBistro. The jobs offered at these sites may be for online or print work.

Targeting specific ezines or websites is much like pitching to print magazines: decide what interests you. There is little point offering to write for Bloomberg if you have no interest in the money markets, or for CNET if computing bores you. The sites you will want to write for are those you would want to read. Don't limit yourself to online publications in your area or even your country: a Hong Kong website may be thrilled to have a UK 'correspondent'; a Los Angeles-based movie site may be interested in articles with a British or European slant.

Once you have found websites where you feel you can make a contribution, you can pitch the editors with specific ideas. Make sure you know the site intimately before you do this: their approach to writing, the subjects they cover and the style guide or guidelines they impose on writers. You may have participated in surveys or questionnaires on the site, posted messages on their boards, spent time and thought considering what the site currently offers and what *you* can bring to it.

Check the About Us (or Contact Us) section of the website to get the name and contact details of the site, or section editor. A concise, thoughtfully worded email should indicate your previous experience and include ideas you have for features you might write. Remember to include a link to your website, where the editor can read your blog (if you are writing one) and get an idea of your writing style from previous work. If you don't have a website, include good and relevant writing samples, or at least the offer to send them on if requested. The writing samples must match the genre: your pitching is likely to be more successful when your samples match the writing in the ezine or website you are targeting. Just as in print publishing, this is a hit-and-miss approach; you do not always receive an acknowledgement of your request. Don't be deterred. If the thought of pitching to websites is daunting, looking at some poor specimens will encourage you. Concentrate on targeted websites as a user, make notes, then rewrite/rearrange material and provide a new sample. If the site is hosted locally, try to arrange a meeting with the site or section editor. While waiting for your big break, you can hone your skills on ezines.

Ezines are the online equivalent of fanzines, and many are produced by a minimal staff and pay little or nothing, but offer an audience and valuable experience in writing for the Web. Even if the ezines you first write for are not very well known, by constantly writing you can develop your voice and with it an audience, which will help you to move forward.

There are several successful and prestigious ezines out there. Many are general interest magazines: look at Slate (owned by Microsoft), which boasts well-known authors/journalists among its contributors; Jackhammer; Salon; or the wonderfully spiteful satire of Capital of Nasty, but there are many more which specialize in everything from classical music to politics. As you would with print magazines, study them rigorously before deciding who to pitch to.

When dealing with ezines, remember the market is volatile and ezines often run on enthusiasm and passion alone. This may not be the most lucrative work, but it is important always to remain professional.

Writing techniques

The values of online journalism are the same as the values of print journalism. As in any medium, your success will depend on the accuracy and authority of your news stories or the style, wit and voice of your features. In the words of Laurie Peterson, supervising producer for iVillage, 'online journalists must have all the skills of those in other media: good interviewing skills, solid research capabilities, tenacity, speed, accuracy, flexibility, a good B.S. detector and crisp and vivid writing.'

The main difference between offline and online writing techniques is that while people buy newspapers and magazines intending to read them, on the Internet people generally browse. You must grab their attention and hold it if they are to read on. This means that, on the whole, online writing is more concise and pithy and should offer the reader greater interactivity.

Before you write, always ask yourself what an online article can offer that print or broadcast media cannot. Time and space requirements mean that print and broadcast media cannot cover every angle of a story. Is there a local angle to a major story or one relevant to readers of your favourite website? Write it! Print and broadcast media are also limited in the context they can provide to news stories. It is difficult to get a full picture of complex events. Ask yourself how you can add to existing stories, provide much-needed context or shed light on a specific angle.

Much is made by online editors of the 'fact' that users won't scroll. As newspapers do, they refer to text 'below the fold', meaning the reader has to scroll the page in order to read on. It is a concern that is overdone. Blogs and online magazines have proved that if you write well, users will scroll and read on. But there is some truth to the cliché: you cannot simply shovel a 4000-word piece conceived for a newspaper onto a web page and hope the reader will be captivated. Reading from a computer screen is hard on the eyes. Readers scan pages quickly and if they don't find what they're looking for, they leave. Mike Ward, in his book *Journalism Online*, suggests you use no more than half of a text written for a print publication. So, rethink the article, breaking it up into manageable pieces and bulleted lists which the web designer can use to create multiple interlinked pages. Make individual sections capable of standing alone. Ask yourself whether graphics, surveys, user polls or multimedia content might make it a more compelling online experience.

Above all, if you are going to write for the Web, be passionate. Talent is not enough. You may start out writing for poorly paid ezines where only your enthusiasm for your subject and for writing itself make the long hours and pitiful wages bearable. A love of writing and a passion for your subject shines through and it is this, just as importantly as your command of English or your store of arcane information, which will help you succeed.

ASSIGNMENTS

1 Produce your own website if you haven't already done so.
2 Join a newsgroup that has a special interest (especially for you), and after a month of involvement write an 800 word feature for a computer magazine relating your experience, entitled 'Bombarded by points of view'.

---

10   Creating the best order

Prose = words in their best order. (Samuel Taylor Coleridge, *Table Talk*)

You've pitched an idea and had it accepted. It's a fairly complex project, 1000 words or above, and if you're new (and even if you're not) you may have had some advice on approach or some kind of briefing, and you have a fair idea of what you want to say. It will help if you have a provisional title that reflects your proposal and any briefing. You've collected a pile of notes and materials. It won't be easy to go straight to drafts without first:

- checking for the right ingredients
- putting your file in order
- discovering what to say
- matching order to content.

At some stage in all this you may want to get back to the editor and make sure any modification of the original idea is acceptable.

CHECKING FOR THE RIGHT INGREDIENTS

You will want to consider which of the following ingredients are needed and are available:

1 A premise or point of view.
2 A thesis or theme.
3 The descriptions, story, points, facts, explanations, arguments that are largely confined to the body, the core of the feature.
4 Supporting material: anecdotes, case studies, quotes, mainly for the body.
5 Illustrations: photographic/other, with captions.

The intro and conclusion will need much more attention than what was required for those simple features of Chapter 3. The intro for a complex feature needs to provide not only a hook but some briefing or orientation to make the reader's journey hassle-free, and the conclusion will need to bring all the preceding teamwork of (provisional) title, intro and body to a satisfying fulfilment. The intro may have as many as three parts to it, as in the example below.

The full armoury would then be:

- title
- standfirst or subtitle
- intro: hook (or teaser, or beginning)
- intro: bridge (or context), which gives any necessary background, or raises the questions to be answered, leading the reader in
- intro: text (or nub or pivot), which indicates what the feature is all about and gets readers into it
- body
- conclusion (or ending).

Let's get an idea of how those ingredients fit into the structure of a published feature. There's no rigid formula of course. No two features are exactly the same in structure, and in any three sections of intro, for example, there's some overlapping of the roles mentioned and their order can sometimes be changed for different effects. With that reservation in mind, here's an example of this sort of teamwork from an 1150-word feature by John Kampfner in *New Statesman* of 5 August 2002:

Title
   'No longer just the bank'

When you've got a fair amount of introductory matter the title can be as mysterious as you like.

Standfirst
   Europe may have been subsidizing the Palestinian Authority, but it has played an insignificant role in the Middle East. Now that will change.

It was useful to explain that mysterious title straight away, clearly and concisely. Now there's room for a bit more mystery.

Hook

> At least on one point the Israelis and Palestinians agree – we in Europe have lost our nerve. From the Palestinians' envoy to London: 'Europe is still an actor in search of a role and we in the Middle East, we have a role in search of an actor. Europe has become too resigned to its marginal role.' And this, from Israel's ambassador to the EU: 'It is our expectation to see our European democratic friends expressing solidarity and responsibility. It is not working and I am distressed by that.'

The same feeling about Europe on both sides but we're intrigued by the different ways that feeling is expressed. We want to know why Europe …

Bridge

> Why do the European Union and its member states appear so powerless to act? Is it because the other players won't let them? Is it because they can't agree a common foreign policy? Is it our dark history? Is it American muscle? Or is it a lack of will?

Interesting questions and we want to read on and get some answers.

Text

> The situation is demeaning. Our diplomats shuttle between Brussels and Washington, between Jerusalem and Ramallah, but their efforts are neither noticed nor acted upon. Miguel Moratinos has been the European Union's special representative in the region for the past six years, although you have probably never heard of him. I spoke to him for BBC Radio 4's *Analysis* programme late last month, in a break between his several meetings.

Body summary

It lists and contrasts the points of view that emerge in considering those questions. It incorporates quotes from the EU's special representative in the region, the head of the Middle East programme at the Royal Institute of International Affairs, Israel's ambassador in Brussels, the UK's Foreign Office minister with responsibility for the Middle East, the Palestinian envoy to London and the EU's high representative on foreign affairs. The quotes are interspersed with the effects of one or two events in the period, and some explanations and commentary. A crucial aspect is the way Europe has kept paying for Palestinian areas damaged by Israeli attacks but doesn't use its economic clout.

Conclusion

We end on a glimmer of hope and a question. Israel's ambassador in Brussels says Europe will have to become not just a payer but a player. But is it up to the task?

A good structure. But Kampfner was first faced with that pile of notes and had to sort his body out first. So let's return to bodies and get back to the shape of the whole in Chapter 11.

PUTTING YOUR FILE IN ORDER

Take more notes than you need but don't take too many is the best practice. You don't want to get bogged down. Here is a typical procedure when the research is done. Read through what you've got several times until you're familiar with it. Go for a walk and sleep on it and see if a clear theme falls into place, with beginning, middle and end coming into focus. Select what you want from your notes and source materials and put the rest aside, just in case there's a change of plan later.

Try dividing your notes into sections with headings: 1, 2, 3, 4, …. Your source materials can be labelled A, B, C, D, … and put to the side.

Research materials for a feature on what treatments are available for alcoholics might amount to research reports and other literature from:

A The NHS
B Alcoholics Anonymous
C Institute of Psychiatry
D Ruttgers University, New York
E Drink Watchers organization
F Edinburgh research unit
G National Institute of Alcohol Abuse and Alcoholism
H *Directory of Psychology* and *Psychiatry Encyclopaedia*.

The notes might come from books, journalism (consult the indexes), literature of the above organizations and from legwork/interviews involved in visits. The notes might provide the following headings, with the sources indicated:

1 Definitions of alcoholism (C, H)
2 The main causes (C, G, H)

3 Recent developments, e.g. among women (journalism, G)
4 Two kinds of cure: controlled drinking and abstinence (B, F)
5 Most successful treatments (D, F)
6 Least successful treatments (D, F)
7 Lack of funding for research/medical facilities/voluntary organizations (A, G)
8 What needs to be done (journalism, D, G).

One way of working with this outline is to allocate half a page to each heading and slot underneath it the most significant or most striking acts, quotes, anecdotes, whatever from the notes and literature. In the margins of the pages you can indicate any links that occur to you.

You may want then to write a first draft from memory, using the second draft to fill in the gaps and polish. A detailed outline of this kind can become the framework for a book.

Some commissioning editors, especially in the USA, like to see your pitch in the form of an outline with research sources indicated, as above, plus a proposed intro. A paragraph summarizing what will come after that might also be welcome. This is especially likely when your feature is to be long, fairly complex and based on a fair amount of research. See, for example, the booklet *Writing for Reader's Digest*, obtainable from the publishers.

DISCOVERING WHAT TO SAY

If you find the theme slow to emerge clearly, you may want to try brain-storming. Get some feedback on your thoughts by discussing them with friends and colleagues. Put the headings on cards and shuffle them as suggested on page 30, to see what new patterns emerge.

Try a mind map

You may want to try a mind map to get you thinking about your material. Have another look at the mind map on page 55. Suppose your idea is 'Do surgeons make too many mistakes? Suppose you have put that in the middle of your page. East and south of the surgery map is your area of interest. You may want to add to these aspects various specialisms – eye surgery, ear, nose and throat, heart, etc., writing them round the centred title.

You will spread out in bubbles such aspects as:

- accusations from patients – false and genuine
- whistleblowers – prejudiced and unprejudiced
- secrecies
- compensation policies
- causes – lack of funding, lack of training, shortage of nursing staff, overwork

and link them up where relevant to the specialisms. You will then spread out your thoughts, questions and points extracted from your research (facts, quotes, anecdotes, examples, etc.) under the relevant bubbles. You will do your lateral thinking, to see unexpected associations and resonances, comparisons and contrasts to get your imagination working towards a compelling theme, and with luck your intro and ending would suggest themselves as well.

MATCHING ORDER TO CONTENT

You may have sensational material but if you depend on its quality rather than how you put it across you can end up with a turkey. 'True ease in writing comes from art, not chance, as those move easiest who have learned to dance,' as Alexander Pope said.

Here we are concerned with the various skills that produce different kinds of order, rather than the whys and wherefores and the armoury mentioned above, which will reappear in the next chapter. How do you find the right order for an effective body of description, narration, exposition (analysis/explanation/demonstration), argument?

Each of these skills demands its own patterns, and a feature will normally require two or more different patterns. Narration usually needs some description and much narration (history, for example) is expository in purpose. Argument of any substance needs exposition to support it as well as straight facts as evidence. For the sake of clarity and convenience we'll deal with each order separately.

Readers' interest order

But first, because we're talking about journalism, any order must take account of where your readers' interest will lie, so let's start with that.

Readers' interest prevents any order becoming too predictable or too rigid. The order required for a how-to feature on cookery or gardening is likely to be firmly dictated by the subject but there are features whose structure is not going to be at all obvious.

Features that require different kinds of material may need all or most of the patterns mentioned above. Then the main criterion determining structure is often readers' interest. Profiles often depend on it.

A profile by Val Hennessy (no relation) in *The Mail on Sunday* told of a 4 ft 5 in., 76-year-old veteran pickpocket called Rose caught again (she'd spent 20 years in prison) at Harvey Nichols. She was given a conditional discharge. Rose mainly tells her own story, which is skilfully linked up with facts and commentary. Here are the bare bones after the intro gives those main facts:

- she lives in a slum: crime doesn't pay
- life in Holloway as it used to be
- anecdotes about Myra Hindley (Moors murderer) and Ruth Ellis (the last woman hanged in Britain) in Holloway
- childhood (during First World War) with prostitute stepmother who neglected her; at 11 sexually abused servant in large houses
- Borstal at 17 and learned skills of the trade
- marriage at 34; defrauded by husband who died while she was in prison
- daughter without reproaches

The feature ends with lunch at a restaurant and Rose saying she's turned over a new leaf ('my fingers are not so nimble').

Attempts to deal with a long life, however much interest there is in certain aspects and events, is difficult to do in a feature. Notice that we needed to know about the subject now before we were taken on the more or less chronological story. Notice how vivid incidents in the subject's life are slotted in to represent a period.

We don't know the questions; what we get in abundance is the answers in Rose's inimitable style. There's some linking and summarizing, but no moral judgements, no explanations. Readers can react in any way they like, but the hidden message, the humanitarian one, is hard to ignore. The questions are easily guessed at, and they are obviously the ones any reader would have asked.

When the first facts you get are that a 76-year-old has spent 20 years in prison you want to know about her prison experiences first before the childhood. Then you probably want to know what sort of childhood produced this sort of character. And then boyfriends, husband, children?

Exposition

Exposition is all about being clear, concise and in logical order. Showing something clearly is what all your ordering and outlining aims to achieve. In its simplest form, explaining how to do or achieve something (wiring your house or tiling your roof, for example), getting the order wrong could do your readers severe damage.

How-to

Straightforward how-to features are legion and in popular magazines and newspaper lifestyle sections, often produced in-house, you will find all kinds of subjects: how to cook, garden, complain, furnish, keep fit, keep healthy, beat back pain, do the plumbing. You have to study the prospects for any freelance contributions carefully to work out which have scope for freelance features and then what sort of treatments they want. How do they use photographic and other illustrations, boxes, charts, and so on?

Readers' interest/exposition

The decline in the world population of dolphins prompted a feature in Glasgow's *Sunday Post* that gave the straightforward facts about dolphins. They were organized under question headings. The questions were put to an expert on dolphins and the order had to be both logical and keep the reader interested:

- How common are dolphins around Britain?
- How intelligent are they?
- How did you become interested?
- How do they sleep?
- Are they naturally friendly?
- Do they adapt well to humans?
- Are they ever dangerous?
- What's the largest species of dolphin?
- Why are they easy to train?
- How do they communicate?

- How endangered are they?
- How are dolphins used in medicine?
- What might surprise us about them?

Description

When you describe in a feature, which means to give a detailed account of a person, an object, a place, a situation, you have to be careful not to write the kind of school essay where you had to evoke something for its own sake, where you tended to show off your store of adjectives and adverbs. You have also to avoid giving a lengthy account of the make-up of something or the process of some activity, as an essay in biology does. Your description must be concise, and must serve the purpose of the feature in an interesting way.

You might want to note the essential details in a good order. For example, a feature about buying tulip bulbs in the *Sunday Herald Magazine* goes like this:

> you'll be tempted by the brilliantly coloured photos on the packets
> but don't buy the dried-up bulbs you get from the shops and supermarkets
> get them fresher from a specialist grower
> from a small bulb grower in the UK
> look at their colour photos online
> last year I bought some excellent bulbs in this way
> they came in paper bags, stamped with their names, wrapped in newspaper
> the tall tulips
> Queen of the Night, dark purple–black
> Shirley, white with fine purple edges
> the small species tulips which were followed by interesting seedpods
> Camassia 'Blue Spires', a beautiful, tall delphinium-like plant
> flowers in May and is perfect for damp soil
> the elegant snakeshead fritillary, *Fritillaria meleagris* …

The feature ends with planting hints.

Exposition/description/narration

More ambitious kinds of description that a feature might need are the creative ability to transport the reader and fill the mind with imagery, and may

167

be combined with exposition and narration. A landscape can be easy enough if it's: to the north … to the south …, etc. But you may need to describe a landscape as seen from an aeroplane or a moving train, or a riot in a marketplace where you would employ all the senses, and you might need to describe the effects of time passing. Your best guides to acquiring these skills are good fiction writers.

Here are a few evocative bits, however, from part of a feature by Paul Evans in *Geographical* magazine of April 2003, with some quoting to indicate the more creative skills. The feature tells how the author joined a team of volunteers helping to monitor wolves in Poland, in danger of being hunted into local extinction:

> It's a sound to chill the blood. In the preternatural stillness that descends with the falling snow, a wolf howls. A reply comes almost instantly … it's a sound that is becoming increasingly rare …

> One of these wolves recently walked along the ridge … the fore print is about ten centimetres in diameter, four large clawed toes and a large heel make an almost circular shape …

> The forests in which this wolf lives form part of Poland's 270-square-kilometre Bieszczady (pronounced Bish-cardy) National Park [whose wildlife includes] roe deer, wild boar, elk, European bison, beaver, brown bear and lynx …

We learn the history of the National Park, the ravages of the hunting, and the more recent conservation efforts of Dr Wojciech Smetana of the Institute of Nature Conservation at the Polish Academy of Sciences. He has trapped a number of wolves and fitted them with radio-collars to track them.

Dr Smetana has also revived the tradition of using Tatra sheepdogs to guard flocks:

> This large, tough hound is raised with sheep in order to form a powerful social bond with the flock. Wolves are very reluctant to risk injury by tackling Tatra dogs and two per flock provide a sufficient deterrent. Smetana uses the dogs to corral flocks at night into enclosures surrounded by three strands of electrified wire. The top strand is 'fladry' – a line of coloured flags that wolves dislike and are reluctant to cross.

The feature ends:

> These tracks belong to an inspiring language, and it is one we should learn. The living creature at the end of its trail may never care, but if we're going

to save it from persecution – and possible extinction – we must (*Geographical*, the magazine of the Royal Geographical Society, April 2003).

Let's see how the main points of a descriptive/expository/narrative piece about mazes and labyrinths in *Active Life* magazine are arranged:

- mazes and labyrinths depicted throughout history
- the difference: each path of the labyrinth leads to the centre
- the Cretan labyrinth myth: Theseus kills the Minotaur at the centre
- the Roman version, square or rectangular, depicted in mosaic
- thirteenth century – a central cross with Christian significance
- turf mazes symbolic mazes, multilevel and unicursal mazes mentioned
- the Archbishop's Maze, created 1981, at Grey's Court; rich in Christian symbolism
- the Hampton Court maze, oldest hedge maze in the UK – a trapezoid design
- various games connected with mazes
- mazes in the shapes of mythical beasts – dragons, etc.
- Hever Castle in Kent: a yew maze and a water maze
- some of the new mazes created every year
- all kinds of designs

Narration

We have seen in Chapter 3 how you can choose between climax order (for example, 2, 4, 3, 1) and anticlimax, without tailing off (for example, 1, 4, 3, 2), when your feature is straightforward narration/exposition, and that a good way of avoiding any tailing off at the end is to provide an echo of some kind of a striking beginning, so that there's a satisfying circle.

The *Reader's Digest*'s TOTS (triumphs over tragedies) and thriller-type crimes and adventures receive a great deal of attention to ensure that the story grips from the start and the suspense or fascination is maintained till the end. The trick is to incorporate the necessary explanation, description, background history or whatever into the piece without losing the momentum of the story. Here's the plan of a 3500-word piece that combines several structural techniques: 'Murder on the cliff' by Helen O'Neill in the issue of November 2003. It goes like this, with gaps as in the original:

- description of the cliff rising from the Wyoming desert: 'loose shale and parched brushwood and swirling dust winds … coiled rattlesnakes …'

- a young mother and her child plunged to their deaths
- two friends grew up in Green River, a mining town: Roger Brauburger and Bob Duke
- they shot rabbits and drank beer
- the older, with connections to small-time crime, Brauburger, at 21 bought Duke a pistol
- Duke's girlfriend got pregnant at 17: Duke married her but felt trapped
- they had a son Erik

- August 1996: Brauburger's mother tells him of the deaths
- it was thought Duke had gone to the jeep for a drink
- Brauburger's sorrow and torment at the funeral
- why had the family gone to such a desolate place?

- Duke moved to Houston to live with brother Mike
- he began to phone Brauburger
- Brauburger's torment increased
- his father said, 'Go to Mont.'

- Green River police lieutenant Mont Mecham had been suspicious about the deaths
- but the case came under Sweetwater County Sheriff's department
- Brauburger reported a call from Duke out of insurance money from the deaths

- then said he'd pay Brauburger $20,000 to kill his parents
- also said he'd 'done family before and didn't like it'
- in the summer of 1996 Duke had offered him $15,000 to kill his wife and child
- the police tapped the next call from Duke and a date for the killing was set

- further phone calls were recorded and the FBI arrested Duke

- Duke was given only 10 years
- Brauburger didn't get his family protection programme asked for
- he had drugs and drink problems, lost jobs

- Tim Merchant of the Sweetwater County Sheriff's Department, re-examined the cliff deaths
- He and prosecutor Harold Moneyhun put together discrepancies in Duke's old story

- on 13 August 2001 the court case faltered
- Brauburger's testimony was rubbished by the defence
- a new witness saved the day – Duke's secret girlfriend at the time
- she said she and Duke had often visited the clifftop and he had talked of finishing with the marriage
- but without having to pay child support
- Duke's story had been that he had lost his way with his family

- the sentence was six life terms, four of them consecutive
- Brauburger could get on with his life.

Notice the way the surprises in the story are saved up to keep the suspense going, change the pace, provide changes in direction. This storytelling technique serves in all kinds of long features. Sections of them will have their own pattern of climax or anticlimax, most important to less important or vice versa.

Argument

A sort of amalgamation of several features I've seen arguing about whether or not many more police should be armed with guns has produced the list below of Against points followed by For points in pairs. This results in a conclusion in favour of a moderate increase in arms.

I'm leaving out the other elements. You might start such a piece by describing a housing estate as the scene of a gun battle between police and criminals and follow up with a bloodthirsty narrative before getting into the argument. You would undoubtedly have some exposition: some comparisons with the situation in the USA and some history perhaps. I've suggested in the notes how some of this lead-in material might go in an intro. But let's concentrate on the order of the argument.

Depending on your point of view, you might order (or rearrange before writing up) as all the Againsts followed by all the Fors when the argument is in favour, or as all the Fors followed by all the Againsts when the argument is not in favour, and split up into pairs perhaps (F-A, F-A, etc. or A-F, A-F, etc.) when the argument is left more open. Let's see how the Against list followed by the For list works. You might have produced this final order after having experimented with a mind map or just put down points in any order as they came into your head.

Intro

Narrate an inner city gun battle involving police and describe the setting.

Give some figures from other countries, indicating both more armed police increasing shootings and more armed police reducing them. Relate the figures to the UK, and indicate point of view. Define 'more'.

Body

(It's a good idea when outlining an argument to put points in sentence form. This helps you to make the logical structure clear.)

1A   Arming more police will encourage more villains to arm. The armed response vehicles (ARVs) are sufficient.

1F   The ARVs rarely get to the scene quickly enough.

2A   The relationship between the police and the community would deteriorate.

2F   People would trade in some friendliness for more effectiveness.

3A   The answer to rising violent crime is stricter gun laws with an amnesty for guns handed in.

3F   The police are at the mercy of increasingly violent armed criminals. Collecting arms from the populace has had limited success.

4A   There's a great danger of trigger-happy police shooting people by mistake or without sufficient cause. Look at the USA experience.

4F   The answer to that is thorough training of the police in the use of arms and clear rules of engagement. More guns would work well if combined with the stepping up of current reforms.

Conclusion

The policy would have to be cautiously implemented. Sum up why it is believed the weight of evidence is in favour. Quote?

It would probably help to flesh out this outline, developing the argument a little and showing the train of thought with some links. For example:

2A   The relationship between the police and the community would deteriorate. One advantage of a friendly relationship is that crimes are more likely to be reported (A).

2F   *But too many of these reports are not followed up. And anyway attitudes to the police are complex and varied.* Some people say that too many violent elements are not brought to justice. Others emphasize the evidence of corruption or racism. Others blame bureaucracy and failure to recruit. Verdict: people would trade in some friendliness for effective reforms in these areas (F).

(*Link in italics.*)

For a 2000-word plus piece on the above subject you might go on to do a more detailed outline, slotting in the contacts and source materials where they will be used before writing up. And your For/Against pattern might be allocated to the different sections of the piece rather than followed straight through: covering relationships with the community, the amnesty policy, training in arms, other reforms, and so on. And you would vary the order of the Fors and Againsts a bit.

ASSIGNMENTS

1 Analyse any published article of 1000 words in the same way as is done in this chapter.

2 After a tutor or colleague has photocopied three published articles, cut them up and paste them on sheets in the wrong order; re-order the paragraphs.

3 Do some research and organize some notes and materials for a feature provisionally titled 'Should the honours system be abolished?' Include at least one interview.

Create a mind map to get you thinking about the subject.

Develop from this a For and Against outline.

Write the feature (about 1000 words), indicating a target publication.

---

11   Making a coherent whole

This chapter concentrates on the teamwork that keeps a feature unified. Title, subtitle or standfirst if any, intro, body and ending must work together. Anecdotes and quotes, examples, case studies, figures, pictures, charts, boxes and suchlike can bring illumination, resonance, relevance and humanity. Key terms and other kinds of links keep the theme focused. It has to be a juggling act, and the ingredients you're juggling with have to be the best you can find, within the time available, not necessarily the first that you find.

You've collected and verified facts. You've represented ('interpreted') interviews accurately. You've got an outline, with a few links inserted to keep you on track. You've got one or two anecdotes and quotes that should serve. You know what you want to say. Surely that's enough?

It depends. Before you start writing up, it will be a good idea to ask yourself one or two more questions. Are you sure that what you want to say is of obvious interest to the readers you have in mind? Are those readers like you? Do you love Bach cantatas and spend a lot of time with your train set? Or are you a heavy metal/down the pub sort of guy?

You have, of course, got certain readers in mind. Your ability to interest them may well be easier if you're addressing people of like mind, if your interest in trains has encouraged you to write for *Trainspotting Magazine*. Otherwise, if you're writing for a general market, which might include readers of both those persuasions mentioned, you will be wise to assume that many of them will be coming to your subject cold. Based on that premise you'll have a much better chance of making those ingredients add up to an article that will capture interest and sustain it throughout. You'll keep in mind that purpose/theme, content and style are in harmony throughout. Let's contrast two quite different features to see the teamwork in action.

EXAMPLES OF TEAMWORK

Triumph over tragedy

First, a typical popular magazine formula in an article by Dawn Doherty.

Title	'My 12-year-old had a nervous breakdown'
Publication	*Woman*
Date	12 April 1999
Length	850 words
Purpose/theme	To give the inspirational story of a child's struggle against a disease, with much success, that can be told mainly in the words of mother and child.

Standfirst
'Yes, children *can* suffer stress and Jamie had so much to cope with he cracked.'

Intro:
(*Hook*)
Tina Kennedy loves to splash out on expensive clothes for her teenage son, Jamie – happily spending £200 a month. She says: 'It means he's getting taller, like any other young boy – and that's fantastic.'

(*Bridge*)
Jamie suffers from a rare illness which stopped him growing when he was 10 and caused his weight to shoot from 5 st. 4 lb to 7 st. Bullied at school and forced to give up his beloved football, he had a nervous breakdown. Tina and her husband, Philip, watched as Jamie changed from a confident boy into a tearful child, haunted by nightmares.

(*Text, moving into the body*)
'We've lost a year of his life, which is sad,' says Tina, 42, from High Wycombe, Bucks. Jamie's future had always seemed so bright. A talented footballer, he'd been invited to join a local club's school of excellence.

Summary of body
The progress of his disease. He had to leave the football club. In hospital his illness was diagnosed as hypothyroidosis, an underactive thyroid gland, and he started a drug treatment. Bullied at school, he refused to leave his house. He had a nervous breakdown and joined a special teaching unit at the hospital; his parents also received counselling. After three months Jamie began to lose weight. Slowly his confidence returned, he began playing with a new club and he gained height and weight.

Ending
> Now 13, he goes part-time to senior school and hopes to go full-time by the autumn. He'll take the drugs permanently and his growth should be normal by 19. 'It's wonderful to have him back.'

Colour photos with captions
Jamie looking stressed: 'Jamie was haunted by nightmares'
'Happy at last – Jamie with his parents Tina and Philip'
'On the pitch, Jamie forgot all his troubles and was his old self'

Text breaker quote
> 'We've lost a year of his life – it's just so sad'

Linking
Key words: breakdown, tears, haunted, nightmares, sad, struggled, devastated, lethargic, underactive, crying, ugly, and then:
confidence, cheeky, better, will, forgot, shot up, good, great, enjoying, growth, wonderful.

Paragraph to paragraph: bullied (mid paragraph) ... the bullies, after that, then, after three months, by last November, since then, finally, no longer.

Anecdotes and quotes
> Slowly, Jamie's confidence returned. 'When his doctor told us he'd been cheeky one day, we knew he was getting better,' laughs Tina. 'Another time he was caught throwing things out of the hospital window. Though he'd been naughty, it was a good sign.'

The elements are carefully chosen to explain and move the story forward at the same time.

The teamwork of purpose/theme, content/structure, style

1 Readers will gain inspiration and reassurance that families suffering misfortune can get much help if they refuse to give up to despair.
2 The case study indicates that with determination, family and expert support, childhood misfortunes can be overcome. The structure effectively brings out the drama of the story.
3 The message is put across with simplicity, using the words of the boy and his mother: the emotions are projected directly, with no tricks.

Exploring the Nazi legacy: description of a place and its people

The second feature is a description/narration/exposition that relates a place with some shameful history to the people living there now.

When you've got three times as many words and more there are more complexities but you can adapt some of those simple structures shown above. The novelist and journalist Angela Lambert had a personal motivation for visiting the small Bavarian town of Berchtesgaden, Hitler's retreat: she was researching a book on the Third Reich and her mother came from Hamburg. We don't discover this until halfway through the feature. Her personal motivation is interesting because it deepens her involvement with the people and guides her to discoveries about the Nazi past. But as readers we want more than her personal odyssey, and we also get a fascinating picture of the Berchtesgadeners today and some reflections on their relationship with the racists of the past.

Title	'In his ideal world'
Publication	*Financial Times Magazine*
Date	4 October 2003
Length	2800 words
Motivation/purpose	To answer the questions: What are the people like? What is their connection with the Nazi past? With the evils committed by both sides in the Second World War?

Standfirst

Hitler chose as his retreat a Bavarian town where the scenery and people met his Aryan desires. Seventy years on, Angela Lambert feels haunted in the Fuhrer's Utopia.

Intro:

(*Hook*)

The small Bavarian town of Berchtesgaden has a disproportionately vast railway station, designed by Albert Speer in 1937 to impress visitors to Obersalzberg, Hitler's mountain retreat. They included Mussolini, monarchs of central European countries keen to curry favour and, on 23 October 1937, the Duke and Duchess of Windsor: 'We thank you especially for the pleasant hours we spent at Obersalzberg,' the former Edward VIII later wrote to the Fuhrer – nothing if not well brought up.

(*Bridge*)

It is more than 50 years since Hitler's retreat was razed and today not many people in the pretty town even know that he once lived here. Fewer still are aware that Speer, his chief architect and creator of special effects at the Nuremberg rallies, was responsible for their grand neoclassical station. Under the three archways designed to frame Hitler or his guests before they climbed into his armoured Mercedes and sped up the mountainside, there is no sign or plaque dating from those years. In the 1930s, thousands of people gathered every day outside Hitler's house (well protected by iron railings and SS

177

guards) shouting 'We want the Fuhrer!' Now, it seems, he has been almost airbrushed out of the history of this peaceful place.

(*Text, moving into the body*)

Germany is waking up from half a century of denial. Books that tell the truth about the Second World War are being published, such as Bernard Schlink's *The Reader* and Gunter Grass's recent novel *Crabwalk*, about the sinking of a German refugee ship by a Soviet submarine in January 1945. More than 9000 people drowned – it was the worst marine disaster ever and was all but forgotten for 55 years. Films and documentaries are being made that reveal the shame and suffering of the German people.

Summary of body, with the main links in italics

28 July 1943: 40,000 people died in the bombing of Hamburg by Bomber Command.

Near the Berghof, Hitler's former home in Berchtesgaden, an information centre, *Dokumentation Obersalzberg*, exhibits Third Reich documents and a video in which former residents describe how their homes were compulsorily purchased and pulled down and rebuilt as villas for the Fuhrer and his circle.

Between 1932 and 1937 the village was colonized by the Nazi leaders. *Dokumentation* tells *also* the story of the annihilation of the Jews through letters and photos of the dead and dying in the extermination camps, while speakers can be activated to hear Hitler's speeches. She spent a week here in a chalet below Hitler's Berghof trying to understand 'how the two decades during which he lived here might have changed it, or the people living here, then and now'.

In a supermarket she was astonished by people's sudden, unprovoked rudeness. People like this, she concluded, became Nazis.

'*It is easy to see why Hitler chose to make his retreat here.*' He was born 75 km away just over the Austrian border. He was nostalgic for this area with its blonde, healthy people, prototype of his idealized Aryan race.

'Toweringly beautiful' Bavaria appealed to the 'blend of the epic and the sentimental in Hitler's nature'.

The pretty doll-like women and the gnome-like men in their *lederhosen* reassured Hitler, who was generally ill at ease with women and suspicious of men. She found them unsettling.

They are well behaved in *this Catholic stronghold*, with respect for order and authority. My landlord's two sons helped him convert a garage into a flat with exceptional obedience.

If Bavarians personified the ideal Germans Hitler, with jet-black hair and greyish skin, was physically lazy. But he knew how to lead these 'good, God-fearing people'.

First though the purifying had to be done: it lasted for more than a decade. There were no Jews here, or handicapped or blacks or Asians. The landlord loaned her books about Hitler's colony, the Obersalzberg, in the 1930s and gave me the address of a bookshop specializing in such books.

The owner of this bookshop … gave her other contacts and she surfed through Second World War websites. Those covering the Third Reich took pains to deny any Nazi convictions.

The next day she went on a four-hour guided bus tour of the area. The guide explained that Obersalzberg was not only a retreat but an alternative centre of government with telephone exchange, SS barracks for thousands of soldiers, and a bunker.

On 25 April 1945 RAF Lancasters bombed the area into ruins, which were later demolished.

For the last part of the tour the bus climbed to the top of the 3000 ft mountain. The German people paid 34 million Reichsmarks (about £100 million today) for the Eagle's Nest, a 50th birthday present for Hitler, ordered by his private secretary, Martin Bormann, now a café with a splendid view. Tourists, mostly German, buy souvenirs. She saw no sign of disapproval at any record of the Nazi regime.

Ending
> In this Eden-like landscape of mountains, meadows, wayside shrines, happy children and hard-working adults, how could Satan intrude? Bur perfection is always flawed. It is not only lager-louts with shaven heads who preach the racist creed. They rant from incoherent rage at their squalid surroundings, lack of opportunity and unvalued lives. Berchtesgadeners have no such excuses. Most, of course, are welcoming, decent people. So why was I haunted by the feeling that the little town's immaculate streets and immaculate citizens hid not just an appalling past but a troubling present? There were many who might still, in spite of everything that happened here, respond to a stirring and seductive call for the purification of the German race.

Colour photos with captions
(*Above the title, no caption*) Hitler in uniform, a mountain in the background.

(*Beside the title*) 'Hitler's *Berghof*, which was blown up and bulldozed after the war.' A spacious two-storey villa seen against the mountainous backdrop.

(*Above the title, no caption*) Picture of Hitler in uniform, grim-faced, with swastika armband outside the *Berghof*.

'Once visited by the elite of the Nazi regime, Hitler's Eagle's Nest now attracts curious tourists.' The picture shows the café perched on top of a high mountain.

Text breaker quote

> As a 50th birthday present to Hitler, Bormann ordered the building of the Eagle's Nest. This was not a good idea: Hitler suffered from claustrophobia and a fear of heights. It is now a café, with a rather good view.

Other linking

> Between 1932 and 1937 the entire village was colonized by the Nazi leadership. 'Staying at the *Berghof* [Hitler's home] in Obersalzberg,' recalls Heinrich Hoffmann, one of Hitler's closest friends, 'was like living in a gilded cage.' The members of the inner circle enjoyed every luxury here …

The quote follows up the first sentence by giving us the experience of one of the Nazi leaders and transports us back in time and place.

Unpleasantness in the supermarket is made dramatic by the angry shopper incident and the quote:

> '*Mensch!* Just pile it back in the trolley, can't you, instead of keeping other people waiting!' He was so vehement and aggressive that I felt physically threatened.

The taxi driver knows the place well:

> There's no crime here. Why should anyone want to commit a crime in this beautiful place?

The teamwork of purpose/theme, content/structure, style

1   The author's main theme is that in Hitler's idyllic retreat there's a disturbing sense that many of these decent, happy, prosperous people could be turned into Nazis again.

2   She puts across this haunted feeling by contrasting the serene beauty of the place with facts about the shameful past, the rudeness of some of the inhabitants and her uneasiness about the Nazi purification scheme leaving no sign of multiculturalism. A skilful collaboration of narrative, descriptive and expositional structures.

3   The style is unobtrusive, letting the facts speak for themselves. The article reminds us that evil lurks in the most beautiful places – that the Nazi evil is still there and could be reawakened – without dramatizing. We are calmly persuaded that the human race will always be capable of evil and to be on our guard.

For a long feature you need resonances and the above summary reveals some. In particular, though, note the way that the ending reminds you of where you started – 'respond to a stirring and seductive call' echoing 'waking up from half a century of denial' – and makes the connection with the journey made into the legacy of the past – 'in spite of all that has happened here'.

Let's zoom in a bit closer on some titles, intros and endings to identify some formulae worth noting. If you work for a publication as staff writer or sub-editor, or write for one regularly, your feeling for titles that are appropriate for it will be finely tuned. Freelances should give special attention to these parts of articles in publications aimed at. They have particular likes and dislikes.

TITLES

Even though freelances' titles are often changed (you don't normally know how the page is going to be designed), a provisional title can help to provide you with the controlling idea, or at least keep the feature on track. A title must first of all grab the reader's attention. It should charm, amuse, intrigue or buttonhole the reader in some way.

The first title of each pair below, in italics, would serve as a provisional title. The second is given an attribution if known. One or two are made up.

1 *The superiority in Russian tanks*
WHY RUSSIAN TANKS ARE BETTER
'Wh' phrases get straight to the point, and it's easy to give them a smooth rhythm. Avoid long abstract words such as 'superiority'. Simple, direct words work best on the whole.

2 *The lack of good manners today*
WHERE ARE ALL THE MANNERS GONE?
The tone of the first is too serious and preachy. The second is helped by its allusion to an old song, 'Where are all the flowers gone?' An example of how a question can sometimes make a good title – though of course any publication would ration their use.

Here are some examples of puns, two of them alliterative as well, a common combination:

1 *The answer to depression – exercise*
EXERCISING THE DEMONS
A pun from *The Observer Magazine*.

2 *Studying a star*
STAR STUDIED
This headed a *Guardian* feature about a Hollywood star. A pun on 'studded'.

3 *Our poor attitude to waste*
DOWN IN THE DUMPS
Another piece from *The Observer Magazine* (25 January 2004) by Jane Withers of around 3000 words deplores the lack of recycling in the UK. It has a standfirst that neatly summarizes the content:

> Every year in Britain we produce millions of tons of rubbish; yet we recycle a mere 12.4 per cent of it. Our bin, burn and bury approach to waste means we are now drastically out of step with our European neighbours and environmentalists who practise the three 'Rs' – reduce, reuse and recycle. So when are we going to clean up our act? (© Jane Withers. With kind permission of *The Guardian*)
> The ending is discussed below.

4 *The unemployed who are happy as they are*
THE RISK OF FINDING A JOB
The irony of the second gives it more resonance.

5 *The problem of obesity*
A JOB FOR NANNY
A title that wouldn't work for many publications these days, since nannies are thin on the ground.

> It needed the standfirst: 'Fat people aren't victims,' says Tania Kindersley. 'They're just fat, and it's time they were urged to shape up.' From *The Spectator* of 6 July 2002.

THE INTRO

Let's label some devices, starting with the intro to the *spectator* piece.

Vivid, surprising or shocking statement

Often in the hook:

> We are all vast now. Columnists, doctors, cross-bench committees and government ministers desperately inveigh against the epidemic of obesity, the rising tide of fat that will swamp us all. We may have put a man on the moon, but we can't get off the sofa to change the television channel.

(We then get a bridge – stark statistics such as 30,000 deaths and £500,000 cost to the NHS annually; and the text paragraph, which lists the several bogeymen to blame, including fast foods, diets, television and amoral advertising.)

A quote can add support to the right to shock:

> There were four ways in which airmen used to come into Ward 3 of the Queen Victoria Hospital in East Grinstead during the war: boiled, mashed, fried and roast. 'Just like potatoes, really,' said one of them. (A *Mail on Sunday* feature on plastic surgery)

Anecdote

> It was 5 a.m. when the fuse-box in the cupboard under the stairs in the Doherty family's house in Ilford, Essex, developed a fault. As it grew molten red, it set fire to plastic rubbish bags near by: acrid, poisonous fumes started to pour out towards the sleeping family.
>
> Then suddenly a small, saucer-shaped object fixed to the ceiling of the landing above the cupboard emitted a piercing, 85-decibel shriek. It woke Olive Doherty, who shook her husband Jimmy. Together they grabbed their three daughters from their bedrooms and rushed down the stairs before the smoke and fumes, already spreading through the house, could engulf them. (From an article on 'Home Fire-Alarms', *Readers' Digest*)

Atmosphere/description

> As the last rays of sunlight caress the evening sky, a fascinating metamorphosis takes place all over Malaysia. Shops close up for the day and traffic on the usually congested streets begins to thin. But as one cycle ends, another unfolds over a few crowded and brightly lit streets bearing such exotic names as Tuanku Abdul Rahman, Chow Kit and Petaling. Here, the night hawkers prepare themselves for another busy night, hanging lights, heating woks, fastidiously arranging their wares and airing the latest Malay hits on their sound systems. It's *pasar malam* time. (From an article titled 'Late-night shopping' by Michael Defreitas in *Geographical* magazine of March 2003. © *Geographical*, the magazine of the Royal Geographical Society)

Not so much trying to grab you, this intro, as trying to cast a spell over you with a sort of incantatory rhythm. The mood was set by the standfirst: 'With its history of trading, colonization and immigration, modern-day Malaysia has an extraordinarily multicultural society. Nowhere is this more apparent than in its night markets, where exotic flavours of the past and present create an intoxicating, unmissable experience.' And of course, if you're new to Malaysia, you guessed that *pasar malam* means night markets, which makes you feel pleased with yourself, even if you're not told so until the third paragraph.

Exposition/argument by analogy

Ironically, the animal whose name is a synonym for everything contemptible in the human vocabulary is in many essential respects the most similar of all animals to man. The basis of this similarity is the fact that men and rats are the only omnivorous animals.

In this example the analogy quickly builds a bridge from the familiar fact to the unfamiliar facts that will be the basis for the article.

We're all in this together

There's an unwritten law among friends – most of whom have small children – that we will never criticize each other's offspring. Nor, for that matter, will we ever raise our voices – or worse still, our hands – to any child that has sprung from the loins of one of our mates. This rule is so vital, it may as well be emblazoned on our foreheads in fluorescent pen.

The *Woman* feature titled 'Don't you criticize my child' can confidently assume that its readers and their friends will have small children and that analysing the contrast in their attitudes to their own and others' small children will be of immediate interest. Including them all in 'we' in the intro emphasizes this bond. From the second paragraph on it's 'my' and 'your' children.

Don't, however, assume your readers are 'we' too readily; you risk being an unwelcome guest.

Significant scene

A hackle-raising howl filled the moonlit valley and died away. The slight young woman with a knapsack stood quietly and listened. Nothing. Then, cupping both hands round her mouth, she howled once more. This time she heard an answering howl, with the playful yapping of pups, coming closer.

Ghostly as puffs of smoke, three young wolves sprang into the clearing. They shot curious glances at the intruder, then darted back into the moon-shadows. (From a *Reader's Digest* article about wolves reappearing throughout Europe)

Significant quote/quotation

'There you are,' said my first-born accusingly. '*The Spectator* is just saying what I've been thinking for some time now. This generation of grannies is a disgrace.'

'They've lost the plot … still careering on and neglecting their duties as parents. I mean, when am I going to get the chance to do half the things my mother does?'

Margo MacDonald in the Edinburgh *Evening News* points out that the social structure today doesn't embrace many extended families living in the same area, and the 'glamorous grannies' with a new lease of life are either finding new careers or careering off to the sun and to the golf course.

You can quote from a person in your story and from a magazine article, as the author does, or from a book or a report or a TV programme or from a book of quotations. But make sure it's relevant.

Literary allusion

April may be the cruellest month in the natural world, but in the world of humanity January is when the fists start to fly …

So begins a feature in *The Independent Magazine* about violence in Britain and an organization that tries to help those addicted to it, reflecting the start of T.S. Eliot's poem *The Waste Land*. Readers of that organ are expected to catch the allusion. To have expectations of this kind further downmarket can be intellectual snob territory; to explain, however, that *Hamlet* was one of Shakespeare's plays can be very patronizing. Of course, if you integrate an allusion as skilfully as Will Self does here, it doesn't matter whether readers catch the allusion or not.

In the same publication is a piece describing a restaurant called Allium, which is the garlic genus, beginning:

> In The Arabian Nights, a young man came to his bride smelling of garlic. Because he had presumed to appear thusly, she cut off his thumbs and his big toes. And never again did the young man forget to freshen up after a ragout …

Celebrity peg

> That great British institution, immortalized by Ronnie Barker in the classic sitcom *Open All Hours*, is pulling down its shutters for the final time.
>
> The modern-day Granvilles and Arkwrights – who have managed to survive against the odds by providing basic home essentials – are having to seek alternative employment as customers turn increasingly to supermarkets.
>
> Every week, 11 independent convenience outlets close as owners find themselves priced out of business.
>
> And these traditional shopkeepers say they are victims of chain stores such as Tesco and Sainsbury's which are opening smaller, 'local' versions on their doorstep. (*The Mirror*)

Cryptic/intriguing/dramatic

> There is an unreported war in progress in Ireland. The island is in danger of being covered to a depth of ten feet by a vicious Turkish importation which eats everything in its path, swallows up whole oak trees, houses and entire colonies of the native inhabitants, and is insidiously and maliciously spread by Japanese immigrants. A vigorous counterattack has been mounted and armies of sturdy Irishmen and their valiant women are to be seen by the alert, North and South, conducting their lonely and arduous campaign as intrepidly they creep through the undergrowth in valley and hillside, up mountains and across the treacherous surface of boglands, their weapons ever at the ready, eyes peeled for the enemy. (From a gardening piece, 'Day of the Rhododendrons', by Stan Gebler Davies in *You*, *Mail on Sunday* magazine; the title echoes that of the science fiction novel *Day of the Triffids* by John Wyndham)

A good beginning can be elusive. It may be found hiding somewhere in your feature. Try removing the first paragraph or two of your first draft and you may find it there. Or have you got a feeble beginning but a strong ending? Can you turn the ending into the beginning and rewrite the ending?

THE ENDING

Here are a few types of endings:

The most important point to remember

The ending of 'Late-night shopping' (see the intro above) is concerned to give you the best practical advice you will need if you are to get off your armchair. It comes on top of a detailed survey of the markets, greatly varied because of the country's multiracial composition: the influences range from traditional Malay through Thai and Chinese and there are Indian and Moslem flavours. The *pasar malam* is 'the social and cultural heart of Malay life' and that, it's also implied, is knowing how to shop in the markets:

> Haggling is an important activity in the night markets, particularly for dry goods (food is very expensive and prices are generally not negotiable). In fact, if you accept the first price offered you will be labelled a *lembik* (for weak or weakling). But there are a number of rules to remember before you enter into any negotiations: never insult a vendor by offering a ridiculously low price; for locally produced clothes, arts and crafts bear in mind how long the goods would have taken to make; start your haggling at around 60 per cent of the asking price and you should end up at about 75 per cent.

> No trip to Malaysia is complete without at least one visit to a night market. So don't spend all your cash during the day, because when the sun goes down it's *pasar malam* time.

Summing up

That often comes with a simple restatement of the thesis. An article in *Choice*, about The Queen's Messengers, who are all over 50, and who deliver state papers to diplomats abroad has:

> Such demanding work and hours ... engenders considerable loyalty and comradeship. No wonder the Colonel can point out with pride that the

Corps has never had a traitor in its ranks in over 300 years and never knowingly failed in its duty.

'A Job for Nanny' (see page 184) had to weave among all those who dole out blame widely for fatness and show how fat people can be encouraged rather than victimized. Kindersley's conclusion, in two paragraphs, is that 'we need something imaginative and left-field'. The first paragraph recommends 'jumping-for-joy meetings' instead of weigh-ins. The final paragraph is a clincher:

Too simple, perhaps, but the point holds: we need to take a fearless approach; to call a spade a spade. The obese should not be abandoned to an imperfect world and crappy food. We must face fat, without flinching, because we need hope; and the blame-culture and political correctness offer only hopelessness.

Final quote

An article on the looting of ancient sites, using metal detectors, quoting an archaeologist:

'Our main hope,' says Gregory, 'is for landowners and police to take a greater interest in what goes on at local sites. It is vital if we are to prevent the small minority who detect illegally from inflicting damage out of all proportion to their number.' (*Reader's Digest*)

Provocation to action

Or at least to think again. An article advising parents how to deal with children's nightmares and night terrors:

If your child suffers three or more night terrors a week over a period of months, you should ask your doctor for advice. (*Living*)

Your provocation to action may benefit from experts' quotes and if you're spreading the problem wide you may need to suggest a solution. 'Down in the Dumps' (has a standfirst) that gives the problem – see page 184. Its conclusion runs for three paragraphs:

As Rethink Rubbish, the waste awareness campaign says, 'recycling has to be made easier for people to understand and do'. It cites disinterest as a problem area: 'Currently, people are neither incentivized to act nor penalized for inaction.' The 'Waste Not Want Not' strategy includes recommendations 'for a third of collection authorities to have tried incentive-based schemes' by 2005/6.

The Dutch already enforce strict penalties. 'In Holland, you only put out rubbish on rubbish day, not the day before or the day after,' says Hettinga [Hester Hettinga, a Dutch marketing consultant who lives in London on and off and is amazed at the litter one sees everywhere in this country]. 'Once I got the day wrong and put my garbage out too early; the environment police contacted me. Because they found I was freelance I got the business fine, not the residential fine – about 400 Euros.'

The truth in this country is revealed in *The Tomorrow People*, where trend forecaster Martin Raymond found that even those who claim to be keen recyclers are in fact only marginally better than the average household. 'Keen recyclers might bank bottles and paper but still discard large quantities of recyclable materials and foods. Radical action is needed before it's too late. I'd vote for the designer Michael Marriot's bolder tactic: "If we have a Swede running our football why shouldn't we have a Dutch government running our recycling". Now that might actually get us out of the waste crisis.'

Note the way that the quotes (indirect and direct) are incorporated seamlessly into the ending.

Future prospects or possibilities

One of Yemen's latest projects, now almost complete, is the building of a new dam here at Ma'rib, to restore the region's former glory. (a travel article about Yemen in *Country Life*)

If your first draft is done and you're not pleased with the ending, try removing the last two paragraphs. Is it there? If not, look elsewhere in the draft. It is usually easy to pull out with a little changing of links.

The ending should make you feel that the writer has achieved their purpose, whatever that was. It should be fulfilling, satisfying in some way, though some daily newspaper features might tend to raise questions and worries that stem from the raw edges of news, while magazine features within their slower process are more likely to answer questions and suggest solutions.

Whatever the purpose of the feature is – to persuade or provoke to action, to create a climate of debate, paint a portrait, move emotionally, argue a case, leave the reader something to think about – some kind of evidence that the purpose has been followed through if not fulfilled should be present in the ending. Make sure your ending grows out of the context of the article, and does not appear to be stitched on as an afterthought.

Make sure you have arrived at as clear a view of things as you can get on the basis of your material. You may have too many points/aspects circling round each other that need to be pulled together in the ending.

Avoid preaching or begging the question. Make sure you have given the evidence throughout the article by which readers can come to their own conclusions as well as follow yours. A proposition can fail if you are seen to have imposed rather than argued your case from evidence.

Both anecdotes and quotes are effective devices throughout a feature but must be used sparingly, with relevance and impact.

LINKS

They keep the theme constantly in mind, threaded throughout the article, but they must not draw attention to themselves. For a straightforward argument or exposition a sentence outline indicating links is effective. Here's such an outline, each sentence indicating perhaps one par (some of the content is no doubt out of date):

Title: 'Warning: Alcohol can seriously endanger your foetus'

- There is much damage done to unborn children of women drinking in pregnancy.
- *This fact* has been evidenced by convincing research.
- *Yet* only extreme cases tend to attract health authorities.
- *This is because* the damage is not very visible unless extreme.
- *Which is defined as* 'well below average size' or 'very noticeably backward'.
- *In fact*, there is no 'safe amount' of alcohol for pregnant women.
- *In spite of this* the warnings given to drinkers among pregnant women are much less urgent than those given to smokers.
- *When visible*, the damage is called 'foetal alcoholic syndrome'.
- *Some of the questions that arise* are the following. Is the government's slowness connected with the revenue from sales of alcoholic drink?

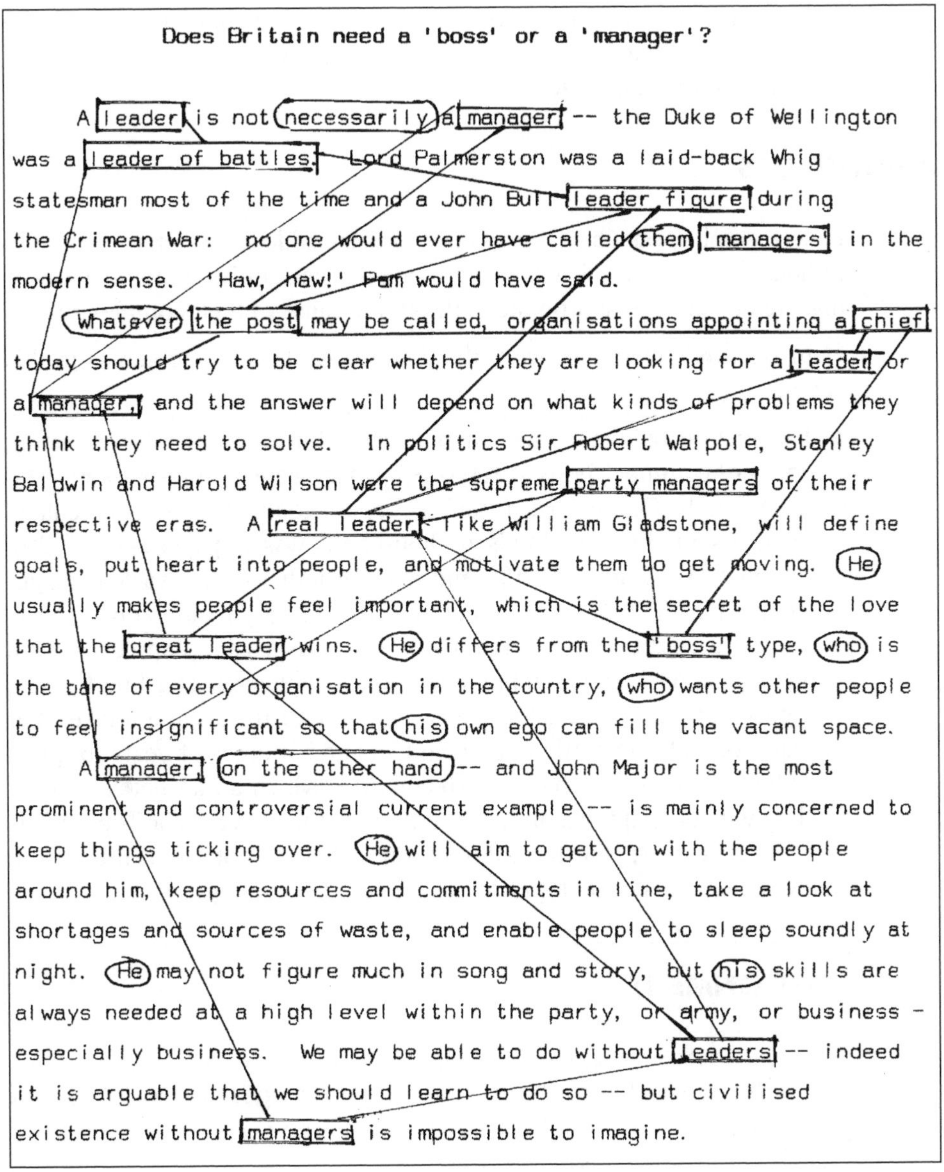

Does Britain need a 'boss' or a 'manager'?

A leader is not necessarily a manager -- the Duke of Wellington was a leader of battles; Lord Palmerston was a laid-back Whig statesman most of the time and a John Bull leader figure during the Crimean War: no one would ever have called them 'managers' in the modern sense. 'Haw, haw!' Pam would have said.

Whatever the post may be called, organisations appointing a chief today should try to be clear whether they are looking for a leader or a manager, and the answer will depend on what kinds of problems they think they need to solve. In politics Sir Robert Walpole, Stanley Baldwin and Harold Wilson were the supreme party managers of their respective eras. A real leader, like William Gladstone, will define goals, put heart into people, and motivate them to get moving. He usually makes people feel important, which is the secret of the love that the great leader wins. He differs from the 'boss' type, who is the bane of every organisation in the country, who wants other people to feel insignificant so that his own ego can fill the vacant space.

A manager, on the other hand -- and John Major is the most prominent and controversial current example -- is mainly concerned to keep things ticking over. He will aim to get on with the people around him, keep resources and commitments in line, take a look at shortages and sources of waste, and enable people to sleep soundly at night. He may not figure much in song and story, but his skills are always needed at a high level within the party, or army, or business – especially business. We may be able to do without leaders -- indeed it is arguable that we should learn to do so -- but civilised existence without managers is impossible to imagine.

Figure 11.1
Connections that make for coherence: an extract from a backgrounder piece (John Major had resigned to bring about a leadership election) by Michael Harrington in *The Sunday Telegraph* of 2 July 1995. Two separate networks are shown: balloons of pronouns and miscellaneous connectives; and linked boxes of key terms ('leader' and 'manager' and synonyms). Note the parallelism device whereby statements about the two key terms are contrasted

How greatly is the government swayed by the brewing interests? By the fact that drinking is a 'socially acceptable' activity?

- *And so* to the conclusions.

APPENDAGES

Panels, graphics, sidebars, boxes and tables are added to a feature, generally in-house, to give facts that can be presented in a usefully memorable way or that are not easy to incorporate in the text because of their complexity.

Here are a few examples from the features we have come across in this chapter:

- The feature on the corner shop has an illustrated panel contrasting prices of common foods at Tesco, Sainsbury's and a mini-market.
- 'Down in the Dumps' has a 'round cheese' graphic showing percentage segments of different kinds of household waste: paper/card 33.2%, compost 28.4%, glass 14.1%, and so on. Another shows waste management: landfill 77%, recycled/composted 12.4%, incineration 9%. A sidebar describes 'Top 3 Landfill Pests': disposable nappies, plastic bottles and packaging, and mobile phones, with some startling figures. Eighty per cent of plastic waste is sent to landfill sites and it takes 450 years for a plastic bottle to biodegrade, and hundreds of years for plastic bags. Another sidebar lists 10 countries which do far better at recycling with descriptions of their solutions. A third gives 'The Top 10 Tips for Compost'. A 'Further Information' list at the bottom of the feature gives addresses of organizations involved in recycling.

ASSIGNMENT

Study the following student's feature (written for a women's magazine) and then rewrite it in 800 words for a general magazine. Indicate your target publication. Update as necessary, having done some research. Some suggestions follow the piece.

House-husbands: how well do they cope?

1 It isn't easy to bring up children and run the home. Men have in the past underestimated the amount of work it involves and have

been reluctant to help. But fathers of the twenty-first century are a different breed.

2 Since the 1950s, when it was recognized that problem children respond well to their fathers taking an active interest in them, fathers have increasingly become involved in the everyday care of their children, from birth onwards. The days of Victorian patriarchs, rarely seen by their awestruck children, are long gone.

3 Today men are comfortable with the gentle side of their nature and many have realized their ability to nurture. A survey conducted by Bristol University showed that 9 per cent of fathers were the main carers for their babies.

4 But men taking on this role need as much support as possible. Until it becomes normal for men to be at home raising children they not only have to deal with the problems women have dealt with for centuries, but additional ones too, because they are men operating in a woman's world.

5 Many thousands of fathers have turned their lives upside down in order to look after the children while their wives or partners continue working. For many families role reversal is the way forward. Films such as *Mr Mum* or *Trading Places* reflect this growing trend.

6 There are many things to take into consideration when making childcare arrangements. Circumstances today mean more couples are choosing to reverse roles. These include increased unemployment, women's improved career prospects and earning power, better attitudes towards working mums, more egalitarian beliefs regarding childcare, and the desire more fathers have to be involved in their children's lives.

7 Role reversal offers women a greater degree of flexibility and choice when looking after children and running the home. Children are not affected by the change, other than the benefit from improved relationships with their fathers. Yet many role-reversed couples return to traditional roles earlier than anticipated because of the difficulties fathers experience with their new position as house-husband.

8 Difficulties stem from the attitudes of others, the way they perceive themselves as house-husbands, the everyday demands of a new role and the change in their relationship with their partners.

9 Research shows that house-husbands meet with disapproval from people around them because they are fulfilling an unconventional role. Although initially friends react positively to their situation, they find scepticism soon sets in, especially among relatives and male friends. One father said his male friends didn't even consider child-care to be an activity, let alone work.

10 Generally excluded from the local groups women form, house-husbands become isolated. They sense that some women feel threatened by them and are reluctant to include them in associated community activities. As Bob, a West Midlands house-husband, explained, playgroups and school circles are closed to him. 'I tried taking my son Damien to a playgroup but it was too embarrassing. I only went once. When I walked in the women stopped talking in groups and just stared at me.' In another case, a man was asked to leave his playgroup because husbands of the Indian women could not allow them to attend if there was a man there. Friendships between house-husbands and housewives rarely develop as women prefer not to invite men into their homes. Consequently fathers lack support and company during the day. One father told me he felt more lonely with a small child than he had ever felt on his own.

11 Fathers are not accepted as equals in the business of child rearing. They are referred to as 'good babysitters' and congratulated on the way they cope. While out with the children they are liable to be approached by women offering such advice as 'you need to keep him well wrapped up in this weather'. Men, apparently, are unable to cope. Men become sensitive to such criticism and feel they have to work twice as hard before they are accepted as good primary parents.

12 A more serious, but thankfully less common, problem for house-husbands is people who suspect them of being abductors. This experience seems to be more common among fathers who look unconventional and are in charge of very young babies.

13 George, a North Londoner, is a full-time parent to his eight-week-old daughter, Chloe. He has dreadlocks, a full beard and casual clothing. He was once followed for four miles. 'I started home from the shops, a journey that involves two buses and a walk. A middle-aged woman was on the first bus and she kept looking at me and Chloe. She got off the bus when I did and waited near me at the depot. She followed me onto the next bus and then when I got off

near my road, she got off too. I walked to my house and she was still behind me. She watched me go indoors and carried on walking.' He is convinced she thought Chloe had been abducted. Men with children have been stopped by the police and asked to prove that they are the father. The children are asked, 'Is this your Daddy?'

14 In our society men are brought up to behave in a masculine way, especially when socializing with other men. Schools, families, films and books educate them to expect to join the workforce and be breadwinners for their families. When they decide to swap roles with their partners they forgo much of this. In many cases this leads to them doubting their function in society and feeling their identity is under threat. They also feel more vulnerable as a result of having to expose the sensitive and caring side of their nature with the children. In one study (Lewis and O'Brien) 40 per cent of fathers said their self-esteem was undermined by leaving paid employment and this was a major disadvantage of their new lifestyle. However, 42 per cent of fathers reported enhanced self-esteem and confidence, possibly a result of successfully fulfilling a new role.

15 House-husbands are often shocked to discover how much work parenting involves. They need to adapt quickly to new tasks, unfamiliar emotions, demanding children and a heavy physical workload; backbreaking buggies, designed at a height for women; and a lack of father and baby changing rooms serves only to exacerbate the situation. Town planners, marketing people and designers should recognize this growing section of society.

16 It is only to be expected that couples suffer relationship problems within the first few months of role reversal. Both parents suffer from stress as they adjust to the physical and emotional demands of new jobs. However, in some cases, these problems are not resolved and, in fact, get worse. Deciding who is responsible for what can be a complicated business, leading to uncertainty and arguments.

17 A common problem is that mothers are reluctant to hand over their responsibility for decision-making when it comes to the home and the children. Some find it hard to trust their partners in this traditionally female domain. As a consequence, fathers resent the fact that they do not have the authority within the home that their wives would certainly have. They are resentful because they don't have the same freedom to manage their new role as their partners do to manage their careers.

18 Joseph, father of two, living near Bristol, said: 'The most difficult thing was my girlfriend's attitude. She was never fully comfortable with the role reversal. She seemed to think that her side of the arrangement meant becoming a "male chauvinist". She didn't value my role as a house husband as highly as her role as the main breadwinner and criticized the way I did things.'

19 Perhaps surprisingly, major problems occur in some families because the working woman does not necessarily support her partner. She may find it hard to accept him in a domestic role and therefore cannot sympathize with his worries and shortcomings. In addition, she may feel hurt if the children go to their fathers rather than to her when in need of comfort. This, combined with being away from the children all day, can make her feel guilty. She may be resentful of the father's closeness to the children. Findings show that coping with the mother's emotional anxieties and exhaustion is a primary problem for house-husbands.

20 To ensure successful role reversal women must accept men as equals in the home just as men must accept women as equals in the workplace. We have a lot to learn from the encouragement house-husbands get in Sweden.

(1100 words approx.)

Suggestions

- Do an outline of what is there, identify faults of structure and produce a new outline, with some links inserted.
- Keep to one topic per par and avoid repetition.
- Provide a more attention-grabbing intro and a stronger ending. The piece suddenly comes to a halt. More is needed on solutions to the problems listed.
- How could the UK government learn from the support system in Sweden? What kind of support is given to house-husbands there?
- Avoid academic style and jargon.
- Find more interesting quotes and anecdotes.
- Avoid constant changes of subject. For example, par 7: 'role reversal ... studies ... children ... couples ...'.
- Inject some humour or drama.
- Provide a standfirst, a sidebar and describe two or three suitable illustrations.

12 Developing writing techniques

Put it before them briefly so they will read it, clearly so they will appreciate it, picturesquely so they will remember it and, above all, accurately so they will be guided by its light. (Joseph Pulitzer)

Literature is the art of writing something that will be read twice; journalism what will be grasped at once. (Cyril Connolly)

Journalists tend to sum up these attributes as readability. The sum of course is more than the parts. Sometimes you can see how it is done. 'Give not that which is holy unto the dogs, neither cast ye your pearls before swine, lest they trample them under their feet, and turn again and rend you' (St Matthew, VII, vi). The anecdotes or metaphors of today's journalists are akin to Christian parables, and if you need lessons in how to get a message moving there are few better places to look than the Bible in its Authorized Version.

Connolly reminds us that the priority for journalists must be immediate communication: simple and direct before vivid. All the other qualities must make the communication more effective. Writing that fails to fulfil its main purpose draws attention to the writer instead of to the content. It is often pompous or pretentious or self-conscious. The writer is either not clear about the content or is not sufficiently engaged with it. Fulfilling your commitment to content and audience is largely what this book is about. But this chapter gets in closer to the tricks of the writing trade.

Good writing is as simple, direct and picturesque as the content and audience require. Those three words sum up all the principles of good writing of all kinds listed by pundits throughout the ages. To picturesque Pulitzer adds the connotation memorable. In journalistic terms we might gloss this as attention grabbing and sustaining, vivid, assailing the senses, moving.

The classic guides to writing techniques are listed in the Bibliography (page 400). They include creative writers, editors, critics and journalists.

They range from Aristotle, through Schopenhauer and Maugham, to Gowers and Orwell, and the Americans William Strunk, E. B. White and Rudolph Flesch. The essentials are:

- Choose the precise word
- Be simple and concise
- Prefer the familiar word to the unfamiliar
- Use the concrete rather than the abstract
- Avoid clichés
- Be positive and honest
- Write as you speak
- Vary your pace and rhythm.

CHOOSE THE PRECISE WORD

Imprecise language follows from not thinking clearly. At its worst, it is gobbledygook, meaningless or unintelligible language, especially when over-technical or pompous. Here's a sample:

> In communicating these data to your organization after fullest consultation with all my colleagues also concerned, I would certainly be less than truthful if I were to say that this has occasioned the Ministry (and this section in particular) no little difficulty but that the delay is nevertheless regretted.

This comes from Sir Ernest Gowers's classic *The Complete Plain Words*. Gowers points out that the writer intended to say something very simple: I am sorry we could not send the information sooner, but we have found this a very difficult case. But the sentence ends up with the meaning: the case was easy and the delay is not regretted. Gobbledygook is a disease of bureaucrats rather than journalists, but because it tends to fall foul of most of the principles of good writing we have to recognize it, and steer clear of it.

Precision takes time and thought, and we are often short of both. Then we tend to take the words and phrases lying conveniently on the storage shelves of our minds. Pairs of words that look like synonyms but are not can be a trap. 'Alternatives' is not the same as 'choices', nor do the following match up: 'chronic' and 'acute', 'comprise' and 'compose'. On the other hand, you have to be on the alert for the way language is changing all the time. Dictionaries do not prescribe on but describe current usage and you have to accept that 'disinterested' can now have the meaning of 'uninterested' as well as 'not influenced by considerations of personal advantage' even though you wanted the two words to remain forever distinct.

Unnecessary adjectives and adverbs are the first words to be blue-pencilled out by subeditors. 'The man is *very* big' may sound as if you are anxious the reader won't believe you when you say he's big. They had an absolutely amazing day by the sea is used to mean that they quite enjoyed themselves rather than that they saw an Immaculate Conception rising to heaven. 'Fantastic' and 'fabulous' are similar gush words, devalued through overuse. Beware of trendy words that can be out of date by the time you get around to pinning them down.

Modifiers can bring precision, of course, when used appropriately. Arts reviewers need them. The arts reviews of the weeklies, for example, have to pack a lot in. Consider how neatly the background information about character and situation is encapsulated by the adjectives and adverbs in this extract from an *Evening Standard* review (28 January 2004) by Nicholas de Jongh of a play called *I'm a Fool to Want You* by Paul Hunter:

> The bare stage boasts a back wall, from whose three exits characters keep popping, and onto which three chairs and a pair of red shoes are horizontally stuck. This design, Zoe Rahman's jazzy piano music and Mark Crown's trumpet improvisations all help shape the dream-struck, improvisatory atmosphere in which Stephen Harper's dark-suited, moustachioed, deadpan Boris falls for his barber Ursula. Seductive Hayley Carmichael invests this latter role with her familiar mix of husky-voiced, waif-like exuberance and childish glee.

The great resourcefulness of English with the numerous synonyms, near-synonyms and different ways of saying things allows us to be precise if we avoid being complacent. We can, for example, choose the English *ask*, or the French-derived *question*, or the Latin-derived *interrogate*, to indicate different usages: ordinary, more formal and more restricted (e.g. professional). We can choose between *freedom* and *liberty*, *answerable* and *responsible*, *lively* and *animated*, depending on the context.

Use a thesaurus if you can't think of the precise word you want. Then you will say *cajole* rather than 'persuade by flattery or deceit', *hagiography* rather than 'writing about the lives of the saints', a *scowl* for an 'expression of extreme displeasure', a *sycophant* for a 'toadying hanger-on'. If you're trying to remember the word that means the church caretaker and gravedigger but can't think of a synonym the thesaurus and a straightforward dictionary won't be much use. Your answer is in the *Oxford Reverse Dictionary*: *sexton*, to be found among the numerous terms under the headword 'church'.

Clear and correct

That wealth of choices in English, however, brings its dangers. It's easy to go wrong with punctuation, spelling, grammar, usage, connotations and registers. A comma missing from a steak flambé recipe can result in a house on fire. Computer spellchecks and grammarchecks are limited. Don't expect a spellcheck to correct 'She combed her hare into two plates'. A common grammar mistake is the misplaced participle: 'Taking the baby into her arms, the bus was boarded with difficulty' (say 'she boarded'). The trouble with the muscular modern sentence is that it can become muscle-bound. To avoid heavy subsidiary clauses, economic phrases can be overburdened and fail to connect, as in 'An avid theatregoer, she became one of the country's top biologists'.

Usage can vary with different constructions. A sign in the window of an Indian restaurant said: 'Once you've eaten here, you'll recommend others'. A chemist sign said, 'We dispense with accuracy'. The ambiguity pointed out, the chemist changed it to 'We don't dispense with accuracy'. The difference in meaning given to a verb when a preposition is added is a source of many traps.

Words change their connotations according to the company they keep. You'll believe in a plausible theory but not in a plausible rogue. Admissible means worth considering in general parlance but when given the law register admissible evidence is much more specific: evidence that can be presented in court.

BE SIMPLE AND CONCISE

The second last paragraph of the draft of an article of mine on human rights needed attention:

> Who doesn't believe in human rights? They are, as the Universal Declaration of Human Rights of the United Nations proclaims, the foundation of freedom, justice and peace in the world. Amnesty concentrates on

a clear, simple programme. It works for the release of prisoners of conscience, who have been deprived of liberty for political or religious beliefs,
and who have not used or supported violence. Early and fair trials for all
prisoners are demanded. And the death penalty, torture, and any cruel or
degrading treatment are opposed in all circumstances.

Note how the rewrite improved the paragraph following the above principles:

In theory, who doesn't believe in human rights? Are they not the foundation of freedom, justice and peace in the world? That's how the United
Nations puts it, in the Universal Declaration of Human Rights. Amnesty
concentrates on working for the release of prisoners of conscience – those
deprived of liberty for political or religious beliefs who have not used or
supported violence. Amnesty demands early and fair trials for all prisoners, and it opposes the death penalty, torture, and any cruel or degrading
treatment, in all circumstances.

Simplicity, directness and the resulting clarity will result from:

1 Keeping to the same subject as far as possible. Don't change the subject
  too often.
2 Putting the meaning where possible into active verbs rather than in passive
  ones or in abstract nouns.
3 Keeping subject and verb near each other.

When editing your piece, also look for:

1 The irrelevant, the digressions, the self-indulgent writing that you're proud
  of ('murder your darlings').
2 The superfluous modifiers.
3 Circumlocutions and tautologies.

Examples

1 Your 800-word travel piece about the delights of Viennese restaurants today
  has 200 words on Mozart's eating habits. You found some fascinating material on the subject during your research. Cut the paragraphs out or reduce to
  a couple of sentences. You may find another place for the material.
2 Superfluous adverbs can hamper a verb's performance. 'Predictably, his
  failure to put in the effort needed caused him to fail' and 'Basically,
  I criticized the council's handling of the problem' try with those adverbs to
  be extra thoughtful. A second thought would have removed them, and also
  these – *quite* perfect, *actually quite* perfect, *totally* ridiculous, and so on.

Superfluous adjectives likewise: 'the true facts', 'an acute crisis', 'the prerequisite conditions', 'under active consideration'. Instead of adding impact these undervalue the nouns. The following earn their keep: 'a damaging lie', 'a lamentable conclusion', 'the hidden facts'.

Put the meaning into the verbs and take your story forward more quickly. Use:

> *stagger*, *lurch* or *wobble* rather than 'walk with an unsteady gait'
> *condemn* rather than 'expressed complete disapproval of'
> *alluded to* rather than 'made an allusion to'
> *ignored* rather than 'paid no attention to'

3 Circumlocutions – talking round the subject – can similarly be avoided by finding the right word. Use:

> *ruined* rather than 'in a ruined condition'
> *except* rather than 'with the exception of'
> *in adult education* rather than 'in adult education situations'.

Use short words rather than long, if they mean the same thing: why say 'implement' if you mean *do*? Prefer *buy* to 'purchase', *live* to 'reside', *only* to 'exclusively'.

Tautology is unnecessary repetition. 'The row of camels had disappeared' is enough, without 'from view'.

The popular papers have no space to be wordy. Positive active verbs achieve conciseness in this story from *The Star*:

> A hero was blasted to death when he tackled an armed robber yesterday. The middle-aged partner in a mortgage brokers challenged the raider when he demanded cash. A scuffle broke out, a shot was fired and Christopher Nugent fell dying in a pool of his own blood.
>
> Mr Nugent tackled the gunman in his offices in Mildenhall, Suffolk, after being alerted by a terrified assistant.
>
> After the shooting the man raced from the offices and leapt into a waiting car which sped off ...

Such action-packed prose works well if the story is short. The hunt for synonyms – for, say, 'moving fast', 'fled', 'whisked', 'swooped' – can become frenetic in longer pieces and then they become popular paper clichés. (See below.)

Sentences average 18 to 20 words in the popular papers. In the qualities they can grow longer, but simplicity is maintained by the same basic structure of subject, verb, object, as in this *Guardian* intro:

> Saddam Hussein is reputed to be a big Shakespeare fan. He particularly likes *The Taming of the Shrew* and, more oddly, *Romeo and Juliet*. For some reason, the ex-dictator believes the tale of the star-crossed lovers teaches children obedience to nation and family.

PREFER THE FAMILIAR WORD TO THE UNFAMILIAR

The commonest kinds of unfamiliar language are foreign words and jargon. Foreign borrowings that have become familiar, such as croquet, gringo (Spanish American for a foreigner, especially English-speaking) and milieu are usually printed without italics. The less familiar (foreignisms) are usually in italics: as with the French *a huis clos* (in private) and *mesalliance* (marriage with a person of a lower social position), the Spanish *manana* (literally tomorrow: in the indefinite future) and the German *Bildungsroman* (a novel dealing with a person's early life and development). The *Oxford Writers' Dictionary* gives general advice on such matters. To get right up to date, though, you may have to check with house style.

You may want to use a foreign borrowing, usually French, when there's no English equivalent. A review of a book about an Italian football club with rowdy fans in *The Sunday Times* refers to the author 'as if seized by some strange *nostalgie de la boue* bringing those fans to life'. The review doesn't explain that the French phrase means literally 'yearning for mud', in other words a desire for degradation and depravity, although the context makes it fairly clear. Somehow the French gets it just right while the English of it doesn't sound right at all. But you can't use such foreignisms downmarket.

You have to judge whether such words or phrases need translation, and your decision doesn't entirely depend on whether there are italics or not. A *Spectator* review of a book about courtesans (no italics needed) in *New Statesman* refers to a 'grisette', which has no italics but is nevertheless translated: 'a seamstress in poor, grey cotton'. In the same review the italicized *demi-mondaine* is not translated.

If there is a good English word or expression equivalent to your foreignism, the latter betrays pretentiousness. For *de haut en bas*, 'condescendingly' or 'patronizingly' will serve. *Weltmacht* makes you sound deeply cultivated, but (do you mind?) it only means world power. *The Spectator* especially and *New Statesman* and the Sunday qualities in the review pages are very fond of foreignisms.

Jargon is 'words or expressions used by a particular profession or group that are difficult for others to understand'. All the professions and occupations have their own jargon. Journalists who write about technology or science have to translate the jargon of the experts, and judge how much translation is required in a particular publication.

There is former slang that, emanating from Silicone Valley, used to signal high-tech credentials, such as *interface, user-friendly* and *input*. They are now as likely to be talking about sandwiches, and why not? *Read-only memory* can refer to a person who never learns anything.

Why jargon has almost become a dirty word is that it has invaded the language of some groups and turned it into gobbledygook, or something close to it. The piling up of abstract nouns is common in the pretentious kind of gobbledygook that *Private Eye* lampoons in its Pseuds' Corner. Many of the extracts are journalism – a piece, for example, about a young woman haunted by the shame of cooking badly says she is not alone:

> According to a new report, the fear of such a kitchen crisis can cause mental blocks, nausea, headaches and difficulty in breathing; all symptoms of a newly identified disorder dubbed kitchen performance anxiety syndrome.

Avoid 'environment phrases': a 'friendly, enthusiastic and cooperative working environment' is better known as an office.

Slang

Slang is informal language more common in speech than in writing. As long as you're sure that you are on the same wavelength as a well-defined audience, slang can be a lively way of addressing it. Its origins are generally among the low-life and rebellious, on the street. Much of it is vulgar. There's schoolboy slang and criminals' slang, and druggies' slang.

Like straightforward jargon slang can be a concise way of getting across the character of a person or a group, so it is sometimes needed when reviewing. A book review in *The Observer* refers to a novelist's style as 'ditsy' (with the quotes), adding that she 'manages to drive her six-in-hand at a cracking pace' by way of explaining the term. Jonathan Green's monumental

Dictionary of Jargon tells us that it meant 'wonderful' in the USA in the 1970s and then came to mean fussy, intricate, and then, 'esp. of women, scatterbrained'. Not fair, is it?

You have to use it in the right context, or it's pretentious, and unless it's vital for your purpose, and needs explaining, you shouldn't have to explain it.

There's slang that lasts because it's vivid or funny. 'To have a guest in the attic' means to be insane. 'Hang someone out to dry', 'sailing close to the wind' and 'letting your hair down': can't do without, or becoming clichés? – you decide. Slang has to be used in moderation and mainly in conversation. You risk ridicule if you overdo it in your writing and rejection if you don't keep up with what's in and what's out and what changed in meaning.

A *Loaded* feature about playing elephant polo in India which required the writer Graham Wray and photographer Dan White to hole up in a five-star hotel mixes their twenty-something argot with that of the more posh variety typical of the Raj:

> As luck would have it, the previous guests in our particular room had been Kate Moss and Christy Turlington, who'd been here on a fashion shoot. A quick recce under the bed for any misplaced scanties proved fruitless so, free from other distractions, we immediately hit the bar. Two hours on the juice and we're all getting along spiffingly. The aforementioned Gurkha officer even seems like a decent sort. Turns out his son reads *Loaded*. 'Yah, bloody good mag. Got some balls. Not my sort of malarkey, you understand. Young person's caper.' Turns out it's his birthday, so we duly get the champers in. Two glasses later and the old boy's completely plastered.

USE THE CONCRETE RATHER THAN THE ABSTRACT

That means bringing people into it rather than theorizing, being specific as well as general, giving figures as well as facts. We've already mentioned the need to ask those basic reporting questions when exploring any subject: who, what, where, when, why and how.

Picturesqueness and memorability are achieved by leaving the reader thought-provoked or wiser or happier. Few features can do this if they don't relate to people in some way. Photographic or graphic illustrations, case studies, anecdotes, quotations or quotes, as we've seen, will help to do this.

Social problems, the tragedies of war, the triumphs to inspire have little impact for most readers in the form of abstract exposition and argument.

The mind can be well engaged by an essay, but emotional involvement is needed if the newspaper or magazine reader's attention is to be captured. There must be a protagonist or victim to identify with or sympathize with. The plight of the civilian victims of the war against Iraq was iconized by stories of such victims as the 12-year-old boy who lost both his arms.

Laurie Lee, travelling in Spain, assails us through all the five senses. Here is a sample, from *As I Walked Out One Midsummer Morning*:

> In the village square I came on a great studded door bearing the sign: 'Posada de Nuestra Senora'. I pushed the door open and entered a whitewashed courtyard hanging with geraniums and crowded with mules and asses. There was bedlam in the courtyard – mules stamping, asses braying, chickens cackling and children fighting. A fat old crone, crouching by the fire in the corner, was stirring soup in a large black cauldron, and as she seemed to be in charge, I went up to her and asked for food. Without a word she lifted a ladleful of the soup and held it to my mouth. I tasted and choked: it was hot, strong and acrid with smoke and herbs. The old lady peered at me sharply through the fumes of the fire. She was bent, leather-skinned, bearded and fanged, and looked like a watchful moose.

We feel we are there, and the effect is assured by the pattern made by the shifting viewpoint as the author walks, from general picture (whitewashed courtyard) to particular detail (bearded and fanged woman).

Make sure your metaphors are still alive. 'Neither cast your pearls before swine' was brilliant when St Matthew first came out with it, but that was a long time ago. You can still use it, with attribution, as I have, or you might find a context where using it without quotes will be apt, assuming your readers will know its origin; in this way you can use any famous quotation.

Learn how to use figurative language from the great satirists, from Voltaire and Swift (who suggested various ways children could be cooked in Ireland as part of the solution to famine there) to today's disciples. Irony is their sharpest weapon.

AVOID CLICHÉS

An occasional cliché has its place, like waving to someone as you turn the corner of the street.

Many clichés are metaphors that are in their last stages of life, or that died some time ago. 'Grist to the mill', 'ring the changes on', 'no stone unturned', 'play into the hands of' and 'keen as mustard' have not yet been buried. They are so easy to slot into any story. To ring the changes on such expressions, you have to be as keen as mustard and leave no stone unturned in the effort, otherwise you're playing into the hands of … I'm sorry, I've lost the track.…

The particular clichés that journalists are prone to are designated journalese and reporters offend more often than feature writers. They generally have less space and less time to produce, so more excuse. The report of a house on fire in a local paper uses the clichés of the popular nationals and can be a template for the tyro reporter.

It might go something like this:

> A family of six cheated death by minutes as a fierce blaze roared through their semi in leafy Laburnum Avenue yesterday. Horrified neighbours looked on shocked and helpless as the house was gutted.

> While police probe the origins of the fire, neighbours lauded John and Mandy, the fearless dad and mum-to-be. They had snatched their tots, aged between two and seven, out of their beds and through the flames.

> The grief-stricken family are now housed with relatives in nearby Middenminster. In a bid to stem the increase of fires in the area, the overstretched fire service is to launch a recruiting campaign. The tragedy has alerted the town to the need for a major rethink about fire precautions and for radical and far-reaching solutions.

Those buzz words of the popular press – 'blast', 'probe', 'snatched', 'bid', 'stem' and so on – were seized for catchy headlines and then infiltrated the texts underneath where more restraint is required. The sort of report given above may well be exaggerated, given more drama and colour than it deserves, because there are a few other papers covering the area to compete with.

'Radical and far-reaching solutions' is the sort of phrase you might find in any report or feature, especially when no space has been found to work out what the solutions might be. Meanwhile, upmarket 'phenomenon', 'inexorably' and 'parameters' are being done to death, while misfortunes, presumably, will come in 'a rash' and demands will come in 'choruses' for some time to come. Events often come 'in waves' and 'trends', profits or losses 'rocketing' or 'plummeting', and numerous expectations and anxieties are usually 'increasing'. There is the same need to upstage competitors.

You can extract humour by sending up clichés and jargon, as *Private Eye* does in its Clichewatch section. Under the heading 'The Neophiliacs' we were given samples from mainly national papers:

> Cricket's mass-marketing is long overdue. The premise that the sport of gentlemen can become the new rock 'n' roll is entirely plausible.
>
> Art ... the new rock 'n' roll.
>
> Nigella has made cooking the new sex.
>
> The trendsetters were all drinking vodka mixed with fizzy pop or cranberry juice ... Cranberry is the new black.
>
> Staying in seems to be the new going out.
>
> Geometric prints may be the new black for the fashionistas of Paris, but May is the new August for French workers.
>
> Going out is the new going out.
>
> Fashion: Small is the New Big.

BE POSITIVE AND HONEST

To keep your readers you've got to have colour of some kind, even for the most factual piece. If there's no drama in your theme you look for some degree of significance to make it rise above the ordinary. That's what journalism is all about. You cannot merely list the facts, you've got to find the story in them, and that word 'story' suggests what the dangers are.

You're going to make your piece as interesting as possible. It's a well-established convention, and you have to assume that your readers will go along with it. But there is a line to draw. The fire report was an example of how you can overstep the line and such exaggerations can easily be recognized for what they are.

The following examples of being economical with the truth (forgive me) are more subtle and are of two kinds:

1 Implying more significance than is warranted by the facts, as in buzz words and fuzz words (tenuous links).
2 Evading facts that embarrass, as in euphemisms and political correctness.

Buzz and fuzz

We've already hit on buzz words above. They are clichés, but of the special kind called journalese or hackery, so they get another mention here. The qualities share some of the populars' monosyllabic buzz words: politicians 'rise and fall' and there are 'splits' and 'spins'.

Qualities have their own species of journalese. Such phrases as 'growing concern', 'growing speculation' and 'sources close to the Prime Minister' are needed when the civil servant or press secretary or whistleblower doesn't want to be identified. These are acceptable as long as the reader is not being given spurious rumour dressed up as fact. Nicholas Bagnall's *Newspaper Language* covers this subject fairly extensively.

'Fuzz' is when you imply linkage between facts and events when there is no link, or at best a tenuous one. It is understandable: how otherwise do you make a pattern, shape a story, out of the avalanche of events? Matthew Parris, as political sketch writer for *The Times*, once spelt out how this works (especially in writing about politics):

> The simplest way is to state a chronological relationship between events, and to imply by this a causal one *but without stating it*. 'After a series of embarrassing attacks on his leadership, Tony Blair yesterday sought to regain the initiative in a speech ...'

Parris points out that the words 'after', 'series', 'embarrassing' and 'regain' suggest links that may not exist. He ends by conceding that a political journalist probably has to use these devices but that readers should be aware of them.

Euphemisms and political correctness

Euphemisms are expressions that use mild or less direct words when referring to something unpleasant or embarrassing. They can be harmless and can raise a smile. English, naturally enough, is full of them. We're aware of the fact and send ourselves up by coining funny ones, such as 'follically challenged' for bald, 'altitudinally challenged' for short, and 'orthographically challenged' for 'can't spell'.

Most euphemisms are straight-faced, at least at the producer end. Many have been born as US spacespeak, where 'a benign environment' means safe, 'a dynamic environment' means dangerous and 'latch integrity' means the door's shut. Well they did anyway.

Some euphemisms, though, can be sinister, calculated to deceive, and can degenerate into gobbledygook. As Mark Twain said, 'to a man with a hammer everything looks like a nail'. In 1987 Israel authorized the use of 'moderate physical pressure', which covered shaking, cold showers and sleep deprivation 'in exceptional circumstances'. In 1999 an Israeli human rights group successfully challenged in court the way the General Security Services interpreted this authorization. It was found that 85 per cent of Arabs arrested each year were given the treatment, including many never charged with a crime. Ten detainees had died from the mistreatment.

Such is the power of the euphemism. More recently Guantanamo Bay and the Blair War Cabinet have spawned a few more. There are sinister euphemisms among stock phrases – attempts to prevent other people from worrying too much – such as 'pacification', 'population control' and so on. Apparently 'collateral counterforce damage of second strike capability' means 70 million dead. Note that string of foggy nouns again.

A lie can be called 'an inoperative statement' (USA) or 'an economical use of truth' (Britain). More tongue-in-cheek, no doubt, an American journalist asked about a call-girl who slept with diplomats: 'Did she horizontalize her way to the information?' Are 'horizontalization' and 'horizontalizationize' on their way?

Political correctness (PC) is the kind of euphemism that attempts to avoid upsetting people by language that might sound discriminatory. Often one welcomes a reminder of what the PC term is, so: disabled please (not 'crippled', to which the dictionary gives the registers *archaic* or *offensive*), Down syndrome (not 'Mongoloid', *offensive*); these are a matter of good manners. It good to see off the racists by insisting on Blacks rather than 'nignogs'. Guidelines are set by local councils and other organizations, especially in the public sector.

The extensive litany of PC language, however, has gathered numerous weasel words and expressions designed to discourage thought. When workers become redundant the company can call it 'downsizing' and losses can be called 'negative profits'. Waste tips sound better as 'civic amenity centres'. Your disagreement with your company or your party policy can be politely ignored by labelling it 'partisan' or 'divisive' or 'inappropriate'.

Such devalued currency turns up everywhere. Fairy tales are rewritten in case the animals in them are upset. A script for Prokoviev's musical setting for *Peter and the Wolf* has the wolf being freed into the wild at the end instead of being put in a zoo. Exam authorities have planned to replace

F for Fail with N for Nearly, and crowd control is sometimes referred to as 'visitor flow management'.

Wrongs are not righted and lies may be allowed to breed by evasions. Sometimes you need to identify the perpetrators by being offensive.

Sexist language has largely been replaced. 'Man's achievements' has become 'human achievements' and so on. But to replace the old tendency to use male nouns and pronouns, when the content refers to both sexes, with female nouns and pronouns seems to me to be absurd. Example: 'If a client complains, she is immediately listened to.'

There are better solutions:

'If a client complains, they are ...' ('they' used as a singular, non-specific sex)
'If clients ... they are ...'
'If a client ..., immediate attention is given ...'

WRITE AS YOU SPEAK

Well, not exactly. You've no doubt taped interviews, and you've watched and listened to live broadcasts. You wouldn't want to put all those 'ers' and 'ums' into writing, or the repetitions, hesitations and infelicities. A piece of writing is expected to be in much better order than your normal conversation and with the qualities outlined above. But the injunction to write as you speak warns you to write as naturally as possible and to avoid, in particular, egotism, pomposity, preachiness and ostentation. Avoid this sort of thing:

I was idly noticing the negligible effect of the *adan* upon the occupants of the neighbouring shops when suddenly my errant attention became arrested. A mendicant of unwholesome aspect crouched in the shadow of the narrow gateway.

So begins a story about Egypt. If you carry on like that you'll be arrested too.

No doubt the people you talk to put a damper on any egotistic tendency you may have. It's all too easy for the tendency to reappear when you write: there's nobody staying your hand. A feature based on personal experience may require you to be the protagonist, but don't assume every one of your thoughts and actions are of interest to your readers because they interest you. Keep the first person to the minimum. How the army of personal columnists sustain interest (or try to) is the subject of another chapter.

Don't prefix what you want to say with pompous impersonal statements such as 'It's important to keep in mind that …' or 'it's not generally realized that …'. Avoid preaching. 'While the British public remains indifferent to the litter-infested streets, nothing will be done about it', presumably insults most of your readers. Include yourself in the complaint.

VARY YOUR PACE AND RHYTHM

However interesting your content, if your pace doesn't vary and your rhythm is monotonous you will lose your readers' attention. These variations should become instinctive. If you need help, study the features that 'read short' rather than long and work out how it's achieved.

Two suggestions:

1 Consider varying the pace as you switch from intro to body and again to ending. A brisk intro may be compelling. The body may need to slow down for description, explanation, argument, expansion with supporting material. Then, perhaps, the pace needs to speed up again as the article gets into the homeward stretch.
2 Vary the lengths and rhythms of words, sentences and paragraphs to reflect the variations in content and to avoid monotony. Occasionally reverse the normal orders. Put the subject at the end, use a few passives.

Here's a paragraph with variations, from an *Observer* column by Francis Wheen, having fun with the sociological stereotype of Middle England which spawned acres of newsprint in the mid 1990s. He has been running, for some years, he says, a little known seat of learning … Formerly the Central English Poly, it now rejoices in the title of the University of Middle England.

> Our curriculum is small and carefully designed. Physics lessons stop well short of chaos theory (far too upsetting a concept for our sensitive undergraduates). In History, the only set books are those of Sir Arthur Bryant, though we do sometimes allow students to refer to Winston Churchill's *History of the English-Speaking Peoples*. The Philosophy course is built around the works of Patience Strong. No foreign languages are studied. To those who ask, 'What should they know of England that only England know?' we reply: quite enough, thank you. Our core subject, as you would expect, is English freed of the continental theory that so disfigures the discipline in other universities. The syllabus includes all the immortals of our native literature, with special papers on Sir Henry Newbolt (rake he in his

hammock till the great Armadas come/Capten, art tha sleepin there below?) and Sir John Betjeman. Our flourishing Dramatic Society performs one Shakespeare play and one Savoy Opera every term. We award only second-hand degrees, since our motto is 'Moderation in All Things'.

R. L. Stevenson, revered as a great stylist, said, 'I wonder if I shall ever learn to write.' You will find me guilty of some of the faults criticized in this chapter. That, of course, will help you to avoid them. Columnists often send up in their columns the lapses of their rivals, their colleagues, sometimes of themselves.

Making it final

Before your final version, put the latest draft of your article aside for an hour or two, or a day or two if you have the time. It will then be easier to read it with the eyes of an editor, freshly and objectively. Read it more than once, concentrating on particular aspects.

Checklist

1 Is the overall *purpose/theme/idea* and *audience* clear? (Why did you write the article? What did you hope to achieve by it? Was it effectively communicated to the readers you had in mind?) Did you digress confusingly from the original idea? Is it now too vague?
2 Is the *content* adequate for the purpose? Is it significant enough? Was some information inaccessible? Did you manage to replace it?
3 Does the *structure* match the idea and the content? Is there good, clear linkage? Does it pass the readability test for interest, directness, pace and linkage?
4 Is the *style* appropriate for the audience? Does it pass the readability test for interest, directness and pace?

ASSIGNMENTS

1 Rewrite the following sentences more clearly and concisely:
   (a) The government building is in a delapidated state, giving you the impression that the administration has reached a state that

could be described as seized up, that the city is in what might be described as death throes, and that the country hasn't really worked.

(b) A major contribution to the creation of ugliness in our towns today is the bad manners of people who leave their litter all over the place and decline to use the rubbish bins provided.

(c) The Palestinians say that the barrier has the effect of rendering it practically impossible to create an independent state on the grounds that the bulk of the Palestinian population will eventually be surrounded by it and half of the West Bank will effectively be annexed by it.

(d) The policyholders of Equitable Life, in their struggle to win £3 bn in compensation, believing that the government was responsible for the failure to regulate the insurer properly, entertained the hope that it would be put in the dock and called to account.

(e) (Rewrite more clearly as two sentences:)
By 11 September 2001 the *jihadis* (holy warriors), having established cooperation with local groups known to be extremists, who had begun to use the kidnapping tactics themselves to further political demands, were according to the reports of reliable sources using Yemen as a major base of operations, resulting most spectacularly in the sinking of an American warship in Aden harbour.

2 Rewrite a *Daily Telegraph* feature of 800 to 1000 words as a 300-word feature for *The Sun*.

3 Rewrite a *Daily Mirror* feature of 500 words as an 800-word feature for *The Independent*.

13 The style for the purpose

Every writer, by the way he [or she] uses the language, reveals something of his spirit, his habits, his capacities, his bias. (E. B. White, Strunk and White's *The Elements of Style*, Chapter 5)

We have identified several qualities that make up a writer's style in previous chapters: notably rhythm, pace and euphony. In this chapter we ask what sort of style is effective in description, narration, exposition and argument, by studying good examples. These may also reveal the less definable quality that will make the whole greater than the sum of the parts, and some of the writer's originality.

DESCRIBING MEMORABLY

Laurie Lee in Spain (page 208) reveals a poet's eye. Such descriptions, plunging the reader into the whole experience, depend on sharp observation and precise detail (which animals, what kind of food, what sort of old woman's face?) and the occasional figure of speech (like a watchful moose?).

When doing legwork, if you know that a description of a place or a person will be required, you will be wise to take plenty of notes, of measurements and other precise details. 'Big', 'fat', 'short', 'comfortable', 'beautiful' and suchlike adjectives are vague if you're trying to create a picture in the reader's mind. For a travel article you might use your camera to record sights you will want to describe as well as to take pics that may be used in illustration. You might use a tape recorder to remind you of interesting sounds as well as to record interviews. Don't get too absorbed with your equipment, though, or you'll forget to use your imagination and may miss the essence of what you're trying to capture.

Description typically moves from the general, or larger detail, to the particular, or smaller. Consider the difference between a scene described from a plane and a scene described from a train. Description for its own sake is out: the reader must see its purpose within the whole.

The modern newspaper or magazine article likes description that is meaty with facts and pacy. Here is Tony Parsons in an *Arena* article, 'Slaves of Milan', inside the cathedral:

> In the cool shadows inside, among the massive white columns and the infinite stained glass windows, Milanesi businessmen in their lunch hour kneel before the Madonna and child, make the signs of the cross and clasp their hands in prayer. One of them – wrapped up against February in a deep camel hair coat, squat and heavy bearded, like a company man Martin Scorsese – catches my eye. He looks like the archetypal hard-nosed, go-getting Milano corporate cowboy. The sight of him – with his head bowed, his lips muttering in supplication, not worried if he gets the knees of his million lire suit messed up – is strangely moving. After long minutes lost in prayer he eventually rises and checks his watch. Five past two. Time to get back to the office.

NARRATING COMPELLINGLY

That generally means sweeping the reader along, wanting to know what happened next, with short, vigorous sentences round meaningful, active verbs. Aidan Hartley in *The Spectator* ('Me Frodo, You Jane') tells how one of Dr Jane Goodall's chimp study groups in Tanzania murdered a child:

> The story begins on a morning in May. The wife and toddler son of Moshi Sadiqi, a park attendant, were collecting firewood in Gombe, on the shores of Lake Tanganyika. Like many staff families, they lived inside the park. The pair ventured into the rainforest. Frodo struck without warning. He swung out of the jungle, snatched up the boy and, as the distraught mother looked on, retreated into the trees. Here, Frodo flung his prey against the branches repeatedly, until the boy was as limp as a rag doll. The mother ran for help and park rangers rushed to the scene. Frodo had by this time disembowelled the boy and eaten part of his head.

Most of the description needed is supplied by the verbs – 'swung', 'snatched', 'disembowelled'.

When your story is expository narrative (history), you will be looking for devices that help you to leap through the years. Here are some in a feature by Kevin Roberts in *FHM* – 'Lockdown' – which told of the extraordinary power of cocaine traffickers in Rio de Janeiro:

> Aged just 34, Seaside Freddy has enjoyed a swift – and vicious – rise to become Brazil's cocaine kingpin. Born into the Rio ghetto, he started out as a slum-dwelling pot dealer and, through a mix of street smarts and ruthlessness, rose to become a major trafficker and the undisputed head of Red Command [a Rio gang with extensive national criminal influence] while still in his twenties. At his peak he was believed to be supplying more than two-thirds of all Brazil's cocaine – an estimated 30 tons a year. Arrested in 1996, he escaped and spent five years on the run. Finally, after a three-month manhunt involving thousands of troops, he was recaptured in the Colombian jungle in April 2001, when his plane was shot down by an air force fighter. Fleeing on foot, after losing two fingers in a gunfight with soldiers, Brazil's Public Enemy No. 1 was collared trying to sneak into Venezuela.

Note how the chronological order is sustained and the leaps economically achieved by the links starting each sentence: 'aged just 34', 'born into', 'at his peak', 'arrested in 1996', 'finally', 'fleeing on foot'. Note also how the sentences pack in the events of many years by the skilful use of adverbial clauses and participles to link up the actions of the verbs.

EXPLAINING FULLY

A great deal of all feature writing is exposition. Newspapers' background features put the daily news into perspective by explaining the significance of the facts. Such features may make forecasts, anticipate problems, suggest solutions.

Much of a foreign correspondent's work is putting into perspective the events of the country reported from, making sure that everything that needs explaining – customs, ethnic balance, the governing system – is explained clearly.

How-to features are legion: gardening, cookery, fashion, DIY, lifestyle, etc. Such a straightforward how-to piece as following a recipe is not as easy to get right as it looks. It is easy to forget to say what you do with a particular ingredient, and putting the instructions in the best order requires careful thought if disaster is to be avoided.

In India they have both class (inherited from British colonials) and caste. In *New Internationalist*'s Equality issue of January/February 2004, Mari

Marcel Thekaekara explored these 'evil twins' from an Indian perspective. After a mention of the only class-free society of indigenous or *adivasi* people, we get two paragraphs explaining the origins of the caste system:

> Then came caste, a system devised by Machiavellian minds to keep an entire sub-group in bondage forever. Caste was invented by the Hindu Brahmin or priestly group some 2000 years ago. They took what were essentially divisions of labour and dictated that everyone had a predestined, preordained station in life. To ensure that the diktat was obeyed, they created an elaborate religious system which insisted that your birth in this life was directly related to your sins or good deeds in the last one. Hence everyone had to accept this rigid system which controlled society and totally prohibited social mobility.
>
> Knowledge was closely controlled by the Brahmins. Disobedience could mean death or worse. For example Manu, the Hindu lawgiver who codified a great deal of caste-dictated social behaviour into rigid laws, decreed that 'a Dahlit' (person below or outside the caste system) who listened to the chanting of the *Vedas* (holy texts) should have molten lead poured into his ears. (*New Internationalist*, www.newint.org)

The tone is reassuringly calm and without ornament. Every word of an exposition should indicate authority. You show that you know your subject, that you have studied it thoroughly and are experienced. If you leave something out because you are unsure about it, the reader will sense that there's a gap.

The extract has the essential qualities of good expository writing: comprehensiveness (as far as it goes), logical order and, as always, clarity. The key techniques to achieve these are:

Analysis

First you see what the elements of your subject are. You divide and subdivide, and then decide in which order what you have to say will best be understood by the reader. Thus the material of books like this is divided into chapters, headings and sub-headings.

Definition

Above, 'caste', 'Dahlit' and *Vedas* had to be defined. Obvious enough. Special care needs to be taken with words that have more than one field or register. It's probably clear when you're referring to a geological depression and not a psychological one. But many legal terms, like 'plead', 'contempt' and 'prejudice', have different meanings outside the law and you may have to point out which field you're in. You use 'cool' in a mention of an open-air concert: do you mean it was successful or that you should have taken a woolly? By 'homeless' do you mean staying with Mum between selling and moving to your new house, or do you mean sleeping rough?

A feature about the effects of divorce on children would need to make it clear by definition what the difference is between care and custody, and we're now talking legal again.

From abstract to concrete

Again (see Chapter 12), you use analogy, illustration, examples, anecdotes and figures to help you explain.

ARGUING CONVINCINGLY

You are engaged in a debate about the Holocaust and Mr A says, 'All right, there were concentration camps, and reportedly, a number of Jews and other unfortunates were exterminated, but six million is just propaganda'. You might try to move the argument forward by asking:

What do you mean by *reportedly*?

How many people do you think were exterminated?

I don't think you'll get satisfactory answers. First because the evidence is against Mr A. Sorry, no space to elaborate here. As a reminder though: to be convincing, arguments must be backed up by good evidence, facts or figures, or both. Keep in mind the gap between the facts and the truth that faces the deadline-pressured journalist, the problems that can make verification difficult and the limitations of different kinds of sources, matters that are spelt out in Chapter 8.

Second, Mr A doesn't convince because his language (*reportedly ... just*) doesn't inspire confidence. To argue convincingly means leaving no doubt about what you mean by your language. Your language has determined how clearly you're thinking as well as how clearly you're expressing yourself.

Defining your terms is crucial, and not only your own terms but those technical terms or jargon that you're confronted with by your subject.

A *Reader's Digest* feature, 'Outrageous! Now We Can't Defend Ourselves Against Burglars' (March 2003) by Alan Judd has at its core what exactly the Crown Prosecution Service means by allowing the use of 'reasonable force' to defend ourselves. Judd cites similar cases of killing or seriously injuring intruders into family homes, where it is hard to see why some defenders were prosecuted and some not.

The feature follows a classical structure of argument. It starts by getting the reader emotionally involved. Two burglaries are described in which householders were injured yet refrained from fighting back and had long waits for the police. We then get the For and Against arguments, concluding with the view that the emphasis of the law needs to be changed.

Judd wants 'a shift of emphasis for the courts to make it clear that there's a strong presumption against prosecuting any householder who injures an intruder'. He counters the anti-gun argument by noting that in the US 'where the law is more robustly on the side of the victim the rate of burglary is less than half of ours'. (No comparisons are made about the rates of murders in the two countries but we'll leave that aside.)

Emotion comes into the discussion again. As well as the phrase 'reasonable force' leading to confusion it is also 'a question of attitude … Increasingly, our legal and judicial officials seem more concerned with covering their own backs in this rights-based culture, turning victims into perpetrators and perpetrators into victims'.

Emotion used appropriately is needed to persuade. It helps you to get past readers' indifference, to encourage an attitude or mood, to make readers receptive. But reason must be in control. Emotion used dishonestly or carelessly can lead to the following common flaws in argument:

Emotionally weighted language

An often used illustration of emotionally weighted language that prevents us from thinking objectively (or from trying to) is: 'I am firm, you are obstinate, he is pig-headed.' Such terms are called 'witch words': they may be used either cunningly or unconsciously (by the prejudiced). 'Freedom fighter' or 'terrorist', 'staunch Conservative' or 'hidebound Tory', 'unemployed' or 'work-shy': whose side are you on?

Non-sequiturs

'More children in this country are becoming obese. The main reason is that they're eating the wrong kind of food.' There are too many other reasons to be sure that's the main reason.

Begging the question

'More police on the streets will reduce crime.' You assume to be true what you're supposed to be proving. The crime might go somewhere else.

Sweeping generalization (or bias)

'The Labour Party are purely interested in getting elected.'

'The Conservatives are only interested in ensuring that the rich stay rich.'

In practice such faults appear in more subtle statements and are not so easy to avoid.

Essays, think pieces and polemics

The Op Ed (opposite the editorial or leader) pages of the national papers, the political weeklies and a few journals offer homes for features referred to as 'think pieces'. They are journalistic essays, and may be designated as such. Some take up controversial topics of the moment and express a personal viewpoint that can vary from the publication's stance. The style may approach that of the deliberately provocative pundits who use their personal columns to stir up debate, but they are more respectful, on the whole, of their content. They may give the email address of the author or publication to encourage readers to respond.

Here are some typical examples, starting with Op Eds plus standfirsts:

'Stress' by Angela Patmore (*Daily Mail*, 2 March 2004). 'For most it's utterly bogus. What's more, treatment can make it worse.'

'The uncomfortable truth about Putin' by Mary Dejevsky (*The Independent*, 11 March 2004). 'On every single count, Russia is a better place for more people now than it was.'

'Never forget, Prime Minister, that Parliament is sovereign' (*The Daily Telegraph*, 11 March 2004). 'Thomas Strathclyde [Lord Strathclyde, Leader of the Opposition in the House of Lords] says the Government will suffer if it tries to break its word on Lords reform.'

'Drug tests need more muscle' by Christopher Caldwell (*Financial Times*, 6/7 March, 2004). 'There are doping scandals at the highest level of sport in several countries.'

'A grotesque choice' by Max Hastings (*The Guardian*, 11 March 2004). 'Israel's repression of the Palestinian people is fuelling a resurgence of anti-semitism.'

'The outlook is prosperous if only the stranglehold of regulation can be eased' by Anatole Kaletsky (*The Times*, 11 March 2004). Anticipating the Budget of the following week.

Some magazine samples:

'A private affair' by Rachel Johnson (*Spectator*, 6 July 2002). 'The amazing ubiquity of private education.'

'Off their pedestals' by Alain de Botton, a 'Books Essay' (*FT Magazine*, 6 March 2004). 'The novel allows us to reject the standard lens through which people's status in society is viewed.'

Among publications offering high level debate are:

'Those I have loved and loathed' by Keith Waterhouse (the quarterly *British Journalism Review*, Number 1, 2004 and reprinted in *Press Gazette*, 5 March 2004). Voted best contemporary columnist by the readers of the journal, Waterhouse discusses what makes a good columnist.

'Which civilization?' by Michael Lind (*Prospect*, the monthly magazine for the thinking classes, 'Politics, Essays, Argument', November 2001). 'The idea of a liberal "west", standing against fundamentalism, is a fallacy. Secular humanism is threatened by American as well as Islamic militants.'

Philosophy Now (bimonthly 'magazine of ideas') collects several essays in each issue under a heading such as 'Philosophy and Sport', May/June 2003. More on this in Chapter 16.

FINDING YOUR OWN STYLE

Your own style must develop naturally out of who you are and what you're interested in. It's integral to your outlook on life and comes from inside.

It's your tone of voice. You can develop your own style as you go and if it has some originality, some distinction, editors will detect and value it. Extracts without attribution from feature writers with inimitable styles (the great columnists being obvious examples) can be recognized just as great novelists can. Meanwhile, you must let your style develop (improve?) naturally: you don't consciously cultivate a tone of voice. Here are some guidelines worth considering.

1 Content must almost always come first, however recognizable your writing is. Don't get too personal. Use the impersonal 'you' rather than the personal 'have you ever locked yourself out of your house?' Edit your features rigorously and complement this with feedback to weed out where you're too self-absorbed.

2 Get on your readers' wavelength so as to avoid (a) overestimating or (b) underestimating them:
   (a) You may be knowledgeable about how chromosomes work and it may be an aspect of your subject. You'll have to explain it without talking down (unless you're writing for *Lancet* or suchlike). If you're not sure how much your readers know, you can say something like: 'The Parliamentary procedure, of course, is …'.
   (b) Few readers will need to be told what a café latte or a chicken en croute is.

3 Be natural. If your writing is based on the assumption that it's leaking wisdom or great humour and it isn't, you won't get past an editor. Avoid showing off in any form. Don't name-drop.

4 'Against the orange glow of the setting sun the towers of the council estate were sharply etched …'. So begins a newspaper feature. 'Sharply etched' – haven't you heard that somewhere before? Didn't you put that in a school essay more than once? Find fresh figurative language and use it sparingly.

5 Read the great originals and learn from them, the journalists as well as the novelists, playwrights and poets.

ASSIGNMENTS

1 Select a feature that you've written recently that has a subject of wide interest and rewrite the intro for three of the following publications:
   (a) *Daily Mirror*
   (b) *Daily Express*

(c) *Daily Telegraph*
(d) *Woman's Own*
(e) *Loaded*
(f) *GQ*
(g) *Cosmopolitan*
(h) *The Spectator*.

2 Select any place that you visit regularly or that you remember vividly that seems to you dangerous, or mysterious or eerie or otherwise memorable. It may be a building (disused warehouse/rundown pub) or a street or a square, or uncultivated land (a wood/marsh). Write four separate paragraphs of 150 words each under the headings:

(a) *Description*. Describe the place and its atmosphere without story or explanation. Use imagery, and all the senses.

(b) *Narration*. Make up a story about the place that fits the description.

(c) *Exposition*. Give factual evidence that explains the nature of the place (isolated?, vandals?, scene of a murder?, haunted?).

(d) *Argument*. The council have to decide to change the place in some way: repair it, destroy it, build on it ... Argue for a particular course of action in a letter to the local paper.

Exchange with fellow students to be subbed down to 100 words for each section.

3 Make notes as you watch someone doing some manual job or participating in a sport. Later, write a description of the way your subject operated. Then deduce as much as you can about the person's character/likely background.

14 Illustrating with impact

Of course, there will always be those who look at technique, who ask 'how', while others of a more curious nature will ask 'why'. Personally, I have always preferred inspiration to information. (Man Ray)

The end product [of magazine design] should be a fusion of words and visuals, a creation that is greater than the sum of the separate elements. (John Morrish, *Magazine Editing*)

Illustration to accompany features in newspapers and magazines means photographs, and that means black and white prints or colour transparencies. It also means non-photographic visual art: both kinds, as Morrish points out, are an applied discipline and not a form of fine art.

That visual art takes many forms: line drawings, sketches, cartoons, caricatures, old prints and engravings, charts, flowcharts, maps, tables, diagrams, graphs, computer graphics. It involves negotiations and briefing (of the experts), cover fee, rights, size of illustration to be delivered, the size it will be reproduced and the deadline.

As a freelance writer you have to decide when to offer illustrations with your features and whether it's worthwhile attempting to provide them yourself. Can you (or can you learn to) produce them to the level of competence required?

As a freelance writer, should you hire the services of a professional photographer or illustrator? Should you do some picture research and deal with picture libraries? (Working as a picture researcher for a publisher or picture library is a good way to start a career as a writer/photographer.) Should you try to obtain free pictures from the publicity departments of manufacturing or retail companies, or the press offices of institutions, agencies, charities and other non-profit-making organizations? If you're freelance and versatile it will be well worth your while exploring the possibilities of taking your own photographs. Raise your standards by taking courses, joining a camera club (a good place to pick up a second-hand camera) and subscribing to a photography magazine. Many magazine features are picture-led and welcome proposals more promptly if they see excellent pictures already obtained or can be assured that they will come with the package. You can sell your pictures over and over again to fit different pieces – it isn't usual to sell the copyright. If you build up a large stock of photographs you may want to do some photojournalism (communicating news by means of photographs) as a sideline, but that is outside our remit. It is also a good idea to take photos of places and objects you're writing about for the record, so that you can refer to them for exact details.

This chapter will help you decide in what ways and how far you want to be involved with illustration. We'll look at the market, the likely subjects, the equipment, the essential skills, the business aspects and the online possibilities.

ENTERING THE MARKET

The marketing guides will suggest likely publications for illustrated features. Try *Freelance Photographer* and *Willing's Press Guide*. Let's concentrate for the moment on photographs. Look for magazines that rely on freelances, even if they have photographers on the staff and a picture library.

Check on the way prospective publications use illustration. What kind of features, how much black and white and how much colour? Glossy or matt for B&W? Sharp focus? What influences the decisions? How closely allied to the text are a publication's pictures? How important is overall design?

When proposing your ideas give details of pictures available or promised. When a proposal is accepted, talk to the editor or art editor and get as much detailed briefing about the photography as you can. When you're established as a writer/illustrator ideas for pictures may come first and you will try them out on those picture-led publications.

RELEVANCE OR ART?

There are obvious places where the art, meaning high quality, of your photographs may be what sells them rather than their relevance, but most often it's relevance that editors look for first. Any photograph sold for publication should:

- have enough impact to make the reader want to read the feature
- engage the attention and emotions more firmly than the words themselves could achieve (a picture isn't always 'worth a thousand words' but it can try)
- help to tell the story; make the message clearer
- conform to the requirements of the publication as briefed – its policy for pictures, format, size and so on
- have high quality, which usually means sharp detail, though special artistic effects such as fuzziness or graininess may occasionally be appropriate.

SUBJECTS FOR YOUR PICTURES

The hundreds of subjects that travel provides? Of course, but the competition is fierce, and picture libraries are groaning under the loads of excellent material supplied by top photographers and writer/photographers. Editors may prefer to use those rather than commissioning you, even if you have a reasonable track record for pictures.

If you're building up that track record, start nearer home perhaps. Try to sell illustrated reports of local events that staff of local papers haven't time to cover. Try a few pieces on spec. Then there are the numerous how-to subjects, hobbies, oddities, people in pictures that tell a funny or dramatic story, arts and antiques, inn-signs, strange animal behaviour (you might need a zoom lens), and so on. These are well-worn subjects but still in demand by popular publications.

There are cliché shots that need to be avoided, unless used as background for a relevant scene: Sydney Harbour and Big Ben, for example. You'll be lucky to have accepted shots of crowded beaches, people lined up posing. Take them off guard, take a bullfighter in action, but there's a caveat: permission may be required (see below).

If you know a fair amount about the techniques the photography magazines have a regular demand for how-to-photograph features. You may be able to use again photographs that have illustrated various of your features for how-to examples: how to compose, how to use different lenses effectively, the use of flash, lighting tricks and so on.

Landscape, apparently easy, needs particular skills and preferably special equipment. You may be able to obtain free photographs of relevant scenery from tourist organizations in the UK and abroad that are of a much higher standard than you could produce. If the scenery is merely a background to interesting people or animals that may be another matter.

Whatever your subject, take many more than you need so that you can illustrate more than one project, offering a different selection to different editors, and so that you'll be prepared for future assignments that are similar. Take shots of different kinds so that editors can choose those that will add up to a good design: vertical, horizontal; distant, middle distance, close-up.

Getting permissions

It is good manners to ask permission from people if you intend to photograph them close up, making their faces recognizable. They may be delighted by the opportunity but they may need persuading – and in some tourist spots there are people who expect payment and make a living at it. Some American magazines (see *Writer's Market*) demand signed permissions from people you've photographed who have recognizable faces.

Some English plane-spotters took pictures at a Greek airport and ended up in a Greek jail, accused of spying. In many countries you need written permission before you photograph in art galleries, museums and archaeological sites. In the UK you need permission to photograph from the National Trust, English Heritage and other places that attract tourists.

Make sure you are on the same wavelength as your editor in the sphere of photographic ethics and legalities, a subject covered in Chapter 21.

CHOOSING YOUR EQUIPMENT

If photography is new to you start with a medium-priced camera, an inconspicuous, 35 mm SLR (single-lens reflex) – which means you see through the lens that takes the picture. It's a general-purpose lens quite adequate for most tasks. This will deliver 36 exposures and accommodate interchangeable lenses. You will be able to switch off the automatic functions and do your own adjusting of apertures, shutter speed and focusing.

Cheaper and less ambitious are the lightweight pocket-sized APS (Advanced Photo System) and the 35 mm compact. Both have automatic functions that produce good quality prints without need of any expertise.

It's probably best to start with automatic exposure and focusing and to avoid the expense of sophisticated, and often heavy, gadgetry. When your work justifies it, and you're getting more sophisticated yourself, wanting to experiment more, then is the time to add equipment. You will have much more scope to create different effects, to take several shots of the same subject with different exposures ('bracketing') for example, comparing the results.

A telephoto lens is useful for interviews, a flash gun if you do plenty of interiors, a tripod if you need plenty of 'mug shots'.

The basic technique

'Fill the frame' is the essential advice. The eye should not be distracted by much space or fuzziness around the target, so that the target makes a sharp image and it's clear at once what the picture is all about. Avoid any kind of distracting background such as fussy wallpaper.

To return to the question of having plenty of choice when you've finished shooting. Expanding on that, an illustrated feature generally needs three kinds of picture: long shot, medium and close. Take these shots from various viewpoints and angles, and you may want to vary the lighting too. Take plenty so that the edition will choose from the best. Figure 14.1 shows a clever choice of pictures to project a feature, with the page design in mind.

Digitally speaking

Increasingly publications are organized to receive digital photographs, and the prices of digital cameras are dropping rapidly. You need the computer programs to change the contents of the camera into something you can send an editor, and that's an extra skill to acquire.

Have a look at the digital photography magazines as well as the digital sections of the general photography magazines. A good website for beginners is Photoexpert, run by Epson (www.photoexpert.co.uk). This provides online tutorials, product reviews and practical advice on getting the best out of digital camera and printer.

Figure 14.1

How display techniques project a feature. Bold pictures are used in this *Sunday Times* travel page to offset a dominant advertisement. The byline is incorporated in the standfirst above the intro, and it is used to explain what the writer is doing. The big capital 'W' at the start of the article is typical of the 'stand-up drops' used decoratively in the paper's travel articles. With kind permission of *The Sunday Times*

Some of the advantages of digital are:

- You view your pictures immediately; you don't have to wait for film to be developed. If they're not right you can erase them and try again. That facility encourages you to experiment.
- It's easy to use pictures to record details of places/objects that you need to describe (see above), and you can build up your picture library online. You can file them under keywords and rapidly locate them.
- You can produce your own illustrations to enhance your website, and these will be of higher quality than any used by scanning photographs.
- There are computer programs that enable you to make all kinds of improvements to digital pictures.
- You can send your pictures along with your feature by email.

Some of the disadvantages are:

- For top quality, greater versatility with lenses and more film speeds, film cameras are best.
- Battery life in digital cameras can be short. This can be solved by using lithium-ion rechargeables.
- Because of 'shutter lag' (the delay in your picture being recorded) digitals are not good for action pictures.

Your choice clearly depends on your priorities.

WORKING WITH A PHOTOGRAPHER

You may prefer to work with a photographer. To find one you might try the press photographers of local publications, the names of photographers credited under their pictures in magazines, the classified adverts in photography magazines, photographers' associations, *Writers' and Artists' Yearbook* for photography agencies, or the *Publishers' Freelance Directory*.

You can arrange for article and photographs to be paid for separately. If the fee is for a package, work out a division with the photographer. Be wary. For speculative projects the photographer may expect a fee whether the feature sells or not. Make sure you're going to get what your editor will want. Ideally, work with a few photographers who can produce exactly what you want.

Photographers who work regularly with journalists can obviously be useful contacts. They will hear of feature requirements and let you know, or recommend you.

PICTURES FROM OTHER SOURCES

Once commissioned, you may prefer simply to pass on to the commissioning editor information about where to get pictures, and the questions of permissions, copyright and credits are taken out of your hands.

Free pictures can be obtained from tourist offices, PR companies and various organizations, including commercial companies, voluntary associations and research institutes. Museums and picture agencies normally charge a reproduction fee. BAPLA (The British Association of Picture Libraries and Agencies) will give advice. Check copyright and licensing agreements.

Digital photographs (images) can be obtained free online and sent directly to your editor. Multimedia companies supply cheap CD-ROMs that contain stocks of picture libraries that have been converted to digital format. If you have the necessary software you can view these pictures and copy those you want to send to your editor.

GRAPHICS

The simplest kind of flow diagrams, charts or maps to illustrate articles require little artistic skill. Use a pen with a fine nib, black ink and drawing paper. Line drawings should be made at about twice the size they will be reproduced. Leave out lettering: indicate it on an attached photocopy – the publication will get it set in type. If your artistic skill is as limited as mine, find a talented friend. If substantial skill is needed try the picture libraries or the *Publishers' Freelance Directory*. Figure 14.2, which illustrated a news feature in *Press Gazette* shows how computer graphics can come to your aid.

Your editor may employ an artist who will do the whole drawing to your rough sketch or specifications. Where precision is needed, the graphics must be done with great care – see the line drawings illustrating a how-to feature (Figure 19.2). Line drawings of the artistic kind – cartoons, caricatures and so on – aim at an immediate and powerful impact and must be done by experts. You can download maps and other graphics on CD-ROM from the Internet.

Figure 14.2
Graphics from *Press Gazette* (30 July 2004). With kind permission of John Rooney/*Press Gazette*

CAPTIONS

Captions anchor the pictures to the text. In photojournalism the captions *are* the text, in effect. Typically the caption is in the present tense: it describes what the picture is saying, the message. It doesn't, of course, merely describe the picture. That's obvious enough as stated but remember that if you're to write the caption you need to know if it's going to be cropped, and if so how exactly? Thus the final form of the caption normally is the concern of the subeditor. Subs and photographers may get together at the final stage of page design.

A caption normally adds something to the picture: it gives information that cannot be obtained from the picture alone, and may give needed explanation. It may have to answer some of those 'wh' questions, identifying people and places without stating the obvious. It can say which meaning out of many possible meanings will relate to the text. It can establish the required mood; it may amuse, entertain. It's a bridge between the title and the text – part of the teamwork of the various presentational elements.

Here are a few samples of captions to photographs:

1 *ENABLER social worker Gaye Petek at her office at Elele, an association that helps Muslim women in crisis.*

   Feature about the enforced use of Islamic headscarves in French schools (*Vanity Fair*).

233

2 *The Trojan war, as chronicled by Homer and depicted here by Jean Maublanc, is now examined in scientific detail by* Horizon.

The painting reproduced is a stirring entree to the documentary produced under the BBC2 TV *Horizon* rubric (*Radio Times*).

3 *Barbara and George Bush joking with fellow Texans Charlie Wilson and former governor Ann Richards.*

An edited extract from a book about congressman Charlie Wilson's support for the CIA-backed war of the Afghan mujahideen against the Soviet army. The names are in left to right order. That has to be spelt out if there are many names (*Financial Times Magazine*).

4 *Light at the end of the tunnel: the memorial to victims of 11 September may yet attract back the visitors.*

The New York memorial at night, festooned in lights. A feature by Jason Cowley in *New Statesman* of 22 April 2002 describes the slow recovery from the trauma of 11 September 2001.

5 *Cloistered gardens and Moorish architecture: the Hotel Babylon offers the ultimate in luxurious good taste – and a regime of salt-water baths and seaweed massages.*

The feature describes the unusual services of this luxurious hotel in southern Spain (*Sunday Times Magazine*).

THE BUSINESS ASPECTS

Illustrations can sell a feature so it's advisable to be well organized. Pictures can go astray, get stolen, be damaged. Be professional in the way you do your negotiating, processing, submitting, storing, and record keeping. Here are a few hints.

Negotiating

Since supplying photographs and graphics, either your own or from various sources, may entail much expense, make sure you have been commissioned for an illustrated feature, establish exactly what is wanted and what the fee will be for supplying them. Editors can assume the feature/pictures package is what is being discussed and may not offer a separate fee for pictures. You should make it clear that the copyright for your own pictures remains with you and that the fee is for one use. See the NUJ's *Freelance Handbook* for guidance on fees.

Processing

It is not usual to send illustrated features out on spec. Get a commission or a 'we'll look at it' first, and it's best to let an editor choose from your black and white contact prints those they like and to arrange for the publication to do the processing. If you're sending from a country where the developing is not of high quality, you may be asked to send a whole exposed roll of film to be developed by the publication.

If you do your own processing, note that B&W prints should be glossy, (usually) borderless, not less than 7 in. by 5 in. and at least as big as they will be reproduced, since quality diminishes with enlargement. Colour pictures must be sent as transparencies (35 mm is the usual size). Cardboard mounts are best, because you can write captions or caption numbers on them (see below). Plastic mounts with glass inserts run the risk of damage in transit.

Most writer-photographers, however, prefer to spend their time writing than processing, which can be time-consuming and costly. Some High Street chemists or developers may not produce the quality you need to reach, in which case find an established photography shop. There you'll get good professional advice as well.

Recording

As you take pictures, make notes on the subject matter, which will form the basis of your captions. These are sometimes best left to subeditors but your label, indicating subject and location, should give them help. Devise a number system for your illustrations, recording the date photographs were taken or graphics completed. For example, 0426 can refer to the 26th picture taken in 2004. You can then list details in a record book or typed list or database, where you can add such details as exact date taken, subject matter of picture, feature(s) which it illustrates (and perhaps the captions used for them).

Storing and submitting

Whether stored in file cabinets, three-ring binders or acid-free boxes, transparencies and negatives should be labelled with the photographer's name, phone number and subject/location. You may want to put this information on cardboard mounts of transparencies. Put 'copyright' (or the symbol) and your name, address and phone number on the back of your own photographs and drawings. Either type the information on self-adhesive labels, or labels stuck on with a rubber solution, or get a rubber stamp made with the details. Put captions for B&Ws on labels. Peel-off labels are useful for photos not your own.

Keep a record book or database separate from that used for features and keep a copy of every letter sent that refers to illustrations, and a record of every phone call made about illustrations, separate from those that referred to the features themselves. Remember that you may want to offer your illustrations over and over again. The records will stand you in good stead when returning to clients.

Find out what size of prints are wanted. Initially, submit copies rather than original illustrations to obtain approval. Send a proof sheet of B&Ws and a laser copy for transparencies or (if you have the computer program and a colour printer) produce your own copies. Send photocopies of graphics.

Once you've been given the go-ahead to send originals, send illustrative material in hard-backed envelopes. Transparencies should be sent in plastic presentation sheets, repeating copyright symbol, name and address. BAPLA supplies printed forms to send with transparencies, spelling out terms and conditions of your agreement with the publication. Send recorded delivery or registered. Valuable photographic material should be insured.

A NOMADIC CAREER

The following is the result of an exchange of emails with Natasha Babaian, who pursues a varied and sometimes adventurous career as a writer/ photographer in the USA (http://www.nomadcamera.com).

In her early thirties, Natasha Babaian has established a career as writer/ photographer/picture researcher. Born in New York City, she has dual American/British nationality and has divided much of her life between New York and London. At the time of writing she is based in Cape Cod, Massachusetts, but she is often on the road, and the road might be almost anywhere in the world. She graduated with a Bachelor of Fine Arts degree from the State University of New York at Purchase, where she majored in Photography.

She has produced illustrated features or photographs for various American newspapers and magazines, written pieces and supplied photographs for Berlitz travel books and Insight Guides, and has done the picture research for these books and for freelance writers.

She uses Canon A1 and Nikon F series SLR cameras. 'I usually shoot 35 mm colour slide film. At this time I have no plans to go digital and am happy shooting slides and negatives that I can scan for professional use when necessary. I don't use a lot of equipment – different lenses, tripod and so on. Since I specialize in travel photography and am often on the go, I try to carry a minimum of equipment and to keep things as simple as possible. I like the immediacy that the 35 mm offers, as compared with larger format cameras, which require more set-up time and bits and pieces.'

She thinks that a writer/photographer starting off would ideally be equipped with a laptop computer (preferably with a built-in CD burner) and a slide/print scanner of sufficient quality to make high-resolution images. 'The scanner is especially important for photographers who shoot negatives or slides rather than digital images. The ability to transmit images digitally (via email, disk or CD) to prospective clients with a minimum of fuss is very useful.' Beginners must keep in mind that competition is strong. 'To be noticed and remembered it really is important to present yourself and your work in the best possible light, and that means to be well organized with your storage and submission systems. Building a body of work and a client base takes time, patience, determination and professionalism.'

She finds that the Internet can provide useful technical advice and instruction, especially when she's off the beaten track, but in general prefers to use it for both picture and story research. 'Many picture libraries have their collections available for online viewing, which can save time and unnecessary travel. Of course the speed with which portals can open is problematic too – one too many clicks and you can get nonsense.'

Babaian's versatility has extended to working for TV film-makers Subtractive Media (director Dave Kennedy, writer Scott Norman Howe) in Wellfleet, Massachusetts, who were doing spoofs of old westerns. Figures 14.3 and 14.4 are examples of her work as a production stills photographer on the set of the film *Spaghetti Vision*. Figure 14.3 shows a hangman's rope in the foreground with a bandito in the background. Figure 14.4 has actor Eric Martinson as a bandito with writer/director Dave Kennedy holding the camera.

Figure 14.3 (left) and Figure 14.4 (above)
Photographer collaborating with a writer on a film set for *The Advocate*. Photographs by Natasha Babaian

'Heat, long days, intense light reflected off hot sand was a challenge,' says Babaian, 'but I enjoyed the work.'

ASSIGNMENTS

1 For any of your recent features use a camera to provide either three B&Ws or three colour prints. Supply appropriate captions. Copy the pictures and print out from your computer or photocopy them. Then devise a layout for a two- or three-page feature, cutting and pasting the text and pix.
2 As above, but cut out appropriate pix from magazines.
3 Take three magazines and study the captions. Improve six that you think need improving. Keep to the same length, within a word or two. Explain your rewordings.
4 Study the travel magazines and come up with ideas for three of them. It's not easy to come up with new ideas for this market, for obvious reasons. Remember to check back some way to ensure they haven't been done recently. One or two subjects that might be developed into good ideas (if they're not overdone) are as follows (there may be cities or countries where the subject might be fairly new):
   - lighthouses
   - children's museums
   - tree houses
   - resorts that cater for people with food allergies
   - the nation with the tallest/shortest/fattest (be careful), thinnest people.

II   Expanding your horizons

15   Writing publicity

I think God is groovy. He had a great publicity agent. (P. J. Proby, quoted in J. Green, *The Book of Rock Quotes*)

Think of the great variety of communications that business organizations produce. There are display adverts and advertising features placed in newspapers and magazines, sales letters, leaflets, 'fliers' (one-sheet mail-shots), brochures, instructional pamphlets, posters and management reports. Public Relations (PR) items in the form of press releases and feature articles are edited to their standards by the publications using them. There are also corporate videos and websites, and the various forms of broadcasting advertising.

The writing skills required for these communications are not often allied to business acumen and administrative ability. Business people need interpreters who can research a subject and know how to get the required message across compellingly to the targeted audience. A job for a journalist, in other words.

Journalists may move into the world of publicity at a point in their careers where there is little scope for promotion or when they find that they will be paid better. Their contacts will be highly valued and so will some of their experience – for example, of rewriting clumsy press releases.

They must, however, be prepared to learn new skills. Rather than one editor there are various groups to please: more than one executive within the employing company and within the client companies. That means a lot of compromises.

To adapt, the journalist-turned-publicity writer needs to develop a sharper focus on the audience too. Although journalists are used to having a definite age group/social class/professional group in their sights, a publicity writer will think of the 19-year-old daughter of a next-door neighbour if a young woman's perfume is being promoted, or a 60-year-old uncle if an insurance policy for those about to retire is the subject.

Surveys are often used to identify a market before the writing is thought about. The social grades scale of readership provided by the National Readership Survey (NRS) will indicate how to pitch the message. Publicity writing aimed at a trade journal, for example, will contain exactly the amount of technical jargon appropriate for that particular audience.

The writer may be asked to write several versions of a press release – about a motor car, for example – for different markets: middle-age upmarket, yuppies, technical, woman's, downmarket, and so on. Different media may be used for one campaign. Peak-hour TV may get the main message to as many people as possible, followed perhaps by adverts in the broadsheet papers, reshaped for the tabloids and then for selected magazines, highlighting the attractions of the message for each market.

This chapter suggests ways of obtaining training in publicity writing and work for the different kinds of organizations that supply it. We look at the main areas first: advertising, Public Relations and publicity as journalism (getting publicity by getting into the media). Then come hints on how to obtain publicity writing work and some guidance on special writing techniques.

ADVERTISING AND PR DEFINED

In a publicity campaign it can be hard to distinguish advertising from Public Relations (PR). Advertising is selling, PR is informing. But the informing is 'selling' an image as part of the process of selling products and services, or promoting a business (or ideas that will promote it). For convenience, let's call all this activity selling the product.

The official definitions will keep us on the right track. Advertising, according to the Institute of Practitioners in Advertising, 'presents the most persuasive possible selling message to the right prospects for the product or service at the lowest possible cost'. Less kindly, Stephen Leacock said it was 'the science of arresting the human intelligence long enough to get money from it'. PR, as defined by the British Institute of Public Relations, is 'the deliberate, planned and sustained effort to establish and maintain mutual understanding between an organization and its public'.

As an example of the former, let's have a look at advertising copywriting.

Subject and market research

Whether it's advertising or PR work the publicity writer needs to do the subject and market research that journalists do, and often much more. The industry or activity being written about must be studied. That means accessing the right publications and Internet sources. It may also mean visiting trade fairs or factories and interviewing industrialists, managers, workers.

To get an advert or a press release or a promotional feature into a publication the writer needs to research the target publications. What sort of content does it want, what sort of readers does it have? Get media kits from them and study the editorial calendars.

ADVERTISING COPYWRITING

An advertising agency invited to apply to a client for a commission presents, after some research, a 'strategy'. This identifies the audience aimed at, media that will provide access to that audience (target publications, etc.), general approach, expenses (for example, any survey that will be needed) and an estimate of fees. It's a sophisticated form of the journalist's query letter, and it ensures that agency and client are on the same wavelength.

Copywriting means providing the words for advertising, whatever form it takes, but it is most readily identified with the most traditional form – display adverts in newspapers and magazines.

What an advert must do is clear enough. It must grab the reader's attention, arouse desire (or stimulate interest in the proposition), sustain interest, provoke to action (buy something or perhaps fill up a coupon) or make the reader remember the name. To do these things, because space is expensive, words must be used with great economy.

Slogans for compression

Great economy encourages experimenting with the various compression devices found in newspaper and magazine headlines. Alliteration, rhymes, puns, catchphrases, references to song or film titles are among the devices.

For a poster or full-page advert a slogan with a picture is enough. Here are some old ones, a few of which survive or resound in the memory: 'We'll take more care of you' (British Airways), 'Don't be vague, ask for Haig', 'It's good to talk' (BT), 'Mars are marvellous'.

Slogans have to fit the times; some buzz words date quickly (as journalists know). Avoid using an idea that can be readily adapted by a competitor. 'Who made the going great?' (Pan Am) was exploited by 'Who made the Boeing great?' of the British Overseas Airways Corporation, as British Airways then was. Conversely, if you try to adapt the latest techniques of competitors to your particular message, the advert may draw more attention to itself than to the product, may have more artifice than life.

The message in all copywriting should be reduced as far as possible, so the prescription goes, to the Unique Selling Proposition (USP), the one concept or idea that will persuade the customer to buy. Journalists are used to finding a 'controlling idea' (see pages 20–1) for a piece of work. Another approach to a good advert is via an 'image', showing that the product satisfies psychological needs. An advert for central heating says, 'Come in from the cold'. Some adverts play on the reader's fears of being left behind in the rat-race, others promise increased sexual powers or opportunities.

Developing the idea

The process of composition, from knowledge about the product, through selection of subject matter, to proposition or image, has close parallels with the process of developing ideas for features described in Chapter 4. A slogan or catchphrase for an advert which neatly encapsulates the idea for the copywriter may come early, just as a title may come quickly to a feature writer. But the research to identify the audience and the subject research can be more extensive for an advert of 200 words than for an article of 2000.

Copywriters do legwork where appropriate. They may visit factories – for example, to see computers, cars, perfume, clothes if those are the products they are writing about. They talk to manufacturers, to journalists who assess the products in trade papers, to customers.

A useful approach to content is to use the five W questions used by reporters but with rather different kinds of questions. Who is involved? What is it? Where will it be most useful? Where can you buy it? When is the best time to use it? Why is it used, and how? Why should this product be bought rather than competing products?

Which subjects grab the attention on the whole? A renowned *Daily Express* editor, Arthur Christianson, said there were three subjects for a mass circulation newspaper: sex, money and sport. Advertisers appreciate the value of these and have added animals, babies, cars, disasters, entertainment, fashion, war and weddings. The triggers must, however, be deployed with imagination.

Special word power

As well as cliché subjects, there are cliché words that have their uses as a kind of shorthand. There's no point in avoiding 'bargain' if it means 10 words instead of one.

Clichés more recently coined or emotive words handled like clichés are called 'buzz' words because they are signals, immediately recognizable, setting up predictable reactions. They include 'new', 'now', 'free', 'introducing', 'announcing', 'secret', 'magic', 'mother', 'unique', 'economy', 'breakthrough', 'guarantee'. Action words should be short: 'phone', 'send', 'take', 'buy', 'ask'.

Adverts often work by being ironic, or by sending themselves up, and using clichés can work as part of this style. The normal rules of grammar and spelling can be broken to good effect: 'Beans Meanz Heinz'. Copywriters have the poets' need to be more than usually concise and to stir the imagination with metaphor. Yoking two kinds of ideas together in a collision, as poets do, produced '*New Statesman*. Things you would not find in a month of Sundays'.

Typography and layout

The design of an advert can make or mar the impact of the words. In an advertising agency the copywriter will normally work closely with a visualizer from the art department, and they will share ideas about design, illustration and words. A freelance writer who does some copywriting may join up with one or two others as a team to share different kinds of expertise. They meet up in the 'situations vacant' columns of the advertising and marketing weeklies.

FROM PR INTO JOURNALISM

Publicity writing aims to get past editors into the editorial pages of newspapers and magazines and must be regarded as journalism. Press releases, specially written PR-orientated feature articles and the content of house journals might be promoting a company or its products or services, but the writers must behave as journalists. The pieces must have the news values and fulfil all the other requirements of good journalism. Let's take press releases as an example.

Press releases

These are of two main kinds: hard news and trade. A hard news release means one that contains news value for a newspaper or magazine. Suppose a new kind of lawnmower is being launched that will expand the manufacturing company, with more jobs in the centres of production. Though the main purpose of the release will be to promote the product, the news value must be projected first. If the release is to be sent to local editors where there are employment gains, it will be adapted to reflect those gains. For a trade magazine, on the other hand, the innovatory qualities of the new machine may become the news value. And so on.

Getting past editors

The general interest in your release for a national market or the local interest for a regional must hit the editor between the eyes. Many releases sound too much like adverts: plug, plug. Many are too long.

Notice the tired phrases (my italics) in this paragraph of a news release for newspapers, no doubt both national and regional in aim:

ANOTHER SUCCESSFUL MOVE
The National Homelink Service, launched by the National Association of Estate Agents two years ago, *has proved a resounding success with the number* of offices throughout the UK and Channel Islands *now amounting to* over 600. A new link has recently been formed with an American Real Estate Company, which has joined Homelink *and therefore extends the service* across the Atlantic. *A valuable addition* which *enhances the links already in operation* in Europe through members in the UK.

This is the service congratulating itself. The words don't seem to be aimed at anybody in particular. What is *important* about the new link? Who will benefit from the service? How does it work? The second paragraph begins to tell us, but again in weary language.

Homelink *was designed to make* house hunting easier, and the *number of enquiries received* show that this free referral service is *of considerable benefit* to anyone moving to another area....

A brighter start would be something like:

HOUSE HUNTERS' NETWORK
House hunters can now link into a national network of over 600 offices. That means speedy contacts, and the referral service is free.

Adapting to different markets

A new building company has been established to exploit a central heating system using solar energy. The system is about to be launched with demonstrations in newly built model houses in large towns throughout the country. Plastics and other materials are used that are cheaper than traditional building materials. Labour costs for building the average three-bedroom house will be greatly reduced.

For a national newspaper the news peg is likely to be the prospect of a revolution (but be careful of that word: radical change?) in the house-building industry. The regional papers will want to cover the nearest demonstration in a town. Trade magazines that cover solar energy and plastics will expect the more technical information that will interest their readers.

This release could be adapted for several different markets (after the necessary market research) by changing only the heading and the first paragraph. The news value would be expressed in those places, and then the interesting facts ordered in a way that would suit all those different markets.

The story must be of intrinsic interest to the general reader of the publication. The facts should be strong enough evidence of the merits of the product to speak for themselves. Avoid superlatives ('excellent', 'world-beating', 'unique') and emotive adjectives ('lovely', 'fabulous').

Writers of releases must think hard about what people need or want to know, whether it's mobile cassette libraries or a new kind of nicotine remover, and then engage their interest with subtlety. A news peg may have to be manufactured (picture of celebrity using nicotine remover).

Trade releases

Some trade magazines have an audience of garden equipment retailers serving owners of small gardens, others have an audience of retailers of heavier equipment for parks. A manufacturer of garden equipment trying to get releases published may have to adapt one for those two markets, or write two separate releases. The owner of the small garden may be particularly interested in extra-close mowing, while the council employee maintaining a park will be more interested in staying power. Those W questions will include: Who will benefit particularly from a certain product? What questions are a particular group of readers likely to ask about the products? And so on.

Retailers are being sold a market as well as a product, so trade releases answer marketing questions as well as the usual questions about the target audience as listed above. Retailers want to know:

- Will the product sell quickly and will it fit marketing plans?
- What discounts/special offers/trade deals are there?
- What is the sales potential? (And is there any research evidence for this?)
- Is the selling pattern likely to be seasonal, occasional or regular throughout the year?
- How will the product be promoted?
- Is there any advertising or press information available?
- Will there be any demonstrations, launch by celebrity?
- Too much specific detail may help competitors to fight back, so some information – about media campaigns, for example – may be put in general terms.
- Many trade releases succeed in listing the necessary facts and benefits but fail to inspire with an idea. To take a simple example, the news value of a solution for polishing metal antiques could be identified by associating the product with growing home ownership and house pride.

Press releases are often sent by email. Don't send long attachments. Copy and paste it into the email itself.

Ending with contacts

Contacts, with telephone and fax numbers and email addresses, should be given at the end of releases: the writer and key sources of information. These could include government departments, local housing departments, manufacturers and suppliers of products. Editors often want to follow up a story suggested by part of a release even if they don't want to use the material as it is.

OBTAINING PUBLICITY WORK

For training courses, see Appendix 6. You can train yourself too. For example, you can go online to sample press release models provided by PR companies and have a go at rewriting them. Otherwise, train yourself by sampling press release and advertising models given online by PR companies and advertising agencies. Look for offers of work, online and in the press; when you have an adequate portfolio, advertise your services in the press. For providing publicity work online, see Chapter 9.

When offering writing services, find out first the name and job title of the most appropriate person to talk to. Promotions director? Publicity director? Sales promotion manager? Marketing manager? Advertising manager? Titles vary greatly. *Campaign*, *Marketing Week* and similar magazines give copious news about publicity about what these people are doing. Before approaching a company you would be advised to do some research into it and to decide what convincing evidence you have that your writing skills would be of particular value to it. Both staff and freelance vacancies are advertised in those magazines.

If you want a full-time staff job, you'll stand a better chance if you can provide cuttings of publicity work published. That work will have given you special insight into the whole process and into the varied responsibilities of staff writers. So let's assume it's freelance services you're offering.

Apply to the promotions or publicity director of a business organization or the director of an advertising agency. *Advertisers' Annual* or *British Rate and Data (BRAD) Advertiser and Agency List* give names. Articles in the advertising and marketing publications will suggest which companies might respond. You can also advertise your services in those magazines.

Consultancies and advertising agencies offer publicity writing services to the publicity departments of companies. Show those departments why you think you could do the job better. Indicate in your letter that you have done your research, that you know what their clients want, and enclose samples of writing backing up your claim.

You may want to try obtaining commissions from the agencies and consultancies rather than directly from client companies. That will save you time spent looking for work. The disadvantage is that you have lost some independence, you are further removed from the client, and you have to depend on the agency briefing you well.

Building your portfolio

Develop a portfolio as you go so that you can back up a letter touting for work. Try to collect samples of various kinds of work. Your original press releases together with what was actually printed may impress.

Once you become knowledgeable about a particular business or industry, organize your workload. Suppose you build up expertise in the hotels and catering business. You might have such long-term projects as books, both general interest (*The World's Most Unusual Hotels*), with ideas for spin-off articles, and specialized (*New Ideas in Hotel Organization*).

Shorter-term projects might include brief career guides for publishers' series and educational texts on related subjects such as diets, home economics, etc. You might write brochures on hotels for tourist agencies or the texts for tourist boards' publications.

Specialist services

This brings us to the opportunities for specialists. If you're something of an expert on, and have published articles on, gardening, computers, DIY, homeopathy, cosmetic surgery, dentistry, mountaineering or sailing, or whatever, there are corporate clients who might be interested to hear from you. Manufacturers of gardening equipment, plant nurseries or landscape gardening firms, for example, will value your contacts, experience and communication skills.

Travel writers obtain commissions to write brochures for travel agents, and writers for trade magazines can obtain commissions to do copywriting aimed at those markets.

Fees are generally much higher for publicity work than for journalism. You may want to secure a contract for each piece of work done or work on a retainer basis.

TECHNIQUES FOR PUBLICITY WRITING

It's worth summarizing the special qualities of publicity writing.

Descriptive

Avoid too many adjectives and adverbs and choose adjectives for precision. If you say a product is 'truly amazing', the 'truly' casts doubt on the 'amazing', a word that has been drastically devalued anyway. Find one precise adjective that will convince. Give the burden of meaning to nouns and verbs. Description means making the reader see, hear, smell, taste, touch. Avoid abstractions.

Narrative

Putting the meaning into verbs will help keep the story moving. Saying *what happened* is essential. Initial thoughts, plans, problems, how it began and how it progressed may not be.

Exposition

Avoid over-long sentences. Planning your piece is essential when explaining something. Make a checklist to make sure no important fact has been omitted.

What kind of order is required – chronological or logical? Who are the target audience? How readily will they understand? How technical can you be? What exactly is being explained? Does the audience have to understand how to carry out a procedure or merely understand, roughly, how a machine works?

Avoid a confusing mixture of pronouns: 'one', 'he', 'you', etc. Consider using the passive. Punctuation is important: a comma in the wrong place can completely change the meaning.

Argument/persuasion

In news releases and persuasive articles the facts must be marshalled clearly and in good order to support the proposition. There's a tendency to 'knock' the opposition simplistically in some releases. It's better to talk generally about the dangers or difficulties that have been surmounted by a new product or service, and concentrate on its positive virtues.

In most writing aimed at persuasion it's useful to anticipate objections/ criticisms before going on to the virtues. State improvements realistically. To repeat: the facts will convince if they are good enough. Superlatives rarely convince.

ASSIGNMENTS

1 Publicity writing has to be concise, which usually means go for the short and simple word. Replace the following words with a shorter or simpler word:
   (a) affluent, (b) contusions, (c) purloin, (d) illumination, (e) allude, (f) intoxicated, (g) exhibit (verb), (h) remainder, (i) verbalize, (j) incarcerated, (k) ambiguous, (l) genuine, (m) residence, (n) lacerations, (o) interrogate.
2 Study a full-page advert in a newspaper or magazine with a fair amount of copy. Note the main points. Put the advert away and rewrite it, using your outline, trying to improve on the original. Compare with the original. Note the differences and make an assessment. Which is best, and why?
3 Write three press releases aimed at a local paper, publicizing:
   (a) the opening of a restaurant specializing in Mediterranean cuisines;
   (b) the opening of a sports centre;
   (c) a talk, followed by a book signing, to be given by your favourite author in the main bookshop of the town.

---

16   Interview features and profiles

> The US Army calls it embedding. Like Hollywood, the Pentagon has nightmares at the thought of freewheeling journalists reporting events outside the embedded system. Is there someone out there in showbiz Babylon still willing to resist embedment and keep the oriflamme of bloodyminded independence aloft? If not, editors might as well send along their secretaries to take the star's dictation. Actually, I'm not sure they aren't already. (Victor Davis, 'The stars look down', *British Journalism Review*, Number 2, 2003)

> The best technique is to make tiny pricks in the subject's ego and let him expel hot air slowly. (Humphrey Bogart, late film actor)

> Our most vivid impressions of our contemporaries are through interviews. Almost everything of moment reaches us through one [person] asking questions of another. Because of this, the interviewer holds a position of unprecedented power and influence. (Denis Brian, *Murderers and other Friendly People: The Public and Private Worlds of Interviewers*)

Skill in interviewing, as Chapter 8 demonstrates, is an essential part of the information-gathering process. In this chapter we analyse that skill more closely. When the feature is based on an interview (or interviews), when the interviewee or what the interviewee has to say is the whole subject, interviewing is a much more complex operation. We get back to telephone and email methods but it is the face-to-face ones that will demand most attention. The terms 'interview' and 'profile' are applied interchangeably to a feature about one interviewee, but I shall use the latter term more strictly – when talking about the longer, more rounded portrait of an individual derived from various sources (sometimes without a byline).

Study the best interviewers. Read *The Penguin Book of Interviews* (1993), edited by Christopher Silvester (republished in the USA as *The Norton Book of Interviews* in 1996), a fascinating anthology from 1859 to 1992, and taking in such luminaries as Karl Marx, Mark Twain (interviewed by Rudyard Kipling), Emile Zola, a taciturn Ibsen, a voluble young Greta Garbo, Freud, Hitler, Stalin (by H. G. Wells), a drunk Scott Fitzgerald, Marilyn Monroe, Margaret Thatcher, Bette Davis and Mae West. A 43-page introduction charts the journalistic interview through its history and analyses some psychological subtexts. Interviewers who are almost celebrities in their own right have published collections.

Note the great number of approaches, ways of asking questions, ways of writing up, and note how these aspects are influenced by the different personalities of interviewees, the different purposes of the features, the different audiences. This chapter will help you to decide what kinds of treatments are likely to be fruitful for different interviewees and different publications. Some subjects will have illuminating comments on the state of the world, others an oblique outlook on the world well worth anybody's attention, or a wealth of humour to tap into, or exceptional courage to inspire. Whether the subject is famous or not, the trick is to discover how to open the tap, how to help the subject to find their best words for what they have to say, and how to develop a style of your own to colour the numerous shapes and tones that will emerge. Women are regarded in many quarters as having the edge when it comes to encouraging people to talk: tact, warmth, intuition and rapport are cited as evidence.

What's certain is that you'll need those qualities, and more. Some interviewees need to be kept on track: they will want to talk about their cats, perhaps, or their garden when your purpose is to talk about their study of a remote African tribe. Other interviewees, even among writers and academics, can be unforthcoming because worried about how you'll represent them. The more famous they are, the more difficult they can be. They may have been asked the same questions over and over, and here they are again. They may have been frustrated by too many interviewers having done little preparation (for example, 'Could you please give me the titles of one or two of your books?' or 'Have you done a stage play recently?').

This chapter covers the following ground:

- choice of interviewee
- getting commissioned
- setting up the interview
- choosing the method
- preparing the questions

- interviewing techniques
- editing the transcript
- formats for writing up
- following up.

CHOICE OF INTERVIEWEE

Before choosing your prospects prepare for these challenges by researching previous interviews and finding new questions. Find out as much as you can about how your prospect performs at interviews (from agents and from friends or acquaintances) and work out a friendly, professional, positive approach.

For the local paper there will be mileage to be got out of the head teacher retiring after 50 years, a businessman planning a factory, a councillor embroiled in a corruption allegation, the local girl who has won a part in a soap opera, the policeman who has been awarded the CBE. You keep your ears open in the pub and on the street and if you're a freelance you try to beat the local paper reporter with the news.

Offbeat characters can be a fruitful field – accountants who are black belts in judo, greengrocers who become steeplejacks on Saturdays, plumbers who fly gliders, surgeons who perform in amateur theatricals.

If there are locally based celebrities (let's call them 'celebs') they might make subjects for interview but have probably been done too often in the local press. You can keep an eye open for other celebs passing through. Thus Pete Best, the original drummer with the Beatles, was interviewed by David Male of the *Kentish Times* when he was on the road with his band, with dates in Croydon and Chatham.

When a book is being published by a well-known person, the author may well be interested in the publicity generated by reviews in the local as well as the national press. Thus Angela Wintle of the *Brighton Argus* secured an interview with Sir Bernard Ingham, Margaret Thatcher's press secretary, when his book *The Wages of Sin* came out. No doubt feature writers of other local papers did too.

'Ordinary but with an extraordinary story' or 'expert' or 'famous' or 'infamous'? You will have your preferences and those will no doubt change as you grow older or ambitions alter. Make sure you have a publication's interest, if not firm commission, to interview somebody before you approach them.

Choose wisely when it comes to celebs. Decide, for example, after some preliminary research on a prospect, whether or not you could avoid increasing their boredom. You may feel that:

- you haven't got any new questions to ask
- you can't get excited enough about the task
- you are so excited that you feel you wouldn't avoid a deadly effect of sycophancy
- you're not yet capable of rising to the occasion.

If it's celebs you're after, note that big names tend to give interviews to established names. When you have impressed a few agents and editors with pieces on minor celebs you will find bigger celebs more willing to talk to you. (On the other hand, as will be seen, it's too often expected that the interview will be on their terms, or the terms laid down by their publicity people, and that can mean a boring interview before you start.)

You have to keep up with the news of celebs, whether major or minor, so that you can get in first with proposals to editors, who will want publication of the piece to coincide with any event/public appearance in the offing.

GETTING COMMISSIONED

Do some preliminary research in order to get the approval of interviewee and editor. Study the press cuttings or the CD-ROMs for features about your subject. (Don't forget the way errors are repeated and double-check where possible.) There may be news about a book coming out or a concert appearance, other news items in the press, a fairly recent magazine interview perhaps (in a different market from the one you have in mind). It will be wise to specialize as an interviewer in one or two fields in case such preparation time doesn't lead to many commissions. Then at least you're becoming knowledgeable about the subject area.

If you're staff you'll automatically get briefing. If freelance, don't ask editors for commissions until you know their publications, know what treatments they give interviews, and know which interviews they've done in the past six months or more. Indicate that the sort of interview, in terms of content and treatment, that you have in mind would fit the target publication. You suggest, perhaps, that the main interest should be in the work, or in the private life, or in the mind or in the personality of the subject. Then you're prepared to discuss the editor's briefing. (Unless, of course, your track record is so good that the editor trusts you not to need any briefing.)

You should have some files of interview cuttings that include pieces done for various kinds of publications which you can compare. Pitch when you feel sure you can secure the interview. At the least obtain a 'we'll have a look at it'. You can then say to your prospect, 'I've been asked to do an interview for ...'.

SETTING UP THE INTERVIEW

The reporter gets used to barging into places, extracting a couple of juicy quotes and barging out again. Arranging to spend an hour or more eliciting substantial amounts of information or personal accounts of lives and careers is an altogether much weightier proposition. Interview feature writers require much confidence to set up an interview, and then various kinds of skills to carry it out. It may be wise to start modestly, if you're new to the game, with a strategy for going up the scale, establishing your credentials in the eyes of both editors and interview prospects.

How to contact your prospect? This can be surprisingly easy. You get the home phone number from the telephone directory and ring up and you may be immediately talking to him/her. The prospect may be much more relaxed at home than in an office or hotel or other public place, but of course may be much less relaxed.

A husband or a wife or a secretary tells you that you will get a call back if the prospect is interested. Or you are asked to contact directly, by phone, email or letter.

It's more likely, however, that there's more than one intermediary: a spouse or secretary, then an assistant perhaps or a press officer, publicist, agent, promoter, show producer, union official, membership secretary or more than one of these. The intermediary listens to your pitch, says it will be passed to the subject (or to another intermediary), and if the prospect agrees to be interviewed you will get a call.

If you've concentrated on a particular field – actors, pop singers, authors, footballers, tennis players, IT experts – you can receive information regularly about prospects and their activities and whereabouts from intermediaries. Actors, writers and others have their unions, guilds and societies, which will divulge agents' names. *Spotlight* directory lists actors and their agents.

Get yourself on such organizations' mailing lists or log on to their websites and keep up to date with the news about their clients' activities. Many of your prospects will have their own websites that regularly keep their story up to date.

Most of the tactics you need in setting an interview up come into play with celebs, so let's use this area to describe those tactics. Otherwise watch the press for celebs' movements. If a pop singer you're interested in will appear at the Hammersmith Odeon in London, find out from the box office the admin number for the venue. From there you will get the publicist's number. Publicists will (you hope) get back to you to arrange the interview. At that stage, ask for, if you're not offered any, information that will help you to prepare: a CD, an up-to-date bio (biography), newsletters, summaries of recent interviews, plans for the next few months (or years). If such information is not forthcoming there are cuttings agencies that supply them.

You may want to subscribe to a service that keeps you informed of the movements of celebs in the entertainment business, if it's worth around £100 a month to you. *The Celebrity Bulletin*, for example, published by Celebrity Service Ltd., will give you daily news of who's arriving in the UK, where they'll be appearing, and whom to contact at venues and agencies, with addresses and telephone numbers.

Some people will appreciate the publicity you'll be giving them, some need publicity to survive: in a famous phrase they 'face the choice between starving and being eaten'. You will be rebuffed by some who have not been treated well by journalists in the past.

Getting past the minders

Without a track record you'll find it difficult to get past the minders. Even with a track record you may be thwarted at the end by film stars and press agents. Silvester, in the introduction to his *Penguin Book*, explains how this works:

> Lynn Barber's first interviewing assignment for *Vanity Fair* was spiked because the interviewee, film actor Nick Nolte, disliked her attitude and

instructed his press agent to refuse to provide exclusive pictures to *Vanity Fair* if they were to go ahead and publish. The Hollywood press agents, of whom there are only half a dozen of any significance, now operate a cartel. Unless the writer's treatment of their client meets with their approval, they are likely to refuse not only future access to the client in question but also future access to any of their other clients.

This was the mid 1990s but things haven't changed much. Fortunately *Vanity Fair* and such magazines will sometimes show their muscle; interviewee's or publicist's approval of the script will not be granted, despite the threats; the feature will be published despite the interviewee's objections (and *Vanity Fair* have often done this); and interviewers will find imaginative ways of completing an assignment besieged by obstacles. But until you are a well-known interviewer yourself, attracting customers who welcome the challenge and the exposure, it's best to probe gently.

You will confront obstacles at all levels and you must be persistent. Here are a few tips:

1 Ascertain from your preliminary reading, and if possible from talking to friends, relatives, colleagues or associates' relatives, what kind of approach is most likely to work. For example, what has pleased your subject most and what has irritated most about past interviews?
2 Try to get agents, secretaries, prospects on your side with that good pitch. Your initial contacts are crucial. You must sell yourself as someone who can bring benefit of some kind to interviewees, bring good publicity, get their ideas or interesting personality across, produce a readable feature.
3 Get across to your subject why the commissioning publication is interested in the interview, your special interest and knowledge, how much you're enjoying reading up about the prospect or the work.
4 Show that you're passionate about the character or the activities of the person or about what you can find out that's exciting and newsworthy.
5 Arouse the subject's curiosity, especially if you have to encapsulate your request in a voice message. Try to avoid spelling out too precisely what you have in mind if there's a chance that it may not appeal or that it may have been raised too often by past interviews. Try instead to indicate that you'll be able to reveal the sort of things that past interviews have failed to discover (giving a clue out of what you've discovered so far).
6 Take any opportunity to convey to your subject that you can correct any misrepresentations that have been unfavourable, which you will no doubt find in past interviews.

7 Agree about the method: email, phone or face to face? Email has its limitations for feature interviews (see below). Even face to face can be done at a distance these days. Ian Reeves explains that his interview with the publishing mogul Felix Dennis in *Press Gazette* is being carried out via videoconference link in his house in Mustique. 'I'm sitting in the Dennis Publishing boardroom in Soho [London], talking to a rather fuzzy, jerky image of its boss in a book-lined room 7000 miles away' in his house in Mustique.

8 If you do get to do the Hollywood stars, don't sell your soul (see the first quote at the start of this chapter).

How to be persistent

Even when agents are trying to be helpful, film stars and showbiz people can require obstinacy beyond the natural. I failed to get an interview with Dustin Hoffman for a magazine. He was at the Dorchester Hotel in London for three days before going to Paris to work on a film. I telephoned his London agent. 'I'll ring you back.' While waiting I rang the Dorchester and was put through to Mr Hoffman's secretary in his suite … 'I'll ring you back.' The press officer at the Dorchester: 'I'll ring you back.' The hall porter: 'If you came along to the hotel you might ….' The London agent called: 'Mr Hoffman is very busy but he's trying to fit you in.' The press office at the Dorchester: 'I'm so sorry. Mr Hoffman has just left for Paris – a day early.'

In one of the Sunday papers I found an interview with Dustin Hoffman. The hall porter: 'Yes, he wouldn't give up. He spent several hours in the lounge, and in the cocktail bar and in the restaurant, continually monitoring Mr Hoffman's movements. He had a fair number of the hotel staff helping him. …'

Some interviews demand extra initiative. Albert Einstein was difficult to pin down. He was staying once in a small-town hotel in the United States. Big-name foreign correspondents crowded the lobby waiting in vain for a word or two. A local reporter put on dungarees, marched into Einstein's room and said he was sorting out the telephones. He had a long chat with Einstein as he tinkered away. It was a scoop.

Come to an agreement about place and time and make sure your subject knows how to contact you in case of cancellation.

CHOOSING THE METHOD

There are face-to-face, letter, email and phone situations, as described in Chapter 8. There's going to be some repetition here of what was said there, to match the different purpose and approaches.

Your choice will depend to some extent on distance, and to some extent on the brief and the format agreed for the write-up. If your subject is too far to warrant the expense and the travelling time for face to face, you (and your subject) will have to decide among letter, email and phone procedures. You're going to need a notebook. Both for face-to-face and phoned interviews you can use a tape recorder as well. Let's contrast these methods.

Face to face

Be as considerate as possible about time and place of meeting. But avoid meeting people who keep late hours early in the day, and meeting people in noisy places – film sets, TV studios, bars, restaurants. After you've listened to a tape of an interview done over lunch in a busy restaurant seated near the kitchen you won't do it again. Avoid rooms with low ceilings where you'll tend to get poor acoustics, or offices overlooking main streets with busy traffic. Try to avoid being interrupted by telephone calls.

Don't sit opposite the interviewee as if you're considering them for a job or suspecting them of a crime. Make it 90 degrees. Make sure you have a spare tape and spare batteries. If you're worried about your tape recorder breaking down, use two. The spare tape may come in useful if your published piece confronts legal problems (see below).

An interview-feature containing a rounded portrait of the subject is best done after a face to face. You can play things to some extent by ear. Like any conversation, it's an exchange of views happening naturally, so that you can judge by body language and facial expression as well as tone of voice how your subject is reacting. Interpreting these signs you can shape the interview accordingly – make the questions shorter and simpler than you had prepared, for example, or more demanding, or you may decide to start more gently when you find someone is more sensitive than anticipated.

Journalists used to have much better memories than they have now. Even a notebook, it was considered, would put an interviewee off. Many journalists would make a few brief notes surreptitiously. Until the 1960s notebooks were mainly used for interview features. The piece would be written up promptly while fresh in the mind. We have so many machines now that remember things for us, from digital diaries to sophisticated computer programs, that the capacity to listen and remember is being eroded.

As tape recorders became fashionable, from the 1970s onwards, old hands deplored the practice of depending on them for interviews. It was maintained, with some justice, that tape recorders encouraged laziness. Younger hands with excellent memories can do wonders with notebooks alone (see Hunter Davies's selection, *Hunting People*, Mainstream Publishing). It's true that tape recorders can encourage the devoting of less time to the actual encounter. They can also encourage the assumption that there's bound to be something good on tape (there isn't bound to be). They can, if you're not alert to the danger, produce depersonalized features, with mechanical exchanges lacking nuances.

Tape recording with skill

There are still these dangers but the skill of interviewing with a tape recorder has been developed so that both parties (with the exceptions that are being noted) tend to be more relaxed than they used to be. The advantages have come to be increasingly appreciated. You can have much more eye contact if you don't have to make many notes. You obtain a record of the intonations, of the manner of speaking, the accent. Much of the personality of a person comes through in these aspects. Furthermore, a tape is an insurance if you're not sure if you'll be able to write up immediately.

Most editors expect tape recorders to be used for features so that the printed account can be backed up if there are any complaints from the interviewee about misrepresentation, or even threats of libel action. People can be astonished when they see their casually bestowed words in cold print. 'Did I really say that?' Some frequently interviewed celebs like to make their own tapes of an interview, even of phoned interviews. It can be welcomed if otherwise the subject is likely to question the accuracy of what ends up in print.

In your unobtrusive way jot down details of setting, facial expressions, body language, clothes, and so on. Note key statements to help your memory to keep you on track. Transcribing will be easier if you select as you go, making a note of the numbers on the tape indicator so that you can quickly locate the best bits. You can compensate to some extent for that loss of listening art with a juggling art.

Write down all names and figures clearly. They may not be clear on the tape. Ask for names to be spelt. Go back over any figures you are doubtful about. 'Did you say fifteen thousand or fifty thousand?'

By letter

Interviewing by letter, a valuable part of research on occasion, is not often done to achieve a piece for publication, unless what is wanted is, say, opinions of weight for an academic journal, with atmosphere and personality not required, and especially when such a subject is distant.

When time is short, the interview for information rather than personality can be done by email or phone.

By email

You or the subject may prefer to get a dialogue going by an exchange of emails, with time allowed on both sides for thinking, rather than have a one-off straightforward Q-and-A session.

Emails are particularly useful for interviewing the expert, when you don't need the sound or tone of the voice. Information is almost everything, though of course some humanity should be allowed to creep in. The interviews with journalists in this book were done by email.

You can't break in to follow up an interesting point raised. The email dialogue, however, can easily continue, so you can come back with new questions that have suggested themselves. Furthermore, the situation is relaxed because both parties choose the time when they want to contribute. Make sure, however, that your interviewee is aware of your deadline.

A word of warning. Make sure with emails (and even sometimes with letters) that you're getting verbatim quotes and not versions of what your subject has to say sanitized by publicists. Print out longish emails that you're responding to. When you depend on scrolling up and down a screen there's a tendency to miss points.

If the email interview is going to be long, questions and answers can be sent, in the form of numbered lists, as attachments.

By phone

Especially when time is short, a 'phoner' can be ideal. This is an interview using a phone with a phone pick-up stuck onto the back of the handset and plugged into a tape recorder. For the phone you need to have a fair number of short questions, placed in a good order in a script, getting deeper perhaps as you go, so that awkward silences are avoided. Getting subtle or ironic on either side is problematic when you can't see each other's faces (a technology that's on the way). You have to remember to put your friendly smile into your voice.

PREPARING THE QUESTIONS

You've been commissioned and you've set up the interview. Now continue studying your subject in the ways described above, going deeper and noting the questions you want to ask. Read one or two of the author's books, a playwright's plays (and see one or two productions), visit an artist's exhibition or at least see some of the work. Walk round an architect's building, watch a footballer play a few times, pore over the annual accounts of the businessman's company. Consult such reference books as *Who's Who*. Note as you do all this what you will want to talk about.

Read past interviews with the subject and collect cuttings. From what you now have learned about the subject, you should be able to discover some gaps – some areas of experience the subject hasn't been asked about. Don't expect interviewees to tell you these things. Pick out also old quotes that will now need to be updated. Note any errors that have been lazily repeated through those interviews and indicate that you're correcting them. Your subject will be grateful for these signs of your research. But your credit will be small if you leave in a few of 'the same old questions'.

It's illuminating to look up past interviews with your prospect done for different publications (see below). As well as giving you different angles on your prospect you'll be engaged in relevant market study: you'll see more clearly what different publications tend to like in their interviews.

In particular, that will make you aware of the effects of length. The longer interview, 2000 to 3000 words or more, provide room to go deeper, to explore the darker or more puzzling sides of the character. In a 1600-word interview with Sting by Serge Simonart in *Saga* (January 2002), we are told about the pop star 'who is devoted to his family and conservation issues'. His communion with nature comes across in this way:

> 'I do most of my thinking in the garden, and bring those ideas back to the studio. I'm glad you can hear nature in my music, because that's one of my big inspirations, you know: listen to the grass, talk to the plants, hug trees.' He laughs at this, but quickly shows his sincerity. 'I mean it though: hugging old trees works, old trees are great ancient spirits, they've been here longer than we have, and will survive us, so they know more. And I think to interact somehow with their wisdom is a great thing to do.'

Sting's interest in nature becomes an active interest in the environment in the profile of over 3500 words in *The Telegraph Magazine* by Neil McCormick (13 September 2003) and there's more probing. We learn about the seven houses, the chef, the butler, the cars, pretentiousness, the lack of popularity in the media. Note the difference in style:

> Sting enjoys the trappings of wealth and success. Yet there is a paradox here that he is acutely aware of, a contradiction between his image as an environmental activist and the conspicuous consumption that goes with being fantastically rich. 'I have no excuses,' he says thoughtfully. 'But this is a conundrum faced by anyone who has a car, central heating, air conditioning.'

When accounts differ

At two extremes are interviews with the film actor Richard Gere: for *The Observer Magazine* (by Harriet Lane) and for *Reader's Digest* (by Nancy Collins). Lane's piece was memorable for the conflict described, which was a refreshing change from the sycophantic norm for such subjects. The encounter was cut short by 20 minutes by the publicist. Gere comes across as without humour, neurotic and repressed, over-earnest and hostile. Around the same time (February 2003) Collins showed the devoted father ('How does it feel?'– 'Incredibly vulnerable'), unpretentious, with his eyes welling up thinking about his father playing the trumpet ('his playing is so connected to his heart').

Make sure, then, if you're preparing to meet Sting or Gere that you assess the different approaches of different publications, that you update what you get from research and that you find the most recent accounts as well as the history. You may find that a less pretentious Sting has become much more popular with the media lately, that a more articulate Richard Gere is in more recent interviews neither obnoxious nor sentimental. You have been helped by your preparation to formulate some questions but you must go into action prepared to have your impressions altered. Your subject may have developed in unpredictable ways.

Delve further into any errors or misleading statements that you have picked up about your subject or their organization by cross-checking through different sources. Showing that you have set the record straight (or at least straighter) will be an encouraging place to start the interview.

When researching note what you will want to talk about. Develop some crucial questions with the five Ws and the How in mind. But don't list questions that have been asked many times before, for which the answers are well-known facts. The more you know about your subject the better your questions are likely to be.

I'm using 'questions' as a convenient term to include points to be raised, topics to be introduced, that are not necessarily introduced in the form of questions. To avoid turning the interview into one question after another, list them in such a way that you won't be tempted to do that. Rather than 'did you enjoy being a cabinet minister or are you happier as a back-bencher?', simply 'cabinet minister and backbencher' will prompt you towards conversation when the moment arrives.

What questions, in what order?

First you make sure you're on the same wavelength as your subject, then you try to make your questions, on the whole, specific, open-ended and well ordered.

On the same wavelength

If you're well prepared you'll be able to get on your subject's wavelength, use the jargon of their profession or trade, hit on their enthusiasms, get under their skin. Your questions will be aimed at obtaining explanation, opinion and interpretation rather than mere facts. You will either know the facts or have access to them – facts such as how long a company chairman has been in the job and what last year's statement of accounts showed profits to be.

Even for a brief interview questions should be devised so as to make the best possible use of the time. Your purpose is to find out what your readers would want to know, things which the subject is most qualified to tell you. Your preparation will help you judge if the answers are comprehensible to your average reader. Have alternative forms of difficult questions ready in case answers are unclear. Be ready to rephrase questions on the spot.

If you're on your subject's wavelength you're more likely to produce a desirable form of discussion rather than an embarrassing inquisition. Put questions into context: 'I was interested to learn that you declined the invitation to join the campaign … Of course many others declined. Is it a fair account of your attitude?'

Specific

Questions should be asked one at a time and be clear and specific. Avoid closed questions, which encourage brief answers or yes or no.

'Do you enjoy being a solicitor?' is not a good question. It's too vague. What good to you is the answer 'sometimes'? 'Which of the jobs you have to do as a solicitor do you enjoy most?' is more likely to encourage articulate response, perhaps followed by 'Which do you dislike most?'

Instead of 'Do you agree with the new Education Bill?' try the open-ended 'Do you agree with the criticism that the Bill is likely to be divisive?'

Avoid questions that take you into a cul-de-sac. 'What would have happened if you'd succeeded in that business?' Answer: 'I would have become prosperous.' (Well, what sort of answer did you want?)

Open questions develop a conversation. How and why questions, for example. Encourage articulate answers by contributing to the subject. For example: 'Your colleagues tell me that you're good at getting the best out of backward pupils. How do you do that? Can you give me an example?' The hunt for anecdotes and examples is especially necessary with abstract matters such as relationships.

Questions for children need to be specific and carefully phrased. 'Do you enjoy your weekends?' is better explored by 'What do you like doing best at weekends? Swimming? Playing football?' Use words they can understand. On the other hand, they may know a lot more about certain aspects of life than you did at their age.

Avoid particularly 'leading' questions, which contain your assumption of what the answer is, whether the prompting is in your words, phrasing or tone of voice. 'You've had a lot of arguments with the players this season, haven't you?' might provoke an angry as well as non-committal response. Find another way to approach the subject. If you know it's true you can say, 'I've heard from some fans [or I've read reports] that you've had a lot of arguments … Is that a fair way of putting it? … Do you want to comment on that?'

In a good order

Arrange your questions in an order you think will make a good conversation and elicit good answers. For example, you can site the awkward ones judiciously – immediately after a particular welcome question might be a good place, or near the end.

INTERVIEWING TECHNIQUES

Let's concentrate now on the face-face interview techniques, which can be adapted to the phone and the email.

To what extent are you interviewing yourself as well, anxious to get across your own opinions or attitudes? There are two extremes. There's the invisible interviewer. The format may be straightforward Q-and-A, where your questions are (almost) entirely designed to get information and opinion from your subject, or you may simply print the answers in a monologue as if you weren't there.

The other extreme is the celebrity interviewer who is just as important as the interviewee and sometimes even more so. And there are all degrees in between. How far you get involved depends partly on what works for you and partly on what kind of interviewee you've got. A very quiet one may awaken any histrionic abilities you may possess.

After much preparation of the kind described above you have a list of well-thought-out questions in apparently the most fruitful order. You seem to be doing everything right. You're using the notebook unobtrusively and effectively and are on the same wavelength. But the interview is unsatisfactory, just as a play performance can be great one night and flop the next, with the same script and the same cast.

Perhaps there are technical difficulties relating to your tape recorder or the venue. There may be unwelcome noise or interruptions although you've done your best to avoid them. Try to take these things in your stride: focused but relaxed. You may have failed to establish a rapport with your interviewee. That has to be done early. Turn the occasion into a conversation so that you take the pressure off the interviewee. Reveal yourself. If you are felt to be friendly and trustworthy they will be more likely to confide. Find some warm-up, non-interview remarks/questions to throw out on meeting. And smile.

Here are a few suggestions for getting the best out of an interview.

Keeping in control

That does not mean sticking strictly to the questions or the order that you've planned. It means creating a conversation in which the interviewee is encouraged to give the answers you require without feeling under pressure. Your list of prepared questions will be organized in a particular order: by topic perhaps or by chronology. This is a guide only. As you get to know your interviewee you'll see how to adapt to the shape the conversation takes and judge how best to phrase your questions so that they appeal.

Listen carefully to the answers so that you can take advantage of any opportunity to follow a promising path. Without interrupting too often, you may want to challenge an argument or put the other point of view. Your interviewee might embark on themes or supply information that you didn't anticipate. If this is interesting and relevant you may want to follow up, perhaps cutting out a few of your less interesting questions. But don't be deflected from your purpose. Return to your agenda, if it hasn't been discarded.

Getting the answer you want

Skilled interviewees become adept at giving what they want to give rather than what you want to receive. However brief, it's a kind of marriage, with seductions and withdrawals involved, and so a trade-off. But don't let the interviewee take over in this way:

> Question: Do you agree that bad language and violent behaviour when criticizing your children are not the best kind of model to present your children with?

Answer: I agree that children should be encouraged at every stage. I constantly give my children encouragement …

Question: Have you now decided that you're not going to use bad language in front of the children?

Answer: Have I now decided to take particular care to say 'Well done' when they do the right thing? Yes I have. …

Sometimes you have to say, 'Answer the question please' while remaining positive and tactful, especially if the question is crucial in terms of facts required. When the discussion is about non-personal, abstract/philosophical/political matters it's often effective to keep your main questions general so that interviewees appreciate that they are free to express their opinions freely. They may even feel that they are influencing its direction to a greater extent than they are.

Getting over a lull

'Could you describe your typical day?'
'If you weren't you, who would you like to be?'
'Which age would you have liked to live in, given a choice?'
'If your house were flooded, what are the first things you would try to save?'

Or find better ones.

Techniques for tough questions

Here are various techniques for tough questions, the first three being various versions of the classic 'did you kill your wife' formula:

1 *Everybody approach*: 'Many people have been guilty of killing their wives. Do you happen by any chance to have killed yours?'
2 *Other people approach*: (a) 'Do you know any people who have murdered their wives?' (b) 'How about yourself?'
3 *The Kinsey technique* (with an air of assuming that everyone has done everything): 'As a matter of interest, did you kill your wife?'
4 *The people say that* formula allows you to be unobtrusively tough: 'There are people who say that killing your wife/husband was going too far …' ('Perhaps they misunderstand your motives. …')

5 *The separate questions* formula is used when the questions one after the other put together would impede a completely frank answer. Put other questions between 'Are the regulations in your company about what can be claimed as expenses quite strict?' and 'I suppose you'd feel freer to pursue those activities if your company could stretch the rules on expenses a little ...'.

6 *Rephrasing the painful question.* If a question appears too painful to answer, you might be able to return to it later, rephrasing it so that it sounds different.

7 *Switching off the tape recorder.* If your interviewee is going through a hard time and is finding it difficult to talk about it, you might try switching off the tape recorder. Or you might invite the person to 'say something into the tape if you like', explaining that you have to leave the room for a minute or two while the tape is running.

8 *Finding the question you should have thought of asking.* A possible last question: 'Is there anything you'd like to add to what you have said?' or 'Is there anything I should have asked but didn't?'

9 *Returning to that evasive answer.* You didn't get a straight or a sufficient answer to a question but it was difficult to pursue it at the time. To repeat what was said in Chapter 8, page 137), you stop your tape recorder, close your notebook, and on the way to the door, or the lift, you bring up the question again casually, in different words, and this time you may get a good, relaxed answer. 'I suppose it's difficult to get on with the mother-in-law when ...?'

For difficult interviewees

The way you actually phrase your questions will depend on what sort of animal you've got in your cage. Busy and important people are often friendlier and more cooperative than hustlers on the way up. Just a hint of criticism or reference to unfavourable publicity in the past can upset some interviewees and big egos can delight in making the interviewer look small.

A drunken restaurateur declared he was the greatest in the world and then vomited over the lunch table. It made a dramatic start to the feature and the final result of such encounters, even when far from the original intention, can be illuminating, entertaining and superior to the more predictable result. But don't aim for it.

Ann Leslie, doyenne of foreign correspondents, has some good advice for dangerous interviewees (she has seen a female colleague with a knife at her neck for asking drunken paramilitaries why they were killing people). Make friends with them first, she says. Discover interests in common and when you see danger signs 'start twittering again about babies and sheep recipes ... My mantra ... is always "one step forward, two steps back".'

The most difficult interviewees, generally, are those who have not a great deal to say. They may be anxious that they'll fail to do justice to themselves or their ideas, or they may be made nervous by the compromise of the interview situation. Establishing rapport thus becomes more difficult than usual. One solution is to get into a conversation where you do most of the talking: you reveal things about yourself that the subject finds it easy to respond to and begins to exchange confidences.

On the other hand, don't finish a nervous interviewee's sentences: you may end up with an interview more with yourself than with the subject.

The tactic with other interviewees can be the reverse. Talking too much your-self will make them clam up the more, and you can find that restraint and judicious silences on your part are more likely to make the subject open up.

Avoiding hidden agendas

You publish a favourable interview with:

- a novelist who happens to be a friend who has reviewed as favourable a book of yours
- a politician with whom you've collaborated in a campaign
- a headmistress who then gives your child a place in her school, but your readers are unaware of the connection.

Matthew Parris, ex-MP, then parliamentary sketch writer and now colum-nist for *The Times*, expresses the dilemma well:

> I am very troubled about the relationship between friendship and journal-ism. I never knew where to draw the line. We talk a lot in this country about corruption, in the sense of back pockets, people being paid money to say things or do things. But a very big corruption in all British journalism is the network of friendship and obligation between people who write and the people about whom they write. We have no codes and we make no decla-rations and we leave our readers in the dark.

If you have a sneaking feeling that you're being sycophantic and you can detect some hidden agenda influencing you, tell the reader about it. But if there's too obvious a friendship that prevents you being objective when you know you should be, it will be best not to attempt the interview.

But the kind of corruption Parris refers to can be insidious and you have to be on your guard against it in yourself, and in your interviewee.

Your job is to produce an interesting interview and it may not be entirely your fault if it's not turning out that way. You know, let's say, that your interviewee, veteran of many interviews, is highly skilled at creating a persona that is for public consumption (courageous, kindly, loving, modest, interesting) but which may be far from the truth. You go along with the picture and encourage it with your questions because you think the alternative would be a dull interview. There's where the trade-off lies. And if your interviewee's skill extends to knowing how to flatter you into submission ('I've always wanted to meet *you*' or 'I knew we were going to hit it off') you have to be even more wary.

The best interviewers get the most interesting interviews by finding ways to get behind the facade.

Encouraging revelations

If you're too friendly it will be easy for the interviewee to take control and hide the things you would prefer to know. Nancy Mitford, the English journalist who became a star interviewer in the US, was good at getting people to reveal themselves. She describes her techniques in the classic *The Making of a Muckraker*, which contains a collection of her articles. The following extract from one of the articles, 'Let us now appraise famous writers', first published in *Atlantic* (July 1970), illustrates her method. She interviewed Bennet Cerf, columnist, TV personality and Chairman of the Board of Random House Publishing Corporation, one of the 'Fifteen Famous Writers' who, according to the advertisements, taught you 'to write successfully at home'. Ms Mitford has indicated that she is critical of the correspondence course:

> 'I think mail-order sell has several built-in deficiencies,' he said. 'The crux of it is a very hard sales pitch, an appeal to the gullible. Of course, once somebody has signed a contract with Famous Writers he can't get out of it. But that's true with every business in the country.' Noticing that I was

writing this down, he said in alarm, 'For God's sake, don't quote me on that "gullible" business – you'll have all the mail-order businesses in the country down on my neck!' 'Then would you like to paraphrase it?' I asked, suddenly getting very firm. 'Well – you could say in general I don't like the hard sell, yet it's the basis of all American business.' 'Sorry, I don't call that a paraphrase, I shall have to use both of them,' I said in a positively governessy tone of voice. 'Anyway, why do you lend your name to this hard-sell proposition?' Bennet Cerf (with his melting grin): 'Frankly, if you must know, I'm an awful ham – I love to see my name in the papers!'

She listens hard, has charm, good manners and firmness, all valuable assets for the interviewer. She wouldn't have got the admissions she wanted without them. Even so, it isn't always easy to analyse why a subject will talk to one interviewer and not another.

Mr Cerf's 'don't quote me' raises the subject of what interviewees can expect to be 'off the record' and what not. The journalist has to be up to date with the law and with the editor's interpretation of it (see Chapter 21). In general, your interviewee has a stronger claim to confidentiality if you are asked for a statement to be made 'off the record' before the statement is made than if you're asked after it is made.

Preparing to follow up

Remember to exchange contact numbers at the end of the interview. You may need to arrange for photographs to be taken, to check points when transcribing, perhaps to ask for some additional information.

EDITING THE TRANSCRIPT

As soon as possible after the interview, before listening to the tape, jot down your immediate impressions of the event while they are fresh in your mind. A heading or an intro might occur to you.

One disadvantage of tape is that you may be inclined to let the interview go on too long, feeling that you can easily edit the transcript – but transcription can take three times as long as the interview. When you've taped a long, relaxed conversation you may wish you hadn't when faced with the task of transcribing it. I have already suggested how you can make this easier by using the numbers on the tape indicator for selected playback. Type the pieces out and then find ways of linking them. Extract an attention-grabbing intro if you haven't thought of one already.

For a major interview, though, you may want to have a complete or near-complete transcript to edit from. If so, it may be worth photocopying your transcript, in case your editing is going to be somewhat creative and you want to have the security of the original at hand. Study the photocopy to find a good structure, producing at some stage an outline to guide you. Paste up sections on A4 sheets, and arrange in the order in which you want to write them up. Space out quoted pieces, indirect speech pieces, background pieces in a satisfactory pattern. Leave space where you will need linking material. When you're a veteran interviewer you'll find your own kinds of shortcuts.

However well controlled an interview is, talk is more rambling and repetitive than written-up material, a quality more conspicuous to the eye than the ear. So cut out the wordiness, but not to the extent of being left with gnomic utterances. Get across your interviewee's way of speaking – 'you know', 'indeed it is', 'not me matey'. Indicate a person's accent at the start if it is interesting or distinctive, but don't produce slabs of incomprehensible dialect. Correct faulty grammar that leads to lack of clarity but leave it in if it's a trivial matter that adds colour.

Summarizing

Summarize some of the bigger chunks that you've removed by using indirect speech. For example:

'Do you think your team will get into the First Division next year?'

'I have no doubt whatsoever. …' (Here follows some history of how the club has gone in and out of the First Division for many years, but unfortunately you haven't got room for it.)

'What makes you so sure now?'

'I'm sure because although they've had their ups and downs over the past few years – for example, last year … Nevertheless when you look at the record as a whole you see that there's improvement more or less in the course of time … And if you look at what's happened in the last three or four games you can see that from all points of view the lads are showing a definite improvement. …' (Another longish answer but you've got what you want.)

So you write: 'He thought his team would get into the First Division next season because it has been constantly improving in the last four or five games.'

Be careful as you edit not to misrepresent with your compressions and rearrangements. When you use quotes it is safest to repeat the actual words said and you must always be completely faithful to the speaker's intention. When you don't use quote marks make sure your summaries or para-phrases are quite comprehensible, that they don't need for full understand-ing statements that you have weeded out.

You have had time to think about the interviewee's character and achieve-ments. Perhaps a feather-ruffling approach has encouraged revelations or psychoanalytic probings have unearthed a much more interesting and impressive person than was suspected at the interview. The editing of the tape or notes and the format used for writing up can produce a positive and informative piece that produces a good result even though the encounter didn't seem promising. Conversely if your preparation was inadequate and if you failed to elicit responses that did the interviewee justice, no amount of tweaking and embellishment in the writing will produce a good result.

FORMATS FOR WRITING UP

The writing up, whatever the format, puts the interviewee centre stage, which is what your readers will expect (even when done by the interviewers who are read as much or more for themselves as for their subjects). You can leave out many if not all of your questions and probing techniques, and apparently yourself altogether, and concentrate on the answers. 'Apparently' because of course your formulating of the questions, ordering them and then reshaping the final result means that you are to some degree a subject your-self (even if readers have to be interested enough to dig you out).

The interviewer is quite invisible in the interviews under such straplines as Relationships in women's magazines. Stories can be described as 'As Told To', about romance achieved out of Internet dating, for example, or about an adoption that had an inspiring message. Similarly there's the case stud-ies format: double-page spreads cover such TOTs as three women who suf-fered mightily from painkillers ('A painkiller nearly killed me' in *Woman*), each briefly introduced by the writer, with highly relevant statistics in boxes. In these ways we feel we're being spoken to straight from the heart. Nevertheless the input from the interviewer may have been considerable.

The essential tasks are to order the material of your interview so that it will achieve clarity and maximum impact. That is rarely the order of the questions, which has to allow for informality, for some digression and the natural tendency of a conversation to be discursive rather than logically structured. Most obviously (to repeat) you don't start with the normal gentle warming up exchanges of the discussion but with something extracted from it that defies you to turn the page.

We'll look more closely now at the two formats that offer most scope: the Q-and-A and the narrative. Whichever of these is used, there is room for experiment as well as the need to create a satisfying structure. The essential principle is to be fair to your subjects and to reveal what it is about them that your readers want to know.

Q-and-A

The Q-and-A format is used for a serious debate leaving out personalities, but it is also used as a way of ensuring that the interviewee is centre stage. At any level debates, discussions or more casual conversations may be preceded by an introduction to the interviewee with perhaps some back story, descriptions of clothes, appearance, setting and writer's comments that would otherwise be difficult to incorporate in the dialogue.

Popular magazines use the Q-and-A format for fast-moving, concise accounts of a person's views, a standfirst or a brief paragraph serving for the introduction. *FHM* has an interview with Ray Liotta under 'The *Narc* [film] star on *Grand Theft Auto* [voice-over on computer game], receiving horses' heads and touching beating hearts …' and *She* does Harry Connick Junior under 'The 36-year-old king of swing talks to *She* about his new comedy role, family life and why his wife couldn't care less about his on-screen loves'.

Some interviewers use the Q-and-A format to get closer to the interviewee. The descriptive material can make an informative introduction. The feature then becomes more like the dialogue in a play, with feelings exposed.

This format doesn't therefore guarantee that the subject is represented more objectively or more fairly than any other format, although it appears to do so. There are still all the many editing activities mentioned. Some Q-and-As, notably those that appeared over many years in *Playboy* and *Paris Review*, were several thousand words long yet distilled from several meetings and many hours of talk. The *Playboy* reviews were for a long time vetted and rewritten by the subjects and/or their publicists.

Let's have a look at one or two examples of this format:

The serious debate

If you're aiming to get inside somebody's highly respected mind, it will be wise to have some research notes alongside your questions, ready for unexpected depths.

The interviews in the bimonthly magazine *Philosophy Now*, which brings philosophy down to earth, are good and entertaining examples of serious debate. The sports issue of May/June 2003 has a Q-and-A introduced by a standfirst only:

> Myles Brand has just become President of the National Collegiate Athletic Association (NCAA). Formerly a philosophy professor, his academic research is into the nature of human action. Tim Madigan finds out how sport's new philosopher-king sees his new job.

Since the interview covers one page only and the questions are short and deferential, one can assume that the longish answers represent the unadulterated views of the interviewee. The beginning of each answer gives the flavour of this kind of interview:

> What is a philosopher like you doing in the crazy world of sport?
>
> This is the first non-university job I have had since I was seventeen and pumping gas ...
>
> What are the biggest ethical challenges you think student-athletes face today? Have these challenges increased in recent years?
>
> They have indeed. One good example is sports wagering ...
>
> What are your views regarding rewarding schools for their graduation rates of student-athletes?
>
> I believe that strong incentives and strong disincentives are necessary for the current reform movement in inter-collegiate athletics to be successful ...
>
> The sportswriter Dick Vitale recently argued that student-athletes should be paid to play sports. What is your view on this?
>
> I am opposed to pay for play ...

Do you still have time to philosophize, and if so, how do you do it?

I cannot stop philosophizing. I am pathologically addicted to it …

This final answer ends:

… I expect that I will expand my interests to philosophical issues in cultural studies. So, rather than diminish, my philosophical interests are likely to broaden and deepen.

On the following page there are comments by two contributors on points raised by the interview and finally readers are asked to give their opinions about what is cheating and what is an unfair advantage.

The Q-and-A profile

This combines several formats in one with the aim of being comprehensive; the life story as well as the now. Adrian Deevoy's account of the Canadian singer Shania Twain in *GQ* (August 2003) has a 1000-word preamble followed by a Q-and-A of about 2000 words.

The preamble is in the commonest narrative form, interwoven with quotes, an interview feature in itself, but stopping just before the present occasion. This means that the life story research can be pillaged for the most interesting facts and quotes. After charting her successes in recent years (34 million sales for the country-pop album *Come On Over*), Deevoy describes his first meeting with her – at the American Music Awards early in the year in Los Angeles. He needs a link between the end of this section and a jump back to her early struggles. He does it like this:

… As Shania walked away, she pecked the air affectedly and flapped her hands in the pampered manner of a ditzy diva. In five days, this was the only sight of Shania's inner bitch.

When asked to describe herself in one word she chooses neither 'kittenish' nor 'playful' but 'impatient'. Others opt for 'professional', 'driven' and 'perfectionist'. You'll also hear 'friendly' and 'fun' but often in the same breath you get 'inscrutable' or 'unreadable'.

Much of this remoteness stems from Shania's sad and strange life. In 1987 her mother and stepfather died in a road accident leaving her, at 21, to single-handedly support her younger siblings …

When the story arrives at now we get the Q-and-A interview.

The narrative

The narrative interview has to keep moving, just as a work of fiction does, interspersing the quotes with the unfolding story and yet juggle at the same time with various insights into the subject. These insights come out of the ways of speaking, the mannerisms, the appearance, the way the subject fits into the surroundings. Note the juggling in these extracts from 'Let your fingers do the nicking' by Val Hennessy (no relation) in *You*, magazine of *The Mail on Sunday*. It starts with a teaser-bridge-text intro:

> Old thieves never die. They simply fade away. Take veteran pickpocket, 76-year-old Rose Jones who, last spring, shuffled out of a London court on her walking-frame and announced, 'I've had a good run for my money. Maybe it's time to call it a day, though. Having to use a walking-frame means I'm not as quick on my feet as I used to be, which is a bit of a drawback in my line of business'.

> The offence, on this occasion, had taken place when Rose went 'on the binge' in Harrods during the January sales and lifted three purses. They had yielded £50 and Rose was just hobbling gleefully into Harvey Nichols to pinch a handbag or two for luck when the law caught up with her. Faster than you can say 'electronic eye' two store detectives were propelling Rose, and her walking-frame, into the back room for a search.

> She drew herself up to her full 4 ft 5 in. and was about to let forth a volley of verbal but, suddenly, her heart wasn't in it. She sensed that the game was up. Harrods had been the last fling in a 'line of business' that has resulted in 30 convictions for pickpocketing, dating back to 1926, and a total of 20 years in prison. This time Rose got off with a conditional discharge and strict instructions to cooperate with her social worker.

A lengthy interview with a celeb will probably need to add to the juggling of some commentary, favourable or unfavourable, on points made by previous interviewers. Sting had suffered from criticism, mainly from popular papers, and McCormick in *The Telegraph Magazine* interview already quoted from applies himself to some of this. Seven houses in different places and the conspicuous consumption that goes with them contradicts his image as an environmental activist. The extract on page 269 continues:

> 'I don't know how to alter the paradox. I could go and live in the middle of Hampstead Heath with a blanket around me and eat grass. Maybe as a gesture that might be heroic and even considered useful.'

> Actually it would probably be considered pretentious and risible, attracting the same kind of risible mockery as did his appearance in 1988 daubed in

body paint alongside Amazonian Indians to draw attention to the destruction of the rainforest. Sting-baiting is practically a national pastime among British journalists. Much fun was had at his expense in 1995, for example, when it was revealed that his former accountant had siphoned off £7 million without Sting's noticing.

'I didn't know how much was in the account in the first place,' he shrugs, which seems quite reasonable when you consider that estimates of his wealth tend to vary wildly between £85 million and £200 million. 'I really resent being on those rich lists that they keep publishing. For one thing, it's nobody's business how much I earn. It just makes people envious. And for another thing if you're on the list then you see that Phil Collins has something like five million more, it makes you so f****** competitive!'

He is joking, by the way. I feel duty-bound to point that out because so much can be lost between the lines when a throwaway comment is printed in hard black and white. Like the twinkle in his eyes (which are a lot warmer than might be judged from photographs). And the sudden burst of comical energy in his voice. Yet he is often described as being humourless.

That interpretation of the 'throwaway comment' reminds us that such comments need to be watched out for and put into context. If there are complaints about the published piece it may be unfair to point only to the words as evidence that you've been fair.

The hatchet job

The Queen of Mean, Lynn Barber, Interviewer of the Year in the British Press Awards more times than anyone else, has a reputation not entirely deserved but her putdowns are memorable. For example (guess who, if you don't know):

'I don't want to give a cool appraisal or even be snide. I just want to boil him in oil.'

To paraphrase, a symptom of the British class system which confers undue respect on gravely talking men in pinstripe suits who are 'uttering complete nonsense'.

'Are you thick?'

'She is a difficult so-and-so. What might be called a proper little madam were she not such an improper and enormous madam.'

The fact is, she gets very good answers and she strings them together to best effect. Way back in 1985 (27 October) an interview with Jimmy Boyle in the *Sunday Express Magazine* is a revealing example of her style and of its merits. Boyle was sentenced to life imprisonment for murder in 1967, was released in 1982, had become an author and was running a rehabilitation centre for drug addicts in Edinburgh. Barber worries that 'the Jimmy Boyle of the present is so respectable, so assured, so word-perfect in the lingo of social concern, it is hard to believe he is the same man ...'

> All this sweetness and light and universal forgiveness has the effect of making me feel more acid and I ask if he has ever read Tom Wolfe's book *Radical Chic*. He hasn't, so I explain: 'It's about the sort of trendy scene where you have terrorists and murderers going to cocktail parties with judges and celebrities, and being treated as celebrities themselves.'
>
> He takes a deep breath before replying: 'Look, let me tell you, I could move into London tomorrow but I don't want to get into that trendy shit. There's all these middle-class trendies and academics who think they've got the answer to everything, and meanwhile they just leave people on the scrapheap while they stand around having intellectual arguments. But really the only people who can find the solution is the scrapheap, and I'm right in the thick of it, working at street level. Yes, I have acquired middle-class tastes, but my roots are still in the Gorbals and I wouldn't be doing the work I'm doing if they weren't.'
>
> A good answer, though any pretence of friendliness between us has now hit the dust. 'Why are journalists so cynical?' he keeps asking. 'Because it's our job to be cynical,' I keep telling him.

Humphrey Bogart's tip at the start of this chapter is useful. But before you become a celeb-interviewer go easy.

The profile

The variously-sourced, research-based assessment is the most fruitful kind of profile for our purpose. The present tense is often used to indicate the cuttings-based origins of quotes. Here are three variations:

1 The personal profile, average length to longer, much like the typical interview feature but drawing on various sources and sometimes various meetings rather than being based on a one-off meeting. Some are too obviously written at a distance, scissors-and-paste jobs with an overuse of material gathered from cuttings and publicists.

2 Serious, overall assessments. They may be unsigned, thus putting the publication's authority behind it, though it is more often signed nowadays. Typical examples are those of *The Observer*, which has been signed for several years, *The Sunday Times* and *New Statesman*.

3 The long literary profile, notably done in *The Guardian*, more like an essay than a piece of journalism.

The personal profile

An example is a 3000-word profile of Elizabeth Taylor in *Woman's Own* in 1985 by Donald Zec, pegged on the film star's emergence from the Betty Ford clinic after treatment for drugs and alcohol dependence. Zec is able to enliven it by memories of a relationship going back over many years:

> I remember early on in our sometimes friendly, sometimes abrasive relation, finding myself alone with her in the back seat of a Rolls, in Rome. Embalmed in the limo's exotic upholstery, with Elizabeth Taylor looking as seductive as (to quote Burton) 'an erotic dream', I had the uncanny feeling that she was nestling all around me. The euphoria ended abruptly as she murmured, 'You know you're a shit, Donald dear.'

> This unsolicited testimonial, I was to learn, stemmed from some taunt of mine printed a couple of years earlier about her role in *Cleopatra*. Something like – '57 varieties of cleavage scarcely adds up to a performance ...'. For some reason she never forgot it.

The overall assessment

Liz Hurley in an unsigned profile in *The Sunday Times* was accounted for by:

- Liz Hurley quotes at key moments of her career, derived from interviews
- Quotes from others: a radio comic, an American film critic, teenage contemporaries
- Anecdotes illustrating key moments of her life: a nose ring, being banned from pubs ...
- The liaisons with Hugh Grant and others
- A picture of someone who is demanding, tactless, determined, ambitious, mellowing.

The anonymous writer doesn't judge.

The *New Statesman* profiles are signed and concerned to balance merits and faults, approaching an elegant essay style, especially in intros. David Cox's profile of the TV interviewer Martin Bashir begins:

> The confessional interview has become the most sacred ritual of our contemporary secular religion, celebrity. At unpredictable intervals, totemic figures sanctified by fame, however acquired, bare their souls for our worshipful attention. From their quavering lips come paeans, sometimes of penitence, but more often of petulant self-justification, their credence depending heavily on the congregation's faith. We, the laity, marvel at the utterances of these demi-gods. If we dare, we snigger a bit as well, and leave the sofa chastened, excited and slightly ashamed. (*New Statesman*, 6 May 2002)

Words indicating his character include 'courteous', 'charismatic', 'elusive', 'pushy', 'therapist', 'diffident', 'self-effacing', 'ambition'.

The long and literary

Even more essay-like are the *Guardian* articles collected in *Lives and Works: profiles of leading novelists, poets and playwrights* edited by Annalena McAfee for Atlantic Books and Martin Amis's *The Moronic Inferno and Other Visits to America*. These and others (see the Bibliography) are a highly recommended read when you feel you need to temper a prurient and contriving mood induced by the more journalistic kinds described above. These books contain pieces that have the length to go much deeper into the works of the subjects, with reliable and relevant insights derived from study of the lives.

Unusual formats

A final tip: after studying the interview formats of the publications you're aiming at, look for unusual ones. Editors want what they usually want but a bit different, newer, something special that fits the subject. If you interview a writer who has a very distinctive style you may want to borrow the style for the whole of the write-up (as was once done in the typically long sentence structures of the columnist Bernard Levin). An interview with an actor who has played James Bond could be related in deadpan, ironic James Bond-speak. Sometimes it's a good idea to send yourself up.

FOLLOWING UP

Check on the phone by reading out extracts or send your interviewee a type-script or paste extracts into an email if you're anxious that points have not been made clearly or that there may be some misrepresentation, but don't normally allow changes or grant subjects or publicists approval of your script.

You may need to make arrangements for your subject to be photographed. Add your subject's contact numbers to your script in case subeditors need to follow up. Add such contact numbers to your own records as well. You may want to do future interviews with a subject or benefit from their contacts.

ASSIGNMENTS

1 Get someone (tutor or fellow student?) to read to you a published interview of 1200 to 1500 words. Test your note-making skills by making notes of the content. Make sure you include the main facts, names and figures. Then write up the interview as if you had been the interviewer in the same length as the original. Compare your version with the original to see what of importance was missed and to see if you've made any improvements.

2 Do the research and write up a 2000-word 'scissor-and-paste' profile of a celebrity. Then do outlines for three 800-word profiles of the celebrity for separate publications, focusing on a separate aspect for each target.

3 Write up one of the profiles outlined.

4 *Group.* If a talk by a feature writer on the skills of interviewing (or of research or of feature writing generally) can be arranged, follow it up with questioning time. The members of the group then produce an 800-word report on the event aimed at a journalism students' magazine.

5 *Group.* A large group can divide into four for this one. In each group an interviewer and interviewee are chosen. The interviewee chooses a subject to be questioned about. The other members make notes of the nature of the interviewee (easy, difficult, articulate, rambling, confusing?) and of the skills of the interviewer. These can include ability to establish rapport, persuasiveness, control of the proceedings, body language.

---

17 The regular columnist

The only times I've regretted a column is when I haven't written it – because I thought I'd regret it. It's a highly self-critical, self-analysing process where you spend 90 per cent of the time deciding what to write, justifying writing it, and then the remaining 10 per cent doing it. And for that reason, perhaps, because I know what I'm doing, no, I've never been sued. If ever I were, it would be on purpose. (Keith Waterhouse, in a letter to the author)

The one problem I never have is choosing something to write about. I don't think a general column can be done for long unless you *are* interested in a wide range of matters. (Bernard Levin, in a letter to the author)

The good reporter and the good feature writer do not encourage us to enquire into things. Even the editorial writer does not often ask us to look on both sides. But the columnist is ever flipping things upside down and wrong side out and inviting us to look and laugh – and think even. (Hallam Walker Davis, *The Column*)

A columnist has a licence to be rude, funny, satirical, prejudiced, provocative or philosophical: in one word, different, depending on the publication's formula and the editor's interpretation of it.

Editors like columns. They provide the security that all regular features provide: at least those spaces will be filled. Regular columns can bring depth and perspective to the consideration of events. They can provoke thought, move to action, inspire, uplift, amuse, to a greater degree than other kinds of feature. Content ranges from 'lifestyle' pieces, through humorists, specialists and pundits with a great variety of styles and formats.

What editors value above all in the regular column is an individual voice. They like a columnist who keeps their correspondence page lively. Many columnists now give an email address and benefit from readers' feedback that provides ideas to follow up.

Let's have a look at a few different kinds of columns and think about ways of working and ways of finding a slot.

LEARNING FROM THE BEST

The presses are currently groaning under the weight of columnists famed in non-journalistic fields. When those fields provide expert knowledge the specialist columns that result can be admirable. Those of former stars in athletics and various sports come to mind, and if they get a little more help than usual from subs the results are ample justification.

When the fame has been derived from exposure in an entertainment industry the resulting column is often tittle-tattle. Amusing for a while, but such columns lack staying power. So what? Who cares?

A general column has to come from within. It stands or falls by how strongly attracted readers are to your voice, your angle on life, what you have to say that is individual. You need an interest in a wide variety of subjects and the desire and the energy to share that interest. The best columns have an urgent inevitability about them. That doesn't often come easily: more often it comes after much reading, thinking, and several painful drafts.

Notice that a sentence or two out of the best columns are enough to identify the author. Study the best columnists to develop your techniques until your medium and your message are inseparable: your aim is to be inimitable. It's not enough to find something to say and then to impose on it clever tricks.

You will find your own ways of learning from the best, but here is a workshop method you may want to try. Cut out columns that impress and paste up sections, or paragraphs, on separate sheets. Write notes on the techniques you identify: for example, what sort of intro, what structure in the body, what sort of ending, use of quotes, anecdotes, etc. Follow-up assignments are given at the end of the chapter.

Have a look at the anthologies, notably *The Penguin Book of Columnists* (1997), edited by Christopher Silvester, which includes American and Australian columnists as well as British; and Karl E. Meyer's collection, *Pundits, Poets and Wits: An Omnibus of American Newspaper Columns* (1990). The former is also overwhelmingly newspaper columns, though the *New Statesman* and *The Spectator* are represented. They both cover the ground from the birth of the newspaper column in the middle of the nineteenth century.

As with personal collections of interviews and reviews, columnists' collections can have the whiff of ephemerality about them, especially when depending on immediate reactions to topical events. The exceptions are those that have resonating qualities of depth and/or humour. Among collections that I think have transferred most successfully to book form are some of *The Guardian Bedside Books*, Alice Thomas-Ellis's collection of *Spectator* pieces, *More Home Life* (Duckworth), *Cassandra at his Finest and Funniest* (Daily Mirror/Hamlyn) and Simon Jenkins's *Against the Grain: Writings of a Sceptical Optimist* (mostly from *The Times*), and more recently Francis Wheen's *Hoo-Hahs and Passing Frenzies* (Atlantic Books, 2002).

Jenkins more than most has given the pieces in his selection special attention (including greater length) to make them more suitable for the demands of a book.

GETTING A SLOT

Even if you have a good idea for a column that you think a publication would like you'll need to produce at least half a dozen examples with indications of how you would continue for many weeks/months after that. Maintaining continuity is particularly important for the more personal kind of column. You may have six brilliant weekly columns in you, but have you any more? As for producing three columns a week for *The Times* it will help if, like Bernard Levin, you have an office next to the editor's or if, like Simon Jenkins, you're an ex-editor.

If you are staff, writer or subeditor, you'll be living and breathing the world of your publication. Replacing your duties or adding to them by writing a column (assuming there's room for one or if a current incumbent is poorly) may well be part of your career strategy. If you're a freelance, before coming up with ideas you must market-study more keenly than you normally do.

Finding the gap

List what you think is missing in the formulas. Would a general column fit in? Can you see scope for a semi-specialist subject that you know something about and would enjoy exploring further? Country matters? Video games?

Approach by giving your background in a brief c.v. that includes any experience that qualifies you to write on the topics or along the lines proposed. Provide several samples plus outlines of several more. You're not likely to get a regular column immediately but you might be taken on as an occasional feature writer and from there you may be able to cross the bridge.

Local paper columns

Typically, local papers find something local to reflect on, in parish-pump mode:

> Lovely cherry blossom trees have been planted round the old folks' home in memory of a patient ... Did you know that Lord Nelson used to watch play at our Cricket Green? And yes, Lady Hamilton used to accompany him.

If you're a visitor you might have a so-what reaction but such columns can reflect local inhabitants' deep feelings about where they live: can make it a microcosm.

A sample of wider reach:

> Men have role models such as Victor Meldrew. Women, unfortunately, have only mad, pigeon-feeding ladies and mad lady owners of many cats. (*Daily Echo*, Bournemouth)

I bet that got the letters pages humming. Culture sometimes comes into it, over a pseudonym: Gargoyle ('The Sage on the Page') in *Kentish Times* gets away with a reference to the Frogs in a column under 'Better latte than never...':

> ... Starbucks has opened for business in Paris – the world capital of café culture ...

> Parisians with a sense of history are ('ow you say?) exceedingly miffed that Starbucks – a relative newcomer to the coffee game – has dared to compete with the likes of cafés where the likes of Ernest Hemingway, Simone de Beauvoir and Jean-Paul Sartre used to slurp caffeine and think great thoughts and say highly quotable things ...

How about a tea culture, with the eccentrics and thinkers that tea attracts?

People like Dave Splarg. Philosophy: Cor, look at the state of that? Catchphrase: Any chance of a cuppa?

ALL KINDS OF DISCOVERIES

The number of columnists are many but the stars are few. If you're ambitious you'll derive warning, instruction and encouragement from the words of the esteemed American columnist Max Lerner, quoted by Silvester. Columnists can expect to be criticized for the prejudices in themselves that they expose and attacked for their stance of omniscience:

> A general columnist, by his nature, must roam widely and set down his assertions, not just his doubts and torments. Remember that he is not sitting in judgement as an expert who has mastered what there is to know about the subject. He is only a traveller who has made unsuspected discoveries for himself in the realms of gold, and he wants to share them.

Some columnists have to know exactly what their discoveries are before they start writing. Others prefer to start sooner, with a germ of an idea, and discover as they go, freewheeling on their words that come. And there are all the degrees in between the two methods. What are regular, general columns about? In content, structure and style general columns experiment more than other features. We'll divide the main contents/styles into four, though any one column might exploit several kinds of content and techniques:

- the world at large
- lifestyle
- argument and provocation
- humour, parody and fantasy.

The world at large

Under this heading we have both the columnists who are closely allied to the publication's politics and policies, and those given more or less free rein to choose their content and express their own opinion, even when that conflicts with the stance of the publication. Columnists receive these privileges when they've established a name. Even then they are advised to have a clear understanding with their editors. Some editors draw a fine line above the amount of controversy they want. Editors and columnists come and go, but the top columnists can be fixtures for many years.

Facts are not lying around in tidy piles ready to be collected, on the Internet or anywhere else. In other words gathering them into meaningful patterns is not as easy as it looks. You need a viewpoint to guide your search, and the integrity to respect and divulge the truth as revealed to you.

Columnists with staying power not only discover such facts but know how to take off from them. Check them as well. In his introduction to *Hoo-Hahs and Passing Frenzies*, a collection of columns and essays mainly from *The Guardian*, Francis Wheen says 'journalism involves telling people things they couldn't have found out for themselves'.

A few samples of Wheenery:

> The prolific Paul Johnson … adds that the Queen Mum 'benefits from a deep-rooted veneration the British have – it is more manly than deference, akin rather to admiration – for the aristocracy'. Speak for yourself, matey. (*The Guardian*, 19 July 2000)

> When Evelyn Waugh grumpily described children as 'defective adults', he was articulating a common national prejudice. We are a nation of child-haters; and, as the size of the prison population demonstrates, we are a nation of punishment freaks. Put the two together and you have a society where physical violence against tiny tots is not only acceptable but also a bounden duty. Hence the undisguised glee of Tory backbenchers when Gillian Shepherd indulged her flogging fantasies on the *Today* programme this week. (*The Guardian*, 31 October, 1996)

Other subjects covered by Wheen in the book are the decline of the sitcom, Hollywood's mauling of film scripts, various kinds of prudery and prurience (usually together), the debunking of sacred cows, whimsical if not weird entries in *Who's Who*.

Op Ed pages of newspapers give space to world-at-large columnists. An attack on Tony Blair by Fathers4Justice, using condom bombs filled with purple flour, was followed by a sympathetic treatment of their case in *The Observer* of 23 May 2004 by David Aaronovitch. As well as pointing out why the law finds custody cases difficult (the unfair treatment of women historically has to be set alongside the changing co-carer view of fatherhood), Aaronovitch can bring humanity into it by getting personal:

> So I put myself in the position of another Mr V who is, say, two years into this process: granted access to his children by the courts, thwarted continually by the actions of Mrs V, and almost certainly continually advised that it would be better to give up the fight. Would I not describe myself (and my children) as being victim of a huge injustice? What would I do

about it? Slope off sadly and try and forget that I'd ever been a dad? Most do.

Politically speaking

The highly esteemed Hugo Young, political columnist for many years for *The Guardian* and *The Observer*, who died on 22 September 2003, published a collection of his political writings under the title *Supping with the Devils*. His first essay, spelling out the high standards he set himself, is an inspirational message for all journalists. It was reprinted in *The Guardian* of 24 September, and in the *British Journalism Review* (Vol. 14, Number 4, 2003) an extract is printed in a tribute by Geoffrey Goodman. Part of that extract reads:

> I've been less interested in influencing events and the ministers who make them than in enlightening readers who may want to understand what is going on. It is important however for journalists to know their limits. In the end we are not players. We criticize decisions but never make them. If we purport to telling it like it is we can't avoid talking to politicians. They own the truths we like to think we are reporting. The line they're spinning is at least half the story and the columnist has the advantage of being able expose the spin and deride it. But he has to talk around to be able to do that. He must sup with the devil constantly … Though writing, I contend, as an outsider he must discover as an insider. But, for me, there's a limit to the intimacy. I can think of no more than three politicians I've regarded as friends. Such fastidiousness is not an advantage for a columnist. It cuts off some of the inside dope. But I think it keeps the water purer.

In Geoffrey Goodman's words 'he was fearless as a scourge of cant and hypocrisy'. That makes him a model for all columnists, who can be loath to risk losing favour or friends. When we don't know who the journalists' friends are, we're not quite sure how generous they're being with the truth, as Matthew Parris reminded us (page 276). Especially when they're political columnists who may have friends in high places.

Simon Jenkins, columnist for *The Times* Op Ed pages and for the London *Evening Standard*, has been a fountainhead of common sense for many years and is a model for both cool reasoning and elegantly incisive style. In *The Times* of 19 May 2004 he conjures up the image of bin Laden chalking a list of scalps on the wall of a cave on the Afghan–Pakistan border: the victims of 9/11, Saddam Hussein, the Government of Spain and several others.

> The wall also celebrates the demise of the Middle East 'road map' and the restoration of the Afghan warlords and the opium trade, easing the return of the Taleban. It celebrates the disarray of European diplomacy and a diplomatic war between France and America. It celebrates the American team not daring to wave its flag at the forthcoming Olympics. All this was beyond fantasy two years ago. Bin Laden can now confidently anticipate anti-Western fanatics taking power in Iraq and the corrupt House of Saud losing its valued American sponsors.

> Not only has the Government of Spain fallen, those of Japan, Italy and Poland have been rocked. But even bin Laden could not have hoped to turn the bonny smile on Tony Blair's face into an ashen mask and have his Cabinet scheming to get rid of him. He could not have imagined Donald Rumsfeld swinging in the congressional wind on charges of torture, and George Bush facing plummeting opinion polls. And all because the World Trade Centre was made of tin.

Jenkins's discoveries are of the facts, of how to select them, make pictures with them, give them meaning and draw lessons from them.

Personally speaking

You may, in contrast, prefer to have a general column whose discoveries are largely personal: of yourself and your relationship to the world. You can put yourself in the middle of it all. But are you interesting enough, and are you passionate or funny enough about what you've got to say?

Too many 'I's' are irritating, especially when the culprits have run out of anything worth saying about current events and mores. Whimsical chatter about domestic upheavals can be groan-making. The gossip columns of the popular papers are parodied by *Private Eye* (see below).

If you insist on being whimsical you may find a market in your local paper or an undemanding magazine. But surely a magazine aimed at the retired is also aimed at retirement if it gives room to such pieces as the one that began:

> I am no Adrian Mole, but he, with another 50 years behind him might well turn out to be just like me. Now 64½ I still search my face for pimples past and principles present (or is it the other way round?). And, having taken early retirement and being on a small pension, I also have difficulties with my pocket money.

295

You can get away with a lot of 'I's' if you're angry and forceful enough. Cassandra (Sir William Connor) was the star columnist of the *Daily Mirror* for many years. He wasn't really talking about himself: he was voicing the frustrations of ordinary people with bureaucratic inefficiency, the waste of taxpayers' money, and the other ills that we're all heir to:

> An extraordinarily large part of my life is spent holding a black plastic object that stretches from my mouth to my ear.
>
> I talk, shout and whisper down it for hundreds of hours a year.
>
> Much of the time when I do this I am in a small red room that is usually filthy, always uncomfortable and frequently ill-lit.
>
> This constricted house of pain is called a telephone kiosk.

The Spectator has some highly readable columnists. You don't always believe (or even sympathize with) what they're saying but they can write with inimitable style, the essential quality for longevity. Let's have a look at the issue of 29 May 2004. Paul Johnson, historian as well as journalist, although proud of his connections as already mentioned, often seems in his columns ('And Another Thing') to be in a world, even a planet, of his own. In this issue he gives a potted history, spiced by personal history, of red hair (at 70-odd he happily tells us that though grey on top, he's still red 'downstairs'). Arriving at his public school he was insulted by a group of boys:

> Their spokesman said, 'Johnson, you are a new squit and a nasty-looking ginger fellow, and we don't like your manners. Can you give me one good reason why you should not be beaten up?' I said, 'Yes, I can. But I will have to whisper it.' Suspicious but also intrigued, he leant over. So I dealt him what I had been taught to call an uppercut ...

I wonder about that. I never believed in those uppercuts in Hollywood films. Now at least they rub the fist that was used, with a grimace of pain. Johnson has met everybody worthy of note, it seems, and is often able to put them on the right track. In the same piece he says that once:

> ... after listening to that tortured writer James Baldwin [the black American author who wrote memorably about racial prejudice] complaining at length about his sufferings and slights, I told him, 'Listen, if you're born in England, as I was, red-haired, left-handed and a Roman Catholic, there's nothing you don't know about discrimination.'

You must admit, you've got to read that sort of thing when you come across it.

At the back end of this issue of *The Spectator* there are columns that trade well under their straplines. High Life (Taki) is high society in its most un-PC form. You weren't safe from punks even on Concorde.

On one trip back from the States he had to witness the sort of 'proletarian brutalism' that 'has made the English loathed the world over':

> I told one of the slobs to keep his voice down as I was trying to read, and he looked at me in that cowardly way punks have – half-smile in case I'm someone well connected, and half defiant because I am, after all, a pensioner – but nothing came of it. I know that BA is in trouble but punks should be told to behave or else before they get on. When I asked the stewardess exactly how much 'these gentlemen' had contributed to fly Mach 1, she smiled ruefully and said nothing. Enough said. I sat with the beautiful Princess Ferial of Jordan, talked about the Middle East, and in no time we had landed.

Taki knows he has to perform – you never know what the next sentence will bring – and the timing is impeccable. An unmitigated snob but you have to laugh.

A Low Life column (Jeremy Clarke) has nightmares brought on by withdrawal from antidepressant drugs and experiments with homeopathic tablets and vitamin and mineral pills. Singular Life, in the shape of Petronella Wyatt, deplores girls being drawn to 'pretty boys' like Brad Pitt, Leonardo DiCaprio and Johnny Depp, and rejecting the classic Hollywood types – Clark Gable, Cary Grant and Spencer Tracy. Other kinds of life are given space from time to time: this week Wild Life (Aidan Hartley) charts the shameful record of the British Government in Rwanda and the bleak prospects for Blair's Commission for Africa.

Lifestyle

The term came in for some well-earned ridicule when it was coined, along the lines of: why don't you try getting a life instead? The term now tends to be used as a convenient catch-all to cover anything that doesn't need a great deal of thought or depth, which reflects consumers' increased spending power and which will bring in the adverts. Thus both newspapers and magazines have rubrics such as Life or Living or Style. Typically they cover some of the areas listed under *The Observer Magazine*'s Life section, which has the headings Relationships, Fashion, Interiors, Gardens, Food and Drink, Living, Health, and What Happened Next?

Since such subject matter is perennial, the newer rubrics may seem hardly necessary, even if you admit some convenience. In a way it's a sad reflection of our over-busy, fragmented lives that we need features telling us how to live. 'Slow down!' is a cry getting louder at present, so paradoxically enough that theme also gets into the lifestyle columns.

Most of those sections are specialisms and a few will receive some attention in Chapter 19. Many of the general columns are aspirational: often pegged to celebs' lifestyles, they encourage living vicariously. There are hypocrisies to be aware of in all kinds of publications that are hot on lifestyles. An American magazine editor for 20 years, Myrna Blyth has published a book, *Spin Sisters*, which shows remorse for the way she went along with the vested interest magazines have in making women feel stressed. They are then more likely to buy the aromatherapy oils and yoga videos in their adverts.

There's conspicuous hypocrisy in the popular nationals: for example, when puritanism looms large on one page and prurience on the next. The sexualization of teenage magazines for girls and of the girls themselves is currently causing controversy. The sexualization of the young men's (lads') magazines reached a boring point and they have had to look for more satisfying or less in-your-face diversions. In other words, some thoughtfulness.

Some of the specialisms, of course, notably Health, are covered by interviewing experts and by using case studies. Relationships is often dealt with by psychologists or psychiatrists, but just as often in personal, somewhat frothy columns. On the Living page of Ireland's *Sunday Independent*, under the strapline Working It Out and the standfirst 'Take a good look at what defines you, and you'll find plenty of room to change ...', an essay-style column begins:

> Take a good look at yourself. What do you see? There are some things that you just are and there isn't a whole lot you can do about it. You are as tall as you are. You are the race that you are. If you are 35, and even though you might tell the occasional fib about it, you are 35. But what kind of 35 you are is up to you. You can veer towards the 30 or the 40 with equal ease.

The conclusion is that we can change more about ourselves if we put our minds to it. There's a worthwhile seam in there, about understanding what it is that influences our decisions. But it doesn't avoid preachiness. Sometimes when you're being personal it can even be a good idea to bring a few more 'I's' into it (and a few more doubts).

A column in *Marks & Spencer Magazine* is full of doubts, which makes us all feel better about ourselves, especially if we're a female writer with three children, but it is rather short on drama. It is headed 'A New Me? Yes Please' and subheaded 'Ever-hopeful of a fitter, healthier and stress-free lifestyle, Fiona Gibson finds that reality has other ideas'. She tells us how she has switched from late nights with her 'goals' notebook to stopping work earlier and having a hot bath.

How a particular decision (or rather lack of decision at a particular moment) changed an outlook on life is the subject of Tom Templeton's (invisible) interview with Frank McGarry, the What Happened Next column in *The Observer Magazine* of 23 May 2004. It's an interesting story about 15 years of the interviewee's life and the short-story structure providing suspense gets us emotionally as well as mentally involved. It works like this:

> Standfirst: 'Date: 8 January 1989. Place: M1, Kegworth, Leicestershire. Facts: Frank McGarry was the last survivor to be pulled from the wreckage of a Boeing 737 flight from London to Belfast that crash-landed on the M1. He is now sales director of a fund-management firm in London and has just had a boy with his wife, Paula.'

The intro:

> My memory of the events from the hours around the crash and the weeks after I'm sure is in there, I just don't go looking for it. When I talk about the crash, I have a kind of after-dinner speech – 'Somebody else sat in my seat and they died, two people in front of me died, three people behind me died.' I'm emotionally detached from the crash when I talk about it.

The body, paragraph by paragraph:

1 In hospital with serious injuries.
2 Was 23, a university graduate, and had been about to join the army.
3 It took over a year to recover but two months after the crash he set up a consultancy business with a friend and got engaged. Became a workaholic.
4 Advice from a doctor dealing with post-traumatic stress disorder: get in control. Finally managed to, meeting a great support, Paula, an old school mate. Now have a baby boy.
5 Four years at various IT consultancies, part of the team that set up Cofunds, the UK's leading fund supermarket. Now Cofunds' sales director.

6 What happened before that crash. The pilot said there was 'trouble with the right engine'. McGarry knew it was the left engine because he saw the sparks and could have forced his way through and told the captain he'd made a mistake. Because he didn't '47 people died'.

The conclusion:

> And now, I do the same thing to everybody else. When something is not right, I just stand up and say, 'Where's that going? That's just wrong.' I speak my mind a lot more and know I can change things, if I really want to.

It's not great writing, but you know it's the truth and he doesn't use the word 'lifestyle' once.

Argument and provocation

Readers are prepared to meet, in general columns, arguments that are less balanced than a straightforward feature would allow. The 'purely political' Op Ed columns, such as the Simon Jenkins example above, have to be firmly based, and seen to be firmly based, on facts. What's certain is that in regular columns that are given leeway there must be evident *respect* for the facts.

But how much time have you got? How many more facts do you want? It's never possible to gather all the facts. So the line is not easy to draw between the columns that depend almost entirely on logical persuasion and those that bring more emotion to bear, that are more concerned to make you think or shake up your prejudices than to persuade. Many factual and emotional argument columns supply the publication's or the author's email address to encourage participation by readers, who may provide more facts, opposing arguments, different experiences, fruitful ideas, all of which help to keep the column going.

The iconoclasts

Because many columnists blandly ramble about nothing very much, a columnist who stops you in your tracks is highly valued. Julie Burchill, who has written for *The Face*, *New Society* and *The Mail on Sunday*, and is at the time of writing in *The Guardian*, is a sociopath. Well, that's how she has described herself in an interview: however you interpret her (not easy to do), it works. The collections of columns (see Bibliography) maintain their edge too. Here she is in *The Mail on Sunday*:

> Was I the only person to drop my genuine Our Lady of Lourdes cigarette lighter in awe when the Papal Tiger gave that amazing lecture to Hollywood on the danger of creating images that 'weak, defenceless, old and unattractive' people could never live up to? Apart from the fact that it's very rude to talk this way about Terry Wogan, it was terminally rich coming from a man who leads a church full of priests – celibate of course – who know enough to advise their flocks on every problem of family life and whose ideal woman is a mother who is also a virgin. The truth is that the idea of being born in original sin has mixed up and maimed more people than a million soap operas ever could.
>
> Not only are half the tarts in London convent-educated, but a large number of the drunks, dossers and assorted human flotsam lying around the streets speak with an Irish accent.

Like Taki she knows how to be noticed.

Humour, parody and fantasy

We have seen humour at work in several of the columns discussed above, some successful and some not. For a column whose main purpose is humour you need a good idea and you need to take off. Too much research or analysis is liable to weigh heavily. Subs are warned not to interfere: the moving of a comma can destroy a carefully planned bit of irony. Extracts that give a fair idea of the whole are for the same reason difficult to find, except for the more outlandish styles – parody and fantasy. To appreciate their satirical effect fully you will need more exposure, but there follow a few tastes.

The prolific Craig Brown does parody in several places. His *Daily Telegraph* column of 11 March 2004, 'Continuing Way of the World's exclusive serialization of the *Unpublished John Gielgud* letters' included: 'To Dr Ian Paisley, 5 May 1972':

> I simply cannot be bothered with intrigues, lies and recriminations. When I bumped into you – a perfect stranger! – in Piccadilly and told you how much I admired your white ankle socks, adding as an aside that you also had the most beautiful hands, I had no idea your mind was already occupied. How was I to realize that you were leading a demonstration of 10,000 Ulstermen, bless them, against this, that and the other? One cannot be expected to notice simply everything.

> You bellowed at me to get out of the way, yet I was only being sweet. I sense you are a bit of a bossy-boots, darling Ian. If you cannot take compliments, then I shall no longer bother to offer them, and then you won't like it, will you? And you so marvellously tall and broad-shouldered, and with such a twinkle in your eye. Oh, but there I go again!

Among the greatest of columnists have been those who have taken off into fantasy while working within journalism and its purposes and keeping to its restrictions of length and deadline.

J. B. Morton wrote his Beachcomber columns for the *Daily Express* for over 40 years from 1924. The best were collected in *The Best of Beachcomber*, from which the following extracts were taken. The law in operation provided some of the funniest moments. The first day of the case of Miss Ruby Staggage v. Broxholme Hydraulic Laundries and Others caused Mr Justice Cocklecarrot much trouble, with laborious talk of multiple cozenage, *ultra vires*, *sine die*, 'tutamen being implicit, with or without barratry, responderia and plonth', and so on.

On the second day:

> Cocklecarrot asked Mr Honey-Gander, counsel for the defendants, what the twelve red-bearded dwarfs could possibly have to do with Broxholm Hydraulic Laundries, and how they came into the case. Mr Honey-Gander made the sensational reply, 'M'lud, I understand that these gentlemen have a controlling interest in these laundries. In fact, they *are* Broxholm Hydraulic Laundries.'
>
> *Cocklecarrot*: Then why do they call themselves 'Others'?
> *Mr Honey-Gander*: I believe, m'lud, that there are others connected with the laundries.
> *Cocklecarrot*: Red-bearded dwarfs, too, I will wager.
> *Mr Honey-Gander*: So I understand, m'lud.
> *Cocklecarrot*: How many?
> *Mr Honey-Gander*: Forty-one, m'lud.
> *Cocklecarrot*: Merciful heavens! Call Mrs Staggage.
> *Mr Honey-Gander*: Your name is Elvira Staggage?
> *Miss Staggage*: No, sir. It is Amy Clowte.
> *Mr Honey-Gander*: I see. You own a rocking-horse factory?
> *Miss Staggage*: No, sir. I act for the real owners.
> *Mr Honey-Gander*: And who are they?
> *Miss Staggage*: A number of red-bearded dwarfs, sir. I see them over there.
> (From J. B. Morton, *The Best of Beachcomber*)

The case is complicated by the fact that the dwarfs are both hydraulic laundaderers and rocking-horse manufacturers, and so are both plaintiffs and defendants.

Samples of the famed column of Brian Nolan, a fore-runner of *Private Eye*, are collected in *The Best of Myles*, Pan Books, 1977. Here is a section under the (strictly Gaelic) heading 'Sir Myles na Glopalean'. Note the similarity of this to 'Pseuds' Corner' in that magazine:

> Myles himself, the brilliant young journalist, will be out of town for 14 days. No letters will be forwarded. An indefatigable first-nighter, he is keenly interested in the theatre and has written several plays. Life he regards as a dialectic that evolves from aesthetic and extra-human impulses, many of them indubitably Marxian in manifestation. The greatest moment in his life (which occurred in 1924) was when he made the discovery that life is in reality an art form. Each person, he believes, is engaged on a life-long opus of grandiose expressionism, modulating and mutating the Ego according to subconscious aesthetic patterns. The world, in fact, is a vast art gallery, wherein even the curators themselves are exhibitors and exhibitionists. The horse, however, is the supreme artistic symbol…
>
> *The Editor*: We can't have much more of this, space must be found for my stuff.
>
> *Myself*: All right, never hesitate to say so. I can turn off the tap at will.

Private Eye of 27 May 2004 has Craig Brown parodying Sir Peregrine Worsthorne's recently published *In Defence of Aristocracy*. Sir Peregrine is qualified to deal with this subject because:

> … I was myself born into the very bosom of the aristocracy. As is well-known in aristocratic circles, my great-grandmother's second husband had a third cousin who was an Anstruther of Godalming. The Anstruthers stand as the veriest beacons of the hereditary principle, having given over their lives to looking after the people of Godalming, supplying them with nutritious scraps in cold spells and taking them to court only when the subsequent bills have remained unpaid. (Reproduced by kind permission of *Private Eye*/Pressdram. Copyright Pressdram Limited 2004)

Boris Johnson, Shadow Minister for the Arts, editor of *The Spectator*, and excellent columnist for *The Daily Telegraph* (winning him Columnist of the Year in 2004), is lampooned by *Private Eye* in the same issue in one of the many anonymous pieces (nobody and nothing are sacred in that organ).

Under the heading 'Boris Johnson on his doubts surrounding the conduct of the Iraqi war' we have:

> Golly! Cripes! What's going on? When I signed up to support the war lark, no one said it was going to turn nasty!

> Makes you feel a bit of a chump! I mean, didn't we go over there to liberate Johnny Iraqi? You know – crowds cheering, flags waving, happy smiling kiddies chewing gum, that sort of thing?

> Nobody mentioned torture. Chaps getting their private parts kicked in. That's a bit strong, isn't it? We didn't even do that sort of thing at Eton. Well, we did actually, but that's not the point.

> The point is that old Boris has been sold a pup by our Yankee cousins, and I'm feeling a bit of a prat. Blimey! (Reproduced by kind permission of *Private Eye*/Pressdram. Copyright Pressdram Limited 2004)

MANY WORKING METHODS

Some columnists don't believe in much preparation and like to work an hour or two before the deadline, especially if they've already spent a good part of a lifetime as a newspaper reporter. They may find it difficult to work in a quiet study and will prefer to produce their columns in the middle of a busy office. They keep up with what's in the papers and on their column day will grab some news item that intrigues them, sit in front of the computer and type the thing straight off. Well, they might need to do several drafts of the intro until they get that right, and then the rest will follow. That's how they used to write their reports.

Others carry cards or a notebook everywhere and as ideas occur they are noted. When decision time comes they look the ideas over and make a decision. They have probably read the papers and a news item that day may associate with one of the ideas. Generally it's not finding the idea that's hard, it is having too many (see Keith Waterhouse at the start of this chapter). What seems like a great idea somehow doesn't have legs; it's probably funny enough already. What looks much less promising can suddenly spark the imagination: you see something funny in what is actually ordinary or boring and it's the observation you put into it and the way you tell it that makes it funny. So acknowledges Miles Kingston (*The Independent* and *The Oldie* magazine).

A more leisurely approach that probably works best for the columnist who produces weekly or monthly an elegant essay is to build up files of cuttings on subjects of interest (as has been recommended elsewhere for the feature writer). To these might be added correspondence if that's coming from readers. When the idea is selected there's a ransacking of the files and a consulting of reference books and perhaps some online surfing, and plenty of note-taking. There may then be several drafts.

Whichever preliminaries are preferred, and however good the columnist is at outlining or ordering the material, the trick for humour is to take wing, to be able to think laterally, to take off with word associations and to enliven facts by linking them to their own experience. Surprise is the essential, and too much dependence on research can inhibit the gift.

ASSIGNMENTS

1 Study a regular column that you admire and do the workshop task described on page 291.
   (a) Put it aside and rewrite it as far as you can remember in the same style. Compare with the original.
   (b) Rewrite it in your style in an attempt to improve it. Compare with the original.
   (c) Outline another admired column. Put the column aside. Add to the points or even replace them and write your own column. Compare with the original.
2 Write a 100-word intro to a column built around one of the following topics, updating as necessary, either developing an argument from them or merely using them as triggers to other thoughts. Find other examples/anecdotes. Aim them at national papers:
   (a) An American tycoon offered his estranged wife £4 million to 'sit down with him and smile' at a party. Timber magnate Joe Hardy ... made the offer to ensure the success of 'Lord Hardy's Feast'. Each year he flies 100 Warwickshire residents on Concorde to Pennsylvania to commemorate his buying of the title of Lord Henley-in-Arden for £85,000 in 1990. Find other anecdotes to build a column round the buying of titles.

   (b) 'Violence on TV does not trigger real-life crime.' Agree or disagree. Do some research first.

   (c) Comment on the compensation paid to victims of medical accidents.

3 Select any news story from a national paper and write a 1200-word argument round it for a general interest magazine. Choose an inside-page home news story rather than the major ongoing political one. Do the necessary research.

4 Write a humorous column, indicating a target publication. Choose one of the following:

   (a) Compare hotels in Britain with those abroad.

   (b) After studying *Who's Who*, produce one or two fake items for the next edition, sending up some of the whimsy you can find. Don't quote anybody.

   (c) 'Dealing with stress.'

   (d) 'Dumbed-down Britain?'

5 After doing the necessary legwork and study of catalogues, and interviewing one or two journalists or student-journalists who use tape recorders, write a consumer round-up piece on tape recorders for a journalism students' magazine, a journalism/media magazine or for a newspaper's media section.

6 Take some items out of *Who's Who* and write a column commenting on them.

18   The reviewer

The critics – you shouldn't even ignore them. (Sam Goldwyn, film mogul)

Critics are like horse-flies. They prevent the horse from ploughing. (Anton Chekhov)

The best judge of a feast is the guest, not the cook. (Aristotle)

What you need is honesty, the bravery to say what you really feel … you have to forget about being liked. (Aleks Sierz, in an email to the author)

Let's call them reviewers if they work in journalism and critics if they are academics. Chekhov the creator was mainly thinking of bad theatre reviewers, who didn't appreciate his new approach to playwriting. Goldwyn, the tycoon producer, could afford to rubbish film reviewers, in imitable style. The two of them remind us that the creator is essential – the reviewer isn't, however powerful a few of them can be in closing down very expensively produced plays in London's West End and New York's Broadway. In the critics' camp Aristotle reminds us that nevertheless reviewers perform a most useful task, that they can help the artist's audience to appreciate the art fully and thus promote the art.

Promoting the art that deserves to be promoted means identifying the art that, in the reviewer's opinion, does not. Artists often complain that reviewers don't know what they're talking about because they haven't done it ('those who can do, those who can't teach'). They even complain about favourable reviews on the grounds that they don't address the right issues. It's true that reviewers can gain from having a go themselves at what they review. Some successful novelists are also successful reviewers of novels.

Theatre reviewers can gain from some acting or directing experience, even at an amateur level. But greater involvement in and direct experience of the creative process by reviewers takes time, and artists' demands for these often ignore the pressures of the deadline. More seriously, those demands can fail to take into account that reviewers' main obligation is to the readers written for.

The creators work from one premise; the producers, including directors and actors, work from another; the reviewers and the critics from another. That is, of course, considerable oversimplification. The point is: because of the differences in perspective it's often difficult to pin down what is fair and what is unfair comment. On the whole each side is aware of this and refrains from joining battle, but occasionally war breaks out in letter columns and TV studios. Libel considerations mean in effect that the reviewer's comments should not directly threaten the ability of practitioners to earn their living, and must be written without malice. (An actress won damages when a reviewer said her bottom was too big.)

The reviewer needs some essential attributes, which will demand attention in this chapter:

- knowledge of the field being written about
- a passion to know and experience more
- a desire to share your passion and knowledge with readers
- the ability to judge perceptively
- the courage to stand by convictions against pressures to please those with other premises
- the writing skill to communicate vividly and entertainingly
- the writing skill to make the assessment clear to the readers.

This chapter charts the particular demands made on the reviewer of books, music, art, theatre, films and television. But first: How do you become a reviewer? What are the tasks? Which are the specific writing skills?

HOW TO BECOME A REVIEWER

As with other byline columns, general or specialist, reviewing is unlikely to be the first task a new writer will expect to be doing. Yet it's an obvious specialism for staff and freelance writers interested in the arts, and there are opportunities for beginners on local papers and small magazines. At all levels in the media, reviewing is dominated by outside contributors.

Popular and quality markets are strikingly different in the way they cover the arts. Prospective reviewers must therefore study markets with particular care, collect cuttings and analyse them, and decide what sort of publication to pitch to. Even within the same category of publication, arts or features editors can have varied demands. Some examples are given below of the way reviews of the same work have varied between publications.

The tabloids put the emphasis on lively, entertaining reading. In several (*The Sun*, *News of the World* and *The People* for instance) arts coverage blurs into showbiz gossip. Many provincial papers (again, a good place to start) cover much amateur work, which requires a different approach, as will be described. Another good place to start is in low-circulation little magazines: arts editors watch them, along with students' magazines, for new reviewing talent.

There are several magazines devoted to the arts that should be studied (see the subject indexes of *Macmillan's Writer's Handbook* and *Willing's Press Guide*). Many consumer magazines, weeklies and monthlies, give space to reviews and there are the freesheets and free magazines to consider.

Aleks Sierz is a freelance with extensive experience in theatre reviewing and related activities. His first job as a theatre reviewer came in 1990 when a friend became arts editor of *Tribune* and asked him to review a show. 'Soon I was hooked,' he tells me. 'Later I did an MA in arts criticism at City University, London [following a BA in History] but I learnt the craft of writing by working as a freelance sub.' He has worked for numerous publications, including *The Stage*, *Time Out* and *What's On*. He has been a broadcaster for the BBC, is the author of *In-Yer-Face Theatre* (Faber), a best-selling account of cutting-edge drama, and since 2002 he has been elected Honorary Secretary of the Critics' Circle. He also writes features for *The Sunday Times, The Daily Telegraph, The Financial Times* and *The Independent*.

He has taught journalism for 10 years 'and it's always helped my own work, kept me on my toes. I've been involved in translating plays, doing drama workshops and, of course, interviewing countless practitioners. But although these experiences have been interesting they have not helped my reviewing.'

His advice to the budding reviewer? 'It's best to develop a career as a general journalist, perhaps as a freelance sub, perhaps as a freelance arts feature writer. In addition, try to get your work published anywhere you can, and build up a portfolio of short reviews. Then network like mad and keep hassling.'

309

THE REVIEWER'S TASKS

Some of the tasks to be mentioned assume that the reviewer has done some research. Full-time reviewers have probably done a fair amount of reading up on the subject and have the time to prepare well for what's coming up. Part-time reviewers should at least have the key up-to-date reference books to hand, and find the time to make acquaintance with previous works of the artist. Previous experience and reviews of the artist's (director's/actor's) work will help. Don't neglect the press releases available from the publicity agents.

First reviewers have to decide on the level of knowledge the readers of their publications are likely to have, and whether or not they may have read, seen or heard the work. Play and film reviews are normally the result of attending previews in studios so generally assume readers haven't seen the works. Last night's TV reviews (or last week's) must take into account that some readers have seen the programmes and some haven't. The following tasks need to be modified accordingly. They need to be selected and adapted, of course, to the kind of art being discussed.

Reporting

Reporting is the basis of reviewing. The disciplines of reporting are reflected in the kinds of questions to answer. For example:

- What is it called?
- What's the genre? (Literary novel or thriller, tragedy or comedy, art-house film or blockbuster?)
- What is it about? What does it mean? What does it represent?
- What is it like?
- Who created it?
- Who produced/directed it?
- Where is it showing? Where can you buy it?
- When and where does the action take place?
- Why was it written/painted/composed?
- How much is it?

Assessing

Your opinion must be informed and you must show it to be informed, by indicating the evidence for your statements and arguments. The evidence will be in the form of facts, examples, quotes. It's good to have strong opinions but readers must feel they are being helped to make up their own minds and that they can disagree while still valuing your piece. Some important questions are:

- What are the work's merits/defects?
- Is it worth your time and money?
- Did I like it?
- Will you like it?
- What sort of people will like it?
- Is it informative/inspiring/interesting/entertaining?
- What are the significant elements and how do they compare generally with other works in the genre (plot or characters, well-made play or post-modern experiment, message or slice of life, melody or in the raw?)
- How does it compare with other works by this creator, producer, director, etc.?
- With contemporaries' work?
- With work of a similar kind in the past?
- How far does the creator (or creators) succeed in achieving what they set out to do?
- How well has the work been served by the interpreters involved – actors, directors, set designers, musicians, etc.?
- If known (e.g. last night's theatre), how did the audience react to the work?

Setting standards

We're not talking about pontificating, but of giving your opinion about whether a work is good or bad and guiding your readers to the former. You're angry when you feel that bad work is chasing out the good. Your readers, to repeat, get to know where you stand on various aspects and can be guided by and interested in your piece even when they disagree on various points.

It's a question of integrity. You react to the work, you analyse your reaction, make your assessment and communicate it honestly, taking your readers' likely reaction into account, and you refuse to let your judgement be swayed by outside pressures. Your readers feel they can trust you to tell the truth as you see it.

What outside pressures? Both the subsidized and commercial theatres, for example, depend heavily on PR and pre-production selling (interviews with the stars, lavish praise of the previews, and so on). This hype has recently been compounded by the practice of casting American film stars in London's West End plays less effective than the very successful films they are based on (see below).

'The water is purer', as the late Hugo Young said about political columns (see page 296), if you don't become too friendly with the denizens of the world you're reacting to and assessing. Matthew Parris made a similar comment in his *Times* column (page 276). The dangers are prevalent in reviewing. Andrew Billen interviews for *The Times* subjects whom he may also critically assess for theatre reviews in *New Statesman*. There's certainly a need for circumspection, he says, at the same time recognizing the profit that comes from this broadening of interests.

THE WRITING-UP PROCESS

An advantage of book reviewing is that you can note passages that impress you together with page numbers and refer back to them as many times as you like. You can put your comments in square brackets after passages you mark to be quoted. You can make notes while watching a play or film with a pen-torch but you can't roll the production back (unless you can get the film video). You can be more generous with your notes if you're reviewing TV programmes for reviewing purposes at home, and you can record TV programmes on video to go back on them. But you may prefer to keep your experience fresh, and write up your film or TV review immediately after the viewing. Furthermore, taking notes in any quantity while reviewing the performing arts can prevent you from being open to the experience.

If your review of a performance can wait until the following day, you may be able to produce a more thoughtful and more polished piece. But some reviewers perform better when they have a deadline an hour or two after the performance. Practise doing reviews with both kinds of deadlines.

Language and style

Strong, well-informed opinions go better with a distinctive style, and a distinctive style is especially required by a reviewer. Firstly, because many readers want to be persuaded memorably to buy it or not to buy it. They are better able to assess how they would react, knowing their reviewer, if that reviewer's words have staying power. Secondly, because many more readers won't have the time or the money to buy it, but want to keep up with what books are being published, what plays, films, art exhibitions and concerts are on at the moment.

Such readers want to read something that gives them a fair idea of the reviewer's experience, and they won't get it from a reviewer who's merely competent. A good reviewer can be memorably excited (in the angry sense of the word) by a bad work of art and have interesting things to say about it. That's one important test of the quality of a reviewer. Bernard Levin once wrote a review of a play in London's West End by describing the set in detail from one end to the other. Bur even he, the doyen of theatre reviewers at the time, could only get away with that once. TV reviewers can and do make a living out of rubbishing mediocre TV (see below).

Conciseness and precision

When writing reviews, especially with a pressing deadline, it's hard to avoid clichés, the clichés of approval and disapproval, that don't give a clear idea of how you arrived at your assessment and don't therefore help readers to decide on their likely assessment. Have a look at these, and if they rise up in front of you, strike them out:

> never less than competent/appealing/engaging
> never more than adequate/amusing, likeable
> these are mere quibbles

Avoid unnecessary modifiers:

> a grave emergency
> an acute crisis
> in-depth research
> under active consideration
> consummate skill

Recognizing the value of precise modifiers when aiming at the necessary conciseness, the tendency is to trot out those adjective or adverb pairs that familiarity has drained of their original force, especially when they are alliterative. For example:

> bouncy and bedraggled
> cruel and conniving
> fast and furious

Avoid also vague words, especially those recently overused to the point of exhaustion, used on their own, without explanation. Such words must be added to, exploited in some way, to indicate why they are being used:

> fascinating, interesting, amazing, beautiful, cool (in the newer sense), wonderful, marvellous, glorious, gorgeous, nice, feisty, funny, amusing boring, uninteresting, ugly, awful, unfunny

Words that say why

You can say why an assessment has been arrived at in various ways. Consider the following attempts, which employ tone of voice, irony, implication, as well as precise modifiers:

> Adebimpe's switch from swooning falsetto to rapid-fire lyrical delivery in King Eternal was mesmerizing to watch. [A concert given by the TV on the Radio band]

> The show yanks Modigliani out of the clutches of the makers of pretty postcards and turns him, instead, into an unsettling Jewish mystic, whose cultural anxieties nourished his work continuously, productively and superbly.

> This is the aspect [the qualities of distinguished women writers] that Le Fanu highlights in this pretty-as-pink biography [of Rose Macaulay], its twirling calligraphy, gracious picture gallery and carmine endpapers, as much as its message, an embodiment of 21st century, soft-focus, optimistic new feminism.

> This is a very dense and detailed book. It is a study of decision-making, painstakingly traced through the chaos of competing Nazi institutions. [*The Origins of the Final Solution*]

> Thriller novelist Patricia Highsmith's anti-hero Tom Ripley – your friendly neighbourhood serial murderer – is played with epicene wit by John Malkovich.

> Shakespeare's problem comedy of love discovered and recovered [*Much Ado About Nothing*] came to us served light and bright, without so much as a provocative thought in its pretty little bewigged head.

Finding a good order

It's helpful to report the main facts or the story of a book or play or film early in the review, so that there's a clear context for the judgements made. Note how this principle guides the authors in many of the extracts discussed.

BOOKS

So many books are published that it's essential that you, or your literary editor, choose wisely. That means books that are well above average and that will lend themselves to informative, entertaining and readable columns for those who don't read much and who are highly unlikely to read the ones you're reviewing, as well as for those who do read a lot and are regularly persuaded by you to acquire them.

To review books you need to read widely. You should know something about other books by the author being reviewed: read one or two of their earlier books. Read or find out about similar books by contemporaries for the sake of comparison.

As always, publicity material will guide you into preliminary research: the blurbs on the covers, publishers' catalogues and handouts, literary agents. The author may be listed in *Who's Who*. Look for references in books of literary criticism. Read published reviews of earlier works and interviews with the author.

Non-fiction

When reviewing a non-fiction book it often helps to measure how far the author has succeeded in avoiding the pitfalls of the genre and gaining its prizes. Adam Mars-Jones considers that Peter Parker's literary biography of Christopher Isherwood, novelist, friend of W. H. Auden, succeeds admirably. The intro to *Isherwood: A Life* (*The Observer*, 23 May 2004) contains a clear context for a 1500-word review:

> Authorized lives have one set of disadvantages (self-censorship, mealiness of mouth), unauthorized ones another: restriction of sources, sensationalism. Parker's book is virtually free of blemishes in either category and comes close to combining the corresponding advantages – fullness, fearlessness.

It was a longish (1904–86), interesting life (England, pre-war Berlin where he wrote acclaimed short stories, California from the start of the Second

World War – where he wrote *A Single Man*, 'a novel changed his exile into art' and some film scripts, and took to Hindu mysticism). Mars-Jones shows how Parker skilfully interweaves the facts of the life with the character of the subject. He paraphrases Parker at key moments rather than quotes him. Here, where he does both, we get a sharp flavour of Parker's method:

> As Parker points out with endearing dryness, there could be likelier converts to ascetic religion than 'a sceptical, sybaritic, chain-smoking, egotistical and morally confused homosexual atheist'. It seems particularly drastic for a writer who was only able to approach ideas by an understanding of the people who held them, to take on the belief that personality is an illusion. Nevertheless it brought him peace as well as frustration.

Towards the end Mars-Jones returns to questions of genre, commenting that modern biography tends to 'enlargement of the spleen'. Parker apparently doesn't suffer it:

> His wit at Isherwood's expense never becomes destructive. He may feel mildly disillusioned by his subject at times, but not betrayed. He passes on a great deal of discreditable material – Isherwood was prickly, misogynistic, a hypochondriac and uncontrolled drinker – yet his own enthusiasm doesn't suffer. Isherwood's charm works even posthumously.

A crucial factor

Before reviewing a non-fiction book be sure you have access to up-to-date reference sources (try online) to enable you to check figures and facts.

A reader finding an error or two in a non-fiction work will lack confidence in anything the author says. Similarly the reviewer's authority is damaged if errors go unspotted.

Here's an example of a reviewer (Peter Kellner in *The New Statesman*) who has done the necessary research and is doing the necessary hatchet work on a book about amateurism in some of Britain's elite groups:

> Harold Macmillan became Prime Minister in 1957, not 1956. David Steel entered Parliament in 1965, not 1964. When George Woodcock stepped down as TUC general secretary in 1969 he was succeeded by Vic Feather, not Len Murray. In the 1979 general elections the Scottish Nationalists did not fall 'from fourteen seats to four' – they fell from eleven seats to two. 'The two-year premiership of James Callaghan' in fact lasted for three years and one month. Today Labour constituencies do not 'insist on reselecting their members every two years' – they do so once in each Parliament.

The error detector should distinguish between author's and printer's errors and may need to fault the publisher's proofreading.

Fiction

It's worth spelling out a little first the main elements that fiction reviewers may have to deal with:

- The *story* is what happens; the *plot* is the structure of what happens with the causality indicated.
- The *setting* – the place, the ambience, the atmosphere – needs special attention when it's unusual: for example, if it's a little known or exotic place, such as an imaginary planet in a science fiction work.
- The *period* or *periods*. Is it about today, or 20 years ago, or a century ago? In reviewing a historical novel you would pick up any anachronisms that damage the illusion.
- The *theme*, or message behind the story, may have to be carefully distinguished from the story itself. The immorality of characters has to be distinguished from the morality of the work.
- *Narrative technique* may need comment. How does the author use time? Is the sequence clear or confusing? Are flashbacks used and are they effective?
- *Characters* may be caricatures as in Dickens; or true-to-life as in George Eliot or Jane Austen; or symbolic, representing ideas, as to some extent in Henry James and D. H. Lawrence. Or what?, as in Martin Amis.
- *Style.* It may be so straightforward as to be hardly noticeable: this may be a case of art concealing art, or it may simply be that an unobtrusive style is more effective for what the author wants to do. The style might, on the other hand, be nearly the whole point, as in James Joyce: his universe is in his language.

A straightforward, clearly constructed review is required when the narrative is the thing, especially when it's a historical novel. David Grylls gets across the gripping story of Paul Watkins's *Thunder God* and manages to pack in the kind of decryption Watkins needed to bring the Age of the Vikings to life (*The Sunday Times*, 23 May 2004).

The following is an attempt to indicate the structure of the review and the way the reviewer's assessment is implied in the details he relays (no space for quoting except once but the flavour of the book comes out in the details). Note also how Grylls deals with the question of accuracy and period atmosphere.

Intro:

> Paul Watkins's latest novel – a tortuous but increasingly tense adventure yarn set in the 10th century AD – follows the turbulent fortunes of a young Norseman, Hakon. Having eerily survived being struck by lightning, he is selected to be a priest, then captured by Danish raiders and transported as a slave to Byzantium. Here he fights for the Varangians, Viking mercenaries in the imperial guard. After serving in Baghdad, Cordoba and on the Nile, he saves the emperor in battle. Released from the army, he returns to his homeland, only to find it besieged by bellicose Christians. At this point the book is less than one third through: the real action is yet to come.

Par 2:

> Watkins's surging, fantastic saga is almost too much to take in: for once the standard hyperbolic blurb ('a riveting tale of epic proportions') is a modest understatement …

> There's much religious mysticism, ritual and sacrifice. Pledged to the thunder god Thor, Hakon 'hopes to pierce the barrier between men and gods'.

Par 3:

> Besides swirling with visions and legends, the narrative is packed with physical detail: vivid descriptions of implements and foodstuffs, cloths and coins, ships and swords …

> It ends with that quote:

> Recalling his time with the Varangians, he remembers the 'scent of cloves and cardamon and the pollen-yellow mustiness of turmeric'.

Par 4:

> Not only the diversity of religion is stressed (Norse, Christian and other more exotic creeds), but also its divisiveness …

> Hakon is disillusioned by the benefits of religion. There are fraudulent miracles and slaughtering.

Par 5:

> Recognizing the deep similarity of myths, campaigning ultimately for secular values, the book is informed by a modern sensibility that can seem anachronistic … In a world in which boys have their fingers chopped off for trivial offences such as spilling food … we are asked to believe that the

ultimate trauma is to suffer from clerical child abuse … Watkins is obviously influenced … by westerns, epics and buddy movies …

Conclusion:

None of this matters once the narrative grips you … Like his Victorian predecessor Rider Haggard he offers adventure plus ideas, but (unlike Haggard) his commitment to ideas never inhibits the excitement … [Finally] Thought-provoking about cultural loyalty and the cosmopolitan world of the Vikings, *Thunder God* appeals primarily as a thundering good read.

When dealing with 'literary novels', those that aim to do what the novelist D. H. Lawrence said the novel can do, reviewers may have higher aims and raised sights: in the upmarket prints they may be called critics. Lawrence said the novel 'can inform and lead into new places the flow of our sympathetic consciousness, and it can lead our sympathy away in recoil from things gone dead'. Other critics and commentators have identified similar achievements of the novel: setting standards above the materialistic, questioning the common assumptions about success and status and about what makes life worth living.

MUSIC

Reviewing music and art has to rise to the challenge of how to interpret in words what is non-verbal. The verbal content of opera doesn't help much, nor does the fact that in representational art the subject is obvious.

A review of a Gilbert and Sullivan operetta by the local amateur operatic society won't cause too many problems. In fact you might get away with giving something of the plot, referring to the performances of the leading singers and to the fun to be had by all. The inadequate phrasing of the baker's wife's coloraturas in the leading female role is unlikely to be dwelt upon.

But reviewing concerts or discs of rock, jazz or classical music needs knowledge and appreciation of what the sounds mean, and skill in translating that appreciation into informative and entertaining words (even when you can be sure that your audience knows the jargon). Here's an extract from a rock concert review by James Smart in *The Guardian*:

Eighties Matchbox … still put on an impressively professional stage show. Their thrashing hillbilly rock is played at a speed that necessitates a certain amount of precision, and the Brighton five-piece does not disappoint, stringing a tight mesh of riffing over pounding rhythms. Any tunes are well hidden.

The monthly *Mojo*, devoted to rock, pop, soul and everything in between, covers all the news, and has lengthy features and profiles as well as reviews of gigs and albums. Readers clearly know all the jargon and the names dropped. A review by Manish Agarwal of The Hold Steady's album ('hard rockin' smarts from Brooklyn newcomers who don't dig punk, funk or irony') goes:

> Their publicity photos suggest tidy Mod revivalists, with their bank clerk hair and matching suits, but The Hold Steady shred with the giddy zeal of rock gods in waiting. This unvarnished debut tempers Thin Lizzy flair with Pixies bounce, dripping melodies that slipped down like six-packs and guitars that aren't afraid to solo if the song calls for it. What makes them stand out, though, is frontman Craig Finn's stream-of-consciousness slalom through contemporary culture. Employing a throaty, sing-speak vocal, he skewers club fashionistas with Most People are DJs, rails against indie scene snobs on the sax-boosted Hostile, Mass., and ruminates on rock'n'roll's transformative power with the piano-laden Springsteen-like beauty of Certain Songs. (July 2004)

Reviewing discs of classical music often need comparisons with other artists' efforts, whether benchmark or just different, as in this extract from a *Gramophone* review of Imogen Cooper's playing of Schubert:

> Again, in the A minor Sonata she takes her time. Certainly her spacious conception of the opening movement allows her to orchestrate it to the full, with a splendidly wide and rich dynamic range. But here I sometimes wondered if there was sufficient underlying tension to sustain a tempo rather slower than we often hear – as, for instance, on the old Decca LP recordings by Lupa and Ashtenazy, both of whom also offer a more urgent finale.

Reviewing opera requires attention to all the usual elements of theatrical production, including set design, costumes and machinery as well as matters of acoustics, and acting as well as the singing and the music playing and conducting. The overall assessment is difficult to get balanced. Reviews in *The Week* of theatre, films and opera are worth studying for the comparisons made between extracts from the quality papers. The following piece in the issue of 19 June 2004 does this for the production of Gounod's *Faust* at the Royal Opera House, Covent Garden,

London and holds lessons for the way reviews of the same production can differ:

> … Charles Edwards's wonderful designs [says Rupert Christansen in *The Daily Telegraph*], 'with a set that is a combination of a Gothic Revival church with the interior of Garnier's opera house' reflect the world that Gounod's music inhabits. And, under McVicar's direction, the characters convey 'a vivid sense of the hypocritical values' that underpin the melodrama.

> The singing is wonderful as well, said Richard Fairman in *The Financial Times*. Angela Gheorghiu was 'in gleaming voice' and sang the role of Marguerite 'with thrilling abandon'. While Bryn Terfel made 'a predictably prodigious Mephistopheles *with voice and character to spare*'. But the real revelation was Roberta Alagna, said Tim Ashley in *The Guardian*. He 'gives the performance of a lifetime'. He is 'physically daring – celebrating Faust's new-found youth by cartwheeling round the stage – and vocally responsive to every psychological shift'.

> On the contrary, said Robert Thicknesse in *The Times*. There is no psychological depth to this production. These 'rarefied stars' were easy to listen to, but the leading pair has taken 'glossy blandness to its lucrative apogee'. Not for a moment do these two stray from the path of convention, 'whether it's in the way in which Marguerite unwraps her jewels, just like another parcel from Cartier, to their colour-by-numbers love duet'. Antonio Pappano conducts prettily, but the rest of the evening is 'mediocre, empty and whorish'.

ART

Reviewing art exhibitions requires assured descriptive powers. Here are a few sentences selected at random from various publications over the past few years:

> The figure is demonic, squatting, eyes like black saucers, teeth bared in a hideous rictus, breasts slung like sacks of flour.

> Painted with a freedom strangely prophetic of Francis Bacon, the sightless singer opens his mouth in a grotesque, gap-toothed smile, caught in the spotlight of Goya's scrutiny.

The fourth century BC olive wreath found on a skull in the Ukraine is so fragile that:

> you notice immediately that the paper-thin leaves of beaten gold tremble slightly at your footsteps.

Brash, misleading and garish, orange features in more than half the paintings in this show ...

... de Kooning starts to evolve from bogus Cubism into a flowing, equivocal, Moro-esque style: floating amorphous blobs, variously derived from dislocated body parts (*Fire Island*) or jagged, deconstructed, heavily worked Cityscapes (*Excavation*).

Brian Sewell first wrote of the Royal Academy's Summer Exhibition in London 20 years ago and his coverage of the 2004 exhibition, organized by David Hockney and Allen Jones, deplores the decline he has seen over the years. He's in favour of the traditional skills, like drawing, and is scathing about a small monoprint of Tracey Emin of 1997 with 'not a line of drawing, nor a hint of colour, the printed legend WELL ITS ALRIGHT AND ID LOVE TO BE THE ONE LOVE IS WHAT YOU WONT', priced at £2938.

Hockney's contribution doesn't please: 'six of his absurdly large, wishy-washy and wholly unconvincing watercolours dominate the end wall of the Academy's largest gallery and can be seen the length of the building'. He does, however, find 'quiet pleasure' to see some of the 'old warhorses' of the academy producing some of their best work, and celebrates the work of the late Terry Frost. His 'final flourish is astonishing – a vast and vigorous lexicon of familiar motifs aggressively stated in red and black on white, all subtleties of tone abandoned – a man not, in his late eighties, going gently into that good night'.

Art reviewers need the courage of their convictions more than other reviewers, such is the volatility of the visual arts. For William Packer in *The Financial Times* this was a classic summer exhibition in which Hockney gets across 'the radiant clarity of the fountains in the Alhambra courtyard' and turns watercolour into 'the most up-to-date form in the world'.

As for the minefield of contemporary conceptual art – of which Damien Hurst's pickled sheep in a glass case is a well-known example – reviewers know they are walking through it on a tightrope. They have to say interesting things about a butterfly sitting on top of a pile of turds called 'True Love'; about an empty gallery with its lights going on and off; a bit of a wall in white and pale blush-pink shades with a tiny smudge on it (a squished mosquito) shipped from Mexico, with the sound of another mosquito transcribed into musical notation displayed on a musical stand – a violinist occasionally playing the piece; a video of a naked man jumping up and down on a trampoline; and so on. The butterfly and the turds are made of paper and we are told that this suggests that the artist 'considers beauty and squalor to be inextricably linked'. The mosquito-inspired work is called 'endemically chancy'.

Sally O'Reilly in *Time Out* of 23–30 June 2004 makes a stalwart attempt when covering an exhibition in the Bloomberg gallery in London's East End to relate the two very different artists: Chantal Joffe with her 'visceral, 10-foot portraits of women from the fashion pages' and Kenny McLeod with a 42-minute video:

> 'Blue Grey' is an oddly impersonal portrait of a city boy falling apart, his behaviour dissolving into the fringes of insanity. A series of set pieces serve both as formal devices and as poignant analogies; the man cuts up his suit, then sews it back together; from a bus he reads out loud every word that he sees in his surroundings. Rather than anything personal, there's a whiff of Wittgenstein about McLeod's word/image loops, which makes them appear diametrically opposed to Joffe's paintings. While the expressiveness of the paintings accentuates the formal qualities of the videos, McLeod's analytical approach makes every dribble of paint seem utterly precise.

You can sympathize with the difficulty of the reviewer's task but that 'whiff of Wittgenstein' and the comparisons make you suspect a desperate attempt at justification. Did her readers catch the allusion?

You don't see any criteria by which much conceptual art is being judged: practitioners don't or can't explain; reviewers of it can frequently be found in *Private Eye*'s Pseuds' Corner. But reviewers must be open to new kinds of art and must try to find ways of promoting what they find promising.

THEATRE

Plays and films, like operas, need reviewers skilled at juggling. They share many of the concerns of the fiction reviewer (see page 319). Genres are many, with different terms (or different connotations) from those used for novels: tragedy, comedy, straight play, farce, and more. The various contributions to the staging and to the production, as with opera, have to be noted. The play reviewer is concerned almost entirely with how well the production is served in a particular performance, so allowances may be made if reporting an early performance and there are signs that it might get better. 'Almost entirely' because the reviewer might want to discuss whether or not justice was done to the text, and will often read the text as preliminary research.

Skill at compression is especially required in reviews of plays and films since you have to juggle assessments of various aspects of the work. Here's a one-paragraph review by John Peter in *The Sunday Times Magazine* (23 May 2004) that does this juggling skilfully:

> Self-improvement used to be a moral issue: you got up, and ahead, by learning and working. Neil LaBute's play [*The Shape of Things*] is about the Botox age – you improve not your mind but your appearance to show that you are where it's at. You feel you've had a nice little moral nip and tuck when you are with the gang you want to be with. Even nerds have their IDs. Adam (Enzo Cilenti) has the slouched bearing, the clumsy little paunch, the boyish fidgeting, the indecisive grin. Enter Evelyn (Alicia Witt), student and artist. Evelyn is smart, sexy, imperious: a rule-breaker, a free spirit. The catch is that free spirits are ruthless. They are best admired from a distance, which is why they have a special loneliness. Evelyn has a project, and Adam is her victim. So are his best friends, Jenny and Philip (Sienna Guillory, James Murray). LaBute's take is that artists are, or can be, such free spirits: destroyers, cannibals, emotional imperialists. So, is art a moral experience or a makeover? Julian Webber's direction crackles with aggression, irony and pain, and the actors give elegantly crafted performances, laid-back and cool. Their impact is anything but.

Meaningful modifiers are most often used in reviews to let you see the characters (inside as well as outside). Nouns have to be meaningful too. Note the combinations in the description above of Adam and 'emotional imperialism'.

The language of reviews must get across the atmosphere of the product and the reviewer's place in the world described, but with a scalpel rather than a sledgehammer: 'you feel you've had a nice little nip and tuck ...' neatly tells us what the playwright is doing with the characters and that the reviewer approves: a good example of how you can exploit such clichés as 'nice little'. Note also how another of the listed cliches, 'cool', gains meaning from the context.

The structure of a review normally needs careful planning so that the evidence is clear that backs up the opinions. A brief analysis of Peter's piece will illustrate:

Intro: Today appearance is all: the theme is broached.

Body: From 'You feel you've had ...': the characters and how their relationships make the story. The artist as possible free spirit and destroyer.

Conclusion: From 'So, is art a moral experience or a makeover?': we are left with the question. The director's and actors' contributions are followed by a summing up of the effect of the whole.

It's a short review, so peripheral matters are excluded. There's no mention of the set, which means there was nothing remarkable about it. Plays these days often have minimal settings. If films and TV can do the realism so much more convincingly there's little sense in trying to compete with them. Of course minimal settings can be a creative contribution.

It's a favourable review and the negatives are not serious, so there's no space for them. Minor negatives could have been disposed of at the start or at the finish. What has to be avoided is a back-and-forthing between the two, which makes for confusion.

Even in a short review, notice how different aspects – characterization and conflict – are juggled to effect in the body, as evidence for the author's 'take' or message.

In these play-safe times for the commercial theatre it's musicals or it's star American names in London's West End and new plays there are few. *When Harry Met Sally* at the Theatre Royal was adapted from Nora Ephron's Oscar-nominated film script of a highly successful film starring Billy Crystal and Meg Ryan. Playing even safer, the production attracted a succession of paired, known (if not well) names. Just as adapted mediocre novels can make great films, so can the adapted scripts of very good films make disappointing plays. Fiona Mountford in *The Evening Standard* of 16 June 2004 covers the pairing of Michael Landis and Molly Ringwald.

There's a positive note:

> Smooth surfaces and slick packaging are what Loveday Ingram's serviceable production is all about, with its Jamie Cullum soundtrack and minimalist white box of a set.

But it doesn't quite come off:

> Marcy Kahan's adaptation … nominally anchors the dithering duo in some kind of reality by providing them with a best friend each, but apart from this they remain absurdly context-free.

> The years roll by, Sally's hair remains slightly out of control and still all they talk about are their romantic entanglements, or lack thereof.

On the whole, the National Theatre production of the rarely revived eighteenth century French classic, Marivaux's *The False Servant*, updated to the 1930s and directed by Jonathan Kent, was enthusiastically welcomed by reviewers. The plot is thick. Lelio (Anthony Calf), the fiancé of a Countess (Charlotte Rampling), plans to dump her in favour of an heiress (Nancy

Carroll). The latter disguises herself as a man, Chevalier, who callously wins the Countess's love and exposes Lelio's treachery. The servant of the title betrays anybody for money. The set is striking: candles, chandeliers, mirrors and Louis XIV decorations.

Let's compare a few extracts from June 2004 reviews – (1) Benedict Nightingale in *The Times* (440 words), (2) Sheridan Morley in the *Daily Express* (350 words), and (3) Aleks Sierz in *What's On* (300 words). Note how you think the lengths affect the styles. First, on the translation, the set and updating effects:

1   … Kent and his enjoyably colloquial translator, Martin Crimp, have given us a brilliant, cynical, scary play that justifies every British prejudice about French sophistication and avarice. Paul Brown's marvellous set … sums up much about the glitter, narcissism and shallow awfulness on show. If I described her [Nancy Carroll's] Chevalier as a gorgeously sexy Radclyffe Hall I would not, I think, be wholly misrepresenting an evening that, since it is set in our knowing era, is bound to take on lesbian overtones.

2   Marivaux … whom nobody bothers to revive over here, largely because he is reckoned too precious, too tricky, too wordy and perhaps just too French.

   Which is precisely why this production is such a joy and such a revelation. Kent and his new translator … have cut through all the high heels, wigs and the verbiage to give us the ice-cold modern miracle, Marivaux on speed as it were … In an infinitely glamorous setting … a cast … seem perfectly to understand the world they inhabit is also that of Marlene Dietrich and Katharine Hepburn in trousers, those Hollywood 1930s in which nobody was quite what they seemed, personally or sexually.

3   Martin Crimp's superb translation, which bristles with pointed thrusts and sharp asides, captures Marivaux's seductive scepticism and elegant irony … The Chevalier comes across as a modern woman, enjoying the freedom that dressing as a man gives her, and happily demonstrating her superior intelligence and wit: the poor Countess has no choice but to melt into the arms of androgyny.

Sierz, however, finds the set 'cumbersome'. Acting honours are varied:

This is a play in which Arlequin (David Collings) has become an oafish old drunk, the servant of the title (excellent Adrian Scarborough) is a depraved Jeeves eager to betray anyone for cash, and the male lead, [Anthony] Calf's Lelio, exudes a mix of fastidious, brutishness and slimy misogyny.

The evening's performance comes from Carroll as a sharp, ruthless, dangerously charismatic transvestite ... lesbian overtones. An opportunity, perhaps, for Rampling to explore her character's emotional intricacies in more depth? If so, it's not one that she seizes.

Morley, apart from the favourable mention of the ensemble above, singles out Charlotte Rampling as the Countess:

At the centre of this web of deception and despair, looking more like the ice princess than ever, we get Charlotte Rampling who, although she trained over here at the Royal Court, has seldom, if ever, been back in 30 years.

Sierz finds much of the acting 'muddled' but is in agreement with Nightingale about Scarborough and with Morley about Rampling:

Only the star ... knows how to move with elegance, and the most memorable moment of the show is when Adrian Scarborough as Trivelin gives a spirited mime of his eavesdropping.

Sierz is something of a champion, naturally enough, of in-yer-face theatre and gets around the fringe to review it. He laments the lack of attention given it by British theatre makers to Sarah Kane, who committed suicide aged 28 in February 1999, although she is acclaimed by our universities and abroad. Also in *What's On* (11 February 2004) he reviewed the first revival here (at Battersea Arts Centre, London) of *Crave*, first produced in 1998.

It's a difficult play, he tells us, but worth the challenge. There are no stage directions; in the text, no plot, no ordinary dialogue and characters called A, B, C and M. It's symbolic, fragmentary, Matt Peover's 'daring direction ... focusing on C, a young woman haunted by memories and fantasies'.

... Four voices echo round her mind. At the same time, the cast talk to each other, which suggests two relationships: one between C and an older abusive man, A, and the other between the needy woman M and the more slippery male B. Direct and explicit language clash with ambiguity and elusiveness.

It's a haunting 40 minutes, with lines of poetry following snatches of conversation: at one moment, we're in a psychiatric clinic, at another, in a wine bar. And while C is clearly suffering as she tries to grapple with her depression, there are passages of unexpected elation and wicked humour. Typically, it is the abusive A who gets to speak Kane's long paean to love.

On a dark, abstract set, which suggests a splintered cityscape, the young cast tackles the play with intelligence and commitment. Not every section works equally well, and some of Kane's choral rhythms are missing, but in general this is a memorable version of a rare contemporary classic. Who could crave for anything more?

FILMS

If reviewing regularly, obtain publicity material from film distributors. This normally gives full cast details, potted biographies of actors, details of the production, etc. It is given out at previews. Reviewers of films and TV plays should have some knowledge of the medium, of the technology and of the production techniques used inside and outside the studio, of the difference between the montage of numerous short scenes and the slow build-up in the scenes of a play.

It's not so easy in film to get inside a character's head in any subtle way, as you can in a novel or a play. Against this there's the power of images. Ingenuity is called for, in the use of flashbacks and voice-overs, and so on.

Films have the great advantage in realism. In a flash we are in Rome or London or outside and then inside a castle (even if actually we're not). A Rolls Royce immediately establishes a character's wealth, poverty is represented by a torn and dirty shirt. The images tend to take precedence over the words. Film is a director's medium: scripts can be mediocre and actors can be unconvincing if the images are overpowering or if the disjointed way of working (scenes not done in the order of showing, for example) makes for some confused acting.

Will Self's review of *The Reckoning* in London's *Evening Standard* (3 June 2004), for example, though pointing out some anachronistic elements in this film about medieval England, welcomes director Paul McGuigan's 'fresh, lively cinematic vision':

> His Middle Ages is dirty, smelly and colourful; as plague-ridden corpses are disinterred by the thespian detectives [a troupe of travelling actors], fingernails are properly chipped and bloodied. He and his cinematographer Peter Sova (who also shot the beautifully stylized *Gangster No. 1*), are a little too addicted to the slomo pan accompanied by an amplified 'swoosh' but, mostly, their interpolations of dreamlike fugues – actors performing gymnastics, water flowing down faces like quicksilver – are apposite as well as atmospheric.
>
> The nameless town looks great, especially in long shot, with its half-timbered houses wattling their way up the flanks of the baronial castle, but too much use is made of the crane shot, which, paradoxically, far from opening out the action, make the purpose-built set feel like just that.

Self takes the opportunity to chart the career of the star, Paul Bettany, who plays an unfrocked priest who falls in with the actors: not so convincing in this one, after impressive performances in *Gangster No. 1*, *Master and Commander* and *Dogville*, which are summarized.

Whereas bad plays come across as pretentious or boring and cannot normally be saved from disaster, even by the most skilful acting, bad or run-of-the-mill films can be enjoyable. There's so much to look at and often you don't have to take it seriously.

Rose Lloyd enjoyed *The Lost Boys* and shared her enjoyment with us in the *South London Press*:

> What's got long hair, an ear-ring, a ghetto-blaster, and fangs?
>
> Well, it's something out of *The Lost Boys*, which … creates a whole new breed of monster – Teenychoppers.
>
> The vampire tradition, now a bit long in the tooth, gets some much needed mouth-to-mouth resuscitation, when moved to pretty seaside town Santa Carla, populated almost entirely, it seems, by creatures of the night.

Despite the chattiness the opening firmly places the film in its genre and tells us what it's about.

There are a 'bunch of motorbike-riding, cave-dwelling, bloodsucking, heavy metal bats, who hang around the fairground savaging anyone who dares stick their neck out'. A vampire killer, who hangs out in a shop selling Batman comics, says, 'We have been aware of some very serious vampire activity here in the town. We are almost certain that ghouls and werewolves occupy top positions at the town hall'. Ms Lloyd's comment: 'Well, could you resist a film with lines like that?' and sums the film up as 'a likeable and entertaining variant on *I was a Teenage Werewolf*'.

A couple of comparisons will conclude this section, of *Monster*, directed by Patty Jenkins, starring Oscar winner Charlize Theron, who had a notable uglied-up makeover. This is based on the true story of America's serial killer Aileen Wuornos, who was abused as a child, became a prostitute and ended up, after killing her clients, on Death Row. Here are extracts from the reviews of (1) Nigel Andrews in *The Financial Times* (4 stars verdict) and (2) James Christopher in *The Times* (2 stars verdict) on 1 April 2004:

> 1 Cheap, brisk, vividly written, the film begins like a shoestring shocku-drama, a 'now it can be told' descendant of the old Warners crime biopics, or Sam Fuller reality thrillers. But the performances of Theron and [Christina] Ricci, as the girlfriend increasingly aghast as Wuornos

keeps returning from a hard day's hooking with bloody clothes or smouldering gun, raise it to superior psychodrama.
(© *The Financial Times*. All rights reserved)

2 The romance is as runny and lurid as egg yolk. It inspires Wuornos to pipe dreams of a job and a home, without having a clue what either entails. She is forced back to the streets and, less inevitably, the gun by the petulant [girlfriend] Selby's demand to be kept in the manner to which she is accustomed. Any compelling dramatic point is lost.

The film [is] a vaguely well-intentioned homily about a damaged woman who loses her grasp on reality, and a spoilt girl who never had her hand on it in the first place. How disappointing that Theron's biggest splash should end in such a shallow puddle.

The monthly magazine *Empire* is for film buffs. It covers all aspects, in general features, dissection of works in progress and news on the technology, as well as numerous reviews of current releases and videos. Although averaging 200 to 300 words, reviews manage to pack a lot in. In the August 2004 issue Patrick Peters reviews *The Flower of Evil* in a hundred or so:

Although Claude Chabrol has sustained his career with thrillers in the Hitchcock mode he's at his best dissecting the foibles and failings of the French bourgeoisie. His real targets here are those seemingly respectable bastions who harbour the neo-fascist prejudices that have scarred Gallic society since the Nazi occupation. What's most notable about this compelling study of class arrogance is the restraint and precision of Chabrol's satire, whether he's commenting on the careless affluence of womanizing pharmacist Bernard Le Coq's semi-incestuous family, or the complacent naivety of Nathalie Baye's campaign for mayor of their Bordeaux neighbourhood. But stealing the show is Suzanne Flon's immaculate display as the matriarch whose good-natured indulgence of her ghastly relations belies a guilty secret. Mercilessly acute and quietly devastating.

TELEVISION

My comments on feature films apply to a large extent to TV plays. The distinction between the two in fact is being blurred: many films are now made with finance invested on condition that they will have plenty of TV as well as cinema outlets. Nevertheless there can be important differences in the way film-makers approach work for cinema and TV. As sweeping generalizations, TV works better for domestic kinds of drama (it is watched in domestic surroundings), cinema better for epic westerns or similar works. One-off TV plays are increasingly rare at present and it's series and soaps that need attention. Appropriately enough, they are treated, on the whole, with less seriousness than theatre, but given credit if they are good entertainment.

Series

The series *Murphy's Law* (BBC1) was carried by James Nesbitt in the title role as an unorthodox CID man. Virginia Blackburn in the *Daily Express* (1 June 2004) recognizes that a good detective story/thriller can sail along on a good deal of preposterousness. A chemical leak from a mysterious biotech company, it is suspected, caused the death of a child, reported as drowned. But it was pulled out of the river alive by Alice and died in hospital. Murphy goes undercover:

> On arrival at the factory, an overall-clad Murphy and his troupe of cleaners are told very conveniently by their boss exactly where they shouldn't go. The first and second levels are fine, she says, but avoid the third level. Got that at the back? The third! It's where the bad guys are! Murphy certainly clocks it, as does Alice who's now also working undercover, posing as – guess what? – a cleaner. She attracts the attentions not only of our hero but also the baddest bad guy, John Simpson (one of those scriptwriters must have a sense of humour), the head of corporate affairs, who soon discovers she's the dead boy's mother.
>
> It becomes clear that Simpson's job description covered murdering anyone who might have been on to the company's nasty secret, which, to cut a long story short, involved manufacturing a drug that made it psychologically easier for soldiers to kill people. It appears that Simpson had become addicted to it …

Earlier in the year Mark Lawson in *The Guardian* admitted to enjoying *No Angels*, full of randy nurses and doctors, condemned by the Royal College of Nursing, just as the randy teachers of *Teachers* (also Channel 4) were condemned by the National Union of Teachers:

> The only obstacle to enjoyment is that armchair psychologists may feel that Channel 4 will soon be diagnosed with erotomania.
>
> The objection to *Teachers* and now *No Angels* is that these visions of sex-crazed educators and loose-skirted nurses resulted not from deep research into what colleges and hospitals are like, but from close examination of the effect on TV ratings of heavy sexual content.

Documentaries

The TV documentary may be compared to the well-researched feature article and a series of documentaries to a non-fiction book. It's distortion of emphasis that the reviewer will find to criticize, however, rather than errors of fact. As mentioned above, the film-maker can manipulate viewers' feelings and thoughts by careful selection of images.

TV documentary makers use a wide range of research material, and the reviewer's job is to indicate how well or badly this is used, and how it all contributes to the total effect. Interviews inside and outside the studio, photographs, drawings, paintings, maps, charts, old newsreels, current newsreels, reconstructions by actors of real-life incidents – these are among the devices used. Documentary producers may overdo the general 'make-it-visual' principle; too many coloured figures may be moved about on to many coloured maps to express the simplest of facts or processes.

Reviewing a documentary generally means asking these general questions:

- Is it part of a series? If so, what contribution is it making to the series, and what is to follow?
- What knowledge did the viewer need to bring to the documentary? How clear was the background to a viewer who did not know much about the subject?
- Was the programme's judgement fair, was the argument convincing? As balanced as it should have been?
- How did the programme compare with similar earlier documentaries that may have been seen? (Keeping in mind of course that readers may not have seen either.)

For preliminary research before reviewing, try the station's Press Office or the office of the programme's producer. Put yourself on the necessary mailing lists if a regular reviewer.

The variety of TV output is matched by the variety of approaches to the reviewing task. There's such a vast variety of programmes that the approach of reviewers vastly varies to match, but whatever the publication, assessment tends to be between the lines, with humour and irony to the fore and a consciousness of those huge telly audiences that are being wooed in a spirit of fierce competition. Here's Jill Foster on 'Today's Telly' in the *Daily Mirror* of 28 June 2004 on a documentary, *Little Lady Fauntleroy*

(Channel 4). Ten-year-old James Harries appeared on TV as an antiques expert (we learn that he was primed by his father) and later turned into a woman.

> James is now Lauren who is a marriage counsellor cum karaoke singer cum doctor of metaphysics and dramaturgy – don't worry, I had to look it up too. Trouble is, all her qualifications are from the Cardiff College of Humanistic Studies – located at the Harries' home.

The self-deluded and snobbish parents are making money from the gullible and are attracting venom from the neighbours. The presenter ends up screaming at them what he thinks of their fake qualifications.

Last Night's or The Weekend's TV can group together several items and can find intriguing or funny ways of making connections between them. In *The Independent Review* Thomas Sutcliffe moves from a Panorama (BBC1) programme *Can Condoms Kill?* (the Aids virus can pass through the holes) to a BBC2 documentary on *The Elgin Marbles*:

> Like condoms, the subject of the Elgin Marbles is an impermeable membrane: on one side you have those who believe they should be returned to Greece, and on the other those who think they shouldn't, and the two rarely make any kind of meaningful contact.

When a genre can be covered (or attacked) by lumping together several programmes, the resulting review can say worthwhile things even if the products aren't worth much. In June 2004 the schedules were crammed with 'reality' shows. Sam Wollaston responded with *Reality Bites* in *The Guardian*, starting with *Hell's Kitchen* (ITV1), wherein three-Michelin-starred Gordon Ramsay is the devil:

> So what you essentially have here is a man who used to be a real chef before he turned into a publicity monster pretending to be cross with some people who are pretending we've heard of them in a restaurant that doesn't really exist. And they call it reality.

> Some of the so-called celebrities eating – or not eating – in the makey-uppy restaurant are only 'famous' because they've been on reality shows themselves. Look, there's Jade off Big Brother. And over there is the coughing major who was on Celebrity Wife Swap. With Jade off Big Brother. The whole reality thing seems to have turned into a terrifying self-fertilizing organism that breeds and evolves, creating offspring that get uglier with each new generation.

Wollaston refers to *Big Brother*'s 'bunch of losers who should be cross that they've been locked up in an old formula'. They get on or don't get on and are voted out one by one. It's not enough. For TV these days, he says:

> You have to properly mess with them – swap their wives, fake their jobs, put them in the past, alter their faces, exchange their internal organs ...

He finds the new kind of Pop Idol, *Bollywood Star*, in which hopeful Brits audition for a major part in a Bollywood film, more promising. And Simon Edge in the *Daily Express* found in it things to smile at and things to be moved at. Like some bad films, some bad TV can be enjoyed for various reasons, and the reviewer can sometimes remind you of the fact.

You can make a living out of sending up TV that's not up to scratch because there's so much of it, if you're Victor Lewis-Smith with a regular whole-page column in London's *Evening Standard*. Early June of 2004 saw several programmes commemorating the anniversary of the D-Day landings in Normandy in 1944. Nothing and nobody is safe, as Lewis parodies jingoistic attitudes. He has refused to have anything French in the house since France 'refused to participate in our glorious mission to destroy Saddam's non-existent weapons and liberate the long-suffering and downtrodden oil of Iraq'. He's also returned to the kennels a German shepherd dog and smashed up a Spanish Yamaha guitar ...

> Come on England! We don't need Europe. Let's stick two British fingers up at untrustworthy Johnny Wog, revive the Empire, reintroduce the groat, and enjoy once again our inalienable ancestral right to quaff a flagon of malmsey or a butt of sack (or even a sackbut). We're still a great nation! We've still got the Falkland Isles and Rockall! Honestly, sometimes I wonder who won the sodding war, really I do.

He's rude about the No to Europe Party, fronted by Robert Kilroy-Silk and Joan Collins, and finally in the second column gets round to reviewing *D-Day Dispatches* (ITV1), which he found, among other things, inconsistent in style:

> 'It's the second of June, 1944,' said John Suchet, dressed in unambiguously 2004 clothing and standing in a contemporary ITN-style studio clutching a plastic clipboard, so why was Sian Lloyd dressed in a Second World War military uniform, and pointing at a map with Forties' graphics?

Lewis has generally got a serious point (whether you agree with it or not). People who 'lived and fought through that period seldom mention the war at all'. He concludes:

> They know that, in truth, there's nothing glorious about war, and as we all hurtle towards WWIII, television should remember that the truth that makes us free is not the comforting celebration of our victories. For the most part, it's the truth we'd prefer *not* to hear.

ASSIGNMENTS

After completing the following reviews of very recent works/shows aimed at target publications, without having seen anything published about them, locate any published reviews and compare them with what you've written. Note especially whether the targets have reviewed the same things – for your special attention.

1 A novel, for the *Daily Mail* or the *Daily Express* (500 words) or a non-fiction book for *The Spectator* (600 words).
2 An art exhibition, or a pop/rock or classical music concert, for *What's On* (300 words).
3 Choose one of the following:
   (a) A play in the theatre, produced in your area/county for a local paper or magazine (600 words).
   (b) A film for *Empire* magazine (350 words).
   (c) A TV column containing accounts of three programmes (800 words).

19 The specialists

> No lesson seems to be so deeply inculcated by the experience of life as that you never should trust experts. If you believe in doctors, nothing is wholesome; if you believe the theologians, nothing is innocent; if you believe the soldiers, nothing is safe. They all require to have their strong wine diluted by a very large admixture of insipid common sense. Letter to Lord Lytton, 15 June 1877; in Lady Gwendolen Cecil, *Life of Robert, Marquis of Salisbury*)

The above caveat may be well over the top but specialist feature writers need to keep in mind that the expert professionals they consult usually have an agenda whether conceded or not. The general principle of checking and counter-checking holds good. We need experts much more these days, of course, as we try to keep up. Experts who turn to journalism, generally as a part-time occupation, are highly valued by editors, especially if they don't need too much editing, if they can acquire the journalistic skills, get on the audience's wavelength, bring in the common sense, avoid a narrow viewpoint and jargon.

This chapter addresses both experts-turned-journalists and journalists-turned-experts (of a kind). We'll call them all specialists, for convenience. Specialists are in demand to fill the regular slots, from the arts to zoology, in the newspapers, in the consumer magazines, in the specialist magazines. Some of the specialist writers start by accident. On a local paper versatile staff writers may cover for the health experts when the established ones are on holiday. The former may become hooked on the subject. The trick then may be to identify gaps elsewhere and make pitches.

Even so, it's wise to remain versatile to some degree: the specialisms (and the publications devoted to them) come and go. There was a moment when there was huge demand for writers about computers; a later moment saw many of the magazines going to the wall.

We have already met specialists in Chapters 17 and 18. The subject matter of the specialist columnists and reviewers, however, is a mix of fact and opinion, of the subject outside and the subject within themselves. (To generalize dangerously.) This chapter moves on to the more professional or more scientific/technical subject matter.

Wherever they've come from, with whatever motives, specialist journalists must have a passion to communicate, a desire to share their curiosity, interest and excitement about the subject with an audience. That often means, as well as the usual informing and entertaining, getting feedback from readers, developing a dialogue with them. Specialist, like general, columnists encourage this by supplying their email addresses, and sometimes some of their sources so that readers can take the subject further.

The techniques described in this chapter have already been covered in this book. The purpose now is to show how to adapt those techniques to specialist writing: to detecting opportunities, devising a marketing strategy, to pitching, deciding on content, structure and style, and to researching. There follow commentaries on some samples of published specialist features.

OPPORTUNITIES GALORE

The pace of change accelerates constantly. People find it hard to manage the flood of information reaching their own patch of expertise. They need experts in their field or in associated fields to guide them in selecting relevant information and applying it.

Specialist writers for the prints thus have the advantage that they are badly needed. Being on top of their subjects gives them the further advantage that they know where to get their information from and they know how new information is being applied. Unless their journalism is strongly research-based, the time needed for research may not be great.

Opportunities, apart from the journalistic ones we're mainly concerned with, are much varied: reports, booklets, manuals, brochures, publicity materials, etc. for government departments, associations, business organizations, PR companies; and books and scripts.

At one time the slowness of top professionals to recognize the need to communicate to wider audiences was compounded by the slowness of editors to seek out their services. Academics, especially Oxbridge ones, were discouraged from publishing outside the journals for their disciplines. A. J. P. Taylor was passed over for professorships in Modern History at Oxford in the 1950s because of his (brilliant) features in the *Sunday Express* and TV talks. This has changed. Larger papers with supplements and a spectacular increase in magazines, including specialist magazines, has attracted many specialist writers, and popularizing is no longer such a dirty word.

Finding up-to-date ideas

Specialist writers keep up to date with what's going on in their field. If you're not teaching it or earning most of your income by being employed in it you need to make special efforts to ensure that you're reading the right literature, having access to the right reference books and talking to the right colleagues.

The right literature includes the newspapers and magazines, and scripts of radio and TV documentaries if available. The indexes to articles (BHI, The Times Index, *Willing's Press Guide*, the specialist magazines' indexes, etc.) will guide you to recently published pieces. You will note on which days the quality papers deal with, or have a supplement covering, your field. For example, taking a random selection at the time of writing, *The Times* has a daily supplement (T2) covering most days the arts and health, the media and education on Tuesdays; and there's a business supplement on Wednesdays. *The Guardian* also has a daily supplement (G2) with similar coverage to T2 and special supplements on the media (Mondays), Jobs and Money (Tuesdays), and Society (Wednesdays). The weekend (Saturday) and Sunday packages of the qualities are bulky, with various kinds of supplements. *The Week* alerts you, as we've seen, to one or two of 'the best' of the week's features on the arts, and it provides the same service for other specialisms.

There are many ways a writer can exploit reference books for article ideas, some of which have been mentioned in earlier chapters. Some ways are not obvious. PR consultancies dealing with specialist areas (see *The Hollis Press and Public Relations Annual*) will provide you with masses of information on your subject. So will the publicity departments of business organizations.

The research sources listed below and in the Bibliography are an obvious source of ideas.

A MARKETING STRATEGY

The research results or latest developments reported in specialist journals can form the core of features for newspapers and magazines. A rule-of-thumb principle for finding information or a story in one kind of publication and adapting for another is to go more than one level up market or down. For example, medical specialists can more easily use the research material of *The Lancet* for an article in *Woman's Own* or their local paper than for such professional magazines as *GP*, *Pulse*, *Doctor* or *Modern Medicine*. For the middle-range professional magazines may be too well aware of the contents of the more specialized journals.

Conversely, the same medical specialists will find interestingly angled stories in the popular markets that they will know how to develop by a little research. A story about an elderly person surviving laser surgery will send them through the specialized geriatric journals for detailed coverage of the subject. They may obtain material to rework in several ways – for a technical publication, one of the health magazines, or for magazines for the elderly like *Saga*, or for those who care for them.

Before attempting specialist features, make two lists, side by side:

1 The sort of features you think you could write.
2 The gaps you perceive in the market.

Pitching to specialist publications

Specialist publications have a clearly defined editorial policy for a clearly defined audience and that's why they need close scrutiny. Ideas for specialist features are often developed in-house and may require careful briefing and ongoing feedback (see Figure 19.1). But the specialist pages of newspapers and general interest magazines should also be market-studied with extra care. Here are some dos and don'ts:

- *Show that you have market-studied* the target publication.
- *Angle your proposal* so that it's right for the readership.
- *Indicate your background and qualifications briefly.* A summary of career might help, and samples of published specialist features (see *Campaign's* briefing policy in Figure 19.1).
- *Don't propose ideas covered recently.*

Campaign Briefings

1

From: Robin Hicks, Special Reports Editor
To: M. C.

As promised, here's a brief for a piece I'd like you to write for a Campaign report on Southern Europe.

(1000 words) – **France's risqué advertising under attack**

This is the idea you emailed me and I think it will make a great feature. Order the piece in the way you suggested. First, the anti-ad movement in France (giving details on protesters in Paris, how big the movement is in France). Second, government legislation.

Then move on to talk about how this could spell the end of the great risqué campaigns of the past, giving examples (and pics please – the more sensational, the better!), and present (I hear there was a recent campaign by YSL where a man's private parts were on display).

We need the opinions of France greatest creative directors – of past and present – on how they feel French advertising could be affected by the legislation. My editor has suggested Jacques Seguela VP of Havas (jacques.seguela@havas.com) as one good person to talk to.

Pictures – please can you arrange for pics to be sent to me: jpegs or tiff files, 300 DPI.

For the market overview piece, we could use a few pictures of people you talk to, a cover of a magazine or TV still to go with a media owner you've talked to, or an ad campaign you mention.

For this piece pics are really important: the more jaw-droppingly dramatic the better.

2

From: Robin Hicks, Special Reports Editor
To: P. C.

(1800 words, 2-pager) – **Locations for shooting commercials**

I hope you don't feel it's too specific for you and also that it doesn't prove too long to complete. I want to include quite a few big location shots so we should be able to get away with fewer words if you're struggling.

The premise for the piece is this. Last year the location of choice for shooting commercials seemed to be South Africa – affordable with a glorious climate and diverse scenery. So where's next?

Given the entry of new member states to the EU, Eastern Europe is gaining in popularity. Where else, why and which ads have been made there? The piece should feature the top emerging locations and weigh up the pros and cons of each.

In terms of dividing the piece up, first I want to run 600 or so words of copy to introduce the piece. This will discuss which locations have proved the most popular in the past and the reasons why production companies/agencies are moving on to pastures new. I expect these reasons range from the practical – cost, casting, rules and regulations, infrastructure, weather – to the aesthetic: terrain, architecture and how fashionable the 'look' of a place is. It will touch on which locations are becoming hot destinations for directors, with quotes from a few well-known UK-based directors.

For the next part, I want to feature 4 of the top emerging locations, 300 words for each. I want to make it as easy and at-a-glance as possible. First, some copy to introduce the location, why it's in vogue,

Figure 19.1
Briefings from *Campaign*'s features editor. With kind permission of *Campaign*

naming a few campaigns to have been shot there recently, but touching on a few of its weaknesses. Then some single/two-line answers to the following:

Why is it so popular at the moment (e.g. climate, cost, talent)?
Which ads were recently shot there?
Which directors are raving about it?
Which are the best production service companies?
Where are the best studios?

Are there any other criteria you feel we should be covering?

3

From: Robin Hicks
To: P. C.

(1000 words) – **The French advertising agency scene**

The feature, who's big and who's clever in French advertising, will ask: who are the big stalwarts (such as the ancient and well established Publicis and Euros) and who are the exciting new start-ups making a splash?

It should include:

– a bit about the history of the established agencies and the positioning the new agencies are taking to stand out
– who's winning the most new business?
– who's got the management team with the best reputation?
– who's doing the best work? (see below)
– conclusion: what are French clients looking for most from their agencies?

Mark Tungate is running a piece on French creativity looking at what makes great – and typical – French advertising. In this piece he will touch on an agency called LEG which has just scooped all the prizes at the French Art Directors' Club. There shouldn't be too much overlap (a bit is inevitable), but the fact that LEG saw off the likes of TBWA Paris, Publicis and BETC Euro RSCG, may make a nice hook for your piece.

Seguela would be good to talk to on this one too, I imagine. He'll contrast nicely with a young hot-shot from the start-ups.

For a list of France's biggest agencies try Secodip (part of Taylor Nelson Sofres) who measure them. A table of the top ten would be good. PR person there is Corinne in Albon (cinalbon@mi.secodip; +33 1 30 74 87 97).

Think you may have plenty of contacts for this (e.g. Marie Catherine Dupuy), but here are a few. Let me know if you want more.

miranda.salt@betc.eurorscg.fr – head of pr for BETC, +33 1 56 41 39 95
eve.magnan@publicis.com – head of pr for Publicis.
charlotte.forst@tbwa-europe.fr – head of pr for TBWA Europe, +33 1 49 09 71 21

As usual, it would be great if you could help out with pics – people and work.

Figure 19.1 (continued)

- *Don't invade the territory* of well-established contributors, unless you've identified a neglected aspect.

PRODUCING SPECIALIST FEATURES

What are the special considerations, in terms of content, structure and style?

Approach to content

Your approach to content has to take account of the vast differences in the needs of specialist markets. Business-to-business publications (previously called trade and technical) will on the whole be happy with features that can assume readers' interest for the subject's sake. For more general and more popular publications the thrust of a piece will need to impinge more practically on the lives of its readers.

In spite of these differences the following approach to content should underlie any piece of specialist journalism:

1 *Pitch the information at the right level.* For example, suppose you are describing a solar plant in operation. At the popular level the aim will be to make the reader appreciate how the plant works, probably with the help of simple analogies, anecdotes and perhaps simple diagrams or other illustrations. If addressing solar plant engineers there will be complex scientific/technical explanations. There are many levels in between. The level of discussion will determine which facts you select, which technical terms you use, which you will explain, which processes you describe.

2 *Remove misconceptions* and clear the ground for the necessary definitions and for fruitful explanation, argument, discussion. An article by Sir Fred Hoyle and Professor Chandra Wickramsingh listed some of the mythical origins of the Aids disease – Haitian pigs, African green monkeys, God, Russians in chemical warfare labs. A psychiatrist noted how readily people (and the media) believed the murderer of members of his adoptive family when he accused his mentally ill sister (also dead) of the crime. 'The mentally ill are mistakenly assumed to be particularly prone to kill others and then themselves.'

3 *Illustrate in various ways.* A verbal explanation may not be enough. Figure 19.2 shows a page from an article about basket-weave bricklaying, by a lecturer in the subject, with illustration backing up the text.

use the centre of the first brick placed in the setting out procedure as the centre point of the panel (Fig 4).

Stack bond

The popularity of stack bond has increased greatly. It is mainly seen in new buildings, such as supermarkets or offices, specified under and over window openings (Fig 5).

This type of bond consists of multiple soldier courses laid on top of each other, using horizontal and vertical straight joints.

When constructing walling in stack bond it is good practice to construct a maximum of three courses. These courses must be jointed and left to allow the mortar to set (due to the lack of stability inherent in this bond). Continue the remaining courses using the same procedure. Stack bond must be reinforced horizontally with expanded metal on every bed joint.

The jointing or pointing of the brickwork is sometimes completed using two types of joint finish, for example, a flush joint used on the vertical or 'perp' joints, and a raked joint on the horizontal or bed joint. The perpendicular joints can be filled with a coloured mortar that matches the colour of the face brick. This is called 'blinding out'.

Alternatives

There are numerous alternatives to the panelling described in this and the preceding article (Building Today, February 4). Figs. 6, 7, 8 and 9, show four of the lesser known forms of panelling.

Interlacing bond

This is an attractive type of panelling where the smallest cut can be left open for decorative purposes. A typical situation where interlacing bond could be used as a decorative substitute, would be in honeycomb garden wall construction (Fig 6).

Diagonal interlacing bond

This bond is the same as interlacing bond but with the panel at 45 deg. A great deal of cutting is required for this bond, as for all 45 deg. panels (Fig 7).

Raking bond

In this bond the bricks are run in stretcher bond with 75 mm laps, from the centre point in opposite directions. This bond is unfortunately rarely seen in modern building (Fig 8).

Flemish unit bond

This bond is so-called because of the resemblance to the sectional bonding used in one and a half brick thick Flemish bond walling. It can produce an eyecatching effect (Fig 9). ☐

Mark Dacey is a lecturer in brickwork at Barry College of Further Education.

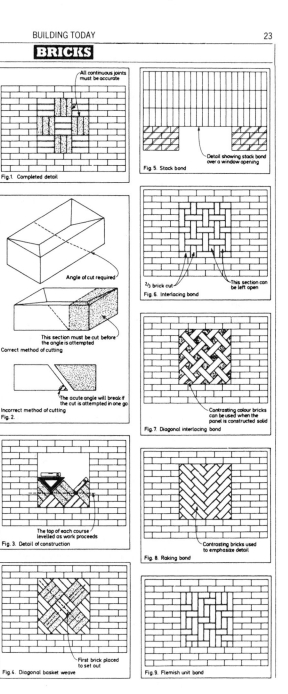

Fig.1. Completed detail

Angle of cut required

This section must be cut before the angle is attempted
Correct method of cutting

The acute angle will break if the cut is attempted in one go
Incorrect method of cutting
Fig. 2.

The top of each course levelled as work proceeds
Fig. 3. Detail of construction

First brick placed to set out
Fig. 4. Diagonal basket weave

All continuous joints must be accurate

Detail showing stack bond over a window opening
Fig. 5. Stack bond

²/₃ brick cut
This section can be left open
Fig. 6. Interlacing bond

Contrasting colour bricks can be used when the panel is constructed solid
Fig. 7. Diagonal interlacing bond

Contrasting bricks used to emphasize detail
Fig. 8. Raking bond

Fig. 9. Flemish unit bond

Figure 19.2
Line drawing with technical detail: from *Building Today*, 24 March 1988, page 23. Reproduced with kind permission

Verbal illustration by such means as simple example, analogy, anecdote or quote is essential in much specialist writing. There are 100 calories in three cubes of sugar. The light from the Pleiades started its journey when Shakespeare was seven years old. Sleep to the brain is 'offline processing'. The lens aperture of a camera is like the pupil of an eye, dilating or contracting in proportion to the light, and so on.

4 *Interpret information by relating it to people.* Identify likely benefits and warn about the possible dangers of discoveries, developments and processes. The education specialist, for instance, considers how current education policies will affect employment patterns. Writers on biogenetics warn that politicians may be tempted to exploit developments in cloning.

Shaping up

Specialist features are read by people avid for information, explanation, instruction. Information must be organized so that it's easy to take in, refer to and remember. The approach is essentially to:

1 *Select points and structure them carefully, using headings if necessary.* Don't make the texture too dense. In how-to features of fair complexity readers will put up with some repetition (but not with digression) because it gives them breathers as they busily ingest all the information, as long as there's a steady progression.

Notice how the repetition of 'brick' and 'softening' and the examples in this paragraph from that *Building Today* bricklaying article spaces out the information so that it is easy to take in:

> When a number of raked cuts have to be completed, as in diagonal basket weave or gable construction, use a softening material under the brick to take the impact out of the blow that a hammer and bolster would create. This decreases the possibility of the brick fracturing. Some good methods of softening are a bucketful of dry sand or a small square of old carpet.

2 *Anticipate readers' questions.* List them, then put them in an order that will create a logical progression and you've probably got a good outline to follow.

3 *Suggest solutions to problems, or raise the most important questions,* and make intelligent predictions about the future. This is often a good way to end a feature.

Outlines in logical order

A 1000-word piece at a specialist level on the current attempts to rehabilitate ex-prisoners in the community aimed at *New Society* or the Society supplement of *The Guardian* might be planned as follows:

Intro

- Hook: setting the scene with a case study or two
- Bridge: background, definitions, removal of misconceptions
- Text: thesis – the rehabilitation must start in prison and there must be adequate follow-up.

Body

- Policies that have failed and why
- The various social problems in the chain
- Likely approaches/solutions, with case studies.

Conclusion

- Summing up/justification of the thesis.

This could be expanded into a detailed outline with sources indicated. It's advisable to work from a more detailed outline for longer features. Let's stay with social problems. A 2500- to 3000-word or longer feature on the treatment of alcoholics would have an intro and a conclusion along the same lines. The outline of the body could have the sources slotted in. You might work in this way:

Your notes can be divided into sections with headings: 1, 2, 3, 4, ... Your source materials can be labelled A, B, C, D, ... and put to the side. They would include, say:

A   The NHS
B   Alcoholics Anonymous
C   Institute of Psychiatry
D   Rutgers University, New York
E   Drink Watchers organization
F   Edinburgh research unit
G   National Institute of Alcohol Abuse and Alcoholism
H   *Directory of Psychology* and *Psychiatry Encyclopaedia*.

The notes might come from books, journalism (consult the indexes), literature of the above organizations and from legwork/interviews involved in visits. The notes might provide the following headings, with the sources indicated:

1 Definitions of alcoholism (C, H)
2 The main causes (C, G, H)
3 Recent developments, e.g. among women (journalism, G)
4 Two kinds of cure – controlled drinking and abstinence (B, F)
5 Most successful treatments (D, F)
6 Least successful treatments (D, F)
7 Lack of funding for research/medical facilities/voluntary organizations (A, G)
8 What needs to be done (journalism, D, G).

One way of working with this outline is to allocate half a page to each heading and slot underneath it the most significant or most striking acts, quotes, anecdotes, whatever, from the notes and literature. In the margins of the pages you can indicate any links that occur to you.

You may want then, if you feel saturated with the stuff, to write a first draft from memory, using the second draft to fill in the gaps by referring to your materials, and to polish.

Some commissioning editors, especially in the USA, like to see your pitch in the form of an outline with research sources indicated, as above, plus a proposed intro. A paragraph summarizing what will come after that might also be welcome. This is especially likely when your feature is to be long, fairly complex and based on a fair amount of research. See for example the booklet *Writing for Reader's Digest*, obtainable from the publishers. A reminder: you don't have to give up your confidential sources.

From the above example it's clear that you could develop a proposal for a book from a detailed feature outline, by expanding research sources and commentary.

Finding the right language

The care to get the approach to content and structure right will be undermined by ineffective language. Check for the three Cs – clarity, conciseness and coherence – in the words, sentences and paragraphs as well as in the overall effect:

- Is every word necessary, immediately comprehensible? Will any of the jargon need to be explained? Would a glossary be useful?

- Is every sentence relevant, comprehensible at first reading?
- Are the sentences and paragraphs in the best order for effective description, explanation, instruction?

The use of jargon

The CED defines jargon as 'words or expressions used by a particular profession or group that are difficult for others to understand'. Explain a term if you think a fair number of readers will find it unfamiliar, but do so unobtrusively so as not to bore others. Readers of *Building Today* were assumed to be familiar with 'soldier course', 'dimension deviation' and 'rebated'. Much jargon, even if unfamiliar, will be understood from the context.

Other definitions of jargon are 'debased language' and 'gibberish'. This is the unacceptable jargon that is developed by some trades and professions as a kind of slang with which only the initiated feel at ease, and which can keep others at a distance. Thus we have the National Health's 'bed throughput', 'the efficiency trap', 'the reverse efficiency trap' and 'increased patient activity' (which has nothing to do with pillow-fights).

Sociologists are accused of 'obscurely systemizing the obvious'. Some of this is done for the sake of political correctness. Is it necessary to call homosexuals 'affectional preference minorities' or stupidity 'conceptual difficulties'? The International Monetary Fund has concocted some euphemistic '-ities' – 'conditionality', additionality', 'mutuality'. Computer nerds like 'functionality'.

Watching that phraseology

Professionals or technicians who launch into addressing large audiences may bring some cumbersome phraseology with them. Here are a couple of samples:

> If that statement appears obvious to the meanest intelligence, it must be realized that …

> This has doubtless been said many times in the past, and doubtless will be said many times in the future, but …

A paragraph from an article about sales techniques runs:

> Our research project starts from the assumption that communication is central to social life; perhaps nowhere is this more important than in selling.

> In this context interpersonal skills appear to be integral features not only of sales success but also of commercial success in general.

This means that business success depends on establishing good relations with people. An article on management in the hotel and catering industries gets tenses in a twist:

> Management ... tends to be very young. It would be surprising to find so many executives in their twenties if the prospect of going into the industries hadn't been so unfashionable in years gone by.

> The image of continental waiters working long hours was a more normal perspective for parents than college graduates, well trained for a worthwhile career. In fact, there are more catering colleges in Britain than in any other EEC country.

This is more clearly and concisely expressed: Management ... *is* young because it *has been* an unfashionable career. The image *has been* overworked waiters rather than college graduates ...

The context needs to be firmly in the present; in other words past situations require the present perfect. The clutter of abstract nouns such as 'prospect', 'image', 'perspective' – in any case an image is not a perspective – doesn't help.

The classics on good English usage that steer us away from gobbledygook (Gowers, Orwell and others – see Bibliography) are well worth the space on our shelves.

On the same wavelength

If you're going to aim at different kinds of publications, study the writers who do it. Dr James Le Fanu turns up all over the place. Here he is in *The Financial Times*, reviewing a book by D. M. Potts and W. T. M. Potts, *Queen Victoria's Gene*:

> Argument centres on how Queen Victoria acquired the haemophiliac gene which she passed down to her various offspring. It could have been a spontaneous mutation, a random garbling of the microscopic part of the DNA that coded for the production of Factor VIII, which is essential for the clotting of the blood.

Moving to *GQ* magazine (in a column called 'What's up, Doc?') he gives us:

> In the 22 years from 1969 to 1991, concentration of all the major air pollutants – sulphur dioxide, ozone, particulates and oxides of nitrogen – declined

by 50 per cent in the city of Philadelphia, while during the same period mortality rates from asthma increased markedly. Even more intriguing is a study of the prevalence of asthma in Britain, which shows that it is more common on the non-polluted island of Skye in the western Highlands of Scotland than in urban Cardiff.

He, like many other doctors and health professionals, find many opportunities up and down market. Dr Vernon Coleman, author of many self-help books, knows how to get down-to-earth for *The People*. Here he advises a caravan couple suffering from the bad behaviour of children in the next caravan whose parents regret that they are hyperactive and cannot be controlled:

> Bollocks. The chances are that if you could stick the little bastards up to their necks in a vat full of warm sewage for 10 hours they'd soon learn some manners. Most of the children diagnosed as suffering from 'hyperactivity' are no more hyperactive than they are rabid.

The best way to annoy people in caravans, says the doctor, is to throw bread on to the roof. The seagulls dancing on the metal roof 'will quickly drive your neighbour potty' and they will then go home.

Me, I make no comment.

SAMPLES PUBLISHED

At the time of writing here are a few recent samples of the numerous specialist subjects covered in features:

Business

The Observer Food Magazine (Andrew Purvis): 'Loaded' – why supermarkets are getting richer and richer.

Financial Times (Roger Bray): 'Flight path to the new Europe' – airlines expect many new routes after eastward expansion of the EU.

Computers

The Sunday Times (Barry Collins): 'Make commuting work for you' – make the most of your laptop on the train by surfing, playing games, and so on.

Internet Magazine (Heather Walmsley): 'Sweet Charity' – interview with Anuradha Vittachi, Director, OneWorld International Foundation, which gives voice to small charities around the world.

Education

The Independent (Steve McCormack): 'I used to bunk off … No longer' – teenager truants take to an employment skills programme in Kingston-upon-Thames.

The Independent (Caroline Haydon): 'Should tots be tuning in?' – pre-school children lack the language skills of previous generations.

The Daily Telegraph (Madsen Pirie, president of the Adam Smith Institute): 'Helping the public to go private' – a Ryanair kind of revolution is recommended to bring private education to a wider public.

New Internationalist magazine (Hugh Warwick, writer and researcher on environmental and social justice issues): 'Smoke' – fuels burned on traditional three-stone stoves are killing at least 1.6 million people yearly.

Food

The Observer Magazine (Dr John Briffa): 'When fatter is fitter' – cutting cholesterol out of your diet can do you harm.

Health

The Daily Telegraph (Barbara Lantin): 'Do you bend like Beckham?' – one leg shorter than the other (which Beckham has) can cause back problems. (Telephone numbers of Health and Fitness Solutions and Institute of Chiropodists and Podiatrists.)

The Observer Magazine ('Getting on top of your troubles is as easy as counting to 81,' says Barefoot Doctor): 'Winning numbers' – exercises that prevent the mind racing and depriving the kidneys of energy, which causes anxiety. (Write or email him, or view his website.)

Daily Express (Dr Adam Carey, ITV Celebrity Fit Club expert and nutritional adviser to England's World Cup Rugby team): vending machines in schools, full of junk food, refined sugar, salt and fat, are causing obesity, which leads to an increase in diabetes and asthma.

Time Magazine (Kate Noble, London): 'Bad drug makes good' – thalidomide, when used in the 1960s to treat morning sickness in pregnant women, caused terrible deformities in their children, but it is now showing possibilities as a cancer treatment.

Media

Press Gazette ('Media misreporting of mental illness is no joke, says Liz Nightingale' as strapline): 'Time for a rethink' – Ms Nightingale is media officer for Rethink, a campaigning membership charity involving people with severe mental illness and carers, with a network of mutual support groups around the country.

For up-to-date commentary on the media see the quality papers on the days when media columns appear, and subscribe to *Press Gazette*. For greater depth, also subscribe to *British Journalism Review*.

Medical science

Marie Claire (Jennifer Wolff): 'Want to freeze your eggs until you meet Mr Right?' – the ethical issues involved, with an account of a business selling models' eggs for between £28,000 and £85,000, case studies of surrogate mothers and interviews with doctors and pressure groups.

Alternative/complementary medicine

She magazine (Linda Bird): 'What's the alternative?' – brief accounts of the most popular forms: acupuncture, homeopathy, nutritional medicine, hypnotherapy, osteopathy and chiropractic.

Psychology Today (Michael Castleman, author of 12 consumer health books): 'The Strange Case of Homeopathy. Miracle cure, placebo or nothing at all?' – its mechanism of action cannot be explained scientifically but Americans believe that the combination of mainstream and alternative medicine will produce the best results.

Psychology

Psychology Today (Marina Krakovsky): 'Caveat Sender. The Pitfalls of E-Mail' – the lack of signals of rapport (tone of voice, nuances, facial expressions, and so on) can mean that emails can sound rude or indifferent, so if in doubt phone first.

Science/technology

Time Magazine (George Johnson, author of *A Shortcut through Time: the Path to the Quantum Computer*): 'The Purr of the Qubit' – an experiment taking scientists closer to the powers of quantum computing.

The magazine gives good coverage of this area, exploring subjects in depth through series of articles on separate aspects: for example, on the DNA revolution.

The Guardian (Life supplement, Ian Sample): 'Science runs into trouble with bubbles' – a US physicist claimed that an experiment triggered nuclear fusion by blasting a beaker of acetone, the key ingredient in nail varnish remover, with soundwaves: sonofusion.

Society

The Guardian (Society supplement, Tristam Hunt, historian): 'Past masters' – we can learn how to revitalize our urban centres from nineteenth century municipal visionaries such as Joseph Chamberlain.

Transport

Daily Mail (Op Ed, Christian Wolmar, writer and broadcaster on transport): 'Le white elephant' – the fiasco of the Channel Tunnel.

SPECIALIST COLUMNS

The specialist byline column can cover a wide range of subjects in a wide range of publications. To ensure continuity, you have to be bang up to date (especially with any new technology), ready with new angles, able to adapt your style to different audiences. *The Oldie* magazine has had two fruitful column formulae based on celebrities: 'I once met …' and 'Still with us …'. Collect such formulae and work out ways of adapting them to your specialism without making it obvious that you've pinched them from *The Oldie*. Devise new formulae, take off from the feedback you get.

Decide on the essential aim of any new specialist column you're about to pitch. Is it mainly to give advice or to entertain or to provoke to action, or all three? Is it to be an essay form, a three- or four-item menu, a catalogue of information (as in a consumer's guide to cameras or computers), an interview feature, a Q-and-A interview, a Q-and-A using readers' queries as in an agony column, a how-to column with headings?

You may want to experiment to see what works with your subject before pitching, so that your column will not look like any other within your subject area. Whatever the formula, your sample material must convince a potential editor that you can keep a column going indefinitely.

RESEARCH AND FACT CHECKING

The British Library's *Research in British Universities*, in several volumes, gives details of research projects being undertaken in the UK, together with the names of experts in specialist subjects. The various *Abstracts* (*Horticultural*, *Psychological*, etc.) summarize the most significant of recent academic texts. You should also have access to the directories listing members of your profession or trade, with details of their work, such as *The Medical Directory*.

Use constant legwork, bringing people into your picture, to make sure you're not rehashing old themes from research materials.

Specialist features need scrupulous research and fact checking. However much of a professional you are, you will depend at different times on interviews/quotes from experts in different disciplines that impinge on your subject, from the people in the middle (the care workers, for example) and from the people at the receiving end (the patients, for example). You're always looking for different angles, to approach the truth. It's advisable to get significant interviewees to check your script (to ensure the facts are right, the quotes accurate).

The much-in-demand medical/health features can be a minefield. Readers will depend on the information and advice given, especially if you're a regular columnist. You need to be able to assess reliably the value to readers of information gathered online, from printed sources, new products publicity, interviews, and so on. Direct quotation may constitute a violation of medical ethics. Indirect speech and cautious summarizing are sometimes advisable: 'cure', 'breakthrough' and suchlike words should be avoided.

Specialists new to journalism may not be sufficiently aware how much information from apparently reliable sources can be inaccurate. It's worth repeating that errors are repeated in newspapers for years. Press releases and other materials from organizations may contain errors of fact and wrong spellings of names. Faulty grammar may make for misleading content.

Professional organizations are listed on pages 389–90 and online sources on page 391–4.

ASSIGNMENTS

Choose two out of the following:

1 The *Marie Claire* article on fertility techniques mentioned above discusses some of the risks and ethical issues. After mentioning that 'some [infertile] couples will pay any price to reverse nature's fate' two procedures were merely mentioned:

> So, how far will we go to have a baby that's genetically our own? The answer: as far as science permits. These days, women are travelling to Lebanon to have their 'weak' eggs supplemented with cytoplasm (the sticky liquid that surrounds the nucleus) from donor eggs, creating babies with three sets of DNA. Other couples are journeying to makeshift medical clinics in Mexico and Colombia, where the blood of husband and wife is mixed and then transfused back into the woman to create (hopefully) an immunity to miscarriage. This procedure has never been proved to be effective and is not available in Britain or the US, where it has been banned.

Write a feature of 1000 words for a popular woman's magazine about these (if still offered) and other procedures, indicating experts' advice.

2 Write a humorous but well-researched column of 800 words on the subject of greed for a target publication. Here to start you off are two paragraphs from an essay in *New Internationalist* of July 2004 by John F. Schumaker:

> When we salute all-consuming America as the standout 'growth engine' of the world, we are in many ways paying tribute to the

economic wonders of greed. William Dodson's essay 'A Culture of Greed' chronicles America's pre-eminence of a greed economy. He writes that the US enjoys a relative absence of constraints, including tax and labour constraints that would otherwise burden corporations with a sense of social responsibility, plus various system advantages and historical traditions, that together allow greed to flourish and be milked for purposes of profit and growth.

Jay Phelan, an economist, biologist, and co-author of *Mean Genes*, feels that greed could be our ultimate undoing as a species. Yet he theorizes that evolution programmed us to be greedy since greed locks us into discontent, which in turn keeps us motivated and itchy for change. In the past at least, this favoured survival. Conversely, he believes, it would be disastrous if humans lacked greed to the extent that they could achieve a genuine state of happiness or contentment. In Phelan's view, this is because happy people tend not to do much, or crave much – poison for a modern economy. (*New Internationalist*, www.newint.org)

3 Rewrite the following extracts, for *The Sun*, *The Mirror*, the *Daily Express* or the *Daily Mail*, reducing each by a half and updating as necessary (indicate the target):

'It's the extended Internet. It's the next generation of the Internet, which will mean the extension of Internet communications to all electronic devices,' says Stan Schatt, vice-president of Forester Research in the US. The idea of devices talking to one another over the Internet has been with us for some time. Fridges that detect when your food stock is low and send an order to the supermarket over the Internet were confidently predicted during the Internet boom.

Such Internet fridges, or at least approximations of them, have indeed become available. Not many people have them. It turns out to be more difficult to get machines talking to one another than some had thought. Yet the technology to allow such communication exists. If devices could talk to one another over the Internet, we could have a world of smart houses and smart offices. (Fiona Harvey, *The Financial Times*, 24 March 2004. © The Financial Times. All rights reserved)

What stimulates this apparently insatiable appetite [for taking control of our health]? Some polemicists argue that, in an age of uncertainty and political impotence, the governance of our health and the reshaping of our anatomy is the only 'power' that punters can wield. It is also the offshoot of both a mistrust of the medical profession and its demystification – witnessed, for instance, in parents who refuse the MMR vaccination for their children, regardless of how much doctor insists that he knows best. Public health campaigns are a whole lot trickier now that the patient no longer swallows large doses of paternalism. (Yvonne Roberts, New Statesman special supplement on health, 24 June 2004)

… three years ago, plants with leaf blemishes and dying stems started turning up in British nurseries and garden centres. The fungus causing this was … found to be P. ramorum. Diseased plants were destroyed by officials from the Department for the Environment, Food and Rural Affairs (defra), but the British version of Sod [sudden oak death], called ramorum, has now been spotted in more than 300 places. Ominously, it has jumped the garden centre fence and appeared in at least nine mature trees in three gardens in Cornwall, a witch-hazel in Wales and an isolated American red oak in Sussex. (Paul Evans, The Guardian Environment, 11 February 2004)

To gain a place on the main board of a public company is the equivalent of a lottery win. Put another way, it gives you access to the bran tub that is shareholders' funds. A huge salary is only the beginning. Now that it is compulsory for companies to reveal much more about their remuneration policies, bemused shareholders are discovering for the first time the extent of their unwitting generosity.

It is not uncommon for directors to have a house in central London on the firm, to have school fees paid, to get free dental and medical treatment, and, for all I know, hair and clothes allowances too. All that, of course, comes on top of lavish share options and pension provisions.

Best of all, however, is that should things go terribly wrong and prove that the pampered voluptuary whom you appointed to the board at immense cost was in fact an overstuffed turkey, he or she still wins. The reward for failure is usually the equivalent of two or three years' salary plus a continuing pension – a system that makes millionaires out of duds. (Iain Murray, Money Observer, June 2003)

20 Selling overseas

1 Any story should have the elements of God, sex and action.
2 All features should be of interest to ...
   (a) New York, the centre of US publishing.
   (b) Finland, because if they have heard of it there, it is probably of interest to all of Europe.
   (c) India, because if the subject is of interest there, it will be of interest all over Asia and Africa.

(BP Singer Features, Anaheim, California, USA, a syndication agency)

The Internet has widened the horizons of feature writers. Perhaps three-quarters of the magazines in the world are in English; some of the others may be interested in translating your offerings, and they are only a few clicks away. Of course there's a great deal of competition and your market study has to be at its sharpest. But there are exciting prospects, both for the traditional prints and for electronic publications.

You can sample some of those traditional prints online and market-study them there. You can arrange for publishers to send recent numbers and arrange to pay by credit card or international money orders. You can then pitch and submit copy by email. Otherwise, if you're something of a traveller you may make a list of likely targets from the marketing guides and pick up copies on holiday. Or you can ask relatives and friends living or travelling overseas to send you publications from various countries.

A feature that will sell without change to different publications overseas requires careful shaping to transcend all the cultural boundaries and you're likely to need a syndication agency (see below). Increasingly magazines are being reproduced in various (especially European) countries in their own languages (with a new title) and they will translate from English, but few features can be marketed in this way without some rewriting. There are, on the other hand, numerous possibilities for rewriting a feature, especially if you've done a fair amount of research which has thrown up a number of different angles that can be exploited.

GUIDES TO THE MARKET

Have another look at Figure 3.4. The various marketing magazines and guidebooks list overseas publications. Remember that names of editors and other details may be out of date and need to be checked. Try online to update these items, or telephone. Other sources for market study are the foreign embassies in the UK, which will give you details of magazines published in their countries, the Foreign Office's and the Department of Trade and Industry's (DTI's) guides to foreign countries.

You must be clear about what rights you will be asked for (American publishers generally ask for all rights), what rights you are willing to grant and how the rights offered should affect the fee you expect. Some overseas publications are not interested in features you've sold in the UK under an FBRO agreement, but many are, as long as you're offering a publication First Rights within its country. Be clear about whether electronic rights are demanded.

Some overseas magazines will accept features in English and translate them. The German periodicals business, for example, will do this, charging you a fee for the service, but often paying well enough to make it worthwhile. Increasingly magazines are producing at the same time in different European countries in their own languages. Again, they may translate your feature for a fee. But keep in mind that features that can be marketed in this way without some rewriting are relatively few. If you're going down this road syndication would seem to be the answer.

Writers' magazines

Although close study of a publication is the best kind of market study, editorial policies can be put into sharper focus by the writers' guidelines that some magazines will send you on request, most likely after an initial pitch. Many American magazines, for example, provide this service. Such guidelines may include a list of subjects to be covered in future issues. These are to be regarded mainly as areas to avoid rather than be embraced – the commissions may have been established – but you may want to check if ideas on such subjects are being encouraged.

Apart from the writers' guidebooks, writers' magazines such as the American *Writer's Digest* and in the UK *Writer's Monthly* and *Writer's*

Forum suggest likely markets for recycling material, including reselling in different countries. Examples of this are provided by Michael Sedge in the latter publication: his feature on the sunken Roman city of Baiae off the coast of Italy had sold at his time of writing more than 20 times, in 12 countries:

> *The Sunken City of Baiae* first appeared in Italy in 1980. As the years passed I continued to find new homes for the feature – *Diver* magazine in Middlesex, *Oceans* and *Los Angeles Times* in the USA, *Mabuhay* in the Philippines, *Going Places Doing Things* in Italy, *R&R* in Germany etc.

and more recently Canada's *Weekend Times*.

Having listed a few overseas publications from the guidebooks and writers' magazines and got a clearer idea of what you can offer to overseas publications, you might then go online to see what more you can find out about them. An online presence? Sample copies? Subscribe? Writers' guidelines? You could also try keying into Google *writers' guides* and *global journalism* and suchlike phrases to sample what's on offer, narrowing the field down to the countries and kinds of publication you're looking for.

Once you're developing a global approach to sales you may find opportunities in English language publications that are international in scope. The monthly magazine *New Internationalist*, for example, published in Oxford, devotes most of each issue with campaigning zeal to an important world issues related to world poverty and inequality.

By email is the obvious way to pitch and submit, especially if you're pitching to several editors in different countries at the same time. You simply copy your query content to your clipboard and paste it into your emails, and then do any editing required.

Play it by ear. How successful are you in getting your ideas accepted in this way? Editors everywhere are getting many queries this way daily. They may find it convenient to reply 'No thanks' but it may be more convenient just to press that delete button. Experiment with follow-up emails when a pitch gets no reply within a week or so. Decide from the response or lack of it whether to keep that editor on your list or not. You have to accept that with the vast increase in opportunities comes a corresponding reduction in the proportion of pitches that are accepted.

The phone may be a better bet for a few editors overseas if you have some track record, or a letter if you have something extra special to offer.

CHOOSING YOUR COUNTRIES

Choose countries you know something about, that interest you, that you can research reasonably quickly. Contacts living in them will be useful to keep you up to date with the journalism there and send you periodicals. They will be able to add a personal slant to your market research. It helps if you, or contacts, have lived or worked or travelled to the countries you select.

The culture study

You must extend your market study. You need to study not merely the target publication but the country – its culture and its people. Features about prison life in the UK, for example, or about sailing round the coast of Britain may well be of interest to overseas markets. But you should have a good idea what the prison life or the sailing is like in the target country and what the target readers would be most interested to know. You will avoid any suggestion that your country is superior in the way it handles things (unless of course that's what you've secured an agreement to do, and the facts stand up and you can do it tactfully). It will help if you know the different varieties of slang and the kinds of English used overseas. A feature sent to the US must use American spelling and watch those cultural references. Refer to a baseball rather than a cricket match.

Start your culture study with guidebooks, encyclopedias, almanacs and the like, going online when you're more sure of what you're looking for. Read, if you can, what they read. If you're aiming at the US, get acquainted with *Time Magazine* and the *New Yorker* and the *New York Times* and have a look at some of the other papers and magazines as well. Then you will need to convince when you pitch that you're clued up. You will show that, first, you have something to offer that might be more difficult to obtain from the natives – a different angle, a different way of looking at things that will intrigue or arouse curiosity; and, second, that you know what sort of readers you're talking to because you've acquainted yourself with their culture.

If you're pitching to an Islamic country you'd be wise to avoid mention of women in bikinis, human body parts, alcohol, dogs and pigs. You would find out how strictly the religion was interpreted. Features are rejected in some European countries because they suggest readers can obtain certain goods at certain international chain stores such as Wal-Mart or can visit a Macdonald's when these establishments haven't arrived yet.

SOME LIKELY OPPORTUNITIES

Many of your opportunities for writing internationally are going to come out of your travelling.

Freelances have an advantage here because they can find more time for it and because they have more freedom to publish in a wide variety of publications. Even when travelling without the specific purpose of producing a feature the benefits of seeing how other peoples live and of broadening your horizons generally are obvious. Travel articles, in the usual sense of the word, were given a little space in Chapter 6 (because there are many good books on the subject). Here we are concerned with features that come out of travel, whatever your interests. If you write about the catering industry, art, architecture, agriculture, sport, banking, zoos, whatever, you can find subjects, ideas, angles, features all over the world to be produced for English-language publications everywhere.

With luck, and increasingly through experience, you'll be able to get your travel expenses covered without using up your fees on them. You might want to do it by producing in the course of each trip a travel article that will attract free travel and accommodation from travel companies, hotels, tourist offices or international trade associations if not from commissioning publications. The latter may well defray at least part of the cost. Where you don't get travel expenses you'll get information.

Apart from the United States the old imperial countries are obviously a good bet. Many of their media organizations have editorial offices in London – the Australian Consolidated Press, for example. Having acquired samples of the magazines such an organization produces, you can make your pitch via London. Spain with its English-speaking tourists and expats has a fair number of English-language publications, and so does the Netherlands where English is widely understood.

SYNDICATION

Assuming you've followed the general advice given in Chapter 3 about multiple submissions, the rights you're selling and on fees, a few more points are worthwhile here. Market-study syndication agencies before approaching them. Their requirements (and their efficiency) vary greatly. Some buy your work outright, others will pay you between 25 and

50 per cent commission from the sales. Some deal with translation fees, others don't.

If you can keep a regular column going that becomes eagerly awaited in many different areas you may be catching sight of substantial rewards. The masters are mainly American, such as Art Buchwald, who could learn the art at home. Agencies are not likely to be interested in taking you on, though, until you are well established. Even then you have to convince the agency that you can produce a column of *international* quality indefinitely.

How to define that international quality? The quote at the start of this chapter gives you a starting point.

Some syndication agencies want a series of columns that will continue indefinitely, and are already being published. When the field is specialized (food, architecture) illustrations will help to sell – photographs or line drawings. Agencies are often interested in finding book publishers to consider putting a writer's work into a book.

ASSIGNMENT

After studying marketing guides, sample issues and writers' guidelines (if you can obtain them), adapt for an overseas publication any three of the feature proposals you have produced while working through this book. (One par of 100 words for each.)

Then follow up any commission or write the feature that is based on what you think was the most promising pitch.

21   Law and ethics

The laws affecting journalists are complex. A script of a staff writer on a national newspaper is checked for libel by a media lawyer for libel and other dangers, and if a case is lost in court the newspaper will cough up. Freelances, in contrast, should remember to warn editors whenever they feel there are any legal dangers in what they've written.

Not only are the laws complex but they are liable to frequent change. You should have the latest editions of McNae's *Essential Law for Journalists* and Tom Crone's *Law and the Media* on your shelves or know where they are accessible. Make sure you are conversant with the NUJ Code of Practice and the Press Complaints Commission's (PCC's) Editors' Code (see pages 375–380) and keep up to date with such magazines as *Press Gazette* and *The Journalist*, and the nationals' media pages.

Here though it's worth underlining the essential points about the copyright and libel laws, and about attribution.

COPYRIGHT

Infringement of copyright means including in your feature or your book a substantial quotation from someone else's work without permission. It's not enough to name the author and the source of the extract. You need that author's permission. (Plagiarism is reproducing another writer's words without any acknowledgement.)

How many words is 'substantial'? Because the word is open to interpretation a measure is supplied by the notions of 'distinctive' and 'fair dealing'. As a rough guide a journalist won't normally need permission to quote 300 words or one or two short pars from another writer's work, as long as full accreditation is given. But to quote a couple of lines of poetry can be considered an infringement of copyright because they are so distinctive in relation to the whole. On the other hand, considerably more than 300 words or several pars (as long as acknowledged) can be defended as 'fair dealing'. To quote Crone:

> The defence of fair dealing acknowledges the wider interest of freedom of speech by allowing considerable latitude in the use of copyright material for certain worthy purposes. The CDPA [the Copyright, Designs and Patents Act 1988 as amended by the Copyright Regulations 1995] limits these purposes to news reporting, criticism and review, and research and private study.

Since each case of infringement that goes to court is judged on its own merits the journalist has to play safe and get legal advice whenever infringement is a possibility.

LIBEL

In 1958 Liberace, the American singer, won £1.5 million against William Connor ('Cassandra'), the columnist, and the *Daily Mirror* for suggesting (though not explicitly) that he was homosexual, although it was well known that the singer had perjured himself in court. Connor was not able to prove that he had. More recently an actress won a libel case against a reviewer who had panned a play she was in. No problem there, of course, but the reviewer had said her bum was too big. Such are the vicissitudes of expressing honest opinions that upset people too much.

The popular nationals occasionally lose a lot of money in sensational libel cases. Sometimes they risk it and succeed in recouping by boosting their circulations. Few freelances can afford to take such risks. Count Nikolas Tolstoy suffered £1.5 million damages for failing to prove that Lord Aldington was guilty of war crimes.

Truth is a defence to libel, but as we've seen the defendant must produce the proof while the plaintiff doesn't have to demonstrate that the words are false. Another important defence is fair comment (based on honest opinion). The Human Rights Act of October 2000, which incorporates the European Convention of Human Rights, marks a move in theory towards greater freedom of expression in the media. But against that right is the right of privacy, so you've got to watch the court cases to see how judges strike the balance.

Avoiding Libel

The main safeguards have been touched on in other parts of this book but it will do no harm to give them emphasis here:

- Check sources (cuttings, passages in books, your notes, your tape recordings and transcripts) to make sure you have reproduced them faithfully and that they contain no falsehoods. It is no excuse to say that printed statements you've drawn on were false – it's your job to check.
- Take care with the spoken words that you have reproduced. Do any of your interviewee's statements look defamatory? Again, check first that you've reproduced them accurately. Then check that you can stand them up before you decide to use them.
- Although the advice given earlier in this book to avoid giving interviewees script approval generally holds, be more generous if you feel there may be legal dangers in any of the words you've quoted. You may, for example, be wise to get the relevant factual parts of such copy checked by a person or organization qualified to do so. To repeat, as a freelance, make a special effort to draw on the advice of a media lawyer.

THE QUESTION OF ATTRIBUTION

Let's add to what was said about attribution in earlier chapters.

You have established contact with a useful source of information. You may, nevertheless, have doubts about the accuracy of the information. Is it the kind of background information that may need careful cross-checking with another source? Is it information offered on an unattributable ('off the record') basis, meaning that you can publish it without using the source's name? The main problem with 'off the record' statements is that the source may have a hidden agenda. A managing director of a company or a government official may want to get a policy idea aired in the press to assess the feedback produced. If the feedback is negative or hostile the source can deny giving out the idea.

The general advice is:

- Avoid using 'off the record' information.
- Get an agreement with your source from the start on what information they want to be 'off the record'.
- Make sure your source means by the phrase exactly what you mean: that you can use the information without their name (some sources mean

background information that will need careful checking with another source or sources).

- If your source is reluctant to go 'on the record', explain why your story needs verification by named sources.
- Never renege on your agreement with the source.

Various kinds of dealings with sources are lucidly covered by David Randall in *The Universal Journalist* (Pluto Press). See Chapter 6: 'Handling Sources, Not Them Handling You'.

ETHICAL CONCERNS

These are covered by the Codes of Conduct and Practice. You try to follow them rigorously, but the defence of public interest can override them on occasion. Check with your editors.

The right of privacy figures prominently in the codes and can cause dilemmas. Celebs complain about journalists' intrusions when inconvenient or allied to unfavourable comment yet want to benefit from favourable publicity. You and your mentors have to do that balancing act again.

Appendix 1 Suggested responses to assignments

CHAPTER 3

Assignment 3

The style is that of an academic essay rather than that of a feature article. It is very wordy. Apart from that, it sounds like a pitch to an editor. Have you removed such expressions as:

the primary question is ...
this article attempts to explore
it is my personal belief that ...

And have you removed most of those 'I's' and 'this's'?

Suggested start:

(First, perhaps, a brief anecdote about a patient who was the subject of euthanasia and the people involved.) Then:

At some time in their careers most nurses will have thoughts of euthanasia. They will meet patients without hope of regaining much quality of life. I talked to two nurses, with opposing points of view. Philippa ... Anne ... (In each case give a brief summary of their struggle to adhere to the principles inculcated by their training.)

CHAPTER 5

Assignment 3

One or two of the points you would need to add:

- Why would you call complaining 'a duty'?
- The different ways of complaining: telephone, face to face, in writing, email, recourse to the law.

- Give examples of when different methods were used and results.
- The pros and cons of each method.

CHAPTER 11

Assignment

The feature 'House-husbands: how well do they cope?'

The jargon includes such phrases as 'reflect this growing trend' and 'maximize our position in the workforce'.

Updating examples: references to such films as *Mr Mum* and *Trading Places* need to be updated and their relevance to the discussion indicated.

'Research shows. ... ' Indicate research evidence more clearly (for example, giving brief details of any survey that provided evidence), but avoid using the word 'research'.

An attention-grabbing intro is needed. Facts, figures, case study, quote? Pars 5, 6 and 7 rewritten might serve.

Consider how to order:

1 Problems/solutions? Or:
2 Problems/solutions, problems/solutions ..., one by one?

Going with the first of these, something like:

- Intro
- The couple's problems (difficulties, disadvantages) as a team
- The individuals' problems separately
- Others' problems
- Solutions (compensations, advantages): follow order of problems
- Conclusion.

The feature is long on problems and short on solutions. The conclusion begins too feebly: 'Let's hope that ...'.

The solutions provided by the various people wheeled on at the end (employers, etc.) should have been discussed throughout.

In what ways should their attitudes change and what should they be doing in the future?

Interviewees 'say' rather than 'said', which suggests it's all over and done with. It's still their opinion, one presumes.

CHAPTER 12

Assignment 2

Was it like this?:

By 11 September 2000 the *jihadis* (holy warriors) were using Yemen as a major base of operations. In cooperation with local extremist groups, also kidnapping to achieve political ends, they sank an American warship in Aden harbour – their most spectacular success.

CHAPTER 15

Assignment 1

Check your words with a good thesaurus.

Assignment 3

Generally, did you get the main selling point upfront?

(a) Did you avoid a blatant plug?
(b) Did you recognize the needs of various age groups?
(c) Did you avoid hyping it up?

CHAPTER 16

Assignment 2

Did you avoid repeating too-well-known facts about the celebrity (that tend to be repeated in the cuttings)? Did you find points in each case that would not be too familiar to the target audience and which would grab them?

CHAPTER 19

Check your pieces for style against similar pieces (even better, pieces covering the same things) in the target publications.

CHAPTER 20

Check that you've adapted cultural references to the new targets. For the USA, for example, find American equivalents for references to British TV shows, meals, sports and so on. Check that you've used American spellings.

Appendix 2 National Union of Journalists – Professional Code of Conduct

THE PUBLIC INTEREST

The NUJ's Code of Conduct has set out the main principles of British and Irish journalism since 1936. It is part of the rules and all journalists joining the union must sign that they will strive to adhere to it.

1 A journalist has a duty to maintain the highest professional and ethical standards.
2 A journalist shall at all times defend the principle of the freedom of the press and other media in relation to the collection of information and the expression of comment and criticism. He/she shall strive to eliminate distortion, news suppression and censorship.
3 A journalist shall strive to ensure that the information he/she disseminates is fair and accurate, avoid the expression of comment and conjecture as established fact and falsification by distortion, selection or misrepresentation.
4 A journalist shall rectify promptly any harmful inaccuracies, ensure that correction and apologies receive due prominence and afford the right of reply to persons criticized when the issue is of sufficient importance.
5 A journalist shall obtain information, photographs and illustrations only by straightforward means. The use of other means can be justified only by overriding considerations of the public interest. The journalist is entitled to exercise a personal conscientious objection to the use of such means.
6 A journalist shall do nothing which entails intrusion into anybody's private life, grief or distress, subject to justification by overriding considerations of the public interest.

7   A journalist shall protect confidential sources of information.

8   A journalist shall not accept bribes nor shall he/she allow other inducements to influence the performance of his/her professional duties.

9   A journalist shall not lend himself/herself to the distortion or suppression of the truth because of advertising or other considerations.

10   A journalist shall mention a person's age, sex, race, colour, creed, illegitimacy, disability, marital status or sexual orientation only if this information is strictly relevant. A journalist shall neither originate nor process material which encourages discrimination, ridicule, prejudice or hatred on any of the above-mentioned grounds.

11   No journalist shall knowingly cause or allow the publication or broadcast of a photograph that has been manipulated unless that photograph is clearly labelled as such. Manipulation does not include normal dodging, burning, colour balancing, spotting, contrast adjustment, cropping and obvious masking for legal or safety reasons.

12   A journalist shall not take private advantage of information gained in the course of his/her duties before the information is public knowledge.

13   A journalist shall not by way of statement, voice or appearance endorse by advertisement any commercial product or service save for the promotion of his/her own work or of the medium by which he/she is employed.

Source: http://www.nuj.org.uk/inner.php?docid=59; © National Union of Journalists 2004

Appendix 3 Press Complaints Commission: Code of Practice for the Press

CODE OF PRACTICE

All members of the press have a duty to maintain the highest professional standards. This Code sets the benchmark for those ethical standards, protecting both the rights of the individual and the public's right to know. It is the cornerstone of the system of self-regulation to which the industry has made a binding commitment.

It is essential that an agreed code be honoured not only to the letter but in the full spirit. It should not be interpreted so narrowly as to compromise its commitment to respect the rights of the individual, nor so broadly that it constitutes an unnecessary interference with freedom of expression or prevents publication in the public interest.

It is the responsibility of editors and publishers to implement the Code and they should take care to ensure it is observed rigorously by all editorial staff and external contributors, including non-journalists, in printed and online versions of publications.

Editors should cooperate swiftly with the PCC in the resolution of complaints. Any publication judged to have breached the Code must print the adjudication in full and with due prominence, including headline reference to the PCC.

1 Accuracy

(i) The press must take care not to publish inaccurate, misleading or distorted information, including pictures.
(ii) A significant inaccuracy, misleading statement or distortion once recognized must be corrected, promptly and with due prominence, and – where appropriate – an apology published.

(iii) The press, whilst free to be partisan, must distinguish clearly between comment, conjecture and fact.

(iv) A publication must report fairly and accurately the outcome of an action for defamation to which it has been a party, unless an agreed settlement states otherwise, or an agreed statement is published.

2   Opportunity to reply

A fair opportunity for reply to inaccuracies must be given when reasonably called for.

3   *Privacy

(i) Everyone is entitled to respect for his or her private and family life, home, health and correspondence, including digital communications. Editors will be expected to justify intrusions into any individual's private life without consent.

(ii) It is unacceptable to photograph individuals in private places without their consent.

Note – Private places are public or private property where there is a reasonable expectation of privacy.

4   *Harassment

(i) Journalists must not engage in intimidation, harassment or persistent pursuit.

(ii) They must not persist in questioning, telephoning, pursuing or photographing individuals once asked to desist; nor remain on their property when asked to leave and must not follow them.

(iii) Editors must ensure these principles are observed by those working for them and take care not to use non-compliant material from other sources.

5   Intrusion into grief or shock

In cases involving personal grief or shock, enquiries and approaches must be made with sympathy and discretion and publication handled sensitively.

This should not restrict the right to report legal proceedings, such as inquests.

6   *Children

  (i) Young people should be free to complete their time at school without unnecessary intrusion.

 (ii) A child under 16 must not be interviewed or photographed on issues involving their own or another child's welfare unless a custodial parent or similarly responsible adult consents.

(iii) Pupils must not be approached or photographed at school without the permission of the school authorities.

(iv) Minors must not be paid for material involving children's welfare, nor parents or guardians for material about their children or wards, unless it is clearly in the child's interest.

 (v) Editors must not use the fame, notoriety or position of a parent or guardian as sole justification for publishing details of a child's private life.

7   *Children in sex cases

1 The press must not, even if legally free to do so, identify children under 16 who are victims or witnesses in cases involving sex offences.

2 In any press report of a case involving a sexual offence against a child:

  (i) The child must not be identified.

 (ii) The adult may be identified.

(iii) The word 'incest' must not be used where a child victim might be identified.

(iv) Care must be taken that nothing in the report implies the relationship between the accused and the child.

8   *Hospitals

  (i) Journalists must identify themselves and obtain permission from a responsible executive before entering non-public areas of hospitals or similar institutions to pursue enquiries.

 (ii) The restrictions on intruding into privacy are particularly relevant to enquiries about individuals in hospitals or similar institutions.

9   *Reporting of crime

(i) Relatives or friends of persons convicted or accused of crime should not generally be identified without their consent, unless they are genuinely relevant to the story.

(ii) Particular regard should be paid to the potentially vulnerable position of children who witness, or are victims of, crime. This should not restrict the right to report legal proceedings.

10   *Clandestine devices and subterfuge

(i) The press must not seek to obtain or publish material acquired by using hidden cameras or clandestine listening devices; or by intercepting private or mobile telephone calls, messages or emails; or by the unauthorized removal of documents or photographs.

(ii) Engaging in misrepresentation or subterfuge can generally be justified only in the public interest and then only when the material cannot be obtained by other means.

11   Victims of sexual assault

The press must not identify victims of sexual assault or publish material likely to contribute to such identification unless there is adequate justification and they are legally free to do so.

12   Discrimination

(i) The press must avoid prejudicial or pejorative reference to an individual's race, colour, religion, sex, sexual orientation or to any physical or mental illness or disability.

(ii) Details of an individual's race, colour, religion, sexual orientation, physical or mental illness or disability must be avoided unless genuinely relevant to the story.

13   Financial journalism

(i) Even where the law does not prohibit it, journalists must not use for their own profit financial information they receive in advance of its general publication, nor should they pass such information to others.

(ii) They must not write about shares or securities in whose performance they know that they or their close families have a significant financial interest without disclosing the interest to the editor or financial editor.

(iii) They must not buy or sell, either directly or through nominees or agents, shares or securities about which they have written recently or about which they intend to write in the near future.

14 Confidential sources

Journalists have a moral obligation to protect confidential sources of information.

15 Witness payments in criminal trials

(i) No payment or offer of payment to a witness – or any person who may reasonably be expected to be called as a witness – should be made in any case once proceedings are active as defined by the Contempt of Court Act 1981.

This prohibition lasts until the suspect has been freed unconditionally by police without charge or bail or the proceedings are otherwise discontinued; or has entered a guilty plea to the court; or, in the event of a not guilty plea, the court has announced its verdict.

(ii) *Where proceedings are not yet active but are likely and foreseeable, editors must not make or offer payment to any person who may reasonably be expected to be called as a witness, unless the information concerned ought demonstrably to be published in the public interest and there is an overriding need to make or promise payment for this to be done; and all reasonable steps have been taken to ensure no financial dealings influence the evidence those witnesses give. In no circumstances should such payment be conditional on the outcome of a trial.

(iii) *Any payment or offer of payment made to a person later cited to give evidence in proceedings must be disclosed to the prosecution and defence. The witness must be advised of this requirement.

16 *Payment to criminals

(i) Payment or offers of payment for stories, pictures or information, which seek to exploit a particular crime or to glorify or glamorize crime in general, must not be made directly or via agents to convicted or confessed criminals or to their associates – who may include family, friends and colleagues.

(ii) Editors invoking the public interest to justify payment or offers would need to demonstrate that there was good reason to believe the public interest would be served. If, despite payment, no public interest emerged, then the material should not be published.

17 The public interest

There may be exceptions to the clauses marked with an asterisk where they can be demonstrated to be in the public interest.

1 The public interest includes, but is not confined to:
   (i) Detecting or exposing crime or serious impropriety.
   (ii) Protecting public health and safety.
   (iii) Preventing the public from being misled by an action or statement of an individual or organization.

2 There is a public interest in freedom of expression itself.

3 Whenever the public interest is invoked, the PCC will require editors to demonstrate fully how the public interest was served.

4 The PCC will consider the extent to which material is already in the public domain, or will become so.

5 In cases involving children under 16, editors must demonstrate an exceptional public interest to override the normally paramount interest of the child.

Source: http://www.pcc.org.uk/cop/cop.asp

Appendix 4   The Society of Authors' Quick Guide 1: Copyright and Moral Rights

Points 1–8: Copyright in the UK

Points 9–17: Copyright in the USA

Points 18–23: Moral Rights

I Copyright in the UK

1. How long does UK copyright protection last?

(a) General rule

Copyright in the work of European authors who died after 1st January 1945 lasts until 70 years from the end of the year the author died (*post mortem auctoris*: pma). Until 1st January 1996, copyright lasted until 50 years pma. For a work of joint authorship, i.e. a work by two or more authors in which the contributions of the authors are not distinct, the period of protection runs from the end of the calendar year of the death of the author who dies last.

(b) Exceptions

(i) Works not published, performed in public, offered for sale to the public on a record or cassette, or broadcast during the author's lifetime

If a European author died before 1st August 1989, literary, dramatic and musical works not published during his/her lifetime remain in copyright until 50 years from the end of the year of first posthumous publication or until 31st December 2039, whichever is the sooner. (If 70 years pma is a longer period, then 70 years pma will prevail.)

Works unpublished during the author's lifetime, where the author died after 1st August 1989, are treated the same as published material, and are protected until 70 years pma.

(ii) Works by non-European authors

The works of non-European authors are protected in the UK for as long as they are protected in the country of origin. For USA works, this is now generally also 70 pma but see also Section II below. For works of other non-European authors, including Canadian and Australian authors, this generally (though not invariably) means 50 years pma.

The protection in the UK of American works which are unpublished or were first published posthumously is complicated. If necessary, consult the Society for further information.

(iii): Revived copyright

The works of European authors who died between 1st January 1925 and 31st December 1944, whose work had gone out of copyright, went back into copyright on 1st January 1996 for what remains of 70 years pma – the new period of protection is known as 'revived copyright'. You are free to use revived copyright material without permission from the rights holder but you have to give notice of your intentions and use and may be subject to payment of a reasonable royalty. If you signed a contract before 1st July 1995 for a work which will include extracts from revived copyright material, you can go ahead without having to give notice or make any payment, so long as the work you are quoting from was out of copyright when the contract was signed.

If the author died before 31st December 1924, the period of protection is 50 years pma.

(iv) Artistic works

Artistic works, whether published in the author's lifetime or not, are protected as at (a) above, with the exception of old photographs, portraits and engravings (see the *Quick Guide to Copyright in Artistic Works*).

(v) Anonymous and pseudonymous works

The period of protection is 70 years from the end of the calendar year in which the work is first 'made available to the public' unless during that period 'it is possible for a person to ascertain the identity of the author by reasonable enquiry', in which case the period is as under (a) above. This would include, for example, newspaper articles where the individual author is not identified. Anonymous and pseudonymous works created before 1st January 1996 are protected for 50 years.

(vi) Crown and Parliamentary copyright

The Crown owns the copyright in works made by an officer or servant of the Crown in the course of his/her duties, and in work made under the direction or control of either of the Houses of Parliament. Different periods of protection apply to such works and the Society can provide further information.

(vii) Copyright in the typographical arrangement of a published work

The publisher owns the copyright in the typographical arrangement of a published work (which means that the work cannot, for example, be photocopied or reproduced in facsimile form without the publisher's consent). This copyright lasts until 25 years from the end of the year in which the edition containing the arrangement was first published.

2. What about the copyright in letters?

Letters are entitled to the same protection as other literary works (see, in particular, point 1(b)(i) above). The letter itself belongs to the recipient, but the copyright in it belongs to the writer and, after the writer's death, to his/her estate.

3. How much may be quoted from a copyright work without permission?

Generally speaking, it is an infringement to quote a 'substantial part' of a copyright work without permission. The Copyright Act 1988 does not define what is meant by 'substantial', but, in one case, four lines from a 32-line poem were held to amount to a 'substantial part'. Other legal precedents indicate that the quality of the 'part' and its value to the user must be taken into account as well as its length in determining whether it is 'substantial'. Even a 'substantial' quotation from a copyright work may not be an infringement if it is 'fair dealing ... for purposes of criticism or review' and provided it is 'accompanied by sufficient acknowledgment'. Again, the term 'fair dealing' is not defined in the Copyright Act.

Further guidance on fair dealing, clearing permissions, and what sort of fees might be charged, is given in the Society's *Quick Guide to Permissions*.

4. Is there copyright in a title?

There is no copyright in a title, but when a title is distinctive and closely identified in the public's mind with the work of a particular author, that author may be able to obtain an injunction and damages if the title is used by another writer. Increasingly these days there is a tendency for established titles and names to be trademarked. (See also the *Quick Guide to The Protection of Titles*.)

5. Is there copyright in a pseudonym?

What we have said about titles also applies here. If an author writes for a periodical under a pseudonym, he/she can, in the absence of agreement to the contrary, use the pen-name elsewhere when he/she ceases to contribute to that periodical.

6. Is there copyright in a plot?

There is no copyright in an idea or in the bare bones of a plot. To succeed in an action for infringement of copyright, the plaintiff would have to show that the combination or series of dramatic events in the allegedly infringing work had been taken from the like situations in the plaintiff's work.

In many cases where judgement has gone against the plaintiff, it is clear that the copying of 'a combination or series of dramatic events' has to be very close before the copyright is held to have been infringed. Proceedings have failed because it has been held that incidents common to two works were stock incidents or revolved around stock characters common to many works. Furthermore, as copyright is not a monopoly, it is a good defence if a later author can prove that he or she had no knowledge of an earlier author's work.

7. What formalities have to be complied with in order to acquire copyright protection?

There are no formalities in the UK or in any country which is a member of the Berne Copyright Union. This Union now includes almost all of the principal countries of the world.

Although copyright is automatically acquired immediately a work is written (or recorded in some other form, e.g. on tape or a computer disk), authors are advised to establish evidence of the date of the completion of each work. One way of doing this is to deposit a copy of the script with your bank and obtain a dated receipt. Another is to post a sealed envelope, containing a copy, to yourself.

8. What is the purpose of the copyright notice?

The copyright notice comes in the form © followed by the name of the copyright owner and the year of first publication.

This is the copyright notice prescribed by the Universal Copyright Convention (UCC), of which Great Britain and more than sixty other countries are members, including the United States (and a number of countries which are not members of the Berne Union). Works bearing the UCC copyright notice are protected in every UCC member state, whether or not that state's domestic law requires registration or other formalities.

II Copyright in the USA

9. The current situation

The Sonny Bono Copyright Term Extension Act came into effect on 27th October 1998. Under the Act, copyright in the USA is extended by 20 years, which brings it into line with European practice. New works are protected until 70 years pma.

Works previously protected until 50 years pma are now protected until 70 years pma, and works previously protected for 75 years from first publication are now protected until 95 years from first publication. There are some exceptions, for instance the new law allows libraries and schools to make use of materials that were about to go out of copyright without seeking permission, if they are not currently being exploited commercially. However, unlike the UK there is no 'revived copyright': works which had already gone out of copyright in America remain out of copyright.

10. Works created before 1996

Until 1996, works that had gone out of copyright in the USA (e.g. through failure to renew copyright, or to include the correct copyright line) could not retrospectively secure copyright protection.

However, works originating from outside the USA, and written by authors who were not American nationals, which lost copyright through failure to comply with the required formalities (of registration and renewal, including the copyright notice and complying with the manufacturing provisions) are now automatically protected by copyright in the USA from 1st January 1996, for as long as they would have been protected in the USA had the formalities been correctly met in the first place. Certain complicated formalities have to be met, however, before any action for copyright infringement can be brought – the Society can provide further information.

11. Copyright in old works

The US Copyright Act of 1909 provided for two separate terms of copyright: a period of 28 years (to the day) from publication, followed by a renewal period of a further 28 years. Until 27th September 1957, when the UK joined the UCC, the two countries never belonged to the same copyright union. One result was that the exact copyright status of old work is often very difficult to assess. Further advice should be sought where necessary.

The Copyright Act 1976, which came into force on 1st January 1978, made fundamental changes in the duration of protection for new works, and also contained some complicated transitional provisions. Further amendments came into force on 26th June 1992. The situation is now as follows:

12. Works originally copyrighted before 1950

Such works had to be registered with the US Register of Copyrights, and were protected for 28 years. Copyright had then to be renewed in the 28th year to gain a further 28 years' protection. As long as such works were registered and renewed, they are automatically protected under the 1976 Act until 31st December of the 75th calendar year from the original date they were secured. In effect this means that all copyrights in their second term on 1st January 1978 were extended for 19 years. This extension applies not only to copyrights less than 56 years old on 1st January 1978, but also to older copyrights that had previously been extended in duration under a series of Congressional enactments beginning in 1962.

Under the Sonny Bono Copyright Term Extension Act, any such work which was still in copyright on 27th October 1998 is now protected until 95 years from the original date in which copyright was secured.

13. Works originally copyrighted between 1st January 1950 and 31st December 1963

Such works had to be registered to gain protection for 28 years. In the 28th year from registration, they had to be renewed with the US Register of Copyrights to gain a further 47 year period of protection, making a total of 75 years. Under the Sonny Bono Copyright Term Extension Act, any such work which was still in copyright on 27th October 1998 is now protected until 95 years from the original date in which copyright was secured.

14. Works originally copyrighted between 1st January 1964 and 31st December 1977

Under the 1992 amendments to the Copyright Act, such works were automatically protected until 75 years from the end of the year of registration, whether or not copyright is renewed in the 28th year. Under the Sonny Bono Copyright Term Extension Act, that period has now been extended to 95 years from the end of the year of registration.

15. Works created on or after 1st January 1978

Works created after the 1976 Copyright Act came into force (on 1st January 1978) are automatically protected for the author's lifetime, and for an additional 50 years pma – now extended to 70 years pma. For works made for hire, and for anonymous and pseudonymous works, the new term is now 95 years from publication or 120 years from creation, whichever is the shorter.

16. Works existing but not copyrighted on 1st January 1978

Unpublished works that were created before 1st January 1978, but have neither been published nor registered for copyright, automatically receive protection under the 1976 Act (as extended by the Sonny Bono Extension Act). The copyright will generally last for the same life-plus-70 or 95/120 year terms provided for new works. However, all works in this category were guaranteed at least 25 years of statutory protection; the 1976 Act specifies that in no case will copyright in a work of this sort expire before 31st December 2002, and if the work is published before that date the term is extended by another 25 years, to the end of 2027. We find it hard to guess why this curious provision was included, but be aware that it does mean that some works may be in copyright for longer than 70 years pma.

17. Registration, renewal and the copyright line

Registration of copyright is no longer necessary to secure copyright protection in the USA. It is, however, advisable. It may be made at any time during the life of a copyright but if arranged within the first three months from publication it secures a claim to statutory damages and attorney's fees in court actions (otherwise the author has to meet his/her own legal fees, even if the case is won). Compliance with registration formalities is important in relation to a complex reversionary provision for old out-of-print works in their second period of protection (the Society can supply further information). It is also generally useful because someone wishing to trace a rights holder will probably refer to the Copyright Office for information. The current registration fee is $30 and further details and appropriate forms are available from the Copyright Office, Library of Congress, Washington, DC 20559.

Until 26th June 1992, failure to register copyright initially, or to renew it in its 28th year, forfeited copyright protection.

Until the USA joined the Berne Convention on 1st March 1989, a work also had to carry the correct copyright notice to secure copyright protection.

III Moral Rights

18. What are an author's 'moral rights'?

There are three main moral rights conferred by the Copyright Act 1988:

(a) the right of paternity is the right of an author to be identified whenever a work is published, performed or broadcast. In other words, book writers, scriptwriters, illustrators, and translators must be properly credited.

(b) the right of integrity is the right of an author to object to 'derogatory' treatment of a work. Treatment is 'derogatory' if it amounts to 'distortion or mutilation ... or is otherwise prejudicial to the honour or reputation of the author ...'.

(c) the right not to have work falsely attributed to you. This is the right of a person not to have a literary or dramatic work or, since 1st August 1989, an artistic work falsely attributed to him/her as author.

19. Are there any formalities?

The right of integrity is automatic, without any formalities. An author does not benefit from the right of paternity unless and until he/she has 'asserted' the right in writing. It is not clear from the Act when the 'assertion' must take place, but we advise authors and agents to include a suitable clause in each publishing contract – the assertion should also appear in the book, generally under the copyright line. The wording is unlikely to be critical. The following is one version:

The Author asserts his/her moral right to be identified as the Author of the work in relation to all such rights as are granted by the Author to the Publisher under the terms and conditions of this Agreement.

Idally the following should also be added:

The Publisher hereby undertakes:

– to print on the verso title page of every copy of every edition of the work published by him/her in the United Kingdom the words 'the right of [the author] to be identified as the author of this work has been asserted by him/her in accordance with the Copyright, Designs and Patents Act 1988'

– to make it a condition of contract with any licensee concerning any edition of the work to be published in the United Kingdom that a notice of assertion in the same terms as above shall be printed in every edition published by the licensee

– to set the name of the author in customary form with due prominence on the title page and on the binding, jacket and/or cover of every copy of the work published by it and to make it a condition of contract that a similar undertaking is made in respect of any licensed editions of the work.

20. How long do moral rights last?

The rights of paternity and integrity last as long as the copyright in the work. The right of a person not to have work falsely attributed to him/her expires 20 years after that person's death.

21. When do moral rights not apply?

The rights of paternity and integrity do not apply when work is published in a newspaper, magazine or similar periodical, or to contributions in an encyclopaedia, dictionary, yearbook or other collective work of reference.

22. Can an author waive his/her moral rights?

Yes. Moral rights cannot be assigned to someone else, but they can be waived by the author in writing (although it is very unusual for book publishers to seek a waiver). Furthermore, moral rights are not infringed by any act 'to which the person entitled to the right has consented'.

23. What happens to moral rights when an author dies?

The rights pass to whoever is nominated in the author's will. If no direction is given in a will, the rights pass to the person receiving the copyright. However, the right of a person not to have a work falsely attributed to him/her is only actionable by an author's personal representatives.

Appendix 5   Useful contacts

This appendix is a rough guide only. For fuller lists check the current editions of the printed marketing guides (see page 396) and online for up-to-date information on addresses, telephone numbers, websites and email addresses, and for details of their services.

GENERAL

The Advertising Association

Association of British Science Writers. C/o The British Association for the Advancement of Science.

Audit Bureau of Circulations. Provides certified circulation data for newspapers and magazines.

Authors' Licensing and Collecting Society (ALCS). Collects and distributes to writers fees for photocopying.

British Association of Communicators in Business. Publishes *Editor's Handbook* for editing house journals.

British Association of Journalists. Trade union.

British Guild of Travel Writers

British Library

British Library National Sound Archive. National collection of sound recording.

British Newspaper Library. Contains archives of national, regional and local newspapers, with microfilm and photocopying services.

British Standards Institution

Campaign for Freedom of Information. Campaigns for right of access by law to public sector information when it is of public interest.

Campaign for Press and Broadcast Freedom. Works for more accessible and more accountable media, with right of reply and with portrayal of minorities.

Celebrity Service Inc.

Central Office of Information

Chartered Institute of Journalists

Communications, Advertising and Marketing (CAM) Foundation

Freelance Press Services, Manchester

The Institute of Journalists. Trade union and (as The Chartered Institute of Journalists) a professional association for writers, journalists and broadcasters.

Institute of Public Relations. Publishes *Getting into Public Relations* pack, careers advice and recommends courses.

The Institute of Scientific and Technical Communicators

National Readership Surveys

National Union of Journalists. The largest union for journalists, working for agreements on salaries, fees and conditions.

PEN. The British branch of International PEN, which is open to all writers. Concerned with freedom of expression throughout the world.

Periodical Publishers Association. Operates the Periodicals Training Council.

Press Complaints Commission. Self-regulatory body of newspapers and periodicals. It investigates complaints and reports monthly and annually.

Public Relations Consultants Association. Publishes information on job opportunities in PR.

Society of Authors. Independent trade union. Advises on negotiations and contracts with publishers, film companies, etc.

Writers' Circles. Will put you in touch with the nationwide network. The Regional Arts Association of your area will put you in touch with local groups if your local library cannot.

Writer's Guild of Great Britain. Trade union, affiliated to the Trades Union Congress.

ILLUSTRATION

Aquarius Picture Library. Specializes in showbusiness.

Barnaby's Picture Library

The British Association of Picture Libraries and Agencies. Publishes an annual directory of its members and a quarterly newsletter.

Bureau of Freelance Photographers. Publishes monthly newsletter and annual handbook. Advises on picture agencies and publishing markets.

The Hutchinson Library. Society of Picture Researchers and Editors.

International Center for Photography

Photo Resources

ONLINE

Online journalism

www.holdthefrontpage.co.uk
wiki.media-culture.org.au/index.php/Main+Page
www.journolist.com

Software

CNET: www.download.com/
Version Tracker: www.versiontracker.com
ZDNet: downloads-zdnet.com.com/

Wireless access

A list of publicly available wireless hotspots can be found at www.wi-fihotspotlist.com.

Search engines

Google: www.google.com
MSN Search: www.msn.com
Yahoo!: www.yahoo.co.uk

Metasearch engines

Visimo: vivisimo.com/
Metacrawler: www.metacrawler.com
Dogpile: www.dogpile.com/
EZ2Find: ez2find.com/
Clusty: clusty.com/

Specialist search engines

Copac: www.copac.ac.uk
British Library Catalogue: catalogue.bl.uk

Guides to specialized search engines

www.searchenginewatch.com
www.searchability.com

Web directories

About.com: www.about.com
Looksmart: www.looksmart.co.uk
Dmoz: www.dmoz.org

Trusted sources

Newspapers

Financial Times: news.ft.com
The Guardian: www.guardianunlimited.co.uk
The Independent: www.independent.co.uk

Daily Telegraph: www.telegraph.co.uk
The Times: www.timesonline.co.uk

News agencies

Associated Press: www.ap.org
Reuters: www.reuters.com
The Press Association: www.pressassociation.co.uk

Reference libraries

Commercial
Encyclopaedia Britannica: www.britannica.com
Oxford Reference: www.oxfordreference.com
   Offers more than 100 works for about £100 per year.
Questia: www.questia.com
   The world's largest online library (more than 400,000 published books,
   journals and articles).
Xrefer: www.xrefer.com
   A reference service for libraries and individuals which aggregates high-
   quality reference works.

Free
Wikipedia: en.Wikipedia.org
Comprehensive, free, publicly edited encyclopaedia.
www.bartleby.com,   www.gutenberg.org,   www.1911encyclopedia.org,
   www.bloomsbury.com/ARC

Finding experts

The Ibiblio Library: www.ibiblio.org
ProfNet: www.profnet.com

Web building tutorials

www.2createawebsite.com/
webdesign.about.com

Blogging

www.blog.com
www.blurty.com
www.bloglines.com
www.blogwise.com
www.blogger.com
www.livejournal.com

Freelance jobs resources

www.elance.com
www.journalismjobs.com
www.dice.com
www.mediabistro.com

Ezines

Slate: www.slate.com
Salon: www.salon.com
Jackhammer: www.eggplant-productions.com
Capital of Nasty: www.con.ca

Appendix 6   Training

A few samples of contacts are listed below. *Press Gazette* produces extensive training supplements.

GENERAL CONTACTS

BBC Training and Development

Tel.: 0870 122 0216
www.bbctraining.co.uk

Broadcast Journalism Training Council

Tel.: 020 7727 9522
www.bjtc.co.uk

National Council for the Training of Journalists (NCTJ)

Latton Bush Centre
Southern Way
Harlow
Essex CM18 7BL
Tel.: 01279 430 009
www.nctj.com

Accredits colleges and universities that deliver newspaper and magazine journalism courses throughout the UK. Offers distance learning courses in newspaper and periodical journalism and subediting, and a programme of London-based short training courses.

Periodicals Training Council

Queen's House
28 Kingsway
London WC2B 6JR
Tel.: 020 7404 4168
www.ppa.co.uk

Publishes an annual *Directory of Magazine Training* and a booklet *A Career in Magazines*.

UCAS

Tel.: 01242 222444
www.ucas.co.uk

Publishes *A Student's Guide to Entry to Media Studies*. (See also *The Potter Guide to Higher Education* (Balebank Books), and *British Universities Guide to Graduate Studies* (Pitman).)

PHOTOGRAPHY

The London College of Communication

Tel.: 020 7514 6500
www.lcp.linst.ac.uk

Offers evening courses.

DISTANCE LEARNING

The London School of Journalism

Tel.: 020 7706 3536
www.home-study.com

Bibliography

BOOKS

Get to know the best local library, with a good reference section, in your area. If you get into writing research features, you can buy second-hand books online and it may be worthwhile to join the British Library. The great majority of the books in these lists have been published a year or two before the date of the edition of this book. Older books are included if they have the status of classics or near-classics. As far as possible obtain the latest editions. Check online for dates of these and availability.

Reference

Basic reference library

The following is a rough guide to a writer's basic reference library. Consider having dictionaries and encyclopedias on CD-ROM. You will add according to the way your interests develop.

1 English dictionary (Oxford or Chambers).
2 Thesaurus.
3 *The Oxford Writers' Dictionary*, compiled by R. E. Allen.
4 *The Oxford Manual of Style*, edited and compiled by R. M. Ritter.
5 *Hart's Rules for Compositors and Readers*, Oxford University Press.
6 *The Oxford Dictionary for Writers and Editors*, OUP.
7 *Longman Guide to English Usage*.
8 *Fowler's Modern English Usage*, OUP.
9 Gowers's *The Complete Plain Words*, revised by Sir Bruce Fraser, Penguin Books.
10 *The Economist Style Guide* or *The Times Style Guide*.
11 *Chambers Dictionary of Dates*.

12 A selection of Penguin dictionaries: politics, economics, religions, etc.
13 A dictionary of quotations.
14 A dictionary of modern quotations.
15 *The New Encyclopedia Britannica*, 30 volumes, available on CD-ROM.
16 *Writers' and Artists' Yearbook*, A. & C. Black.
17 *The Writer's Handbook*, Macmillan.
18 *Writer's Market*, Writer's Digest Books.
19 *Willing's Press Guide*, Thomas Skinner Directories. Magazines classified under headings. Lists important publications of other countries.
20 *Whitaker's Almanack*. Annual. Government names and statistics, etc.
21 World atlas and gazetteer.
22 Atlas and gazetteer of the British Isles.
23 A concise world history.
24 *Chambers Book of Facts*.
25 A website guide.
26 A writer's guide to the Internet.

General

The Advertisers' Annual. Lists advertising rates of publications. Use with *NUJ Freelance Guide* to determine rates payable.

Benn's Media Directory. Volume 1, UK; volume 2, international. Gives magazine under subject headings.

The Blue Book of British Broadcasting, Tellex Monitors Ltd., annual. Contains over 1500 key personnel.

Britain: An Official Handbook, HMSO, London, annual.

British Rate and Data (BRAD), Maclean-Hunter. Gives circulation and readership figures, etc. for newspapers and magazines in the UK.

Central Statistical Office: *Social Trends*, HMSO, annual. Charts the developments in the British way of life.

Chambers Biographical Dictionary.

Concise Guide to Reference Material, ed. A. J. Walford, Library Association, London.

Crone, Tom, *Law and the Media*, Focal Press.

Dod's Parliamentary Companion. Annual. Gives names and backgrounds of MPs.

Greenwood, Walter and Welsh, Tom, *McNae's Essential Law for Journalists*, Butterworth.

Guinness Book of Records.

Hoffmann, Ann, *Research for Writers*, A. & C. Black.
Hollis Press and Public Relations Annual.
International Who's Who.
International Year Book and Statesman's Who's Who.
Keesing's Contemporary Archives. Summarizes world news.
Keesing's Record of World Events.
Kelly's Handbook, Kelly's Directories Ltd, annual. Royalty, nobility, MPS, etc.
Municipal Year Book. For local government matters.
The Ordinance Survey Atlas of Great Britain.
Oxford Companion of English Literature, edited by Margaret Drabble, OUP.
The Spotlight Casting Directory and Contacts. Covers the world of entertainment.
The Statesman's Year Book, Macmillan, annual.
The Statesman's Year Book World Gazetteer.
Titles and Forms of Address: A Guide to their Correct Use, A. & C. Black.
Who's Who. Annual.
Who Was Who. Several volumes.

Dictionaries

Bartlett's Familiar Quotations.
Bartlett's Unfamiliar Quotations.
Brewer's Dictionary of Phrase and Fable.
Chambers Biographical Dictionary.
Dictionary of National Biography.
Newspeak: A Dictionary of Jargon, Jonathan Green, Routledge & Kegan Paul.
Slang Thesaurus.

Directories

Organizations

Advertisers' Annual.
Contact, IPC Business Press Information Services Ltd. Particularly for PROs.

Directory of British Associations. Current British directories.

Directory of Publishing, Cassell/Publishers Association, annual. Gives all main publishers.

Encyclopedia of Associations, Gale Research Co., Detroit, USA.

Voluntary Associations: An NCVO Directory, National Council for Voluntary Associations.

Publications

UK

Benn's Media Directory. Volume 1, UK; volume 2, international. Benn Business Information Services. Gives magazines under subject headings.

British Rate and Data. Gives circulation and readership figures, readership profiles, advertisement rates, etc. for newspapers and magazines in the UK.

The Media Guide. A *Guardian* book published by Fourth Estate.

Whitaker's Books in Print, Book of the Month, Books to Come, Paperback Books in Print, J. Whitaker & Sons.

US

Guide to American Directories, B. Klein Publications, Coral Gables, FL.

Writer's Market, Writer's Digest Books, Cincinnati, Ohio, USA.

International

The Australian Marketing Guide Casebook, University of Queensland Press.

Travel Writer's Market, USA. Gives some 400 markets for travel articles and photographs, in the USA, Canada and other parts of the world.

Ulrich's International Periodicals Directory.

Miscellaneous

Adams, Sally, *Interviewing for Journalists*, Routledge.

Amis, Martin, *The Moronic Inferno and Other Visits to America*, Penguin Books.

Bagnall, Nicholas, *Newspaper Language*, Focal Press.

Barber, Lynn, *Mostly Men*, Penguin; *Demon Barber*, Viking.

Bell, Q., *The PR Business*, Kogan Page.

The Best of Granta Travel, Granta Books.

Bonnett, Alastair, *How to Argue*, Prentice Hall.

Boyd, Andrew, *Broadcast Journalism. Techniques of Radio and TV News*, Focal Press.

Burchill, Julie, *Love it or Shove It*, Century Publishing; *Sex and Sensibility*, Grafton/HarperCollins; *The Guardian Columns 1998–2000*, Orion.

Butcher, Judith, *Copy-Editing. The Cambridge Handbook*, Cambridge University Press.

Butler, Harry, *Teeline Made Simple*, Butterworth-Heinemann.

Campbell, Morag, *Writing about Travel*, A. & C. Black.

Carey, John, ed., *The Faber Book of Reportage, The Faber Book of Utopias*; *The Faber Book of Science*, Faber & Faber.

Cassandra (Sir William Neil Connor), *Cassandra at his Finest and Funniest*, Daily Mirror/Hamlyn.

Caunt, John, *Organize Yourself*, Kogan Page.

Cawkell, Tony, *The Multimedia Handbook*, Routledge.

Cheney, Theodore A. Rees, *Getting the Words Right. How to Revise, Edit or Rewrite*, Writer's Digest Books, Cincinnati, Ohio, USA.

Clayton, Joan, *Interviewing for Journalists*, Piatkus.

Coleridge, N., *Streetsmart*, Orion.

Crofts, Andrew, *The Freelance Writer's Handbook*, Piatkus.

Cutts, Martin, *Plain English Guide*, OUP.

Davies, Hunter, *Hunting People*, Mainstream Publishing. The Introduction summarizes the techniques of some well-known interview specialists – Angela Lambert, Lynn Barber, Ray Connolly, Valerie Crone, John Mortimer – as well as his own. The rest is 44 of his interviews with the famous over 30 years.

Davis, Anthony, *Magazine Journalism Today*, Focal Press.

Dick, Jill, *Freelance Writing for Newspapers*, A. & C. Black.

Dobson, Christopher, *The Freelance Journalist. How to Survive and Succeed*, Focal Press.

Ellis, Alice Thomas, *More Home Life*, Duckworth. A collection of *Spectator* pieces.

Evans, Hilary, *The Art of Picture Research. The Freelance Photographer's Market Handbook*, BFP Books. Annual.

Finch, Peter, *How to Publish Yourself*, Alison & Busby.

Foster, John, *Effective Writing Skills for PR*, Kogan Page.

The Granta Book of Reportage, Granta Books.

The Guardian Bedside Books.

Harrington, Walt, *Intimate Journalism. The art and craft of reporting everyday life*, Sage.

Hastings, Max, ed. *An Inside Story of Newspapers*. Macmillan.

Hennessy, Brendan and Hodgson, F. W., *Journalism Workbook*, Focal Press.

Hicks, Wynford, *English for Journalists*, Routledge.

Hicks, Wynford, with Adams, Sally, *Writing for Journalists*, Routledge.

Hodgson, F. W., *Modern Newspaper Practice*, Focal Press.

Holden, Anthony, *Of Presidents, Prime Ministers and Princes*, Weidenfeld & Nicolson. An anthology of pieces, including interviews/profiles.

Huff, Darrell, *How to Lie with Statistics*, Penguin Books.

Hull, Raymond, *How to Write How-to Books and Articles*, Poplar Press.

Investigative Journalism. Context and Practice, edited by Hugo de Burgh, Routledge.

Jenkins, Simon, *Against the Grain: Writings of a Sceptical Optimist*. Mostly from *The Times*.

Johnson, E. W. and Wolfe (eds), *The New Journalism*, Picador.

Jones, Graham, *The Business of Freelancing*, BFP Books.

A Journalism Reader, edited by Bromley, M. and O'Malley, T., Routledge.

Keeble, Richard, *The Newspapers Handbook* and *Ethics for Journalists*, Routledge.

Keene, Martin, *Practical Photojournalism*, Focal Press.

Kervin, Alison, *Sports Writing*, A. & C. Black.

Knightley, P., *The First Casualty: The War Correspondent as Hero and MythMaker from the Crimea to Kosovo*, Prion Books.

Larkin, Philip, *Required Writing: Miscellaneous Pieces, 1955–82*, Faber & Faber. The late Philip Larkin's reputation rests on his poetry, but he was also a reviewer (mainly of poetry but also of jazz music) of wit and insights.

Legat, Michael, *The Writer's Rights* and *Writing for a Living*, A. & C. Black.

Levin, Bernard, *Enthusiasms*, Hodder & Stoughton; *I Should Say So*, Jonathan Cape; and other collections.

Levine, Michael, *The Address Book: How to reach anyone who's anyone*, Perigee (USA).

Littlejohn, Richard, *You Couldn't Make It Up*, Heinemann.

Macdonald, Janet, *Travel Writing*, Robert Hale.

McAffee, ed. *Lives and Works: profiles of leading novelists, poets and playwrights*, Atlantic Books (from *The Guardian*).

McKay, Jenny, *The Magazines Handbook*, Routledge.

McLeish, Kenneth, *Good Reading Guide*, Bloomsbury Publishing. It takes you to the highly recommended books, mainly fiction, under many headings, including journalism.

Media Ethics, edited by Matthew Kieran, Routledge.

Mitford, Jessica, *The Making of a Muckraker*, Quartet Books.

Morrish, J., *Magazine Editing*, Routledge/Blueprint.

Mortimer, John, *Character Parts, Penguin Books*. A selection of his interviews, all but one of which appeared in *The Sunday Times*.

Morton, J. B., *The Best of Beachcomber*, selected and introduced by Michael Frayn, Mandarin Paperbacks.

Northmore, David, *Freedom of Information Handbook: How to Find out what You Want to Know*, Bloomsbury Publishing; *A Guide to Investigative Research. Global Issues*, Continuum International Publishing, 1996.

O'Brien, Flann (Myles na Gopaleen), *The Best of Myles*, Picador. The best of the humorous columns in *The Irish Times*. His real name was Brian Nolan.

O'Farrell, John, *Global Village Idiot*, Doubleday. Columns from *The Guardian* and *The Independent*.

Orwell, George, *The Collected Essays, Journalism and Letters of George Orwell*, Secker & Warburg.

The Oxford Book of Essays, edited by John Gross, OUP.

Paice, Eric, *The Way to Write for TV*, Elm Tree Books.

Parris, Matthew, *Chance Witness. An Outsider's Life in Politics*, Penguin Books.

Parsons, Tony, *Dispatches from the Front Line of Popular Culture*, Virgin Books. A collection of his pieces from various newspapers and magazines.

Peak, S. and Fisher, P., *The Media Guide*, Guardian Books, Fourth Estate.

The Penguin Book of Columnists, edited by Christopher Silvester, Penguin Books.

The Penguin Book of Interviews, edited by Christopher Silvester, Penguin Books.

The Penguin Book of Journalism. Secrets of the Press, edited by Stephen Glover, Penguin Books.

The Penguin Book of 20th Century Essays, edited by Ian Hamilton, Penguin Books.

Periodicals Training Council, *Your Future in Magazines*.

Photographer's Market, Writer's Digest Books. Annual.

Pilger, John, *Hidden Agendas*, Vintage/Random House.

Pritchard, John, *The Penguin Guide to the Law*, Penguin.

Pundits, Poets and Wits. An Omnibus of American Newspaper Columns. Gathered, annotated and introduced by Karl E. Meyer, OUP. An anthology of the best American columnists, from Benjamin Franklin (1706–90) to Anna Quindlen (1950–).

Purcell, Ann and Carl, *A Guide to Travel Writing and Photography*, Harrap Publishing.

Randall, *The Universal Journalist*, Pluto.

Rigg, Diana (compiler), *No Turn Unstoned*, Arrow Books. The worst ever theatrical reviews.

Rudin, Richard and Ibbotson, Trevor, *An Introduction to Journalism. Essential techniques and background knowledge*, Focal Press.

Shrimsley, Bernard, *The Silly Season*, Robson Books.

Siegel, David, *Secrets of Successful Web Sites*, Hayden, Indianapolis.

Southwell, T., *Getting Away With It. The Inside Story of Loaded*, Ebury Press.

Strunk, William and White, E. B., *The Elements of Style*, Macmillan Publishing, New York.

Time Out Interviews 1968–1998, edited by F. Broughton, Penguin Books.

Todd, Alden, and Loder, Cari, *Finding Facts Fast*, Penguin Books. The essential research techniques.

Turabian, Kate, *A Manual for Writers of Research Papers, Theses and Dissertations*. Heinemann.

Ward, Mike, *Journalism Online*, Focal Press.

Wardle, Irving, *Theatre Criticism*, Routledge.

Waterhouse, Keith, *Waterhouse on Newspaper Style*, Penguin Books; *English Our English (and How to Sing It)*, Viking.

Wells, Gordon, *The Magazine Writer's Handbook* and *Photography for Article Writers*, Allison & Busby.

Whale, John, *Put it in Writing*, J. M. Dent.

Wharton, J., *Magazine Journalism. A Guide to Writing and Subbing for Magazines*, Periodicals Training Council.

Wharton, Michael, Collections of 'Peter Simple' columns from *The Daily Telegraph*, Telegraph Publications.

Wheen, Francis, *Hoo-Hahs and Passing Frenzies. Collected Journalism, 1991–2001*, Atlantic Books.

Whittaker, Kenneth, *Using Libraries*, Andre Deutsche.

Wilson, John, *Understanding Journalism. A Guide to Issues*, Routledge.

Wimbs, Diana, *Freelance Copywriting*, A. & C. Black.

Wolfe, T. and Johnson, E. W. (eds), *The New Journalism*, Picador.

Writing for the BBC, BBC Publications.

Writing for Reader's Digest, Reader's Digest.

Young, Hugo, *Supping with the Devils*. A collection of his political writings. He was a political columnist for many years for *The Guardian* and *The Observer*.

Young, Toby, *How to Lose Friends and Alienate People*, Little, Brown and Company. After being sacked by several publications in the UK, the author spent five years in New York, from 1995 to 2000, during which he was sacked by *Vanity Fair*. Good for a laugh – and for learning how to avoid …

Indexes to articles

(Many publications produce indexes. Some, like *The Times*, put them into volumes annually. Other annual volumes select from various publications. The following is a sample.)

Applied Science and Technology Index.

Architectural Periodicals Index.

British Humanities Index, Library Association. Selects from quality newspapers, weekly reviews, selected magazines and professional journals.

The Clover Index. General and specialized interest magazines.

The Clover Newspaper Index. The quality newspapers and selected magazines.

Current Technology Index. Scientific and technical journals.

Reader's Guide to Periodical Literature, H. W. Wilson Co., New York.

Research Index. Indexes articles and news items of financial interest in the national press and business periodicals.

Guides to the Internet

Bradley, P., *The Advanced Internet Searcher's Handbook*, Library Association Publishing.

Chisholm, Malcolm, *The Internet Guide for Writers*, How To Books.

Dorner, Jane, *The Internet: A Writer's Guide* and *Creative Web Writing*, A. & C. Black; *Writing for the Internet*, OUP.

Edmonds, Graham, *The Good Web Site Guide*, Orion.

Kennedy, Angus J., *The Rough Guide to the Internet*, Rough Guides Ltd.

Kent, Peter, and Young, Rob, *Complete Idiot's Guide to the Internet*, Que.

McGuire, M., Stilborne, L., McAdams, M. and Hyatt, L., *The Internet Handbook for Writers*, The Guildford Press, New York.

Morrish, John, *The Really Simple Internet Guide*, Virgin.

Online Journalism Review, www.ojr.org.

MAGAZINES

The Author, Society of Authors. Quarterly, available to non-members on subscription.

British Journalism Review, BJR Publishing Ltd., quarterly.

Campaign, Haymarket Publishing Group, weekly. For the advertising industry.

Freelance Market News, Freelance Press Services, Cumberland House, Lisadel Street, Salford, Manchester M6 6GG, monthly.

Index on Censorship, Writers and Scholars International, bimonthly. Reports on the struggles against censorship of all kinds of writing.

Magazine News, Periodical Publishers Association.

Media sections in *The Guardian* on Mondays, and *The Times* and *The Independent* on Wednesdays.

Media Week, EMAP Business Publishing. A bridge between the media and advertising.

PR Week, Haymarket Publishing Group.

Press Gazette, Maclean-Hunter.

Writers' Forum, Writers International Ltd.

Writer's Monthly.

Writers' News/Writing Magazine, Yorkshire Post Newspapers.

Index

Aaronovitch, David 293–4
Abstracts 353
Accounts, keeping 14–15
Active Life 169
Advertisers' Annual 251
Advertising 244
  copywriting 245–7
    buzz words 247
    ideas 246–7
    slogans 245–6
    typography and layout 247
*Against the Grain: Writings of a
    Sceptical Optimist* 290
Agarwal, Manish 320
Alternative medicine 88, 351
Amis, Martin 286
Andrews, Nigel 329–30
Anecdote 183
Appendages 192
Arena 216
Argument 171–3, 219–22
  in columns 300–4
  in publicity writing 254
Arts reviews 307–8, 309, 321–3
  See also Reviewing
*As I Walked Out One Midsummer
    Morning* 206
Attribution 365–6
Audit Bureau of Circulations (ABC)
  75
Authorship books 73–4
Authorship magazines 73

Babaian, Natasha 236–9
Backing up work 11
Bagnall, Nicholas 209
Baird, Eric 63
Barber, Lynn 283–4
Barber, Richard 81
Barker, Paul 85
Beckenham and Penge Advertiser
  64
Best of Beachcomber, The 302
Best of Myles, The 303
Big Brother 334
Billen, Andrew 312
Bird, Linda 351
Blackburn, Virginia 331
Blogging 153, 390
Blyth, Myrna 298
Book reviewing 315–19
  fiction 317–19
  non-fiction 315–17
Books:
  as spin-offs 38
  authorship 73–4
  ideas development 50–1
Bottin, Alain de 222
Bowron, Steven 118–19
Brainstorming, computerized 56
Bray, Roger 349
Brian, Denis 255
Briffa, Dr John 350
Brighton Argus 257
British Airways 70–1

British Humanities Index (BHI) 28, 76
British Institute of Mental Handicap 70
British Journalism Review 222, 255, 294, 351
British Medical Journal 89
British Rate and Data (BRAD) Advertiser and Agency List 251
Broadband 143
　See also Internet
Broadcasts 48
Brown, Craig 301–2, 303
Buchwald, Art 362
Building Today 343, 344, 347
Burchill, Julie 300–1
Burnie, Joan 119
Business, specialist features 349
Business-to-business magazines 50
Buzz words 207, 208–9
　in advertising 247

Caldwell, Christopher 222
Camera equipment 228–31
Campaign 339, 340–1
Capital of Nasty 156
Captions 233–4
Carey, Dr Adam 350–1
Cassandra at his Finest and Funniest 290, 364
Cassandra (Sir William Connor) 296
Castleman, Michael 351
Celebrity Bulletin, The 260
Celebrity culture 81–3
Celebrity peg 186
Chambers Dictionary of Dates 50
Chatrooms 150
Children, writing about 83–4
Choice 187–8

Christansen, Rupert 321
Christianson, Arthur 247
Christopher, James 329–30
Clarke, Jeremy 297
Clichés 206–8
　use in advertising 247
Clover Index 76
Coleman, Dr Vernon 349
Collins, Barry 349
Collins, Nancy 267
Columnists 288–90, 292
　getting a slot 290–1
　working methods 304–5
Columns 288
　argument and provocation 300–4 ·
　humour, parody and fantasy 301–4
　lifestyle 297–300
　local papers 291–2
　personal 295–6
　political 294–5
　specialist 352–3
　world at large 292–4
Commissioning 98–9
Commissions:
　obtaining 22–5
　　by email 102–3
　　by fax or letter 103
　　by telephone 101–2
　　interviews 258–9
　　multiple proposals 106–7
　　preparation 99–101
　　publicity work 251–3
　　sending specs 110–11
　organization 108–10
Complementary medicine 351
Complete Plain Words, The 198
Computer equipment 10–11
　backing up 11

Computers, specialist features
     349–50
Connolly, Cyril 197
Connor, Sir William (Cassandra)
     296, 364
Contacts 119–20, 385–90
   establishing bonds with 137–8
   in press releases 251
Copyright 363–4, 380–3
   First British Serial Rights (FBSR)
     14
Cosmopolitan 73
Country Life 189
Cowan, Anne 63
Cox, David 286
Crave 327
Crime 84–6
Critics 307
   See also Reviewing
Croce, Maria 64
Crone, Tom 363, 364
Croydon and Purley Advertiser
     64
Cuttings 48–9, 116

D-Day Dispatches 334–5
Daily Echo 291
Daily Express 302, 326, 331, 334,
     350–1
Daily Mail 221, 352
Daily Mirror 296, 332–3
Daily Telegraph, The 222, 301–2,
     321, 350
Davenport, Walter 97
Davies, Hunter 264
Davies, Stan Gebler 186
Davis, Victor 255
Deevoy, Adrian 281
Defreitas, Michael 183
Dejevsky, Mary 221

Description 167–9, 215–16
   in intros 183–4
   in publicity writing 253
Dictionary of Jargon 205
Digital photography 229–31
Directories:
   organizations 395–6
   publications 396
Directory of British Associations
     (DBA) 28
Doherty, Dawn 175–6
Donovan, Paul 139
Dorner, Jane 145–6
Dover Express 63–4

Economist Style Guide, The 26,
     35
Edge, Simon 334
Edinburgh Evening News 63
Editors:
   dealing with 111–13
   requirements of 98–9
Education:
   issues 86–7
   specialist features 350
Email:
   enquiries 102–3
   file submission 10–11
   interviews 136, 265
   programs 144
Emotionally weighted language
     220–1
Empire 330
Endings 187–90
Equipment 10–11
Essential Law for Journalists 363
Ethical concerns 366
Euphemisms 209–10
Evans, Harold 118
Evans, Paul 168–9

Evening Standard 85, 199, 325, 328, 334–5
Events 47–8
Excavation 322
Expert sources, searching for 149, 389
Exposition 166–9, 217–19
  in intros 184
  in publicity writing 253–4
Ezines 156, 390

Facts, checking 30
  specialist features 353
Fairman, Richard 321
False Servant, The 325–7
Feature file 109–10
Features 16–20, 60
  content 17–18, 342–4
  new emphasis on 61
  specialist features 62, 342–9
  structure 18–20
Fees, negotiating 14
FHM 217, 279
Fiction reviewing 317–19
Film reviews 328–30
Financial Times, The 51, 222, 321, 322, 329–30, 348, 349
Financial Times Magazine 177–81, 222, 234
First British Serial Rights (FBSR) 14
Fisk, Robert 18
Flower of Evil, The 330
Foreignisms 203–4
Formulas, idea development 53–4
Foster, Jill 332–3
Free magazines 70–1
Freebies 92, 93–4
Freelance Market News 36, 37
Freelance Photographer 226

Freesheets 65
Fuzz 209

General Medical Council's Register 89
Geographical 168–9, 183
Geological Magazine 94, 111
Gibson, Fiona 299
Girl about Town 70
Glamour 73
Goodman, Geoffrey 294
Gower, Sir Ernest 198
GQ 281, 348–9
Gramophone 320
Graphics 232
Green, Jonathan 204–5
Grylls, David 317–19
Guardian, The 20, 83, 182, 203, 222, 285, 286, 293, 294, 319–20, 331, 333–4, 338, 352
Guardian Bedside Books, The 290

Harrington, Michael 191
Hartley, Aidan 216
Hastings, Max 222
Haydon, Caroline 350
Health:
  issues 87–9
  specialist features 350–1, 353–4
Heat 81
Hello! 83
Hell's Kitchen 333
Hennessy, Val 165, 282
Herald, The (Glasgow) 63
Here! 82
Here's Health 88
Highlife 70–1
Hoffmann, Ann 28
Holder, Deborah 88
Hollingsbee, Bob 64

Hollis Press and Public Relations Annual 28
Hoo-Hahs and Passing Frenzies 290, 293
Hook, Antony 63–4
House style 34–5
How to Lie With Statistics 140
How-to features 166
Howells, Lisa 88
Huff, Darrell 140
Human Rights Act (2000) 364
Hunt, Tristam 352

IdeaFisher 56
Ideas 20–2
  development of 52–6
    computerized brainstorming 56
    for publicity writing 246–7
    formulas and word associations 53–4
    imagination 52–3
    lateral thinking 55–6
    linear-logical thinking 54–5
  freelance writers 44–52
    broadcasts 48
    computerized sources 51–2
    conversations noted 47
    events observed 47–8
    personal experience 46
    printed sources 48–51
  specialist writers 338
  staff writers 41–4
    from inside 43
    from letters page 43–4
    from news 42
    from press releases 43
Illustrations:
  captions 233–4
  getting permissions 228
  graphics 232

market 226
negotiating 234–5
photographic equipment 228–31
processing 235
recording 235
relevance versus art 226–7
sources 232, 387
storing 235–6
subjects 227–8
submitting 236
Imagination 52–3
Independent, The 18, 221, 350
Independent Magazine, The 185–6
Independent Review, The 333
Indexes 401
Information gathering, *See* Research
Instant messaging 144
Internet 142–5, 357
  connecting 143
  guides 401–2
  instant messaging 144
  market guides 74
  newsgroups 145
  online market 155–6
  research 116, 145–50, 387–90
    evaluation of online sources 147–8
    finding experts 149, 389
    premium content 148–9
    search engines 146–7
    trusted sources 148–9, 388–9
    virtual communities 149–50
    web directories 147
  RSS 145
  web browsers 144
  wireless access 143–4
  See also Email; Writing online
Internet Magazine 350

Interviews 28–9, 122–38, 255–7
  approaches 122–4
  by letter 136, 265
  choice of interviewee 257–8
  editing the transcript 276–8
    summarizing 277–8
  elicitation of good quotes 134–5
  email 136, 265
  face to face 137, 263–5
    tape recording 264–5
  follow up 287
  getting commissioned 258–9
  logging and ordering 126–8
  persuasion techniques 131–4
  question preparation 28, 128–31,
    266–70
  quoting and paraphrasing 125–6
  setting up 259–62
    getting past minders 260–2
    persistence 262
  techniques 270–6
    avoiding hidden agendas
      274–5
    difficult interviewees 273–4
    encouraging revelations 275–6
    keeping in control 271–2
    preparing to follow up 276
    tough questions 272–3
  telephone 136, 266
  writing up formats 278–86
    hatchet job 283–4
    narrative interview 282–3
    profile 284–6
    Q-and-A format 279–81
    unusual formats 286
Intros 182–7
Isherwood: A Life 315–16

Jackhammer 156
Jackson, Ian 62

Jargon 204, 347
  specialist features 347
Jenkins, Simon 290, 294–5
Johnson, Boris 303–4
Johnson, George 352
Johnson, Paul 296
Johnson, Rachel 87, 222
Jongh, Nicholas de 199
Journalism Online 157
Journalist, The 15, 363
Journals, professional 50
Judd, Alan 220

Kaletsky, Anatole 222
Kampfner, John 160–2
Keers, Paul 84
Keesing's Record of World Events 29
Kellner, Peter 316
Kentish Times 257, 291
Kindersley, Tania 182, 188
Kirby, Judy 88
Krakovsky, Marina 352

Lambert, Angela 177–81
Lancet, The 89, 339
Landesman, Cosmo 81
Lane, Harriet 267
Lantin, Barbara 350
Lateral thinking 55–6
Law and the Media 363
Lawson, Mark 331
Le Fanu, Dr James 348
Leask, Anne 64
Lee, Laurie 206, 215
Legwork 27, 116–19
Lerner, Max 292
Leslie, Ann 274
Letters page 6–7, 43–4, 49
Levin, Bernard 290, 313
Lewis-Smith, Victor 334–5

Libel 364
 avoidance of 365
Lifestyle columns 297–300
Lind, Michael 222
Linear-logical thinking 54–5
Literary allusion 185–6
Little Lady Fauntleroy 332–3
*Lives and Works: profiles of leading
 novelists, poets and
 playwrights* 286
Living 188
Lloyd, Rose 329
Loaded 205
Local papers 62–5
 columns 291–2
 local and national interaction 67–8
Lost Boys, The 329
Lott, Tim 8

McAfee, Annalena 286
McCormack, Steve 350
McCormick, Neil 267, 282
MacDonald, Margo 185
Magazine Editing 82
Magazine, The (Sainsbury's) 88
Magazines 67–70
 authorship 73
 business-to-business 50
 free 70–1
 ideas development 48–50
 online versions 148
 sources 402
 subjects 68–9
 writers' magazines 358–9
Mail on Sunday, The 119, 165, 301
 You magazine 186, 282
Making of a Muckraker, The 275
Male, David 257
Margolis, Jonathan 84
Marie Claire 88, 351

Market guidance 72–4
 contributors' guidelines 72
 from authorship books 73–4
 from authorship magazines 73
 from publications directly 72
 from the internet 74
 overseas markets 358–9
 promotional literature 72
Marks & Spencer Magazine 299
Mars-Jones, Adam 315–16
Media, specialist features 351
Medical Directory, The 89, 353
Medicine 87–9
 specialist features 351
Mental Handicap Research 38, 70
Metasearch engines 146, 388
Meyer, Karl E. 289
Mind map 163–4
Mirror, The 186
Mitford, Nancy 275–6
Mojo 320
Monster 329–30
Moral rights 384
More Home Life 290
Morley, Sheridan 326, 327
Morrish, John 82, 150–1, 225
Morton, J. B. 302–3
Mountford, Fiona 325
Ms London 70
Muhibah 71
Multi-purposing 36, 106–7
Multiple submissions 35
Murphy's Law 331
Music reviewing 319–21

Narration 167–71, 216–17
 in publicity writing 253
Narrative interviews 282–3
National Council for the Training of
 Journalists (NCTJ) 391

National papers 65–7
  local and national interaction 67
National Readership Survey (NRS)
  75
National Union of Journalists (NUJ)
  15
  Freelance Guide 14, 235
  Professional Code of Conduct
    371–2
Networking 107–8
New Internationalist 217–18, 350,
  359
New Statesman 86, 160, 203, 204,
  234, 285, 286, 316
New York Times 118, 360
New Yorker 360
News agency websites 149, 389
Newsgroups, online 145, 149
Newspaper Language 209
Newspapers 61
  cuttings 48–9
  local papers 62–5, 67
  national papers 65–7
  online versions 148, 388–9
Nightingale, Benedict 326
Nightingale, Liz 351
No Angels 331
Noble, Kate 351
Nolan, Brian 302
Norton Book of Interviews, The 255–6
Note-taking 29–30
Notes, ordering of 162–3

Observer, The 204–5, 212, 285, 293,
  315
Observer Food Magazine 349
Observer Magazine 181, 182, 267,
  297, 299–300, 350
OK! 81
Old age 89–90

Oldie, The 352–3
O'Neill, Helen 169–71
Online Freelance Directory 15
Op Ed pages 221–2, 293
Opera reviewing 320–1
O'Reilly, Sally 323
Outlining 31–2
  specialist features 345–6
Overseas markets 36, 37, 357
  choice of countries 360
  culture study 360
  market guides 358–9
  opportunities 361
  syndication 361–2
Oxford Reverse Dictionary 200
Oxford Writers' Dictionary 203

Packer, William 322
Paraphrasing 30, 125–6
Paris Review 279–80
Parkin, Diane 73
Parnell, Kerry 73
Parris, Matthew 209, 274, 312
Parsons, Tony 216
Patmore, Angela 221
Penguin Book of Columnists, The
  289
Penguin Book of Interviews, The
  255–6, 260
Penguin Book of Journalism, The 71
People, The 44, 349
Periodicals Training Council 392
Personal columns 295–6
Personal experience 27, 46, 116–17
Personal profile 285
Persuasion techniques 131–4
  in publicity writing 254
Peter, John 324–5
Peters, Patrick 330
Peterson, Laurie 157

Philosophy Now 222, 280
Photographers, working with 231–2
Photographic equipment 228–31
Photographs, *See* Illustrations
Pictures, *See* Illustrations
Pile, Stephen 91
Pirie, Madsen 350
Pitching, *See* Queries
Plagiarism 363
Playboy 279–80
Political columns 294–5
Political correctness (PC) 210–11
Popbitch 82
Postal interviews 136, 265
Press Complaints Commission: Code
     of Practice 378
Press cuttings agencies 116, 117
Press Gazette 7, 49, 66, 73, 120, 139,
     232, 233, 262, 351, 363
Press releases 43, 248–51
  adapting to different markets
     249–50
  contacts 251
Private Eye 208, 295, 303–4
Professional journals 50
Professional organizations 15
Profiles 284–6
Promotional literature 72
Proofreading 112
Proposals, *See* Queries
Prospect 222
*Provincial Press and the Community,
     The* 62
Psychology Today 351, 352
Public relations (PR) 244
Publicity writing 243–4
  advertising copywriting 245–7
  obtaining work 251–3
    portfolio building 252
    specialist services 252–3

press releases 248–51
research 245
techniques 253–4
Publishers' Freelance Directory 231,
     232
*Pundits, Poets and Wits: An Omnibus
     of American Newspaper
     Columns* 289
Purvis, Andrew 349

Qualifications 4
Queries:
  by email 102–3
  by fax or letter 103–6
  by telephone 101–2
  sending specs 110–11
  specialist publications 339–42
Questioning, in interviews 28,
     128–31, 266–70
  asking specific questions
     269–70
  getting on subject's wavelength
     268–9
  order of questions 270
  tough question techniques 272–3
  See also Interviews
Quotes, elicitation of 134–5
Quoting 125–6

Radio Times 234
Randall, David 366
Reader's Digest 81–2, 169–71, 183,
     185, 188, 220, 267
Readers' interest 164–7
Readership analysis 74–5
Reality TV 82–3
Reckoning, The 328–9
Records, keeping 12, 14–15
Reeves, Ian 262
Reference libraries 389, 393–5

Rejections 112–13
  responding to 113
Reporting experience 65
Research 25–30
  background study 116
  computerized sources 51–2
  legwork 27, 116–19
  note-taking 29–30
  online 116, 145–50
  printed sources 27–8, 48–51
  publicity writing 245
  specialist features 353–4
  See also Sources
Research for Writers 28
Research in British Universities 353
Retirement 89–90
Reviewing 307–8
  art 321–3
  becoming a reviewer 308–9
  books 315–19
  films 328–30
  music 319–21
  tasks of 310–12
  television 330–5
  theatre 323–7
  writing-up process 312–15
Rewriting 33–4
  for overseas markets 357
Roberts, Dan 8
Roberts, Kevin 217
Royal Brunei Airlines 71
RSS (Really Simple Syndication)
  145
Ruhrmund, Frank 64
Russell, Jenni 86–7
Ryall, Melody 7

Saga 88, 266
Salon 156
Sample, Ian 352

Sarler, Carol 71
Schools 86–7
Science, specialist features 352
Search Engine Optimization (SEO)
  153
Search engines 146–7, 388
Sedge, Michael 359
Self, Will 328–9
Sewell, Brian 322
She 84, 279, 351
Shorthand 29
Sierz, Aleks 309, 326–7
Silvester, Christopher 255–6, 260,
  289
Simonart, Serge 266
Slang 204–5
Slate 156
Slogans 245–6
Smart, James 319–20
Smith, Will 65
Sources 115–22
  acknowledgement of 137
  assessment of 120–2
    online sources 147–8
  contacts 119–20, 385–90
  experts, searching for 149, 389
  legwork 116–19
  pictures 232
South London Press 65, 329
Specialism 56–7
Specialist columns 352–3
Specialist features 62, 342–9
  research 353–4
Specialists 62, 336–7
  marketing strategy 339–42
  opportunities for 337–8
Specs 110–11
Spectator, The 87, 182, 203, 204,
  216, 222, 296–7
Spin Sisters 298

Spin-offs 35–8
Spotlight 29, 260
Star, The 202
Statesman's Yearbook, The 29
Stevenson, Neil 82
Stevenson, R. L. 213
Style:
  house 34–5
  individual 222–3
  reviews 312–14
Submission of work 10–11, 34–5
Summing up 187–8
Sun, The 71
Sunday Express 338
Sunday Express Magazine 284
Sunday Herald Magazine 167
Sunday Independent (Ireland) 298
Sunday Post, The (Dundee) 118–19
Sunday Post, The (Glasgow) 166
Sunday Telegraph, The 191
Sunday Times, The 60, 118, 203, 230, 285, 349
Sunday Times Magazine 91, 234, 324–5
Sutcliffe, Thomas 333
Syndication 36, 106–7, 361–2
  RSS 145

Taki 297
Tatler 84
Taylor, A. J. P. 338
Technology, specialist features 352
Teeline shorthand 29
Telegraph Magazine, The 267, 282
Telephone:
  enquiries 101–2
  interviews 136, 266
Television reviews 330–5
  documentaries 332–5
  series 331

Templeton, Tom 299–300
The Moronic Inferno and Other Visits to America 286
Theatre reviews 323–7
Thekaekara, Mari Marcel 217–18
Thicknesse, Robert 321
Think pieces 221–2
Thomas-Ellis, Alice 290
Thunder God 317–19
Time Magazine 351, 352, 360
Time Out 323
Timeliness 76
Times, The 209, 222, 294–5, 321, 326, 329–30, 338
Times Stylebook, The 35
Timing 76–7
Titles 181–2
Tolstoy, Count Nikolas 364
Trade releases 250
Training courses 4, 391–2
Travel writing 90–5, 361

UCAS 392
Universal Journalist, The 366
Using a Library 28

Vanity Fair 233, 260–1
Verification skills 138–40
Virtual communities 149–50

Walmsley, Heather 350
Ward, Mike 157
Warwick, Hugh 350
Waterhouse, Keith 222, 288
Web browsers 144
Web directories 147, 388
Website creation 151–4, 389
  promotion 153–4
Webster, Aroha 63
Week, The 320–1, 338

Western Morning News 31, 64
What's On 326, 327
Wheen, Francis 212, 290, 293
White, Dan 205
Whittaker, Kenneth 28
Who's Who 28, 266
Wi-Fi hotspots 143
Wikipedia 149
Wilkes, Angela 88
Willing's Press Guide 29, 226
Wintle, Angela 257
Wireless Internet access 143–4
Withers, Jane 182
Wolff, Jennifer 351
Wollaston, Sam 333–4
Wolmar, Christian 352
Woman 175–6, 184, 278
Woman's Own 285
Word association 53–4
Words, choice of 198–200
Work experience 5–8
    getting printed 6
    staff versus freelance 7–8
    writing for the letters page 6–7

Wray, Graham 205
Writers' and Artists' Yearbook 22, 23,
    72, 231
Writer's Digest 73–4
Writers' Digest 358
Writers' Forum 358–9
Writers' Handbook 22, 24, 72
Writers' Market 22, 228
WritersMarket.com 74
Writing for Reader's Digest 73–4,
    163, 346
Writing Magazine 73
Writing online 154–8
    techniques 157–8
    understanding the market 155–6
Writing up 32–3
    reviews 312–15
    rewriting 33–4
Wyatt, Petronella 297

Yes Minister 65–6
Young, Hugo 294, 312

Zec, Donald 285